The Study of Real Skills
Volume 3

Management Skills

The Study of Real Skills

Series Editor: W. T. Singleton, *Applied Psychology Department, University of Aston in Birmingham*

Volume 1

The Analysis of Practical Skills

This book attempts to bridge the gap between laboratory studies of human skill by experimental psychologists and behavioural studies of man at work.

Volume 2

Compliance and Excellence

Reviews the methods used in skills analysis from work study to process control study with detailed analyses of two extreme kinds of jobs and effort: Compliance, where the individual learns to cope with a hostile situation; and excellence, where the individual dominates the situation with superb performance.

Volume 3

Management Skills

Reviews the conceptual background to management skills with the emphasis on a systems approach.

Volume 4

Social Skills

Reviews the conceptual background to social skills with emphasis on the variety of criteria for effective communal effort from productivity to quality of life.

The Study of Real Skills
Volume 3

Management Skills

Edited by
W. T. Singleton MA DSc
Professor of Applied Psychology
University of Aston in Birmingham

University Park Press
Baltimore

Published in USA and Canada by
University Park Press
300 North Charles Street
Baltimore, Maryland 21201

Published in UK by
MTP Press Limited
Falcon House
Lancaster, England

First published 1981

ISBN 0-8391-1683-7
LCC 81-50284

Printed in Great Britain

Contents

Contributors

Ken G. Burnett

BOC International
Chartridge Lodge
Chesham
Bucks HP5 2TU

After accountancy training he was initiated into Sales and Marketing with Procter and Gamble in the late 1950s. In 1964 he joined P. A. Management Consultants and in the next seven years completed more than 40 assignments in the UK and Eire. Since 1972, he has worked freelance in four continents. Currently he is also Sales and Marketing Tutor at British Oxygen's Management Centre at Chartridge, Bucks. He is a member of the Institute of Management Consultants and a member of the Institute of Marketing.

Peter F. C. Castle

4 Chemin des Bougeries
1231 Conches
Geneva
Switzerland

After serving in the Navy throughout the War, he studied psychology at Cambridge at the time when Professor Bartlett was developing his ideas about skill. He then worked for some years in London at the National Institute of Industrial Psychology and at Kodak Ltd. He has masters and doctoral degrees in psychology and professional qualifications in psychology and personnel management. Since 1956 he has been an international civil servant with the ILO in Geneva.

Norman Chell

Manager Training and Development
Dunlop Ltd.
Company Training Department
Co-operative House
Prince's Street
Stafford ST16 2BT

In a first career in the aerospace industry he started as an aircraft apprentice working on bi-planes at RAF Halton and finished with responsibilities for work on guided missiles for Hawker Siddeley Dynamics thirty years later. In a second career, which commenced in 1968, he held appointments as Group Management Tutor and Senior Instructor Management Studies with the Dunlop Company's Central Training Department before taking up his present job with the Dunlop Company as Manager-Training and Development. He has wide experience of management development in Europe, Africa and the Far East.

Stuart Cumella

MSC Employment Service Division
Employment Rehabilitation Research Centre
Vincent Drive
Edgbaston
Birmingham B15 2TD

Educated at the London School of Economics (BSc Econ), the University of Strathclyde (MSc Politics) and the University of Stirling (professional qualification in Social Work). He has worked in Birmingham Social Services Department, Edinburgh Social Work Department and Lothian Region Social Work Department. He has experience as a social worker in area offices, a health centre, a mental hospital and a community home. Since 1977 he has been employed as Social Worker/Researcher at the Employment Rehabilitation Research Centre, Birmingham.

Alan Hedge

Applied Psychology Department
University of Aston in Birmingham
Gosta Green
Birmingham B4 7ET

He graduated from the University of Sheffield with Bachelor's and Master's degrees in Zoology, he then attended the University of Aston in Birmingham and graduated with a Master's degree in Applied Psychology. He returned to the University of Sheffield for doctoral research in Experimental Psychology. From 1974 to 1976 he worked on environmental research for two Metropolitan County Councils, since 1976 he has been lecturer in Environmental Psychology at the University of Aston in Birmingham.

E. B. McGinnis

Department of Health and Social Security
Friars House
157–168 Blackfriars Road
London SE1 8EU

He joined the Civil Service after graduating from Cambridge, and has been concerned at various times with the War Pensions Scheme, with benefits for others who are impaired or handicapped, with retirement and unemployment benefits, and with Establishment matters. Currently he is an Under Secretary in the Department of Health and Social Security.

Philip Moorhouse

3 Chichester Lane
Hampton Magna
Warwick

After graduating from Queen Mary College (University of London) with a degree in mathematics with social sciences, Philip Moorhouse attended Stirling University to read a Master's degree in mathematical psychology. He then joined Dunlop Ltd., and through a collaborative postgraduate scheme with Aston University, undertook doctoral research into managerial skills to assist in Company management development activities. He has subsequently joined a managerial team at one of the Company's operating Divisions.

Captain M. R. H. Page, RN

Ministry of Defence,
Ensleigh,
Bath, Avon.

Michael Page is serving in the Ministry of Defence as a Deputy Director of Ship Weapon Systems. His Service career has embraced a broad range of sea and shore based jobs within the Weapons field. Early engineering experience was reinforced by a masters course in Applied Psychology during a sabbatical year at Aston University. These together provided the theme for his doctoral research into Personality and Leadership in the Technical Environment of the Royal Navy. He is a convinced advocate of the multi-disciplinary approach to team formation and project management, claiming that Human Factors are not given sufficient weight in UK affairs.

Neil Pendleton

44 Woodhouse Lane
Sale
Cheshire M33 7JY

Graduate in psychology and sociology and as a qualified teacher from the University of Sheffield. Later obtained a Diploma in Town and Regional Planning from Leeds Polytechnic. He has worked since 1974 in local government planning departments on a wide range of strategies, corporate and local planning exercises. Currently he is a Senior Planning Officer in Manchester City Planning Department and is involved in inner city planning and land availability systems.

John H. Plumb

Dairy Farm
Arnolds Lane
Maxstoke
Coleshill
Warks.

He was brought up on the family farm and gained further practical farming experience in various European countries. After graduating from Wye College with a bachelors degree in Agricultural Economics he joined the South American Missionary Society for two years working on development projects for the Indian tribes of Northern Argentina. He now manages his father's tenanted farm in Warwickshire, which produces milk and corn.

Gerry Randell

University of Bradford Management Centre
Emm Lane
Bradford
West Yorkshire BD9 4JL

He started work as an industrial chemist but later graduated in psychology and worked as an industrial psychologist in the Operational Research Department of J. Lyons and Co. and for LEO Computers. He then spent seven years on the staff of the University of London at Birkbeck College, where he obtained his Masters and Doctorate degrees. Currently he is Senior Lecturer in Occupational Psychology at the Bradford University Management Centre. He is consultant in staff development for many companies.

Brian L. Richardson

Solihull Area Health Authority
21 Poplar Road
Solihull
West Midlands B91 2BQ

After qualifying as a chartered accountant, his National Service was in Secretarial (Accounts) Branch of the RAF. He left accounting in 1964 for University Administration and in 1975 joined the re-organized National Health Service. Currently he is Treasurer of an Area Health Authority.

W. T. Singleton

Applied Psychology Department
University of Aston in Birmingham
Gosta Green
Birmingham B4 7ET

After graduating in Natural Sciences and in Moral Sciences (Psychology) he stayed in Cambridge as a member of a research unit in the Department of Psychology. Later he worked for six years in the industrial Midlands on Human Performance and spent a similar period at the College of Aeronautics, Cranfield in engineering production. For the past fifteen years he has been Head of the Department of Applied Psychology, University of Aston in Birmingham.

Brian Wilson

Head of Organization
and Human Resources Group
Cranfield School of Management
Cranfield
Bedford MK43 0AL

Graduated in Chemistry with Maths at the University of London and obtained his doctoral degree from London University in Organic Chemistry. Started his working career as a research chemist with the UKAEA but, pursuing his interest in people, he moved into plant management and then into organization development with ICI, and finally into Personnel Management with BOC and Babcock. Currently he is Professor of Organization and Human Resources in The Cranfield School of Management.

Introduction

W. T. SINGLETON

THE CONCEPT

This is the third in a series of books devoted to the study of real skills. The topic is management. A book on social skills is still to come and it might seem that the sequence should be reversed on the grounds that social skills are obviously one element in management skills but it is appropriate to deal with management first on the criterion of increasing complexity. Management skills are easier to understand than general social skills. This is because the defining characteristic of a skill is a purpose. The purpose of organizations in which managers operate and the tasks in which they are engaged are not easy to define but they are certainly less obscure than are the more general purposes of communities and people interactions in which the complete range of social skills is practised.

Skills, like purposes, are inherently to do with people. It follows that the 'skills view' of management will be as a people-based activity. Individuals carry out management tasks and these tasks always involve other individuals, of whom some are subordinate, some superior and some equivalent within the hierarchy of the particular management organization. The concept of a hierarchy is as central to management as it is to skills. The alternative to hierarchy is anarchy.

Management is not solely concerned with people. The manager's job is to deploy the available resources – space, equipment, money and people – in an optimum way to achieve some purpose. Although every experienced manager is aware of the importance of the human resources of the enterprise he often does not give them the attention they deserve because the current fashion, particularly in higher management, is to rely on numerical data. The standard data are financial since they are generally applicable to all resources but this only provides negative information about human resources. We can estimate the cost of the human resource of an organization in terms of expenditure required to acquire, maintain and develop it. This is important because there must be economy in total resources, but it is not crucial. What really matters is the value of the human resources to the achievement of purpose, that is, to the success of the enterprise as a whole.

The point was made in the first skills book that only a human being can make trade-offs between measurements or descriptions in different domains and that this is a general characteristic of skilled performance. Managers have to be human because they are essentially trading off costs and values. The key resource in organization costs is money; the key resource in organization value is people. For any enterprise and any resource it is so much easier to estimate a cost than it is to estimate a value. It is therefore not surprising that the unskilled manager concentrates on the relatively easy issues to do with space, equipment and money. He may try to avoid the values issue completely by relying on other people, his customers, to translate the value of his enterprise back into costs, in other words to pay for his products. This is the principle of the market place. The perfect market requires complete information, skilled customers and a clearly defined product.

Enterprises in modern societies are much too varied and complex for their success to be judged solely on rewards arising from what the customers pay. In many enterprises (perhaps most) someone at some level in the organization or outside it, has to make value assessments and convey these to people at various levels in the organization. The simple market discipline may operate for a small manufacturing or service company but even here there are many complications to do, for example, with the ability of the customer to assess what he is receiving. A National Health Service and a United Nations Organization are typical of enterprises where the value of the output is extraordinarily difficult to assess. One partial solution to this issue is to rely on the close relationship between the effectiveness of the organization and the effectiveness, that is the skill level, of the people in the organization. If the personnel are appropriately skilled the organization will be effective. This would be tautologous if we could only define skills in terms of achievements but this is not so. There are general principles of skilled performance which are independent of the particular achievement. In so far that these can be clarified, skill appraisal need not be entirely in terms of criteria such as organizational objectives. This is contrary to much current management thinking that the meeting of objectives is the beginning and ending of all criteria of management activity. This has become such an unquestioned axiom that the possibility of having to cope with situations where objectives are not definable is simply ignored. It has emerged in the earlier books in this series that skilled individuals function at the highest level when objectives are neither 'known' nor 'not known' but rather become increasingly clear as the activity proceeds. The hypothesis on which this book is based is that this proposition is as valid for managers as it is for all other highly skilled performers. If we can clarify the skills of management we can avoid the oversimplistic reliance on management by objectives.

SKILL APPRAISAL

The objective is to identify skills in particular management contexts with the hypothesis that there will be skills which are relatively independent of the context. The detailed description of such skills is a necessary stage of any process of systematic management selection, training, assessment and development. In short we wish to embark on a skills analysis for the manager to provide the foundation for methods of improving management and managers.

Even when the analyst is very familiar with the job (for example, he is himself an experienced practitioner) it is necessary to start by doing a task analysis so that the main tasks within the job can be separated and described. This involves clarifying to whom he is responsible for what, for whom he is responsible and what is delegated to subordinates. He relies on the skills of others as well as his own skills and he may not have or need many of the skills needed either by his subordinates or his superiors. The power of an effective organization comes from the complementary skills of the members. Some impression of the relative importance of the various tasks is needed; this can be done partly on the performers' estimates, partly on the discernible consequences of success and failure and partly on the time allocation. Generally the higher the level of functioning the more variability there is in the tasks and skills of the practitioner. Even at the middle level of management it is rare to find two individuals with the same job title who in practice carry out the same range of tasks, but nevertheless there may be a core of basic skills.

Having identified the range of tasks, one or more should be selected for detailed analysis aimed at describing exactly what the practitioner does. This is invariably a process rather than a structure; that is, there is a series of events in time often in several streams but converging on the key decision which is the hall-mark of a particular task. Even though this description might be at a minute level of detail we are still, at this stage, in the task domain. At some point the analyst must make his fundamental creative leap from the task domain to the skills domain. This is a very difficult step partly because how to do it cannot yet be described in general terms and partly because it usually involves a new taxonomy which the practitioner uses but which he himself has probably never identified. However, there are certain tests which can be applied. Negatively if it looks like a computer programme, a training programme or a responsibility chart then the analyst has not escaped from the task domain. More positively he is moving in the right direction if it is becoming clearer why and how the really effective practitioners differ from the less effective and why increasing experience makes a difference.

It is clear from the earlier books that skills analysis can be conducted only by intercommunication between the analyst and the practitioner. The two main sources of evidence are the observed performance of the skilled operator and his introspections about what he is doing and how he is doing it. These latter include how he formulates and modifies his objectives and how he achieves progress in relation to these objectives. His freedom for manoeuvre is always restricted by external constraints not only of available resources and time but also of potentiality for modifying objectives and for the need to conform to procedures acceptable to the organization as a whole. There are also internal constraints set by the attitudes of his colleagues. His key resource lies in the skills of the people including his own and those of his subordinates. This is not a static resource; on the contrary, one of the objectives of any system is the further development of skills so as to extend the human resources of the enterprise.

Although no practitioner will be able to convey the answer directly to the analyst some practitioners are much better than others in introspecting about their strategies and tactics. One valuable step forward is the location of these 'gold mine' sources of evidence: they are not necessarily the most prestigious practitioners. Most practitioners enjoy talking about their job so that although the skills analysis process is time consuming, few people object to taking part in it. Almost all practitioners will recognize the right answer to their skill description when the analyst provides it. In fact they often behave in the 'eureka' mode: 'You are absolutely right but I never thought about it that way before.' One criterion of success for the analyst is this response from his subjects.

THE PRECEDING BOOKS

The first chapter of the first book surveyed the contribution of experimental psychology to skill psychology with particular emphasis on experiments conceived in an information theory setting – often called studies in human performance. The first chapter of the second book described the history of skills analysis in the context of all the related observational techniques including time study, motion study, task analysis, error analysis and process control analysis as well as skills analysis. The first chapter of this book will examine the emergence of the systems approach from general systems theory to the more specific theories of man–machine systems, social systems and management systems. In each book most of the chapters are concerned with studies of skills as manifested either in particular jobs or in relation to general human activities such as designing and creative thinking or in relation to particular disabilities such as those to do with deafness and aging.

In the first book, an attempt was made to encompass the range of human work from the primary industries of forestry and farming to the quaternary industries dealing essentially with information processing. The coverage was comprehensive also in terms of the parallel range from jobs where the practitioner has support for his muscular effort through sensory supplementation to the beginnings of intellectual supplementation by computers and by creativity enhancement techniques. The studies concentrated on ordinary people doing ordinary jobs at the ordinarily achievable level of skill. One exception to this was R. B. Miller's study of the information system designer where he highlighted the differences between ordinary performance and virtuoso performance. There was considerable emphasis on this last theme in the second book which was entitled *Compliance and Excellence.* An attempt was made to illustrate the variety of human skills across the range from compliant tasks which involve coping with difficult external or internal circumstances (e.g. commercial diving and mental retardation respectively) to tasks where the practitioner is characterized by excellence (e.g. the expert pilot, golfer, rock-climber, musician or scientist).

From this point of view, the present book is similar to the first in that the intention is to sample across a wide range of jobs, all of which can be called management. There is a final section on some more general management issues. The term 'issue' is used to distinguish a situation where there is extensive ambiguity and scope for debate in contrast to a 'problem' to which there is a complete solution which can be deduced once the relevant information has been identified. In this terminology there are, in management, few problems and many issues.

SKILLS SO FAR

In the first book the concept of skill was introduced as a way of modelling human behaviour which takes particular account of learning and purpose. The basic question to ask in relation to any behaviour is: 'What is the performer trying to achieve?' It is the immediate temporary goal which gives unity to the activity and meaning to the effort. The purpose defines the boundaries of the unit of behaviour and provides the anchor in relation to which the elements fit together. The fit is always dynamic rather than static; one characteristic of skilled behaviour is that the timing is precise and adaptive. Elements run in parallel or appear in smooth succession so that the activity seems to converge towards the goal. The proposition is that differences between more effective performance and less effective performance are due to differences in skill. Skills are hypothetical constructs at many levels; in the way things are done, in the way the situation is comprehended, and in the way the whole thing fits together. Hence the concepts of motor skills, perceptual skills and executive skills respectively. The legacies of learning can be located in these various kinds of skills.

Motor skills make possible the smooth routines of human outputs which involve the coordination of a great variety of muscle and joint activities. As with all skills their development and reinforcement is a consequence of success in practice. The individual tries to achieve something, he initiates some activity and simultaneously an internal record becomes available from which the activity could be reproduced and against which the feedback of the success of the activity is checked. This feedback of information may be partly through the eyes and ears but, in the case of motor skills, it is predominantly internal, through the kinaesthetic and tactile senses. Motor skills are manifested in precisely timed and positioned movements which can be as different in purpose as a hand movement which changes gear on a car to one which obtains silence at a board meeting.

Perceptual skills can be thought of as models which are updated by selective information through the eyes and ears, particularly the eyes. Normally auditory, tactile and other data are used to reinforce that which has been established through the data from the visual system. The basis for decision and action is usually the model rather than the direct sensory input. Models can vary from simple rules to complex conceptual maps containing extensive symbolism. The human information processing system appears at first sight to be symmetrical with skills as selecting and organizing mechanisms on each side of the decision point; on the input side are perceptual skills and on the output side are motor skills. This is an oversimplification. It implies that the two kinds of skill are somehow equivalent and that they are separated by a third set of processes to do with decision making. Both these propositions seem to be inaccurate. The perceptual skills dominate the motor skills and they are inseparable from what have been called cognitive skills. The difference between perceptual and cognitive skills is just that the former are more directly in touch with new sense data. Decision is not a process which necessarily follows the organizing of information: it emerges during the organizing.

Executive skills are conceived as master programmes which select and coordinate appropriate perceptual and motor skilled activity in the light of some purpose. This can be a useful concept in explaining differences in performance at very high levels of skill and in describing what happens as a consequence of stress and fatigue. The executive programme seems to be more sensitive to disruption than do the component skills and correspondingly the achievement of excellence is very much a function of this high executive level of skill. The key to superb performance is in 'getting it all together' rather than in the separate activities. Nevertheless it is not possible to define an interface between perceptual skills and executive skills. We are probably trying to conceive of a continuous hierarchy by a subdivision of upper and lower levels along what is really a continuum from perceptual skills through cognitive skills up to executive skills.

Even the apparently qualitative distinction between perceptual skills and motor skills tends to diminish with closer analysis. This is because the organization of perception seems to be intimately related to action and correspondingly the organization of actions seems to be related to distinguished streams of inputs. Thus the interface between the perceptual and motor skills, the decision point, vanishes. Decisions emerge as a consequence of skilled activity at the perceptual and motor level.

A different but not necessarily contradictory model of skilled behaviour can be constructed in terms of schema; developing internal records of activity. The most primitive schema are strongly associated with the total body image. There are called enactive models. They develop from earliest infancy. When the reference system shifts from the body itself to the physical environment we have the beginnings of perceptual skills. These are called pictorial models because the behaviour seems to be monitored by an internal representation which corresponds topologically to the external world. However, this correspondence can become increasingly abstract through iconic models to entirely symbolic models which use languages and other abstract communication systems as their vehicle.

Human development from the neonate to the adult can be described in terms of increasing complexity of available skills along this hierarchy: enactive, pictorial, iconic and linguistic: correspondingly the adult can be described as functioning with the aid of all these varieties of internal model and indeed with hybrid models. These internal models or schema develop in line with real time as new data are received through the senses or as spontaneous restructuring occurs. Nevertheless this mode of operation is such that the behaviour of the individual is not tied very closely to the specific inputs at a given time and correspondingly the specified outputs are not merely a function of the immediate situation. The central point of internal modelling or simulation as the basis of control is to escape from real time. A model can incorporate various scenarios for the future with attached likelihoods as well as a record of the past and an indication of the present. The greater the skill of the practitioner the more effective his modelling of reality in terms of both goodness of fit and extension into the future. With some degree of anthropomorphic licence it can be said that the individual reacts to the model and not to reality; this has its disadvantages and advantages. If the model does not match reality he is in serious trouble as an adaptive organism but when it does then he has achieved enormous flexibility in being able to react to a total situation rather than to separate stimuli in succession. Correspondingly his output is not isolated responses in sequence but integrated patterns of smooth activity.

Anthropomorphism is a useful aid to understanding but it is also misleading. There is not a separate individual or internal little man watching the schema develop; the schema are the expression of the individual as well as the model of the situation. Similarly, perceptions, memories, decisions and cognition generally are not separately located processes. They are descriptions of functions which the schema can perform. Self-development, self-control and self-monitoring all proceed as spontaneous automatic consequences of the developing schema.

However, this abstract conception of the internal cognitive system is not essential for the understanding of skilled behaviour at the practical level. It is sufficient to note some of the consequences, that is, skill characteristics which hopefully will apply to management skills as well as to the skills of coping with the physical world which were studied in the first and second books. The following is a summary of the sections headed 'concepts of skill' in the previous books.

(1) The skilled practitioner will utilize any technological facilities which usefully supplement his energy expenditure or information processing and there will be corresponding changes in his skills as he comes to rely on the new facilities.

(2) There could be a relationship, although it is rather an elusive one, between physical and mental dexterity. Precision in thinking has its complement in precision in action.

(3) A basic attribute of all skills is precise timing. This applies across the whole range of activity from single movements in fractions of a second to nicely phased innovations over periods of years.

(4) One general term implying a high level of skill is 'professionalism'. This appears in invariant standards and adaptive functions which do not transgress accepted rules and procedures.

(5) In common with other human activities and attributes, skills can be thought of as person centred, function centred or society centred, depending on the purpose of the particular study.

(6) High-level skilled activity cannot be understood in terms only of the person and the process; the context is equally important.

(7) The skilled individual can be considered to be operating within an overall life-plan which includes a heterogeneous mix of variables such as events and people. This encompasses his motivation and his values and drive which he brings to a situation.

(8) Even the more primitive skills which depend on the body image can incorporate an ideal goal and associated tolerance margins.

(9) Means are a dubious source of evidence on skill level; the successful achievement of ends is more informative. Thus, achievement is the key criterion although insight into procedures can contribute to assessment.

(10) Risks are inseparable from purposes. The skilled practitioner can minimize risks in given contexts (hence his reputation for being lucky) but he cannot eliminate them.

(11) Skill implies optimal effort in relation to achievement: that is, skilled performance is efficient. This applies to energy, information and time and also to other less well-defined resources in the affective domain such as personal commitment and involvement.

(12) Optimal self-monitoring is another characteristic of skill. Too little and the opportunity to learn will not be fully exploited; too much and self-absorption will replace the more appropriate situation-absorption.

(13) The skilled practitioner can select the essentials and then get the order right.

(14) He can appear to concentrate with great specificity on one procedure or objective and yet can notice and react swiftly to the unexpected.

(15) Diagnostic skills involve the weighting and integration of many different factors. These factors vary from those which have been clearly identified and measured to others which are equally important but are collected together in the term 'context'.

(16) The skilled performer will devote considerable effort to 'getting the picture' and will be distressed if he feels he is 'losing the picture'.

(17) The same demand can result in the employment of very different combinations of strategies and capacities by different skilled individuals.

(18) In creative activity the proposed solution is always a function of the solver as well as of the situation.

(19) Differences between skilled performers are more obvious on the perceptual side, e.g. in assessments and judgements, than on the motor or action side.

(20) Different organizational systems suit different kinds of people. The skilled participator partially adapts to the system, partially changes it and partially evades it.

THE WAY FORWARD

Having generated some characteristics of skill which have intriguing potential for the study of management it is necessary to examine in this context what working managers of many different kinds actually do. It may then be possible to detect some general principles which not only fit with human skill theory but also extend it. If skill theory is to be universal in its applicability across all levels and kinds of human activity then the theory must be based on evidence from the correspondingly complete range of human tasks. So far these skills books have concentrated on situations where only one practitioner is involved; we now embark on the study of tasks in which there are many people interacting with the key individual we identify as the manager within the organization.

The concept of an organization, that is a communicating network of people and other elements working in relation to a common purpose, has another theory. Such an organization is a system and there is a theory of systems which we need to explore. The first chapter deals with systems theory and its relationship to skill theory. In the second chapter, the first case study is introduced, one of management in a primary industry – farming. This is followed by eight chapters dealing with the tertiary industries or service sector in which, in our society, the vast majority of people, including managers, work. There are then three chapters dealing with specialized aspects of secondary industry – manufacturing. Finally there are four chapters on wider themes: three across some general issues of management in a skills context and the fourth returning again to the theory of skilled performance.

1 Systems Theory and Skill Theory

W. T. SINGLETON

INTRODUCTION

Two very different methods or philosophies are followed in scientific studies. One is mechanistic, reductionist and analytical, the other is teleological, holistic and synthetic. This latter is now generally described as the systems approach. The former is the one most readily understood; it has been used widely and has proved to be extremely successful in the physical sciences and engineering. The general idea is that the investigator will understand things better if he takes them apart either physically or conceptually. He analyses what happens, reduces a great variety of objects or phenomena to the smallest possible number of universal components or elements, and constructs explanations in terms of the combinations and interactions of these elements. The distinction between a teleological and a mechanistic explanation is lucidly explained by Russell (1946). 'When we ask "why?" concerning an event, we may mean either of two things. We may mean: "what purpose did this event serve?" or we may mean: "what earlier circumstances caused this event?" The answer to the former question is a teleological explanation, or an explanation by final causes; the answer to the latter question is a mechanistic explanation.'

In discussing skilled performance it always seems to be necessary to generate the boundaries of a particular activity in terms of relevance to a given purpose. Correspondingly, the distinguishing feature of a skilled activity is the progressive development of the pattern or form of the activity in time and space; we have to identify the structure and the process rather than the elements. The concept of skill is holistic and synthetic rather than reductionist and analytical. Thus the study of skill clearly requires a systems approach rather than the more traditional elemental scientific approach.

These two approaches are neither antagonistic nor mutually exclusive; they are simply different. Each is more or less effective depending on the topic of study and the style of thinking favoured by the student. They can be complementary, particularly in a young science where there is extensive uncertainty about the usefulness of particular concepts.

Even in the old discipline of physics we still have field theory as well as element theory. There was a time of dispute between the two approaches; e.g. whether light was really made up of packages of energy (photons), or whether it was really waves, was considered as a problem which would eventually be settled one way or the other but these views are not now regarded as antagonistic: for some phenomena one model is more effective but for some other phenomena the alternative model provides a more elegant description of what is happening. Similarly in psychology it is quite tenable, particularly in the laboratory, to take a behaviouristic approach and to examine, for example, the details of the connections between stimuli and responses in a given context and to generate rules and principles about stimulus–response relationships. However, for high level behaviour and for behaviour in the complex, multifaceted real world it seems more apposite to take a systems or skills approach and to start by identifying the purpose of an activity.

The systems approach is relevant in other ways in the management context. O'Shaughnessy (1966) identifies three schools of thought in business organization theory: the classical, the human relations and the systems. In the classical approach the emphasis is on issues such as concepts of subdivision, authority and its delegation, span of control, criteria of meeting or missing objectives and so on. In the human relations approach the emphasis is on the organization as a collection of people, each with his own needs and limitations. These people interact as groups and the groups again have their needs and limitations and interactions. The idealized prescription is that authority is delegated and distributed so that working individuals and groups are as autonomous as possible. There is emphasis on job enlargement, job enrichment and job satisfaction generally in the optimistic belief that the organzation will be maximally efficient when all those who work within it have the greatest flexibility and personal responsibility. In the systems approach the central emphasis is on optimal division into subsystems so that communication between the subsystems can be most effective. Attention is focused on the flow of information, particularly feedback in relation to movement towards objectives. Thus the organization itself is considered as the central system, with machines, procedures and people as interacting subsystems.

It is clear, even from these very brief descriptions, that the three approaches are not exclusive alternatives. The same central issues are identified in all of them; formulation of objectives, information needed for control requirements and the integration of many separate activities. All of them can be considered as systems approaches and skills approaches in that there is a general underlying model of an organization which exists for some purpose or purposes and which must be flexible and adaptive so as to achieve the ends by a variety of means or to modify the ends depending on progress in an essentially unpredictable environment.

Since both the concepts of the organization and the concepts of skilled performance can be considered in the context of systems theory it is desirable to consider the systems approach in detail and from many points of view. Accordingly this chapter is divided into sections concerned with general systems theory, biological systems, man–machine systems, sociotechnical systems and management systems. These topics are the background to the consideration of the central theme of the organization and its management by skilled practitioners.

GENERAL SYSTEMS THEORY

Although general systems theory is often considered to be a post-war innovation its origin can be traced to 19th and even 18th century physics when field theory was first developed conceptually by Faraday and mathematically by Gauss and Ampère (Dampier, 1942). The parallel development of the ideas and the mathematics has always been fundamental to the physical sciences. For example, the resolution of the photon and wave theories of light already mentioned occurred not simply by the acceptance of alternative visualizations but more fundamentally because the general equations which resulted from these apparently very different concepts were found to be identical. This is obviously a highly satisfying situation; the equations are the precise description of the phenomena, while the pictorial models are alternative ways of thinking about their implications. The earliest principles of mechanics were expressions of a model of forces acting between bodies in physical contact. These had to be extended to cover gravitation, magnetism and radiation which involved interactions or transfers of energy at a distance. Here there are still systematic changes in time – that is, processes – and there may be multiple interactions which are best perceived as patterns. It was necessary to postulate an electromagnetic field of force – this is essentially a structure. Thus physics had now incorporated patterns in space and time: structures and processes respectively. The more recent reconciliation of concepts of matter and energy by Maxwell, Einstein and many others again occurred as a parallel development of ideas of waves travelling respectively in circles and in straight lines and of general equations such as the famous $E = mc^2$.

Another profound advance occurred with the introduction of a new fundamental concept – entropy. Eddington (1935) identifies this as the key change in the ideas of physics: 'From the point of view of philosophy of science the conception associated with entropy must I think be ranked as the great contribution of the nineteenth century to scientific thought. It marked a reaction from the view that everything to which science need pay attention is discovered by a microscopic dissection of objects. It provided an alternative standpoint in which the centre of interest is shifted from the entities reached by the customary analysis (atoms, electric potentials, etc.) to qualities possessed by the system as a whole, which cannot be split up and located – a little bit here, and a little bit there.' Shannon (1948) selected entropy as defined by Boltzman in statistical mechanics, $H = \Sigma p_i \log p_i$, as an appropriate measure of choice, uncertainty or information. Entropy is a measure of disorganization and the amount of information in a system is the reverse of this – the degree of organization. Thus, entropy and information content are concepts which can be applied across all sciences and, in psychology, they can be applied to the mind as well as to the brain. This is not true of energy; we talk about 'mental energy' but this is nothing more than a loose analogy. Energy is used in brain function but its consumption is only a very remote indicator of brain activity, just as measuring the electric power consumed by a computer tells us very little about the functions of the computer. This is why we need the additional concept of information.

Although information is a functional rather than a physical concept Shannon was mainly interested in physical processes of communication and it was Weiner (1948) who developed the wider application of statistical mechanics to control mechanisms, including the nervous system. He coined the term 'cybernetics' to mean the study of control and communication whether in the machine or in the animal.

In general systems theory the ideas are extended even further to cover organizations such as factories, cities and societies. The point about the emphasis on entropy and information, that is on communication rather than energy, is that we are primarily interested in the preservation of structure. This is a fight against the physical world which, left to itself, will steadily decrease its degree of organization. Again this is beautifully expressed by Eddington (*op. cit.*). 'The law that entropy always increases – the second law of thermodynamics – holds, I think, the supreme position among the laws of Nature. If someone points out to you that your pet theory of the universe is in disagreement with Maxwell's equations – then so much the worse for Maxwell's equations. If it is found to be contradicted by observations – well these experimentalists do bungle things sometimes. But if your theory is found to be against the second law of thermodynamics I can give you no hope: there is nothing for it but to collapse in deepest humiliation.' Managers are sensitive to this aspect of their task within organizations; invariably they express the feeling that there are unremitting pressures towards chaos in the systems for which they are responsible and that only continuous skilled effort opposes this natural tendency.

In the biological sciences there has always been an interest in structure or morphology because the beginnings of biology – both botany and zoology – were in classification. The key determinants of classification are usually in shape and form. The ideas of evolution propounded by Lamarck and Darwin introduced the importance of the process as well as the structure. Early in the 20th century the new biological science of psychology rapidly divided into two main schools; behaviourism which was and is essentially mechanistic in philosophy and gestalt psychology which, as the name implies, is concerned with structure and form. The influence of systems thinking on the development of biological thought will be discussed in more detail in the next section.

Returning to general science and general systems, the progress of the physical sciences up to the Second World War had been in terms of deterministic mechanics – basically the interaction of two variables and the explanatory model of cause–effect sequences together with the other extreme of statistical mechanics dealing with very large numbers of interactions in 'unorganized complexity'. The intermediate region where there are ten, a hundred or a thousand interacting variables is the focus of systems theory. The relevant mathematics is developing only slowly. The first important book was by von Neumann and Morgenstern (1944). The mathematics of the theory of games is not widely used or even understood but the principles and the jargon have entered into the system thinker's vocabulary *viz.* minimax criterion which involves minimizing the maximum possible loss, the payoff matrix, the regret matrix, pure and mixed strategies, zero-sum or non-zero-sum games and so on. Morgenstern (1967) points out that the fundamental complication of social sciences compared with physical sciences is that one has to take account of purposeful behaviour. Game theory attempts to describe and predict decision-making in situations of indeterminacy where one player may be following a systematic strategy; it may or may not help his opponent to know what this strategy is. The situation is similar in relation to catastrophe theory (Zeeman, 1975) where the mathematics quickly becomes very difficult but the principle of locating discontinuities in multiparameter interactions has wide appeal and application.

The zero-sum game is one formal expression of the general system concept of a closed system as distinct from an open one. This distinction is important. As with all fundamental ideas it has appeared in philosophy in other guises and with different terminologies. For example Broad (1925) described the difference between what he called 'Conservative Systems' and 'Non-Conservative Systems'. Nevertheless it was van Bertalanffy (1962), one of the main pioneers of general systems theory, who set out the distinctions between closed and open systems. Van Bertalanffy summarizes the common characteristics of systems approaches in this way: '*Firstly*, they agree in the emphasis that something should be done about the problems characteristic of the behavioural and biological sciences, but not dealt with in conventional physical theory. *Secondly*, these theories introduce concepts and models novel in comparison to physics: for example, a generalized system concept, the concept of information compared to energy in physics. *Thirdly*, these theories are particularly concerned with multivariable problems. *Fourthly*, these models are interdisciplinary and transcend the conventional fields of science. *Fifthly*, and perhaps most important: concepts like wholeness, organization, teleology and directiveness appear in mechanistic science to be unscientific or metaphysical. Today they are taken seriously and are regarded as amenable to scientific analysis.' The van Bertalanffy approach is typical of the empirico-intuitive method where one starts from the examination of existing biological systems and attempts to proceed upwards to general principles. The complementary method is exemplified by Ashby (1952, 1968) who starts from the general logical principles which an information handling or control system must follow and proceeds downwards to look for examples of these principles in real systems (Figure 1.1).

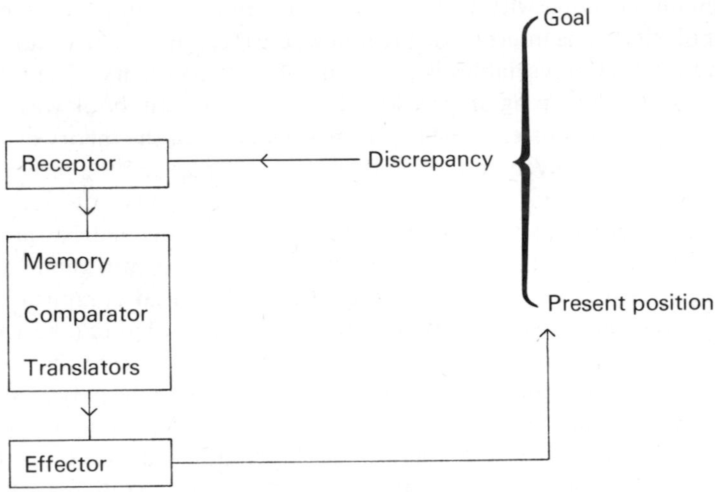

Figure 1.1 General concept of a purposive system: the system must deal in energy and information. This concept can be arrived at either by generalization from the study of working systems or by deductive logic from principles of control and communication

Another exponent of deductive system theory is Mackay (1950, 1969) who, in addition to pursuing the principles of automata, has made a fundamental contribution to information theory. He has pointed out that two of the pioneers of information theory, Fisher and Gabor, did not produce rival versions of the concept of information but rather they defined complementary kinds of information. Fisher, in 1935, was describing metrical information which comes from evidence about the situation while Gabor, in 1946, had defined the structure of the information in either space or time; this is called the logon-content as distinct from Fisher's metron-content. The average manager might feel that the Shannon measure of information is complicated enough without introducing others but it is desirable to have some idea of all three kinds of information content and Mackay has identified the difference; Shannon defined the selective information, the information needed to locate one of a known set of possible messages, enabling the observer to make an identification, while Gabor defined the structure or the measure of dimensionality and Fisher defined the weight of available evidence. Thus we have selective information content (bits), structured information content (logons) and metrical information content (metrons). Shannon assumes that we already know what might happen; communication is needed only to identify what has happened. This is valid only for very restricted behavioural situations, typically those met with in the human performance laboratory.

In real situations the entrant has the primary problem of working out some reasonable range of contingencies. To develop a concept of the main events that might happen he builds a picture based not only on the presented situation but also on the recollections of similar situations experienced in the past. Thus he calls up the most relevant model or schema acquired by previous experience and modifies it to match the present as closely as possible. This model obviously has some structure – that is, some logon content – but it also incorporates precise evidence from the present, namely some metron content. The two are not independent. Mackay (1950) suggests that logon and metron content are flexibly interchangeable within some total limit; for human behaviour this must be a capacity. In other terminology this is discussed as the capacity of short-term or immediate memory. Crossman (1961) pointed out that, in examining the capacity of immediate memory, we need to distinguish between order (which is an elementary form of structure) and content which he discussed in Shannon terms. Returning to skill concepts: observation and introspection confirm that, in entering a situation, the skilled person begins by 'getting the picture'. This is a necessary precursor to information processing in the Shannon sense and it would be interesting if it could be explored more in Gabor/Fisher terms. There seem to be no reports of studies using this latter approach.

BIOLOGICAL SYSTEMS THEORY

In its broadest sense this is the same as general systems theory but the biologists have developed their own concepts about the place of living organisms within the total scheme of things as well as their structure and behaviour, e.g. Boulding (1956) places plants and animals about halfway along a hierarchy from static frameworks to transcendental systems (Table 1.1).

Miller (1978) concentrates on living systems from the cell to supranational systems and suggests that at each of the seven levels the same nineteen subsystems can be identified: eight which process matter – energy, nine which process information and two which deal with both. A summary is given in Table 1.2. There are two subsystems which process both matter – energy and information. The Reproducer makes possible the transmission of the template of the system so that a new generation can appear and individ-

Table 1.1 Hierarchy of systems (Boulding, 1956)

Level	*Name*	*Characteristics*
1	Static	Frameworks: sets of items in fixed relationships such as brick walls or crystals
2	Dynamic	Clockworks: some changes in time but in a regular predetermined way
3	Cybernetic	Self-regulated systems: adaptation to changes in time but again in ways predetermined by rules built into structures, e.g. thermostats
4	Cells	Open systems with self-maintenance: adaptation to change which involves resisting change
5	Plants	Open systems with growth and development
6	Animals	Increased mobility and technological behaviour; some self-awareness
7	Humans	Self-aware; can utilize symbolism
8	Social systems	Organizations of humans with shared values and more extended life cycles
9	Transcendental systems	The relationship between ultimates and unknowables

Physical sciences centre on levels 1–4
Biological sciences on levels 4–7
Social sciences on levels 6–8
Level 9 is the domain of religions as well as arts and humanities

Table 1.2 Hierarchy of systems and subsystems (Miller, 1978)

System levels	Subsystems	
	Matter–energy	Information
Cell	Reproducer Boundary	
Organ	Ingester Distributor	Input transducer Internal transducer
Organism	Convertor Producer	Channel and net Decoder
Group	Store Extruder	Associator Memory
Organization	Motor Supporter	Decider Uncoder
Society		Output transducer
Supra-national system		

uals can be supported until they become self-sufficient. A less obvious subsystem is the Boundary which holds together the components by permitting or excluding various matter–energy or information exchanges. Thus a barrier, a filter and a steady-state differential is provided between the system and the environment. Since matter–energy is coming in and going out then there has to be a set of subsystems which facilitate this process. This set contains, in order: an Ingester, a Distributor, a Converter and then a Producer which generates the temporarily enduring materials needed for growth, repair or replacement within the systems. Storage facilities for these materials are needed and so also are Extrusion facilities for waste products. The Motor subsystem is concerned with moving the system in an environment or adjusting the environment and also with the sending out of markers bearing information. The Supporter is the subsystem which maintains the structure in the sense of the spatial relationship between components. In higher animals this is an exoskeleton or an endoskeleton. The information subsystems are self-explanatory. Transducers are needed because the 'information-bearing markers' change at the system boundary (in the sense organs and muscles) and sometimes at subsystem boundaries. Information flow within the system requires Decoders, Associators and Memory. The Decoder is like an amplifier in that it is a node with fewer outputs than inputs; the outputs of decoders exercise control of the system within a hierarchy. Biology in general can be regarded as the study of how these functions are performed by various mechanisms.

A different use of systems concepts in biology is to consider the properties of continuity in time exhibited by organisms from survival, through stability to maintenance of direction in the broadest sense. The simplest version of this is Cannon's (1939) theory of homeostasis, which emphasizes the broad tendency to return to a balanced state as a reaction to any disturbance from outside. Waddington (1972b) proposes that the notion be extended to homeothesis: stabilized pathways of change rather than stabilized situations. These pathways of change he calls 'chreods'. A chreodic system has built-in end results which will be attained in spite of considerable – but not too much – variation of inputs. He uses the example of rain which falls in a given valley: it doesn't matter which stream it goes into; it will eventually emerge in the same river unless it falls beyond a watershed whereupon with equal inevitability it will come out in a different river. The notion can be applied not only to biological entities such as embryos but also to minds, where chreods are concepts and programmes. This is an interesting way of describing the stability of progress towards goals which are achieved in the face of extensive variations in environments with the associated disturbing forces. It emphasizes the importance of history and the continuous nature of all biological processes. 'Every biological unit has a history, indeed one might say it *is* a history. . . . In place of the maximization of entities whose essence is independent of time, biology deals in the main with optimization, or balancing or "Golden Rule-izing" of things which are very complex. . . . The central theme of biology is the problem of optimizing the components of a system so as to maximize the whole, rather than maximizing any single component.' (Waddington, 1972a). Substitute 'management' for 'biology' throughout this quotation and it remains valid.

In a later exposition Waddington (1973) distinguishes between two different ways in which chreods may come into existence; there are 'generative chreods' where the theme is established and the details appear to be fitted to the theme, and there are 'assimilative chreods' where there seems to be chaos to start with but the theme gradually emerges. This again can be applied to the mind as well as to biological entities. For example, the development of walking seems to suggest a generative chreod – it appears to be a natural development dictated by the structure and maturation of the child – but swimming, by contrast, suggests an assimilative chreod – the swimmer has to be taught how to coordinate his movements to achieve his purpose and there are several quite different styles, i.e. 'strokes'. Human progress is facilitated by a 'jackpot phenomenon' which appears in that many chreods appear to be more unified and coherent than was essential for their primary purpose. Chreods have an extensive affinity with schemata; they appear to be slightly different formulations of the same general concept of developing processes within the mind which have an identity in terms of an objective and which demonstrate stability in terms of progression towards the end, while allowing flexibility in means. Means and ends may not be qualitatively different but merely expressions of particular levels within a more general hierarchy of human values.

MAN–MACHINE SYSTEMS

Ergonomics emerged in post-war Europe as the selective combination of anatomical, physiological and psychological expertise applied to the design of work and the working environment (Murrell, 1965). For example, a man working may have problems of energy expenditure and heat stress which are most appropriately studied from a physiological background; the dimensions of the work space and the kinds, sizes and directions of forces exerted are best determined by anatomical data, while the processing of information needed to control the working activity is within the province of the experimental psychologist. It seemed appropriate to put these operationally related topics together to create a new discipline – ergonomics.

In the USA there were two streams of research and application similar to ergonomics: an activity oriented towards safety and health generated by the occupational health personnel (MacFarland, 1953) and an activity orientated towards effective performance based on the application of experimental psychology to military engineering design (Chapanis *et al.*, 1949). During the 'cold war' era the extensive research and development activity in this latter area began to show utilization of the systems approach (Gagné, 1962).

Industrial ergonomics had run into difficulties because it invariably took the form of criticizing decisions about work design already made by engineers and managers and proposing modifications which required additional expenditure. Systems ergonomics avoided this by introducing human factors consideration at the design stage. To communicate effectively psychologists and engineers needed a common language and a common purpose. The common language was in the description of functions as distinct from mechanisms and the common purpose emerged from the detailed discussion about objectives. The agreed objectives had to be met by a combination of human and hardware activities and the key issue was the allocation of function between man and machine. As functional thinking became more general it was gradually appreciated that the human operator is a superbly designed system in his own right: he has energy generation, storage and distribution subsystems all beautifully integrated towards meeting human needs and purposes. Hardware can thus be seen in a new perspective as simulations and extensions of human functions (Singleton *et al.*, 1967). The characteristics of systems ergonomics are a detailed attention to objectives, the separation of required functions and their allocation between man and machine (or delegation from man to machine). The required human functions are to do with setting up and maintaining systems as well as on-line control. Training and interface design are regarded as complementary aspects of the same systems problem of effectively linking the man and the machine (Singleton, 1974).

The appropriate mathematics for these exercises are models of human performance derived from information theory, control theory and decision theory (Sheridan and Ferrell, 1974). The appropriateness and power of these mathematical tools comes from the functional nature of the underlying concepts; within limits they can be applied indiscriminately to human performance, hardware performance or total system performance. All working systems can be subdivided into a power system and a control system for which the appropriate metrics are respectively energy and information. There must be input and output links with the outside world which can process energy, data and materials and there must be central processes to do with storing and restructuring. Describing the system requires consideration of capacities, speed and precision.

Information theory in this context is Shannon–Weiner theory, in which the source and the destination share an agreed alphabet or ensemble of what might happen in terms of range of events and their probabilities. Information transmission reduces the uncertainty at the destination about what has happened at the source as distinct from what might have happened. Information measures describe actual rates of transmission and capacities per item and per unit time. Errors can be traded off against speed, and losses can be separated into ambiguity-insertions in the output and equivocation-losses from the input. The theory covers continuous information as well as discrete events. All the measures are averages over time.

Control theory is concerned with stability in relation to varieties of inputs and outputs. Optimal control implies some weighted minimization of all the 'cost' variables such as error, energy and time. The simplest form of control is open-loop, where actions or outputs follow according to known rules from given inputs. Most control systems are of the closed-loop kind where an aspect of the output, usually the error (the difference between the ideal and the actual), is fed back as an input to cause the system to reduce the error. This is a servomechanism. Energy and information are involved. Timing is invariably critical: some models are based on the time domain directly and others on the frequency domain. Control theory is straightforward for systems that are linear and stationary (an increment of input is followed by a corresponding increment of output after a constant time interval) but inevitably the human operator is neither. He exhibits non-linearities in terms of thresholds, capacity limits, learning, fatigue and so on; he is non-stationary not only in that his response time can vary but also in that he has a variable weighting of anticipatory and remembered cues which modify his reaction to the current state of the controlled system. Nonetheless for highly restricted situations which are common in big systems these models can accurately describe and predict human performance.

Decision theory is mainly prescriptive in describing how people ought to behave but there can be some descriptive content. In any case, empirically noted departures from supposed ideal behaviour are always theoretically interesting. The basic notion of utility was first introduced by economists to explain certain apparent paradoxes; e.g. people do not always attempt to maximize their financial rewards. A central aspect of decision theory is the distinction between kinds of errors. For example, in signal detection theory cases where the signal was present but the response was not made are separated from cases where the signal was not present but a response was made. Give this separation and certain theoretical assumptions it is possible to calculate two relevant measures of operator performance: the real difficulty in discriminating between the alternative situations and the degree of confidence or caution in making these choices. This theory can be used to describe behaviour in discrete decision situations such as inspection and vigilance tasks. In the case of interdependent sequences (series) of decisions the most useful form of analysis is the decision tree, where the operator is conceived as playing a game against nature. This can be related to game theory mentioned earlier by substituting a second decision-maker in place of nature.

Man–machine system concepts now have an essential part to play in all big systems designs such as those used in aerospace, power generation and distribution and chemical processing. The functions of machines, procedures and people within these systems have to be planned in detail before the systems are realized in physical terms. The performance limits of each subsystem including the personnel must be predicted. The reliability must be as high as possible; this follows when the probability of errors has been minimized. In particular, human errors in such high-powered systems can readily lead to catastrophes. The high power of these systems is such that there is always potentiality for disaster and the high complexity can lead to 'cascading' of faults. Paradoxically the human operator is the main source of unreliability but also the main bulwark in coping with unreliability. In short, he remains the key element in these big systems just as he is in all other man-made systems.

SOCIOTECHNICAL SYSTEMS

The pre-war development of the 'human relations' school (Mayo, 1933) had changed the emphasis in organization theory from the study of the principles of authority and its delegation – 'plan, organize, command, coordinate and control' (Fayol, 1916) – to the study of individual and small group behaviour in which the attitudes of the worker are seen as the key factor in production. After the war Trist and others working from the Tavistock Institute of Human Relations (Trist and Murray, 1948) noted what they called the 'responsible autonomy' of groups of miners, who carried out a complete cycle of operations and recognized the interdependence not only of individuals within the group but also of groups within teams. They noted also that the social and psychological aspects of behaviour could be understood only in the context of the particular technological system in the underground environment. They were able to study the work of groups with different degrees of mechanization in the same type of coal seam (Trist *et al.*, 1963) and also the behaviour of different groups with the same technology but different social systems (Trist and Bamforth, 1951). In this last case the composite group (a variety of tasks and a commitment to the whole group task) had a higher productivity and a lower absenteeism than a conventional group (commitment only to a single part task and to an isolated group). A similar approach was used by Rice in Indian cotton-mills (Rice, 1958).

The conceptually interesting aspect of this approach was in the recognition that, although technical factors and social factors have their independent properties, each in practice imposes constraints in the other domain and in addition the sociotechnical interactions are within further constraints from the economic domain. The key factor in the organization is seen as the task which is to be completed by the joint functions from the technological domain (the things) and the sociopsychological domain (the people). These define the substantive dimension; the economic dimension measures the effectiveness with which human and technological resources are used to carry out the primary task (Trist *et al.*, 1963).

This was very much a systems model, essentially of the closed system type. Emery and Trist (1965) extended the model further by taking a more open system approach and examining what they called the 'causal texture of the environment'. They use the word texture to emphasize that a 'system behaviour' cannot be understood by examining interdependencies within the system and between the system and the environment but it is also necessary to consider interdependencies within the environment. They distinguish four types of causal texture. The first they call the *placid randomized environment* where there are no important external interactions or influences of the organization on the environment; this is the economist's classical market. The second is the *placid clustered environment* where there are interactions within the environment but this is not seriously affected by the organization; the economist's imperfect competition. The third is the *disturbed reactive environment* where the organizations must recognize that there are also other organizations operating in the same environment and there are effects on the environment. The fourth is the *turbulent field* where the environment must be seen as continuously changing, sometimes in unpredictable ways and with complex interactions between the organization and the environment. In the first type of environment forward planning is not necessary; in the second type it is useful; in the third type it becomes essential for survival; but in the fourth type it becomes so difficult as to be almost impossible so that basic stability is threatened. A useful summary of the sociotechnical systems approach is provided by Emery (1969).

The social and technical interaction concept has had a considerable influence within management training at the Tavistock Institute and elsewhere. Perhaps because organizations have been attempting to survive in the fourth type of environment for the past decade or so, the theoretically interesting ideas do not seem to have made much further progress. As one experienced worker in this tradition comments: 'Systems concepts, including the concept of the sociotechnical system, I take at the moment to be formulated at such a high level of generality as not to be, by themselves, operationally very useful. A great deal still has to be done to make them operational and in the meantime, the attractiveness of systems concepts in theory should not delude us into thinking that we have the tools to deal comprehensively with the problems of job design in practice.' (Klein, 1979). Instead there has been a return to more traditional psychological methods as exemplified by the 'Quality of Working Life' movement, (Davis and Cherns, 1975; Warr, 1976) which is a psychometric rather than a systems approach with emphasis on the interaction of external factors and internal traits within the working situation but with a very vague conception of objectives.

ORGANIZATIONAL SYSTEMS AND SOCIETAL SYSTEMS

The consideration of human behaviour within a sociotechnical structure leads naturally, in systems terms, to the consideration of the structure of organizations within society.

In the context of industrial organizations, Woodward (1965) found that the kind of production technology, e.g. batch, mass or process, was related to organization structure; the more complex the production technology the more elaborate became the management hierarchy, and the ratio of managerial staff to other personnel increased. As the managerial staff increases there arise difficult problems of management structure: tall or flat, the grouping of responsibilities (e.g. functional *versus* product), integration and centralization and problems of adapting that structure to the changing environment (Child, 1977). Burns and Stalker (1961) describe the 'organismic structure' as one well adapted to an unpredictable environment. An *organismic structure* is one in which information and authority are decentralized; there is emphasis on horizontal communication and on individuals coping with complex tasks. This contrasts with the *mechanistic structure* which has centralized decision-making, mostly vertical communication and specialist tasks. The so-called bureaucratic/mechanistic structure can be very effective in a stable organization functioning in a stable environment but as the environment becomes increasingly variable and unpredictable so there is a need to move towards the adaptive/organic organization. In the latter, the manager becomes more of a coordinator of diverse groups. These groups function and interact mostly on their own initiative and rarely appeal to the authority of superiors in the management hierarchy (Kast and Rosenzweig, 1970).

Pugh *et al.*, (1969) have examined on the basis of empirical evidence the relationship between structure and context. Each of these is, of course, a multidimensional concept and the major contribution of Pugh and his colleagues has been in the clarification of these dimensions. They see the context variables as origin and history, ownership and control, size, products, technology and independence; and the structural variables as specialization, standardization, formalization, centralization and configuration (Payne and Pugh, 1978).

Johnson *et al.*, (1973) separate the systems approach into systems philosophy, systems analysis and systems management. By *systems philosophy* they mean the way of thinking in terms of objectives, interrelationships of components and hierarchical levels. *Systems analysis* is the method of problem-solving or decision-making based on multifactor analysis and synthesis. *Systems management* involves the application of systems concepts to managing organizations. This last is divided into issues to do with flow systems, automation, program management (conception–design–production–delivery–utilization), planning–programming–budgeting systems and data-processing systems. For the individual manager they define the attributes now required in this way: 'Conceptual ability, tolerance of ambiguity and a sense of situation are becoming essential for managerial effectiveness. The systems approach fosters the development and refinement of these skills.' Similarly, for the organization they define the new requirement as an 'open, problem-solving system' rather than a mechanistic-bureaucratic structure. However, they point that although this approach is dramatically successful for entirely new ventures such as the National Aeronautics and Space Administration it runs into difficulties with the many vested interests in more traditional organizations and environments.

More adaptive organizations are required not only to cope with fluid environments and with rapidly changing material-processing technology but also with the even more rapidly changing information-processing technology. The ability to generate, store and manipulate vast amounts of information at a low cost has itself created new problems for organizations. These will only be solved by more attention to the scientific study of information (Stamper, 1973) and also to structuring the organization to adequately process and reject or utilize all these data. To do this adequately we probably need a combination of two parallel organizations: one support system of the traditional mechanistic-bureaucratic kind which performs all the routines of handling materials, money and information and a primary activity organization of the adaptive, organismic kind. The key design issues are the allocation of functions between the two, their procedures for interaction and, in particular, procedures to prevent the routines dominating the reactive processes.

The conflict between the two goes on at national or societal level as well as at company level. Every society has – and needs – its institutions which preserve the formal routines aimed essentially at reinforcing the inertia so that stability is assured. On the other hand the society must adapt to internal and external forces originating in technology, in the new ideas of young generations and so on. Often those in charge of the adaptation, the politicians, are not sufficiently skilled – partly because they are not systems thinkers. This is where the society systems theorists have a part to play. They often use elaborate computer-based models which ordinary people including politicians do not understand and are therefore not in a position to assess the strengths and weaknesses of the propositions which emerge as conclusions from the manipulation of these models. The most common and influential models are of various aspects of the economy or of various political concepts of an economy (Dalton, 1974) but there are also technological/economic models of social systems (Forrester, 1961; 1969). The Forrester approach is very much a broad systems one aimed in particular at avoiding the fallacies of generating isolated solutions to short-term static subsystem issues. For example, he points out that one of the problems of inner cities is not shortage of housing but an excess of poor housing. Low-cost housing beckons low-income people, until there are more people than jobs; this causes incomes to fall even further and housing to get worse. The isolated action of increasing or improving the housing causes the situation to deteriorate further because it attracts even more people. These societal structures with multifeedback loops can only be successfully modified in the light of a better understanding of their dynamic behaviour as total systems.

SYSTEMS THEORY AND SKILL THEORY

The central concepts of skill theory parallel those of systems theory; or to put it another way, skill theory is a special case of systems theory. The skill unit is defined by its objective, and the descriptive language is functional. There is an awareness of a specific level within a hierarchy; it is possible and informative to consider the parent system and the subsystems bracketing the systems within the hierarchy. Skills are open systems; there is always exchange of information with the environment. In particular the results of activity are fed back so as to modify the activity in line with the objectives. There is receptivity but also resistance. The *principle of equifinality* holds; the final results may be obtained in spite of differing initial conditions and a different series of perturbations from the environment. There is no direct cause-and-effect relationship; interactions are in both directions and can only be understood in the context of the process and the objective.

In psychological terminology the person has aspirations which are partly determined by physical and mental capacities, the gap between capacities and aspirations being bridged by the development of skills. The combinations of capacities and skills are called abilities. The combination of aspirations and capacities are called traits, while combinations of skills and aspirations are the expression of interests. This is at least one approximate summary of what these terms mean (Figure 1.2). Unfortunately different psychologists do attach different meanings to some of them and even go as far as to call it a theory when a new interpretation or restriction of one of the terms is made.

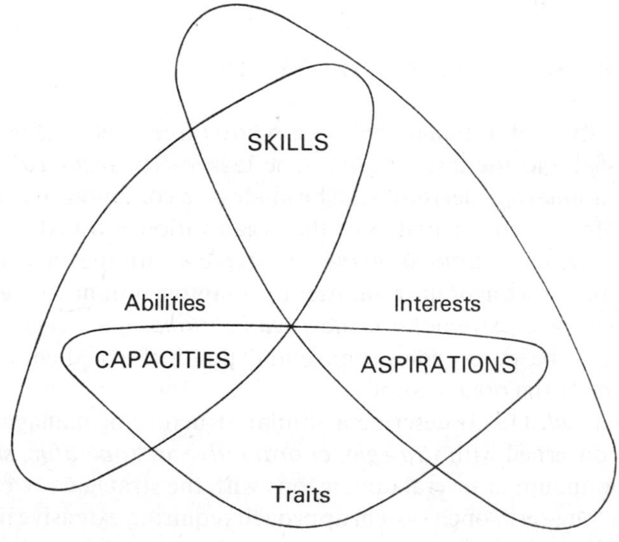

Figure 1.2 Attributes of the individual

It is important to conceive of a person's attributes as dynamic; only the capacities are relatively fixed. Skills can be developed to compensate for capacity limitations, while aspirations are modified by skills and capacity limitations. Individuals can achieve particular aspirations by different combinations of capacities and skills. Skills are developed by activity and by monitoring the consequences of activity in terms of success in relation to aspirations. Feedback or knowledge of results has two distinct consequences; it facilitates the process of achievement – in other words it motivates and it provides awareness of the success of certain strategies and thus reinforces those strategies, i.e. it promotes learning. The residue of learning following performance is skill which, in turn, is made manifest in further performance. This performance is observable not only as dexterous locomotor activity based on motor skills and perceptual skills but also as spoken and written activity based on perceptual and cognitive skills.

Thus, skills are characteristics of individuals but the individual as a stable self-maintaining unit exists within an environment of many other individuals. In other terminology man is a social animal, and he has developed a collective technology. He achieves many of his aspirations by working in concert with other people. This collective of people working to a common end is another system which again demonstrates all the common properties of systems: it is a hierarchy and there is extensive use of feedback to orientate its activities. There are specialist individuals called managers whose task it is to conceptualize the objectives at a given level, to organize the activities of others towards those objectives, to attend to the feedback and to reorientate the activities accordingly.

MANAGERS AS SYSTEM COMPONENTS

Petit (1967) divides the managerial system into three levels: the technical, the organizational and the institutional. The task of *the technical manager* is essentially rational and decisions can be made on a computational basis. He is responsible for the core activities of the organization – transforming inputs into outputs. *The institutional manager* interacts with the environment and deals with the consequent uncertainties by adaptive or innovative strategies. Between these two extremes are *the organizational managers* who have a mediatory role based on compromise and political expediency within the social system of the organization.

Johnson *et al.* (1973) describe a similar structure of management tasks into those concerned with *strategic, coordinative* and *operating subsystems*. This is a continuum in several dimensions with the strategic extreme characterized by a long-term open system approach requiring extensive non-routine judgment where satisfying rather than optimizing is the aspiration. By contrast the operating extreme involves a short-term closed system approach where decisions can be based on computational routines and there is the possibility of optimizing. These distinctions of management level are based on kinds of decision making: computational, mediatory or judgmental.

There is another distinction to do with methods of implementing decisions which might be called 'management style'. This has at least two more or less orthogonal dimensions; the manager may be democratic or autocratic and he may be active or passive (Singleton, 1972). The *active democrat* is a consensus seeker, continually asking for the opinions of others and attempting to make these opinions as coherent as possible. This is expensive and tedious but it can be satisfying to those involved providing that the environment is stable and sudden changes are not required (common in State-supported organizations). The *passive democrat* pursues a *laissez-faire* policy. Each member is allowed to pursue his own objectives and it is hoped that there is enough information and goodwill to keep these objectives reasonably in line; again an organization managed in this way cannot adapt readily to environmental changes (common in educational establishments). The *active autocrat* is the visionary leader; providing he is adequately skilled he can provide a stimulating organizational climate and a system which can adapt readily to environmental changes (common in small businesses in growth situations). The *passive autocrat* automatically vetoes any proposal for change. He believes in the *status quo* and, providing resources are adequate, he will maintain it (common in financial organizations). None of these is inherently inferior or superior to any one of the others; success or failure depends on history, resources (particularly people), objectives and the kind of environment. Broadly, democratic organizations suit their members best and autocratic organizations serve their customers best but even this generalization has exceptions. The culture of the parent system will obviously have a considerable influence on the tolerance of autocracy and democracy, activity and passivity.

In international businesses there can be culture clashes between two different parent systems, that within the business and that within the particular country where there is a branch of the business. The basic advantage of the multinational business apart from the security of size is that differences between environments can be assessed and exploited. Weinshall (1977) distinguishes five environmental systems; the employment-market system, the money-market system, the consumer-market system, the technology system and the sociocultural system. He suggests that such organizations require a multiple structure across the basic alternatives of *entrepreneurial, functional* and *decentralized management.* This is related to size and length of life of the organization as well as to the multinational attribute. New, small organizations are usually entrepreneurial; they then move through centralized functional structures to decentralized adaptive structures to the formalized multistructure where there may be five or even ten thousand managers within the decision-making processes. To achieve stability in such an organization, communications are crucial and the individual managers are subject to strong pressures from the culture of the organization as well as the cultures of the particular countries. Nevertheless they remain individuals, each with his separate skills in the three main managerial processes of perception, cognition and implementation. General systems theory will assist in clarifying the multidimensional context of these processes but it is to skill theory which we must turn to understand the processes as such.

References

Ashby, W. R. (1952). *Design for a Brain.* (New York: Wiley)

Ashby, W. R. (1958). *An Introduction to Cybernetics.* (New York: Wiley)

Boulding, K. E. (1956). General Systems Theory: the skeleton of a scheme. *Management Sci.*, April, 197

Broad, C. D. (1925). *The Mind and its Place in Nature.* (London: Kegan Paul)

Burns and Stalker (1961). *The Management of Innovation.* (London: Tavistock)

Cannon, W. B. (1939). *The Wisdom of the Body.* (New York: Norton)

Chapanis, A., Garner, W. R. and Morgan, C. T. (1949). *Applied Experimental Psychology.* (New York: Wiley)

Child, J. (1977). *Organization.* (London: Harper & Row)

Crossman, E. R. F. W. (1961). Information and serial coding in human immediate memory. In Cherry, C. (ed.) *Information Theory.* (London: Butterworth)

Dalton, G. (1974). *Economic Systems and Society.* (Harmondsworth: Penguin)

Dampier, W. C. (1942). *A History of Science.* (Cambridge: University Press)

Davis, L. E. and Cherns, A. B. (1975) (eds.). *The Quality of Working Life.* (New York: The Free Press)

Eddington, A. (1935). *The Nature of the Physical World.* (London: Dent and Sons)

Emery, F. E. (1969) (ed.) *Systems thinking.* (Harmondsworth: Penguin)

Emery, F. E. and Trist, E. L. (1965). The causal texture of organizational environments. *Hum. Relat.*, **18**, 21

Fayol, H. (1916). Administration industrielle et general. In Chapter by Rackham, J. In Pym, D. (ed.) (1968). *Industrial Society.* (Harmondsworth: Penguin)

Forrester, J. W. (1961). *Industrial Dynamics.* (Cambridge: MIT Press)

Forrester, J. W. (1969). *World Dynamics.* (Cambridge: MIT Press)

Gagné, R. M. (1962). *Psychological Principles in System Development.* (New York: Holt, Rinehart & Winston)

Johnson, R. A., Kast, F. E. and Rosenzweig, J. E. (1973). *The Theory and Management of Systems.* (Tokyo: McGraw – Hill – Kogakusha)

Kast, F. E. and Rosenzweig, J. E. (1970). *Organisation Structure.* (New York: McGraw-Hill)

Klein, L. (1979). Some problems of theory and method. In Sell, R. G. and Shipley, P. (eds.) *Satisfaction in Work Design.* (London: Taylor and Francis)

Mackay, D. M. (1950). Quantal aspects of scientific information. *Phil. Mag.*, **41**, 289

Mackay, D. M. (1969). *Information, Mechanism and Meaning.* (London: MIT Press)

Mayo, E. (1933). *The Human Problems of an Industrial Civilisation.* (New York: Macmillan)

McFarland, R. A. (1953). *Human Factors in Air Transportation.* (New York: McGraw–Hill)

Miller, J. G. (1978). *Living Systems.* (New York: McGraw – Hill)

Morgenstern, O. (1967). Game Theory: a new paradigm of social science. In Zwicky, F. and Wilson, A. G. (eds.) *New Methods of Thought and Procedure.* (New York: Springer-Verlag)

Murrell, K. F. H. (1965). *Ergonomics.* (London: Chapman and Hall)

O'Shaughnessy, J. (1966). *Business Organsiation.* (London: George, Allen and Unwin)

Payne, R. L. and Pugh, D. S. (1978). Organisations as psychological environments. In Warr, P. B. (ed.) *Psychology at Work.* (Harmondsworth: Penguin)

Pugh, D. S., Hickson, D. J. and Hinings, C. R. (1969). An empirical taxonomy of structures of work organisations. *Admin. Sci.*, **14**, 115

Petit, T. A. (1967). A Behavioural Theory of Management. *Acad. Management J.*, 341
Rice, A. K. (1958). Productivity and Social Organisation: the Ahmedhabad experiment. (London: Tavistock)
Russell, B. (1946). *History of Western Philosophy.* (London: George, Allen and Unwin)
Shannon, L. E. (1948). The mathematical theory of communication. *Bell System Tech. J.* – reprinted in Shannon and Weaver (1959) (below)
Shannon, L. E. and Weaver, W. (1959). *The Mathematical Theory of Communication.* (Urbana: University of Illinois Press)
Sheridan, T. B. and Ferrell, W. R. (1974). *Man – Machine Systems.* (Cambridge: MIT Press)
Singleton, W. T. (1972). *Introduction to Ergonomics.* (Geneva: WHO)
Singleton, W. T. (1974). *Man – Machine Systems.* (Harmondsworth: Penguin)
Singleton, W. T., Easterby, R. S. and Whitfield, D. C. (1967) (eds.) *The Human Operator in Complex Systems.* (London: Taylor & Francis)
Stamper, R. (1973). *Information in Business and Administrative Systems.* (London: Batsford)
Trist, E. C. and Murray, H. A. (1948). Work organisation at the coal face. In Emery, F. E. and Trist, E. L. (1965) The causal texture of organisational environments. *Hum. Relat.*, **18,** 21
Trist, E. C. and Bamforth, K. W. (1951). Some social and psychological consequences of the longwall method of coal-getting. *Hum. Relat.*, **4,** 3
Trist, E. C., Higgin, G. W., Pollock, A. E. and Murray, H. A. (1963). *Organisational Choice.* (London: Tavistock)
van Bertalanffy, L. (1950). An outline of general system theory. *Br. J. Philos. Sci.*, **1,** 134
van Bertalanffy, L. (1962). General systems theory – a critical review. Reprinted in Beishon, J. and Peters, G. (eds.) (1972). *Systems Behaviour.* (London: Harper & Row)
von Neumann, J. and Morgenstern, O. (1944). *Theory of Games and Economic Behaviour.* (Princeton: University Press)
Waddington, C. H. (1972a) (ed.) *Biology and the History of the Future.* (Edinburgh: University Press)
Waddington, C. H. (1972b) (ed.) *The nature of mind – Gifford Lectures (1971 – 72).* (Edinburgh: University Press)
Waddington, C. H. (1973). *The development of mind – Gifford Lectures (1972 – 73).* (Edinburgh: University Press)
Warr, P. (1976) (ed.) *Personal Goals and Work Design.* (London: Wiley)
Weiner, H. (1948). *Cybernetics.* (New York: Wiley)
Weinshall, T. D. (1977) (ed.) *Culture and Management.* (Harmondsworth: Penguin)
Woodward, J. (1965). *Industrial Organisation: Theory and Practice.* (Oxford: University Press)
Zeeman, E. C. (1975). Brain Modelling. Presented at *Symposium on Catastrophe Theory*, Seattle 1975, Springer Lecture Notes. (University of Warwick)

2
The Farm

J. H. PLUMB

INTRODUCTION

Farm management is concerned with the application and coordination of resources in order consistently to achieve the established objectives. This is made difficult by the uncertainty of nature, which is both variable in its effects and unpredictable in its presentation. The farm manager must be able to minimize losses in a bad year as well as maximize profits in a good year in order to obtain the optimum level of profit over a number of years. He operates within a framework of constraints which set the boundaries of his activities. The basic factors of production are land, labour and capital; each may be partly or totally limiting, and one factor may severely limit the use of another.

In Britain, land availability is normally the greatest constraint to the scale of a farming business, and farm size tends to limit the amount of capital and labour applied, though greater intensification may partly overcome this restraint.

Labour availability can be limiting, perhaps due to a shortage of housing near the farm, and the seasonal nature of farm work may cause critical labour shortages at peak periods. This has normally been overcome by using high output machinery and by paying for extra overtime when necessary.

Capital in agriculture is divided into landlord's capital and tenant's capital, which is further subdivided into fixed and working capital. On rented farms the capital load is shared between the landlord and the tenant, with the landlord normally being partly responsible for the upkeep of buildings, which means that a high proportion of the farmer's assets are actually involved in running the business. The owner–occupier does not pay rent but in some cases where land has been bought expensively, the interest and repayment may become prohibitive, thus limiting the availability of working capital. This may sometimes be released by mortgages and lease-back agreements.

The scope of a farm business is also limited by the constraints of topography and soil type, position in relation to supplies and markets, and climate. Development may also be restricted by the needs, attitudes and preferences of the owner, farmer or manager.

The definition of farm manager covers a wide range of farming operators, from, for example, the smallholder who operates single handed or with family labour, to the working farmer who employs staff and who is at the same time running the farm, to the salaried manager who is employed by a farmer or landowner to run either the whole business or an enterprise within it. Traditionally farms have been small-scale family units whether owner-occupied or rented, but present trends show an increase in holding size and a greater degree of specialization which have tended to increase the role of the employed manager, while a decrease in the overall labour force has tended to decrease the role of the farm foreman.

Just as farms vary in type, size and intensity, so there are varying needs in management skills. On smallholdings with no employed staff, the farmer is concerned principally with the direction of his own time and effort. He relies heavily upon his own technical skills in effectively completing the physical tasks on his farm and his job could be described as part-time manager and part-time farm worker, though the boundary between the two is not clearly marked. On the larger farm there is an increased emphasis on the skills of man-management and communication, though technical skills are still relevant. In the case of the manager of a single-output enterprise, the skills required are much more specific; for example, the oversight of a modern automated pig or poultry unit involves skill akin to those required in controlling a manufacturing process. The biggest farming complexes require a hierarchy with a division for management purposes either into enterprises including an arable manager, a beef and sheep manager, a dairy manager and so on, or into land blocks with all the enterprises on each block coming under the jurisdiction of one manager.

An important skill of the modern farm manager is his facility to innovate. This does not mean that he must always try every new idea, but that he must learn to discern that which could be beneficial to his own business. Agriculture has an excellent record of improved productivity throughout the post-war period, and new technology and application of scientific research continue to push up yields and output per man. This improved productivity has always been taken into account at the annual government review of farm prices and the industry has been penalized for its own increased efficiency, which means that no farm can afford not to take advantage of newly available resources and methods. Machines have replaced men in agriculture as much as in any other industry, with consequent changes in the requirements of management skills.

Whilst the modern manager still faces the same basic difficulties caused by the vagaries of our climate, he does so with a greater range of equipment at his disposal. This does not mean that modern machinery enables the arable farmer to continue operations whatever the conditions; on the contrary, heavy vehicles will only cause greater damage to soil structure if used when the fields are not fit. But faster working rates do enable him to cover a greater area when the going is good. Therefore timeliness becomes an increasingly important factor in the manager's thinking. To be completely ready to commence and continue operations at the optimum time requires forward thinking, ensuring that staff are available, and are not involved elsewhere at the critical time, and also that machinery is repaired and maintained during off-peak periods of the year, and not just before it is required. Timeliness is somewhat less critical in the livestock sector though smooth continuation of routines is important and forward planning is necessary in ensuring adequate feed supplies and in the maintenance of field fences, winter housing and the various ancillary equipment.

Development of agriculture over the years has thus changed the structure of farms and has therefore changed the skills needed in farm management. The farmer has to accept change in order to survive, but he should only accept fully tried concepts and methods. The farm manager's job is becoming relatively less involved with man-management due to the general reduction in the labour force, but more involved with forward planning due to the increasing importance of timeliness. Farming is carried out at an accelerating pace, though the work has become less arduous and tedious through mechanization. Whatever else may have changed, however, the requirement of good husbandry of fields and livestock remains an essential ingredient for every successful farm business whatever the scale or intensity.

THE TASKS OF THE FARM MANAGER

In any successful undertaking it is necessary to set out objectives, to make plans in order to fulfil them, and to effectively implement those plans. These stages in management tasks cannot always be separated or taken in that order, as most decisions stem from something that already exists, but they do provide convenient headings.

Recognizing objectives

Objectives will depend upon the situation as it already exists and upon the attributes of those responsible for formulating them, and will become adapted as conditions change. The self-employed farmer has first of all to recognize his own ambitions and the limits of his own capabilities. The employed manager has to find out the objectives and limitations put on him by his employer. Both the farmer and the manager may be forced to alter their objectives according to current constraints.

It cannot be assumed that profit maximizing is the only objective of a farm business, and it may not even have a high priority. It is of fundamental importance that whoever has to plan and run the farm primarily comes to a full understanding of what are the objectives that he is seeking to fulfil. It is quite valid for a farmer to maintain a way of life that he finds satisfying, at the expense of innovation and improved profitability, provided that there is no confusion as to what his aims really are. There are those, however, who excuse their own inefficiency and lack of objectivity in this way, and who have probably never really tried to isolate and evaluate their objectives.

The objectives of a farmer will vary according to his own ambitions and according to his present circumstances. For example, even the least profit-orientated individual may be forced to raise profitability on his list of objectives in order to survive during hard times. Also the farmer with a son to follow him into the business may be more eager to develop and improve the farm than if he had no heir. A farmer who is keen on field sports may in the course of time orientate his land to the harbouring of wild life, to the potential detriment of his crop yields. He accepts the resulting loss in profit because it has ceased to be the prime objective, given that the land is still capable of providing a reasonable income. Certain of the less common livestock breeds may be kept out of preference, and many other practices may be adopted by the farmer for aesthetic or display value which will adversely affect profitability but which are nevertheless valid objectives, provided that the farmer understands what they cost him in real terms.

Objectives inevitably change as people grow older and as situations and conditions change, while the ability to recognize them usually increases with maturity and experience. Recognizing objectives rarely occurs as a spontaneous decision and it may be a gradual realization of what seems obvious with the benefit of hindsight.

Farm planning

Having identified key objectives and placed them in their order of importance, the manager must now make certain decisions relating to the future policy and activities of the business. He must produce comprehensive plans for each enterprise within the business and decide upon courses of action to bring about those plans. Correct decision-making depends on the ability to assimilate a large quantity of relevant information and to use it in such way that the resulting course of action has the greatest probability of success. Much skill is involved in putting together information in the right way; by careful analysis and correct presentation of facts and figures a decision may be rendered obvious or even unnecessary. At the level of planning there is normally little room for decisions made by feel or by pure inspiration. It is always important to have a detailed knowledge of the farm and its potential, and to have recourse to physical records of inputs and outputs as well as financial data of the business in total and in part. Plans should be subject to a continuous feedback of information from the performance of the business. Having said this,

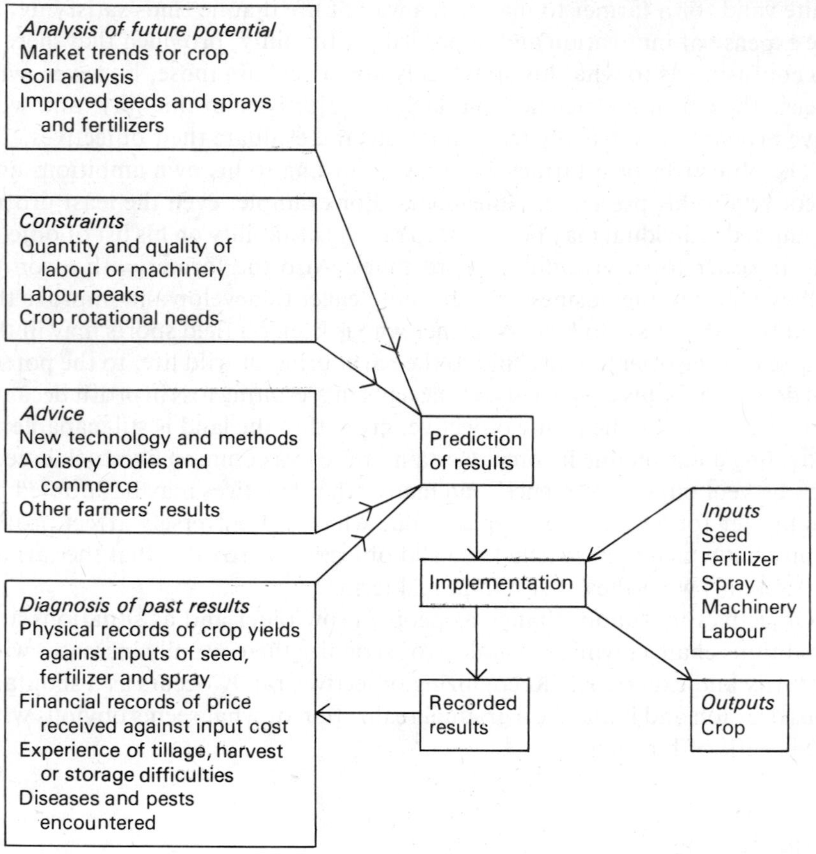

Figure 2.1 Farm planning of field crops

different managers may appear to make similarly successful decisions in different ways, from pencil calculations on the back of an envelope to sophisticated budgeting procedures and even the use of computers. Different kinds of planning skills may frequently produce the same end, but utilization of adequate information is common to all effective planning.

Figure 2.1 applies in particular to field crops, but the principle is equally valid for horticulture and for animal production.

Information for planning

There are many sources of information which aid the manager in his planning. The farm production cycle is a very long one and may appear to give plenty of time for considering a market, but even so the very first step must be to guarantee an outlet for a crop and to have at least some idea of the value of the final product. The farmer must then consider whether the climate and soil are suitably adapted to the crop. There may be difficulties relating to location and market availability, and there may also be internal constraints such as management attitudes, worker ability and limited machine capacity.

In Britain, advice is freely available for all aspects of farm planning. There is a healthy competition between most of the ancillary agricultural industries which ensures good service and free advice to the farmer. There are also professional advisory bodies as well as an excellent service provided by the Ministry of Agriculture. With such a wealth of accessible information it could be said that one of the skills in farm management is in learning when to seek and take advice.

Feedback of information from past results is also essential to planning. Both physical and financial results must be monitored and there must be records of yields against inputs from year to year, preferably on an individual field or individual animal basis, as well as annual accounts and a cash flow record. This information can be used to budget for the future of the business and also to make immediate plans for the separate enterprises.

Making a planning decision

Effective planning depends firstly on the recognition of the fact that decisions have to be made. Considerations are, as far as possible, placed in a logical or chronological order and possible deadlines are set. Alternatives are formulated for each decision, which may legitimately include no change, or a postponement of the decision pending further information or experience. Comprehensive information relating to all aspects of the situation is then gathered and presented in a way which can be understood, and which gives a fair basis for comparison. The object of the decision-maker is to reduce the probability of error to a minimum by examining all the possible outcomes of a course of action through having the relevant information at his disposal. Only in the final stage of making the decision can he allow personal preferences to influence him, as the cost of adopting a preferred course of action should be realized. A preference for a quiet life may be at the expense of efficiency and profit, while conversely the drive for maximum profit may be at the cost of time and energy.

The way in which different managers arrive at a conclusion varies considerably. Some may be more skilled than others, while some may be equally skilled but in different ways. One manager, for example, may be expert in accounting and budgeting while another may have a natural eye for livestock or a feel for crop husbandry. Sometimes there may be so many permutations, or so many possible outcomes of a decision, or information may be so sparse, that it may be necessary to make an inspired guess or do what feels right in the circumstances. This is the special problem of an industry which is constantly dependent upon nature, and such decisions highlight the acquired skills and the particular style of a farm manager.

Implementation of plans

Plans are the logical outcome of objectives within a framework of possibilities and constraints. The success of those plans is in their implementation which is effected by dividing plans into a series of tasks and subtasks. At this level there is much more room for flexibility of method and style in management, provided that the original objectives and plans are not forgotten in the process. On the smaller farm a greater proportion of the tasks may be performed by the manager himself whereas on the larger farm the tasks may be totally delegated to staff. Clearly it is easier for the man who prepares the plans to physically carry them out as there is no need for communication, but it is much harder for the small farm manager to delegate work and all too often planning decisions are clouded by the immediate needs of the task in hand. The manager should be closely involved in implementation, though the level of physical contribution to the work will vary between farms, and each manager must learn to recognize the point at which he must delegate.

Long-term implementation includes the acquiring and retaining of the right amount of land through purchase or tenure, negotiating capital and investing it in suitable buildings and machinery, and hiring staff with skills relevant to the tasks on the farm. Short-term implementation involves the control and coordination of the daily tasks, and the bringing together of materials and equipment in the right place at the right time. The staff must be briefed in their individual tasks and responsibilities, and this briefing should always be a two-way communication in order to make maximum use of the knowledge of both the manager and the operator concerned. Whereas policy and planning are solely the concern of management, daily implementation should be discussed by manager and operator on an equal level to obtain optimum results – given of course that both sides take a responsible and intelligent attitude to their work. While work is in progress it should be continually monitored and, where necessary, activities within the task should be adapted.

To take crop spraying as an example, the manager must first identify the best chemicals for the job and ensure that he has suitable equipment and an operator capable of using it. The operator must be correctly briefed in dosage rates, spraying techniques, safety precautions and the weather conditions needed for an acceptable performance. High winds or wet field conditions, or perhaps just threatening rain are sufficient to halt operations and normally it must be the man in the machine who must make the decision, as more often than not he is working some distance from the farm centre.

Most field operations are dependent upon the weather to a varying extent, and the main characteristic of the British weather is that it is both variable in form and unpredictable in presentation. Timeliness of operation is vital, so decisions have to be continually made as to whether conditions are favourable enough to start or continue a task. These stop-and-start decisions are made more difficult in that there are no constant criteria on which to base them. As the farming season progresses it becomes more urgent to complete tasks in the face of possibly deteriorating conditions, so the manager must be progressively less selective of conditions or risk not completing the task at all. Different managers will vary in their attitude to this risk, but what is important is that they are consistent in their judgment of a situation. A farmer could perhaps be forgiven for making irrational leaps in his decision making when machines break down when conditions are optimal and then the weather changes when everything is running smoothly again, but successful implementation depends to a great extent on keeping cool at such times.

There are many so-called incompatible trade-offs in farming operations, where a positive action is pursued at the expense of another factor. For example, rarely is the corn harvest completed in ideal conditions, as there is a relatively short time between ripening and the corn shedding from the ear, and the objective is to harvest the grain as dry as possible. Some grain is inevitably taken off the field in a moist condition in preference to risking crop loss through later weather damage and shedding.

At peak times in the farming year, particularly spring and autumn, labour and machinery are often required for two or more jobs at the same time. Under conventional systems land is ploughed, cultivated one or more times, and drilled, in that order. Ploughing takes the longest time and is the precursor to the other operations, but it may be continued in weather conditions unfavourable to cultivating or drilling so that during dry weather it may be better to abandon ploughing in order to complete operations on land already ploughed. Thus the various operations may be going on concurrently in different fields and it is often difficult to decide where to place the emphasis at any one time.

Perhaps another common example is that of allowing an inexperienced operator the opportunity to perform a task in order to give him experience at the expense of performance and work quality. In all but the very large businesses, farm managers are usually competent operators in most of the practical work as well as in administration, and it may be difficult for them to delegate to a trainee work in which they themselves are fully competent. Clearly, however, training is important and a lower level of output must occasionally be accepted in this cause.

THE SKILLS OF THE FARM MANAGER

So far we have studied the various tasks in the management of a farm on which to base our skills analysis. Now we turn to the particular qualities that the successful farm manager possesses, and especially those attributes gained through experience which we call skills. There are many skills required in the whole process of management. On a small farm one man may be in total control of all the decisions made, as well as conducting most of the tasks on his farm. At the opposite end of the scale the management of a large agricultural business may be shared between directors, managers, and foremen, and perhaps also individual enterprise managers. Within the range of management there is a variety of jobs which are subject to changes in specification as the industry progresses.

Skill in mapping out policy

The most fundamental skill of the manager is to grasp and fully understand the objectives of the business he is running and also his own objectives. These two may be quite divergent in the case of the employed manager who must be prepared to fully accept objectives set by his employer and act upon them to the best of his ability. This acceptance is not always easy, particularly when profit is not the only measure of success. Nevertheless it is something which can be practised and learnt through experience. It is most important that the business activities of the manager are limited to within the objectives set for him.

The manager who owns and controls his own business must learn the skill of deliberately formulating his own objectives and relating them to what he does every day. It is possible to find farmers who have never really reasoned out what they want before setting out to achieve it, and who may even be carrying through a tradition set by a previous generation. This state of mind may be exacerbated by a drudgery of daily feeding and caring for livestock which may at the time seem to be the only course of action for a continued existence as a farmer. In this situation it is quite possible for a man to continue in a previously set rut and not find his way out of it, by failing to think objectively from a standpoint of his own needs, ideals and ambitions, and to relate them confidently to his work. He may be unnecessarily spending long and uncomfortable hours for a relatively small return, measured in terms of income or satisfaction. This is not to say, however, that there are not farmers who find immense satisfaction in a low expenditure/low income level economy on the land. The life certainly has its attractions, but it is found that those who truly appreciate the life have taken a positive approach in mapping out ideas, objectives and plans and relating them to a daily routine on the farm. This mapping-out process may not be recognizable as the same as that created by the manager of the highly intensive farm, but it is nevertheless valid and just as important in the job satisfaction of all participants.

Expertise in mapping out objectives is found partly in the manager reaching an understanding of his own mind, and partly in the evaluation of the circumstances in which he finds himself. Limiting circumstances should always attenuate the map produced, even though objectives may reach beyond the present limiting circumstances. For example, the acquiring of extra land in order to enlarge the business may originate as an impossible dream, grow into a possibility and hence become a feasible objective, and finally become a reality, so providing a new base for forming further objectives. The experienced and skilled manager learns to discipline himself into planning those things which are real possibilities, thus avoiding fruitless time and energy spent in striving to achieve the impossible. On the other hand, objectives that are somewhat ambitious are an added stimulus to a business. Though styles and abilities vary between different managers, a general quality is that they should learn to be fairly optimistic in their approach to objectives and the forming of an overall plan, but pessimistic in the setting of annual and monthly planning targets, always allowing a percentage in the cash-flow projection for unforeseen costs such as machine breakages or death of livestock, as well as being fairly conservative in the estimation of future yields.

It is most important that a manager should learn to cope with his own nature by recognizing his particular capabilities and limits. This is possibly the most difficult skill to acquire and extends well beyond the bounds of management. Some men are introspective and good at self-criticism, but are perhaps prone to disparage their own efforts, while others are extroverts and good at ambitious planning, but perhaps fall down on the detailed analysis of results. The former type tends to make the better manager, though he may not gain as high a level of job satisfaction as the latter. The most important point is not that a man should try to change his style or attitude – that would be to deny his very make-up and could result in sheer misery. But he must adapt his activities to cope with his failings and get the best from his strong points. Thus the over-ambitious man should consistently allow a margin for lower than anticipated performance, while the pessimist should do the reverse.

Skills in decision-making

Good management stems from a series of decisions ranging from those concerning timing and method in daily and hourly tasks, to those concerning long-term planning in enterprise formation and substitution.

The nature of much of the short-term decision-making is such that many tasks are carried out as a result of apparently subconscious reasoning. As a result of experience the manager gains skills which render it unnecessary to follow a series of conscious thought processes in order to arrive at a conclusion. In retrospect it is normally possible for him to give logical reasons why he arrived at that conclusion but the actual process of deciding has been a matter of 'reflex'. The logical steps of gathering information from a situation, diagnosing problems and possible needs for change, enumerating possibilities and weighing them one against another, are all conducted in one rapid thought process and the answer is clear and known to be correct. Any practitioner in his own field should have this ability to make mundane and short-term decisions by this manner of automatic thought. This quality is a skill gained only through personal experience of the work and practice, and is not very dependent upon natural capacities, though an inborn aptitude for speedy reasoning may enable the manager to acquire the skill much faster.

Through the manager getting accustomed to his job much regular decision-making becomes automatic. Such expertise is demonstrated in his reaction to an unforeseen change in operating conditions such as machine breakdown or a sudden change in the weather. Every such predicament is unique and there are no definite rules to follow. A good example is that of deciding the very optimum point in time at which to start harvesting a field of barley, or to start baling a field of hay. Putting such a decision into a series of logical steps would be to first consider how ripe and how dry is the crop and any special difficulties relating to it. Then he must consider the weather both at present and in the immediate future in order to consider the risk of delaying operations. Finally he must consider the time and upheaval necessary in mobilizing men and machinery from their respective locations. In practice the skilled manager normally weighs all these factors together unconsciously and one careful look at a crop tells him whether he can go ahead or not. This is because his mind has already been conditioned by all the factors external to the crop itself and inspection of the crop completes the information and provides the answer at one and the same time.

The very special thing about farming decisions is that the relevant information is provided often through all five senses at once, and also that nature is subject to a continual transformation. If asked to explain a decision in retrospect the manager could probably say that a crop looked, felt, smelt, tasted and even sounded right, and that he perhaps sensed an imminent deterioration in the weather and so there were no grounds for delaying operations further.

This intuitive approach is also used in decisions concerning livestock. A livestock manager who is tuned in to the caring of his animals will often know that there is something wrong with an animal even before the onset of the obvious symptoms of a particular disease. A true stockman may not even be able to explain why he has taken certain steps in disease prevention, but nevertheless a valid decision has been taken as a result of certain enactive skills of stockmanship.

The use of memory is also an important skill for the manager to acquire, though this is not to say that he must seek to remember every single factual detail concerning the farm or the enterprise which he controls. It is valuable to have certain financial and physical data at his fingertips, but it is also necessary to turn to records for a detailed understanding of an enterprise. Some people have better memories than others and hence tend to lean somewhat less on written evidence, so here again it is important that the manager knows the limits of his own capabilities. Clearly it would be disastrous for an intrinsically forgetful person to feel that as a manager he must remember everything without committing it to written records. What every manager must learn, however, is the use of pictorial skills which give him a familiarity with the factors which make up the domain under his charge. These skills come into play in the area of communication with staff about the tasks which they are performing, and also in consultation with external advisors.

With the exception of the very intensive livestock enterprises it is quite possible for a manager to be aware of the appearance and characteristics of every cow, sheep or pig on the farm, or at least those of the somewhat more permanent breeding stock. Animals (like people) have differing physical characteristics and can be distinguished accordingly; their appearance may be related to a name or a number just as one can put a human face to a name. This ability to recognize and remember is a natural facility but it can be cultivated by deliberately studying markings or unusual features on each animal. It is also aided by marking and tagging systems which help in identification, but should not replace complete recognition. Behaviour patterns should also be studied and remembered; some animals are more friendly or more aggressive for example, and this is important because slight changes in behaviour can be heralds of changes relating to the oestrous cycle, which is information vital to timely breeding. Such information is especially important in dairy-herd management, where both the timing of breeding and accuracy of feeding are main ingredients of profitability. This pictorial information can be related to a written historical record of calving dates, milk yields and veterinary attention for every cow, providing a sound basis for issuing instructions to staff and also giving meaning to the information returned by the staff to the manager. Therefore discussion is more productive and decisions relating to individual cows are reached more quickly.

The same sort of pictorial skills are applicable to the arable manager, whose knowledge of the characteristics of the soil type of a particular field and how it behaves in varying conditions is a great help in discussing and deciding upon the various tasks that have to be performed in the field, as well as in planning crop rotations. Here again, discussions between manager and tractor driver regarding soil conditions and hence tillage requirements are much more productive when both have a good pictorial idea of what they are talking about.

Longer term decisions relating to farm planning require more deliberation and it is not safe to rely solely on the aforementioned enactive and pictorial skills. It is essential that a farm business is equipped with some sort of recording and accounting system, though this will vary in depth and complexity according to the size and type of farm. Different managers also have differing attitudes to records and printed advisory material. Some may rely more heavily on their own knowledge and intuition in almost every decision, while others will exploit every possible source of statistical information before allowing themselves to draw any final conclusions. It is important that each makes the most of his own abilities in reaching successive decisions.

The manager must learn to sift and select the right information that is relevant to the current situation of the farm and apply that information to daily practice. It is not very difficult to record data and most prudent farmers have a reasonably accessible recording system. It is less easy to make the system mean something more than just historical facts, and harder still to make it fit into regular decision-making at both the planning and daily implementation levels in order to increase profitability.

Financial and physical data are essential tools for farm planning but there is a host of other factors which may influence a decision. For example, on paper, wheat may seem to be a more profitable crop to grow than barley; it requires the same equipment and needs only marginally more effort. Thus it may seem right to the arable farmer to substitute all his barley for wheat, but consideration must be given to the fact that repeated wheat crops may reduce soil fertility, causing a gradual reduction in yield in successive crops. In the long term, therefore, it may be more profitable to grow a combination of wheat and barley in rotation. Better still may be to introduce a further break in the rotation in the form of a grass ley carrying beef cattle or sheep. On paper these livestock enterprises may appear to be less financially attractive but may be included for their beneficial effect on soil structure and fertility, which in turn may increase overall farm profitability.

It is very difficult to quantify the improving effect of these rotations and break crops, due to the climatic variation from season to season with its effect on crop output, as well as the variation caused by fluctuating levels of pests and diseases. Nature is such that no two years are ever identical, and furthermore the effect of adverse conditions may be more obvious in some crops than others, and there may even be a varying effect between fields. Thus a drought which disastrously reduces the yield of potatoes on light, free-draining soil may be hardly noticed in a low-lying pasture. There are no constants in the commercial farm situation and a farm manager does not have an accurate measure of the success of his crop rotations, though trends do become clear over a period of years.

Only through learning from years of experience can the farm manager become fully equipped to balance wisely the many alternatives before him. There are so many different decision criteria and so many possible outcomes and performance levels that a manager is liable to make irrational leaps in the decision-making process due to some newly introduced factor. This is particularly true when the manager is closely involved with the daily work load of the farm. In this case it is perhaps helpful to him to turn to an independent but experienced observer who may have different insights. There is an unfortunate stigma attached to the seeking of this kind of advice and sometimes a mistrust of would-be advisors, but there should be no pride lost in seeking an objective point of view of possible improvements in method. As well as the public and commercial advisory bodies there is a wealth of management expertise held within the farming industry by many farmers who are effectively employing their own resources and whose skills are under-exploited. There is always a need for a continuous transfer of these farming skills between managers, and especially from one generation to the next, to the general benefit of the industry.

Communications

Most managers of the larger than average holdings would probably agree that it is in communication that their experience has benefited them the most, though it is the least tangible of skills. Labour management is one of the greatest problem areas facing industry as a whole, but few industries can claim the good labour relations upheld in agriculture. This is partly because of the high level of job satisfaction in most farm jobs, but also because of the relatively small working units and the close relationship between management and staff, which induces mutual loyalty.

The aim of the manager with respect to the staff under his authority must be to produce a working relationship conducive to the fulfilment of the plans of the business. The contribution of a farm worker to successfully implemented plans depends partly on his own skills and his willingness to use them, and partly on proper deployment of his time and energies by his employer. A worker's relationship with his boss is one of many contributing factors to his job satisfaction, though it is not the most important, and the popularity of a manager tends only to be significant if it is in the negative. Thus a manager who has an excellent rapport with the staff only marginally increases output, while the very unpopular man destroys morale eventually to the extent of defeating the objects of the business. This is because as long as there is not a specific problem between a manager and a worker such as a clash of personality or an inconsistent temperament, then the other factors in job satisfaction such as working conditions, hours, pay, or a domestic situation loom much larger in significance. It is also frequently found that employers with quite an authoritarian approach to man-management succeed in retaining a stable and contented work force. However, it is obviously desirable for reasons other than efficiency that a manager is of a congenial nature, though a danger for the unskilled manager is to overrate the importance of his own popularity.

He runs the risk of making concessions to that end which are injurious to the farm policy. Farm policy and planning must always remain firmly in the hands of the manager, and what is more important than popularity is simply an ability to direct operations in a competent and timely manner. It is impossible to lay down absolute guidelines in this area of communication as character plays such a large part, but the key is certainly a consistent and fair approach to men.

At the level of implementation the skilled manager recognizes the importance of full participation of the staff in the way in which tasks are carried out. Discussion is essential and some tolerance is required to accept that different men have different styles and capacities, and different ways of going about a task. The manager has to recognize these differences and has to advise and assist constructively without too much interference which may cause frustration or resentment. Men learn by their mistakes, though a good working relationship between all the members of a team can reduce serious errors and time loss. There is also an erroneous belief in some quarters that the success of a manager depends mainly upon his ability to carry out every task on the farm better and faster than the various operators under his direction. Whilst in many cases he may have this ability, continually demonstrating the fact may only detract from an attitude of independence and responsibility by the staff. When considering a series of tasks and a number of men to carry them out, the manager has to apply the principle of comparative advantage. That is to say that even if one man is able to perform all the tasks better than anyone else, it is to overall advantage that each man carries out what he can do best. The manager should apply this principle to the planning of his own time as well as to that of the rest of the work force.

3
Management of Military Organization

M. R. H. PAGE

INTRODUCTION

When I joined the Royal Naval College Dartmouth as a cadet just after World War II, there was no place in the military vocabulary for phrases like 'management skills'. Everyone had been so busy exercising these skills that there was neither the need nor the spare capacity to study what these skills might be. Shorthand phrases like 'the Divisional system', 'the seaman's eye' and 'officer-like qualities' said it all. The Royal Navy at that time was large and manpower intensive and the young leader learnt the skills of managing his responsibilities by what today would be described as on-job training. He was expected to get it right but if not, the 'snotties nurse' was there to make sure he learnt from his mistakes.

My Service, the Royal Navy, is still a large and complex organization with a budget in excess of £1350M a year and with this deploys ships and aircraft world-wide. There is a Vote A strength of uniformed personnel of 78 000 people. This is supported by civilians totalling a similar number working in Headquarters Department of the Ministry of Defence and in various dockyards and stores organizations throughout the country. However, following 35 years of relative peace, pressures have built up to economize; this means that learning opportunities are fewer, and the management of resources takes on a special significance. The rate of change in military affairs led by the thrust of a rapidly expanding technology has added an extra dimension to the imperative need for special insights and skills. These skills in managing naval affairs in many respects match the normal repertoire found in the country at large but there are differences. Judgment and decision-making under conditions of uncertainty probably heads the list. Today the Defence Budget is under continuous pressure. Despite attempts made to reduce the money provided, the declared policy is to keep the allocation at a fixed percentage of the gross national product. This means that the serving Naval Officers who are members of the Admiralty Board are faced with a complex balancing activity. Between them they must propose policy to the politicians designed to ensure that the Fleet achieves a minimum acceptable level of effectiveness within the budget in the short term and at the same time make provision for maintaining this capability in the future. This calls for much management skill as well as the more conventional forms of leadership, plus a generous pinch of political sensitivity.

Unlike the nationalized industries, and even the Civil Service, the Armed Services of the Crown have to select the top people from within. This requires organizational stability of a remarkably high order. Management skills change as the manager progresses, both in maturity and in experience. Initially, the focus is on short-term material affairs and the immediate circle of people involved. The time span of discretion expands and the preoccupation of the manager tends towards concepts and policy as he becomes more senior. This general rule applies particularly to management skills in National Defence. The young officer is concerned about his men, 'daily orders' and the well-recognized, traditional leadership skills. In mid-career there is more concern with planning ahead but largely in the same environment and concerned with the problems of the 'sharp end' or 'teeth' of the defence machine. Those selected for higher command enter a field of concept shaping and politico-military management, where the skills are quite different.

The basic skill in managing military affairs is difficult to distil because any acceptable criteria are obscured by the overriding emphasis of external events. Furthermore, the total activity embraces a wide spectrum of endeavour in many different time-frames, but from experience inside the environment it is possible to note a pattern. This look at defence management is through the eyes of a serving officer, and will try to identify some keypoints in this family of skills.

SPECIFIC ASPECTS OF MILITARY MANAGEMENT

Fryer (1973) in the context of 'Management by Objective' and other systematic management techniques said: 'If the shore-based officers discovered it was difficult thinking of themselves as middle-managers, those on ships, such as the Leander Class frigate which docked at Portsmouth last week, find it really hard going.' This view of the Royal Navy's attitude to modern management methods failed to reflect an awareness that there is a problem, even if no one looked to M.b.O. as the great panacea. An ability to manage is an essential but not sufficient attribute of the efficient naval officer. This has been recognized for some time and is seen in many aspects of the way the Service conducts its affairs. The naval officer performs in an environment with a large measure of uncertainty which must be inherent in a life at sea. At a course in Operations Research, a lecturer said, 'In my experience, naval officers are magnificent in crises but do very little to avoid them.' He implied a criticism. It could be a compliment to a group which has recognized its true role and played it successfully. The naval officer is frequently in no position to do more than respond to crises. He must develop a repertoire of response and be sensitive to situation. Provided he is selected and trained with this in mind, the Royal Navy will prosper. A slavish adoption of 'technique' in management can result in a naive concentration upon the obvious to the exclusion of the important. This is particularly true when the time span of decision is extended and flair based on experience is necessary to success.

Discussion about the relative place of leadership and management developed in the 1970's as more thought was given to what was meant in a naval setting. How much influence does an act of leadership have when the principal actor might be at one end, the Captain, and at the other end of the scale a Leading Rate? A measure of this would be to consider the influence of each member. Then it becomes apparent that for management to be successful it must be kept within sensible bounds. Once the Captain tries to lead his ship's company by regularly addressing them over the broadcast, or by clearing lower deck, he whittles away his subordinates' powers. This may be necessary occasionally to establish a common bond and to make certain that everyone is on the same wavelength. As a general rule and especially in emergencies, the 'chain of command' should be used and encouraged. The cliché that 'the anchor chain is as strong as the individual link' applies because each leadership act at each level, from the Captain through the Officers, the Chief Petty Officers, to the Leading Rates and other Junior Rates is of equal importance. The more these links can be balanced, the more likely the ship is to function in an efficient, quickly responsive way.

The outsider often questions how management skills exercised by a Leading Rate can fit into this overall picture. What must be remembered is that the Navy has many more Leading Rates than there are roles within the Navy for them to fill. This is an unfortunate consequence of linking pay with rank, rather than linking it with the task done. Those who are actually called upon to lead have a most important, often a vital task to do. Of these, the most crucial is as Leading Hand of the messdeck. He is the key to a scheme whereby the management have a representative within the small peer group who live, eat and sleep together on the messdeck. The man put in charge, responsible for all sorts of decisions about communal life, is given a very narrow path to tread, and if he does it successfully the ship is a long way towards being a happy and efficient one. He provides the ears for the management. Further, the Leading Rates interpret the management's view for the majority of the ship's company. When there is a close relationship between the Leading Hands of the messdecks, their divisional Petty Officers and the 1st Lieutenant, there is no reason at all why grievances should develop or why demands for unexpected action should appear unreasonable. This is a role which has much in common with the shop steward in industry. The big difference is the all-pervading effects of the Naval Discipline Act, embodying draconian penalties for disobedience. This makes service life an acquired taste not always aligned to the public mood.

There is no doubt that the Navy faces a difficult challenge in recruiting the right sort of people and in deciding how to allocate them. It is almost certain that in terms of total numbers we are not short of the men to run the Fleet efficiently. The problem is one of balance and how to allocate the resources of men and of training opportunity. This balance is not only difficult in terms of annual requirements but is also complicated by the needs to balance branch structures and to balance the long-term expectations of the individual. The problem is magnified by the lack of insight which is inevitable because of rapid developments in the technical fields. It is believed that the problem is less serious than is often stated and that it will respond to the application of basic management principles aimed at making a man most effective while in the service, and confident and well satisfied when he returns to the outside world. There is difficulty in finding acceptable definitions for general discussion of the problem, however, and a general taxonomy of tasks and individual skills would help in clarifying the fundamentals.

The Service has, until recently, successfully used rank structure as a frame of reference for manpower planning and control. The national trend to less formal structures has tended to soften boundaries between ranks. This in turn has resulted in the reduction of the effectiveness of this taxonomy as a predictive tool. The success in the past relied on the relationship between individual characteristics and rank. If it is truly no longer useable, a solution would be to identify a more accurate measure of individual difference. One such dimension is 'experience' and another is 'personality'. Both of these are abstracted into the concept of rank. Separating these constituents would provide freedom to examine the contribution which each makes to effectiveness. More important perhaps, a more meaningful interpretation of likely consequences from proposed actions would be possible. This is particularly important when examining management skills and the case for precision in this area of application cannot be exaggerated. The cost of any change is always underestimated and in the personnel field the cost is rarely brought to account.

PREVIOUS RESEARCH ON NAVAL MANAGEMENT

About ten years ago the Ministry of Defence instituted a scheme of study by individuals into important areas of concern. These Defence Fellowships created new opportunities for serving officers to study some aspect which they felt was central to the affairs of national defence. Some of these studies made a significant contribution to the understanding of management skills in the Services. Wright (1970) reported on a study of the contemporary British officer in the three Services. The work threw light on the self-image of the officer corps and highlighted some of the stresses inherent in a period of rapid change. The study used the disciplines of sociology and developed some very valuable insights into the problems facing the Armed Forces of the Crown. Baynes (1969), Bensham-Booth (1969) and Baylis (1970) studied subjects which were closely related to man in his working environment, but all looked at the global problem and did not consider that individual differences were significant elements in the discussion. Eberle (1971) studied the politico-military aspects of operational command and because this is an area where very few people are fortunate enough to be involved, of necessity had to consider individual style and ability.

At about the same time officers were given sabbatical opportunities for post-graduate studies in areas of interest. Groves (1970) used a number of advanced techniques to examine the organization of a technical department in a warship. One aspect of the report highlighted the stresses generated on-board by weakened authority in the middle strata of the Service. This weakening has been caused by the granting of rank to those possessing certain expertise as a means of providing better pay and living conditions. Problems identified were attributed to conflict between the need to maintain viable lines of military succession, the need to reward technical skill and the need to provide adequate sea experience for Senior Rates and Officers. Groves claimed that the study threw light on organizational weaknesses which could be remedied once they were clearly defined. He identified one of the causes of stress in an operational warship as being the overriding need to provide a 'training environment'. This resulted in about one third of the technical officers at sea being in a complement billet for the first time. The proliferation of intermediate ranks, now including the Fleet Chief Petty Officer, had created an image of weakened authority. Inevitably, the result was a reduction in the span of control (Janowitz and Little, 1965). The organization in the fleet has been forced to develop to minimize the effect of this and other stresses. Two of the major mechanisms which emerged were duplicaton of lines of authority and role-splitting.

Role-splitting is identified as typically the 'one-over-one' situation where the head of department has a deputy and the head of section has one senior technical rating as his immediate subordinate. It was suggested that the head of department felt he had to be constantly on his guard against losing control while the subordinate resented the lack of authority which he felt was rightly his lot. In the case of younger officers working with experienced senior rates, the officer was frequently forced to leave technical aspects to the senior rating, causing a number of maladaptive reactions. In particular these younger officers felt that their technical expertise was under-utilized, and there was a reaction by seeking outlets into the fields of innovation and administration.

At the same time, the technical lead was taken by a group of very good Chief Artificers who established the role of 'link man' on most material matters, thus filtering much essential but detailed information (Likert, 1961). This further isolated the young and inexperienced officer. A similar phenomenon has been observed by Sir Derek Rayner in his 1980 Study of Aspects of the Civil Service. He observed that the proliferation of management levels generates nugatory work and his proposal was reported as being the abolition of two levels of management; the Assistant Under-Secretary of State and the Senior Executive Officer. A very important observation was made by Groves in discussing the assessment of subordinates who are working below their capacity, concerning the difficulty of identifying the marginally incompetent role-holder. This was seen as being particularly difficult when the subordinate was from a different professional background to that of the reporting officer, or where the role had been amended or changed, probably unconsciously to match the individuals concerned. Much damage can be caused by such distortions, and considerable managerial skill is called for to avoid such an outcome. The situation is much improved if position power at each level is strong and clear cut.

Gardner (1970) conducted a long term follow-up of naval officers' careers. For this work, he used multivariate techniques of analysis to identify key relationships between individual characteristics and success in both the short term and longer term. He concluded that the research showed the need for important changes in selection, training and career development of RN officers. His work was based on an analysis of historic data held at Headquarters in the organization's Personnel Management system. His results indicated shortcomings in the selection process of the period under examination which extended from 1947 to include about three hundred entrants. He also criticized the numerical reporting system used for periodical assessment of officers in the performance of their duties. This scholarly work lacked one perspective. It appeared to fail to take account of the great social changes which were occurring during the period in which the reports were written. Two critical forces were at work. The first was the transition to a peacetime force with a traumatic reduction in the numbers required. This made reporting very much more uncertain because of turbulence at all levels. Secondly, the Royal Navy changed its attitude to Engineer Officers. Prior to 1956, Executive Officers headed by the gunnery branch were at the top of a clearly remarked pecking order, with distinctive cloth between the gold on the arms of the lesser breeds. After that date, all officers were of one company, and most were on the General List. The respective esteem of the various branches was not homogeneous for many years. This had a great bearing on the fortunes of otherwise equally well fitted officers.

Among other studies undertaken during this period as a result of the upsurge of interest in management, Evans (1970) recommended that systematic management be introduced into the Fleet. In the discussion of the manner of its introduction he stated that authority and accountability were ill-defined and performance was seldom measured against set standards. It was claimed that this situation could be changed by stating objectives, stating limits of authority and specifying mandatory procedures to limit the discretion of individual officers. It was recommended that nominated ships operate under these constraints for a trial period. This approach is now general throughout all spheres of the Royal Navy.

It can be seen that there has been considerable interest in understanding management and manpower problems, but the place of an individual's personality in the equation was less well understood. For this reason selection procedures are worth some examination in the context of management skill. Selection has two major connotations within the Royal Navy. There is selection for service by the Admiralty Interview Board or by the recruiting organization and there is selection for promotion within the Service. Gardner (1970) describes the selection procedure as concerning itself with the identification of individuals who would benefit from an intensive and lengthy training period and who would eventually become effective leaders in the Service environment. He described prediction of success in these two distinctive roles of 'student' and 'practitioner' as the vital balance. My own career has provided a special vantage point to observe this balance. Mid-career retraining to match new tasks was a feature of naval life in the 1960's and personal experience as both a student and Training Staff Officer brought home the many complexities within such a programme. This experience focused in sharp relief on the old naval adage that the sailor – the man – is the greatest single factor in military success. Research into the effects of personality on leadership in the very technical environment of life at sea (Page, 1973) confirmed the importance of individual differences. Equally important is the need for management skills to be developed in a way which would allow the individual to grow in his work and feel challenged at every stage to strive for greater competence. Such an environment is only possible when a conscious decision is taken to provide it. This calls for an understanding of many different disciplines; bringing together the necessary skills in a multidisciplinary team is itself a demanding management task.

THE ROYAL NAVY IN PEACETIME

When considering management skills in the formal organization in peacetime, it can be shown that the allocation of function is achieved on lines which are established traditionally and are adjusted by a process of evolution. In this way the various skills are brought together in packages which permit some continuity from one generation to the next. These various skills are determined by the job activities which are necessary to operate the Fleet, but will of course change as a result of changing technology. There is also, within this balance, a relationship between the various jobs which must be coordinated and controlled. This packaging of management skills is achieved in the formal organization by the rank structure. To make sure that objectives are met, an element of leadership is required. This model of the formal organization can be equated to a department within a small ship, to the ship itself or to the Fleet commander and his various seagoing units. It applies equally well to the description of the organization of the various headquarters departments and dockyards.

The informal structure is also important. Material and psychological satisfactions generated by the members cannot be considered only in relation to the formal organization but must recognize the existence of some less formal grouping of people. The interactions between jobs mould and interact with the attitudes and personalities of the individuals who form the working group. These people, having already been moulded by the strong links in the Service, in their turn determine the norms established within that working group. The impact of the informal organization on the formal can be traced through a number of chains. An example of this interactive effect can again be found in the life of a messdeck. It is often organized on functional lines, being composed, perhaps, of all the junior rates of one branch. The Leading Rate in charge of the mess has the difficult task of belonging to the group while representing 'authority'. Thus, he is very vulnerable to conflicting pressures when there is any change in expectations from above. This is recognized in the old naval maxim of starting a commission with strict discipline and then gently slacking back as the situation permits. This is one example of a very specialized management skill linked to an employment cycle of two-year commissions; it is also an example of the hidden cost of change, however desirable the change itself may be.

Cost-consciousness is a characteristic of the formal structure and is resisted by the informal. In post-war years financial pressures on the Defence Budget from increasing costs of ships and equipments were increased still further by manpower costs rising just as fast. At the same time, life-cycle costing studies had shown that in the course of 20 years' service, 50% of the cost of keeping a ship in the firing line is represented by the money spent on the crew. The realization of this combined with the increasing difficulty in recruiting the men necessary to maintain the Vote A strength generated a mood to reduce the complement of ships. Reacting to this perception the Admiralty Board decreed the upper limit on complements for new design warships. Temporary, smaller manning standards for the existing fleet were applied. Work study techniques were used to look at ways of reducing the total work load, while studies of manpower utilization examined the macro-aspects. Later, the introduction of standardized management methods for the organization of ships took the RN further down the bureaucratic route so familiar in long periods of peace. This encouraged the attitude – 'I have completed my maintenance routines; if it fails now it is not my fault.' Ways to redistribute the skills necessary to fight and maintain the ships of the Fleet were sought in studies into new branch structures. These spread across into new design philosophies for total ship systems which recognized that savings in manpower were vital to the viability of the future fleet. All this activity resulted in the identification of areas where investment could lead to a reduction in complements. For example more attention paid to reliability and maintainability at the equipment development stage would result in a reduction of time spent on corrective maintenance and reduction of level of skills required to complete this maintenance. Again, it was thought possible to reduce the need for user personnel by increasing the automation of weapons and machinery.

In the event, the initiatives were only partially successful. There was not the range of management skills available to ensure that system designers responsible for hardware and software understood the manpower aspects. Equally the 'human factors' experts and especially psychologists missed the opportunity to influence the shape of the future fleet along sound and integrated principles. Part of the difficulty arose from the weakened position of serving officers in Defence Procurement as a result of the Rayner reorganization (Cmnd 4641). Their selection and employment have a big influence in this respect.

Technical officers represent a special case in this context because the characteristics welcomed in a technical officer in his first career are not the same as those required for higher command. It may be necessary to restructure the employment pattern of the small number recognized as suitable for consideration for promotion and earmark them in the early stages in the same way as those identified for sea command. If this is necessary it may prove difficult to find suitable employment for this special group which allows them to progress through the intermediate ranks without becoming disenchanted or having the required features of their personality blunted later by the intervening experiences. In considering the characteristics required in a successful project team, for example, it is recognized that there are different parts to play and that each player has a different set of attributes. It is conceivable that an 'uncomprehending' selection process could exclude all those who embrace the necessary mix of attributes for a particular role in a given area of employment. When it is recognized that the total officer corps of the rank of Commander and above is selected on the basis of confidential reports it is quite conceivable that the multi-stage selection process will have weeded out all those who have an essential quality. Alternatively it is possible that because of the regenerative process involved, the trend in selection creates a shift towards an extreme in some attributes. During research into this aspect one subject said, 'I was forced into considering leaving when I found I was completely unable to identify myself with the sort of person who became a senior officer, not only could I not see myself in that mould but I could not find it in me to do the sort of job they were doing.' This attitude was reported a number of times and is difficult to counter.

Selection for high command is important as a management function because of the existence of a potential mismatch between actual holders of the senior posts in the service and the image held by a new generation of officers. It may be necessary to adopt a concept of selecting men suitable for high command or project management and consciously protecting them during the intervening stages of development during which they gain the appropriate experience and maturity. This is based on the premise that men who are required as leaders at that level are less likely to succeed in the type of job which demands their attention in a peacetime environment. It is the lack of such favourable conditions in peacetime which generates the high stress levels reported by so many middle-ranking officers. It has been noticeable that Seaman Officers chosen for command and Engineer Officers who were closely integrated in project management always reported a high degree of involvement with their work and a satisfaction with the prospects offered by the service. Where an officer was unable to find this involvement because he was not selected for these jobs a greater degree of frustration was reported and there was a marked tendency to leave the service and find employment elsewhere.

Rejection by failure to be selected for promotion bears very heavily in the service being less blatantly obvious in civilian employment. This public recognition of failure when an officer passes through a zone for promotion forces the individual to make some deep readjustment in his goals for himself and his family which determines his approach to the service thereafter. While there is undoubtedly an important part to be played by experienced officers who nevertheless are not eligible for further promotion, there is a danger of having too many such people in the organization. The means of controlling this proportion is difficult to arrange and calls for particular interpersonal skills on the part of the Directors of Naval Officer Appointments.

PREPARATION FOR BATTLE

Preparation for battle in times of peace also requires special management skills. Until the Great War (1914–1918) men in this country had never, strictly speaking, been forced to go to war. 'Volunteers' were rarely in short supply and should the numbers fall off there were always pressgangs at the ready to swell the ranks. The nobility would be called upon to raise an army for the monarch and, indeed, part of the privilege of having title and lands was the requirement to provide men for battle. During World War I the drain on manpower was so great that it became necessary to conscript men into the forces. This happened again in the Second World War and continued in the form of National Service into the 1950's. Men were no longer volunteers and the face and role of the Services was rapidly changing. Equipment had become more technical and sophisticated and the modern servicemen had to learn considerably more than his historic counterpart. The management of the Services changed to keep pace and itself increased in complexity.

Management skills in the preparation for battle now focus on two distinct areas. There is the equipment to procure and maintain, and there is the recruiting and training of the right men to fill the billets in an entirely volunteer force. The years since World War II have seen the Services being concerned more with the threat and deterrence of that threat than actually fighting it. There have been two or three generations of highly sophisticated equipment developed which have never been tried in battle. Also, men have to be trained to use such equipment in realistic conditions. Management skill in this environment is very different from a war setting and probably more difficult to instil. The situation is further complicated by the lack of sufficient opportunity for officers and men to practise flair and initiative. The difference between training for war in peacetime and developing skills in battle has always been recognized. The difference today is in the magnitude of the gulf between success and failure.

The importance of individual difference in matching skill against the management task cannot be overestimated. The formal organization sees itself as selecting men carefully and, by training and experience, moulding them to match this task. The logic of all subsequent activity is based on the assumption that there is an 'average' man. These average men are considered to be completely interchangeable when they hold similar ranks and belong to the same specialization. This actuarial approach is a legitimate simplification required for global manpower planning but tends to result in an oversimplification of subsequent utilization. Men are not equal. Men of similar rank may differ widely in age, motivation, latent ability and experience. Further, the organization is not homogeneous (Emery and Trist, 1969). Summing these 'tolerances' results in a wide range of potential response to a challenge. Because failure is frequently not acceptable when considering outcomes, elaborate precautions are taken to avoid it. It would appear that as a result, men are employed at a level which will minimize the likelihood of such failure. Evidence to support this is provided by statistical analysis of casual wastage.

This policy of caution in utilization is normal in peacetime and has the consequential effect of generating posts where the task may not match the talents of the incumbent. Efforts have been made to reduce this to a minimum by very complicated hierarchical structures. This, however, earns the penalty of a reduction in flexibility in the deployment of individuals. This stereotyping, while serving a purpose, can become maladaptive when the organization is experiencing high rates of change. Further, it does not take note of any personality variables other than a gestalt interpretation at the selection stage. The research literature, naval selection procedures and individual experience all point to a recognition that it is the personality of the individual and the way he reacts within the environment which determines his success as a manager and a leader.

KINDS OF MANAGEMENT TASK

Military management consists of a continuous choice-making process that permits the organization as a whole to proceed towards its objectives despite all sorts of internal and external perturbations. As every officer knows, problems occasionally arise that are not amenable to the available and customary methods of analysis and solution. Although uncertain about which choice to make, an officer may nevertheless have to make a decision. It is in situations of this kind that many of the popular traits attributed to leaders find their justification: quickness of decision, the courage to take risks, coolness under stress, intuition and even luck. There is no doubt that quick, effective, and daring decisions are a highly prized commodity in a crisis, but just as precious a commodity is the art of planning and organizing so that such crises do not occur. The trend in the Royal Navy has been to remove as many of its decisions as possible from the area of hunch and intuition to that of rational calculation. More and more it is choosing to depend less on the unique abilities of rare individuals and to depend instead on the orderly process of analysis. The occasions and opportunities for personal leadership in the old sense still exist, but they are becoming increasingly rare and circumscribed. This trend does not eliminate the role of personal leadership, but it has significantly redefined it. Under normal conditions both afloat and ashore, leadership in today's navy no longer consists of personal decision-making but in maintaining the effectiveness of the decision-making system. The picture of the leader who 'keeps cool and in the nick of time makes the crucial decision' is out of date. The popular stereotype now is the thoughtful officer discussing information supplied by a staff of experts. It is possible that the brilliant leader is becoming as much an organizational embarrassment as he is an asset.

This, reasonable though it may appear on the surface, conceals two serious dangers. First, we may be giving up the opportunity of utilizing the highest expressions of personal leadership in favour of arrangements which, although safer and more reliable, can yield at best only a high level of mediocrity. And second, having committed ourselves to a system that thrives on the ordinary, we may, in the interests of maintaining and improving its efficiency, tend to shun the extraordinary. In the context of management skills in peacetime this may seem unimportant, but when considered in terms of developing a philosophy for the fighting of ships and the managing of the Fleet, it presents, it is believed, a much more alarming picture. It can be seen as a serious threat to the small number of 'agents of change' in a computer-based navy.

The Royal Navy takes an ambivalent view of management, avoiding any fine distinction between 'leadership' and 'management'. Heath (1969) represents the view that leadership is a form of authority and a function of management and claims that Adair's (1969) definition of functional leadership amounts to no more than personalized management. This notion is further substantiated by Groves (1970) who says that management is the exercise of sanctioned authority over resources of men and material towards defined objectives. The concept of functional leadership has a considerable following in all three Services, and can be shown as a dynamic balancing of the needs of the group being led. These needs fall into three basic categories: task achievement, individual needs and team maintenance needs.

The opposite naval school of thought sees management as a lower level of activity than leadership, which is considered especially important in the war environment. The official naval view, as exemplified in the Naval War Manual, tends towards the 'qualities approach' which says that leadership is 'individualistic, should not be copied, but studied for guiding principles'. Whilst this idea supports those who believe leadership to be an art not a science, it has serious draw-backs when used as a basis for managing the selection and training of leaders. The pendulum of opinion swings back and forth and meanwhile the Royal Navy expends a great deal of effort on leadership training at Officer, Petty Officer and Leading Rate level and this embraces those management skills seen as essential.

A considerable effort is also expended on generating efficient teams in ships and ashore. A special management skill is involved in the building of Command Teams in ships. It must be recognized, for example, that Commanding Officers of ships have considerable autonomy in the choice of officers to lead their ships' companies. Thus, a more experienced senior Captain is in a position to form his command team in any image he sees fit. This process may take a number of paths. He may perhaps ask for certain officers whom he has known in the past. He may refuse to accept an officer proposed by the appointing authorities. Finally, he may 'sack' an officer at some stage of the building up of the team into a trained group. Although individual examples of this method of team formation may cause an eyebrow to be raised, it is recognized that the concept is strong in equity and works well in practice. If the Captain is to take full responsibility for every aspect of his ship, he must have the power which enables him to accept it. There should be no suggestion that this power be diminished. What is of interest, however, is that on occasion a Captain goes to endless trouble to bring together a most carefully selected team of officers who are all recognized as 'flyers' in their own field. Most officers can bring an example to mind and the result is frequently judged as a disaster. Few such ships are happy ships and neither the individuals nor the group seem to benefit in the long term. This phenomenon has been called 'the ministry of the talents' in research into team formation and even at the superficial level of playing in a 'business game' the same lack of success is apparent. It is possible that this example of how team formation may fail can be interpreted as a warning against tinkering with the system. That is not the intention.

There are many examples of great success following the bringing together of a carefully selected group. An example can be found in the setting up of the Polaris Project Team within the Ministry of Defence. The establishment of this project was judged to be of great national importance and particular care was taken in the forming of the team. The Director had first call on anyone in the parent organization and the result was a classic example of an 'in' group, which might have been expected to be counter-productive. However, the magnitude of the task faced by the resulting work force generated great co-hesiveness so that members were totally committed and a 'steam-roller' image was presented to the outside world. The success of the group in achieving the declared aim within both the budget and the timescale has stood out as a shining example of what can be achieved. The uniqueness of this achievement has been reflected in the subsequent success of a large proportion of the individuals who were involved. The eventual replacement of a 'first eleven' was by the normal processes of personnel management. The organizational aim of the project was blurred by time. As a result of these two factors, the corporate image became very different. Because of a reduction of individual commitment from the level held previously, it is likely that group effectiveness was also different. It will be interesting to observe how the management of the Polaris successor system is brought together.

A BASIC MODEL

A very simple model of the way a person with all his individual characteristics and skills reacts to a situation to achieve a desired result is shown in Figure 3.1.

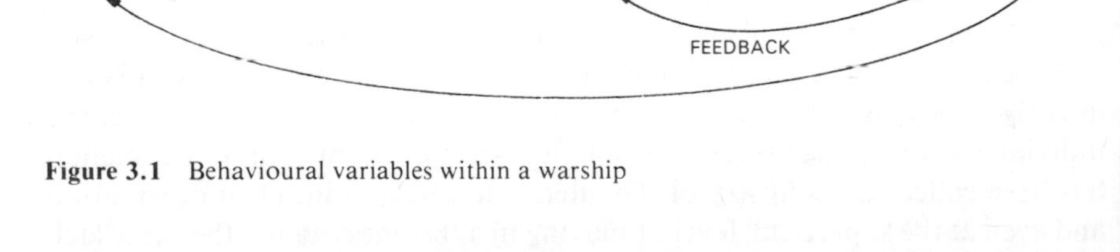

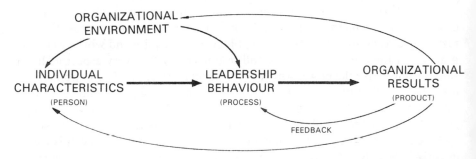

Figure 3.1 Behavioural variables within a warship

The environment is predetermined by the organizational constraints and these affect both the person in his perception of himself and his behaviour in attempting to manage his affairs. The resultant effects of his management and leadership behaviour will usually modify that behaviour but in addition reflect into the organization and the person himself. The effect of this reflection is a measure of the style of both. The conditioning process of training the manager and preparing the organization to react appropriately is lengthy and not always predictable.

Bringing a warship up to an acceptable level of fighting efficiency is a typical example of a desired organizational result. In this it is the central position of the 1st Lieutenant (who is second in command) which gives him the vital role in creating the environment for leadership and management to flourish. He will be dependent upon his captain's wishes and his success will rely on the other heads of department as well. This lynch-pin position identifies the role holder as possibly the most important single person in the ship from the management point of view. A person–process–product is struck which because of the very firmly constrained environment of the steel hull is closely controlled by the feed-back loops. It is very quickly obvious to everyone if, through inexperience or incompetence, the results of his endeavours are inadequate.

From this description emerges a picture of the post-war military establishment which is stressful, competitive and introspective. The individual within this organization needs to be competent, confident and cool. He must have a high resistance to stress – in the early years predominantly physical in nature but mental stress with an intellectual and emotional base will become more dominant as his career progresses. Training and experience will prepare him for coping with these stresses and the corporate image is of great assistance also.

Cheerful optimism as a 'front' is the stock-in-trade of the military leader. Recent management techniques have extended the focus of attention of the military onto future probabilities which engender only pessimism. The resultant conflict between goal and achievement is creating a very difficult management environment. At a personal level, the balance between capacities and aspirations is achieved by the acquisition of skills. If despite these skills the mismatch remains, the result is neurosis. A similar result occurs in large organizations, and working within such an environment requires a robust and resilient approach. This is particularly noticeable if the work environment is based on advanced technology. By definition this implies increased uncertainty and the person in charge must demonstrate by his competence and self-confidence that he is in command of the situation. This is difficult in the face of failure but is crucial for ultimate success. In this context seaman skills, for example in coping with disaster at sea, are well understood and both training and career patterns are well attuned to such demands. In advanced technical areas, the old practices do not necessarily apply and intellectual stress is less well managed. For example, computer maintainers require considerable intellectual stamina to cope with fault diagnosis when documentation is poor and the superior is, through lack of relevant experience, unable to give support. Self-confidence and a strong self-image are essential to success in such people and the organizational structure must foster them.

LEADERSHIP AND SELECTION

The different demands placed upon the officers and ships company will be appreciated by considering the range of activities involved in the many roles played by a frigate. It should be clear that there is a need for both management skills and leadership skills and that these are different. Beyond the dichotomy of peace and war there is the need to balance the demands of the material with the reasonable expectations of the men. Thus although frigates were running with what Fryer (1973) described as 'poor management systems' the fact that they were achieving satisfactory results reflects that they were well led. Prior (1977) in commenting on management education suggested that much of it may have been counter-productive. He says: 'The spark of initiative, the subconscious urge in leaders to make their mark, Lord Wavell's 'irrational tenth' in the aspiring leader are all of far greater importance than whatever happens to be the currently fashionable management science.' I would agree, but a balance must be struck. A nice illustration of this goes back to the trenches. Getting one's men back from the front line for rest and regrouping called for certain management skills; getting them back into the trenches again when the break was over required real leadership!

The balance between leadership and management skills is intimately related to the establishment of criteria for selection. An examination of the total numbers of General List officers will show that about a fifth are of Commander rank and a third of that number are Captain rank, a very small percentage are of Flag rank. It would therefore appear fair to assume as Gardner does that one of the aims of the selection procedure is to provide material for promotion to Commander. It follows that a criterion for the success of the selection procedure could be promotion. In fact, however, the organization requires a certain number of more senior officers and it is a closed system which can draw on candidates for promotion only from within its own ranks. Therefore the process of identifying the ones most likely to fill the higher ranks is more akin to the process of allocation and is governed by different considerations from the ones facing the Admiralty Interview Board. It also has to be recognized that there is considerable elapsed time between the initial selection for service and the successful completion of the first career leading to eligibility for promotion. One stage in the provision of the high command demands the identification quite early of those likely to be suitable for it. These selected few have to be given experience at an accelerated rate to enable them to fit the profile of the potential Flag Officer; for example the operational commander of a seagoing fleet has himself to have had sea command. As has been mentioned earlier, consideration of experience as a resource makes it necessary to restrict the number of individuals who can be allowed sea command. The identification of the officer suitable for an early appointment to command of a ship therefore commits the system to considering him and not his less fortunate peers in a subsequent selection process for Flag rank.

DEVELOPMENT OF SKILLS

Training young officers both ashore and afloat highlights the importance of the self-learning process which takes place when pride is at stake. Early tasks such as running boats, taking charge of a shore patrol or the replacement of a piece of equipment can be predominantly manual in content. The task is defined, supervised and completed well within the working day. Very soon the young manager faces tasks which conflict with the interests of others and the skills for resolution of conflict must be acquired. As his repertoire extends, foresight and planning become second nature and he develops the flair for 'smelling success'. Experience and achievement consolidate these skills to enable him to cope with every new challenge as it is presented. To illustrate this process, the Leading Rate and the young Midshipman receive orders which they don't always fully understand but carry them out to the best of their ability and learn from any mistakes. The people they are managing probably know the drill better than their leaders. The Petty Officer receives more generalized instructions and translates them into well-proved recipes which he knows his men understand. He is likely to be down-to-earth and ill at ease with abstract concepts.

The fully qualified officer has received much education and has applied his training to a variety of challenging activities. To have survived this far he must have shown competence and is likely to be tough, arrogant and ambitious. Other people's management difficulties inevitably reflect their incompetence. His thinking is abstract and closely tied to timescales. At this stage he may be promoted and exposed to the Ministry of Defence. Here he discovers he has lost all his power and has to rely solely on influence. Interpersonal relationships take on a dominant role. The change is traumatic and many officers fail to adapt. He also finds himself in a world of monopoly money and elongated timescales which have always to be initiated in a great hurry for obscure reasons. Those who survive learn from experience and return to the Fleet as wiser men. After a period of rehabilitation some will be ready to re-enter the corridors of power as directing staff. By now, the repertoire of management skills will be catholic with a sound and broad base of experience. Their relevance to the problems of the hour is where luck comes in. By this stage, the officer manager has a complex model of scenarios, cash limits, long-term costing periods, military worth and people problems constantly rehearsed in his brain, hoping that a flash of insight will illuminate a path out of his presently impossible dilemma. When and if he does have that flash of genius he will then face the long hours of convincing his peers and his superiors that he is right. Once more luck enters the equation, but by this stage political considerations take an increasingly important part and the management skills is replaced by political skill.

By the time an officer has reached a position where he can influence events, he will have demonstrated a high level of capability in many different fieids. This is an inherent feature of the selection process. It goes without saying that the selected individual will bring a rich mix of intellectual ability and relevant experience: it is the amalgam of these and the comparison of the result with those of his peers which will determine his subsequent effectiveness.

A naval officer employed in Headquarters at director level will be dealing with a group of people, both service and civilian, who have themselves been selected by similar criteria. Managing departmental activity in this environment calls for a skill which is quite different from that practised in a naval setting. The main difference is in the identification of aims, and the evaluation of outcomes. Previously, there would have been a clear cut black-and-white dividing line between success and failure. The new environment has many shades of grey. This shading reflects the political imperative of the art of the possible. The decision-maker has to identify the preferred outcome and then moderate it to take account of the expectations of his colleagues and the resources which can be won from a limited pool.

The usual reaction by most people to this environment is one of frustration, feeling threatened and afraid of failure. The frustration emerges because the goals of the organization are very diverse, and the timescales in which events mature are very extended. The frustration will occur because the mechanisms for reaching agreement are those of influence rather than authority. The authority to say 'yes' is less easy to identify than the authority to say 'no'. The system apparently operates by a type of blackballing and it is sometimes difficult to identify the underlying rules. Fear of failure is normally contained by the essential and therefore well developed naval trait of ambitious self-interest being closely matched to the aims and goals of the service. As a divisional officer, in command of a ship, and even as a Commander-in-Chief, the aims of the individual and the aims of the service are well matched. The situation in a government ministry is much less clear cut. It is this which creates uncertainty and the fear of failure because of the inability to identify the real challenge or threat to a successful outcome. At this stage in an individual's career all those who are thus employed are likely to have the potential to do more. The ones who are called to contribute the most will usually demonstrate an added dimension of unusual integrity and stamina which stands them in good stead in the critical moments of crisis. It is this, combined with an intellectual penetration and clarity of thought, which allows them to bring order and purpose to a constantly heightening sea of related but chaotic information.

Leaders who survive in this environment develop very special skills and, in particular, the corporate management skill is a tapestry of the skills of individuals refined to a peak and usually deployed in a complementary manner. The highly regarded 'ideas' man of rare vision who can see and describe the unfolding scenario will be faced with so much need for change that he is frequently inhibited from taking action. This vision is usually complemented by a strong decision-maker who can take the conflicting options and pick a way forward that is acceptable to most. The implementation of these decisions is usually delegated to one or two levels below that of the decision-makers. In bringing together these various skills and range of experience which vary so much between individuals, it is necessary to 'group-up' the various specialists. The person in charge of such a team has to consider many aspects which are novel to his experience and this group officer will find that he is facing areas of uncertainty in step with his appointing pattern of two to three years. This develops the earlier characteristics into those of someone who keeps his own counsel, develops an information network for information exchange, and an ability to respond quickly to outside stimuli.

From this mid-career 'group officer' stereotype, the final stage produces a professional decision-maker who is calculating, extremely well informed and usually decisive with a very high resistance to stress. Experience will have made him politically aware in terms of his working environment and he will have learned to tolerate considerable uncertainty in his day-to-day affairs. In short, the system will have selected the man best fitted to make the difficult decisions and will have given him a shell to protect him long enough to do it.

References

Adair, J. (1969). *Training for Leadership.* (London: Macdonald)

Baylis, R. (1970). A contribution to the application of systems analysis to manpower planning with a naive model. *Defence Fellowship Report*, Southampton University.

Baynes, J. C. M. (1969). The influence on the army of change in the British society. *Defence Fellowship Report*, University of Edinburgh

Bensham-Booth, D. F. (1969). The sociological problems of integrating the military and civil communities in the UK. *Defence Fellowship Report*, University College, London

Cmnd 4641 (1971). *Government Organisation for Defence Procurement and Civil Aerospace.* (London: HMSO)

Eberle, J. H. F. (1971). A study of politics – Military aspects of operational command. *Defence Fellowship Report*, University College, Oxford

Emery, F. E. and Trist, E. L. (1969). The causal texture of organisational environments in systems thinking. In Emery, F. E. (ed.) *Systems Thinking.* (Harmondsworth: Penguin)

Evans, D. (1970). *Practical Management in Ships. Western Fleet Report.* (Harmondsworth: Penguin)

Fryer, J. (1973). A victory for the work study sailors. *Sunday Times*, 14/3/1973

Gardner, K. E. (1970). Selection training and career development of naval officers. A long-term follow-up using multivariate techniques. *PhD Thesis*, City University

Groves, L. B. (1970). Some techniques of organisational analysis reviewed in a naval context. *MSc Dissertation*, Brunel University

Heath, P. C. (1969). Management and leadership or the chicken and the egg. *J. Work Study and Management Services*, **2**, 8

Janowitz, M. and Little, R. (1965). *Sociology and the Military Establishment.* (New York: Russell Saye)
Likert, R. (1961). *New Patterns of Management.* (New York: McGraw–Hill)
Page, M. R. H. (1973). A study of personality and leadership in a technical environment. *PhD Thesis*, Aston University
Prior, P. J. (1977). *Leadership is not a Bowler Hat.* (London: David and Charles)
Wright, P. D. (1970). 'The British Officer.' *Defence Fellowship Report*, Reading University

4
Universities

W. T. SINGLETON

INTRODUCTION

Tertiary education has expanded enormously in the past thirty years. Defining a university as an institution financially supported by the University Grants Committee, there are now 44 such bodies in the UK. The national allocation made by the UGC has increased from less than £5 million just after the war to over £1000 million currently. The university student population was about 50 000 in the 1930's; it is now about 300 000 and there are now a similar number of students studying for degrees through other institutions. About one third of students are female. There are about 40 000 academic staff in universities and about 10% of these are professors. This large investment in what was formerly regarded as a highly esoteric activity is usually explained as something made necessary by the increased elaboration of society and the services needed to maintain it, but it is a consequence of as well as a support for technical change. We can now afford to have these people not gainfully employed in any production sense but hopefully engaged in self-development, so as to increase the richness of society now and in the future. These increases in numbers together with other changes in society have radically altered the image and the reality of what staff and students are like and what they do. The internal mores have changed surprisingly little, perhaps because the staff form an isolated self-selected group. They select the students, and also select the criteria and measures of success in performance as a student. The job is so attractive that, on the whole, the formally most successful stay within the system and join in repeating the process of selecting for entry and allocating merit in their own image.

The dominant selection measure is success in written examinations although these do become steadily more open-ended from the school-leaving level to the doctoral level. Promotions of academic staff are made mainly in terms of performance as a research worker; performance as a teacher or administrator is given little weight partly because this latter is more difficult to measure but partly also because there is a potent, if unstated, belief that such skills are either trivial or unnecessary. Thus the university population is dominated by a narrow concept of human capacities based on a very few attributes which focus on intelligence, memory and facility for self-expression associated with a specialized curiosity drive – the need to know within certain selected areas of knowledge called academic disciplines. These mores are uniform and pervasive throughout the academic world which would therefore be liable to complacency if left to itself; because of the growth in size and expenditure it is no longer left to itself and the outside world is increasingly critical of the values and achievements of universities, so much so that the expansion of the system in the Western world has been almost eliminated over the last few years. However, the experience of current academics is limited almost entirely to the expansion phase; the new skills and new organizational structures which will inevitably emerge in the next phase of either contraction or stable size have yet to appear.

Universities everywhere are strong on tradition, and the continuous change which has gone on throughout the centuries tends to be overlooked. The currently accepted concept of the ideal university is essentially a late 19th century one, as expressed for example by Newman (1873). 'A university training is the great ordinary means to a great, but ordinary, end; it aims at raising the intellectual tone of society, at cultivating the public mind, at purifying the national taste, at supplying true principles to popular enthusiasms and fixed aims to popular aspirations, at giving enlargement and sobriety to the ideas of the age, at facilitating the exercise of political power and refining the intercourse of private life. It is the education which gives a man a clear conscious view of his own opinions and judgements, a truth in developing them, an eloquence in urging them and a force in expressing them. It teaches him to see things as they are, to go right to the point, to disentangle a skein of thought, to detect what is sophistical and to discard what is irrelevant. It prepares him to fill any post with credit and to master any subject with facility. It shows him how to accommodate himself to others, how to throw himself into their state of mind, how to bring before them his own, how to influence them, how to come to an understanding with them, how to bear with them. He is at home in any society, he has common ground with every class; he knows when to speak and when to be silent, he is able to converse, he is able to listen; he can ask a question pertinently and gain a lesson seasonably when he has nothing to impart himself; he is ever ready, yet never in the way; he is a pleasant companion and a comrade whom you may depend upon; he knows when to be serious, when to trifle, and he has a sure tact which enables him to trifle with gracefulness and to be serious with effect. He has the repose of mind which lives in itself while it lives in the world and which has resources for its happiness at home when it cannot go abroad. He has a gift which serves him in public and supports him in retirement, without which good fortune is but vulgar and with which failure and disappointment have a charm. The art which tends to make a man all this is, in the object which it pursues, as useful as the art of wealth or the art of health, though it is less susceptible of method, less certain, less complete in its result.'

The traditional and ideal method of teaching is seen as one in which the student works under a particular don or professor famous for his expertise in a specialized academic field. The students are his pupils and identify themselves as having served their apprenticeship under him. The impact of much larger numbers of universities and students, and the consequent need for responsible, formal organization and financial accounting has resulted in the creation of the department as an organization which now pervades the university system. To counterbalance the academic department there are now other formal associated organizations such as student unions and university administration departments. These latter engage in a dialogue with academic departments on the one hand and national government on the other. This dramatic change within a staff generation may not have been desirable but in retrospect it seems to have been inevitable.

Administrative departments have interesting problems of organization and skill development. A new profession of university administrator has appeared but he has much in common with administrators from the same profession in other large industries. An accountant, a systems analyst or a personnel specialist does a similar job whether he operates in a university, a health service or a nationalized industry. For this reason, this chapter concentrates on academic departments in universities.

THE UNIVERSITY DEPARTMENT

An academic department is primarily a collection of individuals dedicated to a particular intellectual discipline, that is to a coherent set of knowledge and techniques. Such a people-centred enterprise can be approached in terms of either systems theory or task/skill theory or social psychology. Systems theory stresses the importance of clarifying objectives, of analysis by description of inputs and outputs and of allocating functions between man and machines and procedures. In general man is regarded as a systems component but a key component in that he holds the rest of the system together. A more specific focus on personnel is provided by the task analysis approach which centres on what people actually do. This is supplemented by the skills approach which considers how task performance changes with experience, that is with learning. Man is seen as essentially rational, as an information processor and as a goal seeker. In social psychology the frame of reference is the interaction between people. The basic characteristic of man is that he is a member of a group or a herd. This is man as a social animal. The application of each of these points of view to the business of a university department can be considered separately.

The system

A department can be described by an input/output diagram as shown in Figure 4.1. It is a system which generates graduates, papers and techniques

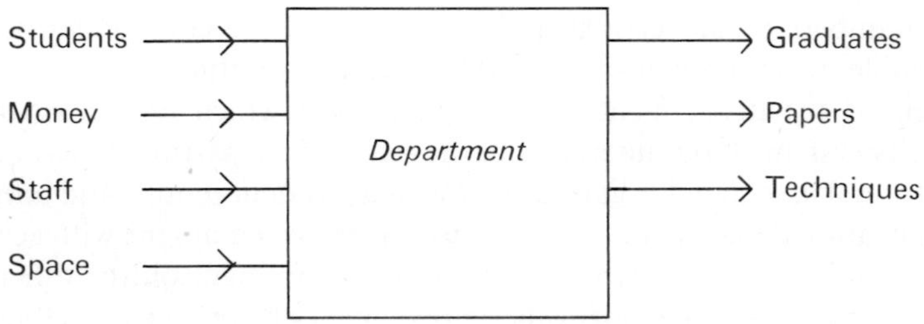

Figure 4.1 The inputs and outputs of a university department

after taking in students, money, staff and space. This analysis already reveals one unnecessary complication in that money, staff and space are regarded as three separate kinds of asset with no trade-offs between them. This is a primitive form of organization or bureaucracy. Greater flexibility could be obtained if there were one basic currency, namely money, which those concerned with running the department could manipulate. The department has an administrative load in that there are offices, laboratories, equipment and reports which need to be organized by relatively routine processes. There is then the teaching function which generates its own routines concerned with admissions, timetables, the organization of tutorials and the generation of references for past students. There is a research function where the content varies depending on the topics of the department (Table 4.1).

Table 4.1 Departmental infrastructure in universities

Administration	Offices, Laboratories, Equipment, Reports
Teaching	Admissions, Timetables, Tutorials, Assessment, References
Research and application	Scholarship, Laboratory studies, Field studies, Implementation and evaluation

In summary, the main functions of an academic department are: teaching, advancing knowledge and administration. To have some measure of efficiency, productivity, or even purpose, it is valuable to have a criterion for each of these. In the case of teaching the ideal situation seems to be the close contact between the single dedicated teacher and the single motivated pupil, or the small group of interacting pupils. All other teaching situations compromise on but attempt to retain the standards of this ideal. From this point of view, teaching technology is merely a method of saving or utilizing more widely the individual teacher time but it can never be a complete substitute for it. On the advancement of knowledge there are no adequate criteria. Various simple measures have been suggested, the crudest one being the measurement of the output of an academic by weighing papers he has written. This has been refined into counting the number of papers published in various kinds of journals and even further by attempting to count the number of citations of papers. This latter appears superficially to be a reasonable approach but it is subject to the vagaries of fashion. That is, if one happens to publish in a fashionable field there will be many citations regardless of the quality of the paper, whereas if one happens to be working alone in a novel area there will be few citations however high the quality. For administration, about 90% success seems to be optimal; to attempt a greater level would be inefficient in wider terms in that it would take up too much time of academic staff. If the professional administrators of a university never complain, then the academics are spending too much time on administration; if on the other hand they complain continually then too little time is being spent.

The tasks

Task analysis is the art of describing what a human operator does in the course of his specialized activity. The analysis of the tasks of the university lecturer is shown in Table 4.2. The tasks are graduated in increasing order of difficulty; thus lecturing on special topics is regarded as the easiest kind of lecture while presenting introductory courses is regarded as the most difficult. With this kind of model in mind it is the duty of the senior staff to ensure that new lecturers are introduced sequentially to more difficult tasks under each of the four headings. In this sense the on-line training of a university lecturer takes about seven years. The complete lecturer is defined as a person who has experience and skill in each of these areas. The same kind of analysis can be applied to the Senior Lecturer. The art of coping with committees is questioned because it is arguable as to whether or not the good senior lecturer or reader must have this kind of skill or whether it is merely a desirable feature for the majority. The equivalent for a professor must include the political arts which can be defined as the pursuit and manipulation of power in an organizational setting. Occupational guidance is regarded as of key importance starting from the axiom that a department is a collection of dedicated and skilled individuals. It therefore follows that the progress of the department is basically a matter of the progress of individuals and it is the duty of the professors to facilitate and nourish their development.

Table 4.2 Task description

Lecturer	
Teacher	Special topics Advanced courses Standard courses Introductory courses
Tutor	Demonstrating Subject tutoring General tutoring Moral tutoring
Individual supervision	Bachelor course projects Master's course projects Master's level research Doctoral level research
Team supervisor	Class experiments Case studies Group projects Seminars
Senior lecturer	
Administration	Department University
Extra-mural work	Professional Regional National
Staff development	Academic Clerical Technical
Political(?)	Internal and external committees Mass media appearances
Professor	
Specialist research reputation	
Academic occupational guidance	
University politician	

Seniority in academic life is somewhat unusual in the respect that individuals rarely drop tasks completely. A senior professor goes on doing everything that a junior lecturer does. University dons and hospital consultants are about the only two professions where the senior practitioner refuses to stop doing the tasks which he did when he first entered the profession. The chief constable does not go out on the beat; the general does not lead a platoon into action; the managing director does not take over from a foreman, but the consultant still examines patients and the professor still does his lectures.

Social aspects

It is orthodox to describe the university as a self-governing community of scholars. It is less common to find any clear descriptions of what this means or what it implies. That a university is a community would be accepted by everyone and in this sense social psychology should be able to make a contribution. A university must, of course, be more than just a community; in particular it must be a centre of excellence, the quality and the integrity of what is done must be beyond question. These matters are very much a function of leadership and there are many kinds of leader and styles of leadership. It is clear that each kind and style has its advantages and disadvantages and its appropriateness to particular times and situations. The university dean or head of department, like the leader in any other field, tends to change his characteristics to suit the context and to employ a combination of styles, partly rationally but mainly intuitively.

As centres of intellectual activity, universities invariably over-estimate the rationality of human behaviour. In this sense they are naive in their attitudes and in their structures. They have closed their collective mind to the concepts and ideas developed for at least a century which emphasize the inherent irrationality of human behaviour, particularly of human interactions. In the 19th century, for example, Newman wrote that 'Many a man will live and die upon a dogma: no man will be a martyr for a conclusion'. Trotter (1916) developed and clarified this point; in particular he emphasized the strength of the herd instinct as a dominant factor in human behaviour, '. . . that belief of affirmations sanctioned by the herd is a normal mechanism of the human mind, and goes on however much affirmations may be opposed by evidence, that reason cannot enforce belief against herd suggestions and finally that totally false opinions may appear to the holder of them to possess all the characters of rationally verifiable truth, and may be justified by secondary processes of rationalization which may be impossible directly to combat by argument'. A wider understanding of these ideas would reduce expectations of university decision-making to a more realistic and accurate level.

It might be argued that academics are above this kind of thing; their belief in the rational man and in human intelligence is supreme and they act accordingly. Trotter would point out that this is just another manifestation of rationalization. Intelligence does not protect a man from the dictates of herd sanctions and beliefs, it merely provides him with more and more elaborate ways of justifying what he is already committed to believing.

Objectives and values

As one would expect from intelligent people, university staff construct the most elaborate ideational structures to justify themselves and their activities not only to others, but also to themselves. It remains a privileged and elitist way of life and in an egalitarian age, statements of objectives and values have to be most carefully propounded so as to maintain the status quo whilst not offending against the broader national *zeitgeist*.

There is a need to be careful to maintain internal consistency between three key aspects of university philosophy which are not readily reconcilable. Firstly, universities are monuments to rational man; there is respect for evidence and for systematic progress, notably in the accumulation of evidence but also in the use of that evidence in the construction of theories and new hypotheses – in short in increased understanding. Secondly, it is recognized that advancement of knowledge and teaching require creativity as well as mere factual evidence and deductive logic. Creativity is notoriously erratic and unpredictable, the antithesis of the systematic. Thirdly, as to what it is for, there is an almost inevitable lapse into mysticism. The storage and pursuit of knowledge and the development of young minds are such worthwhile aims as to be axiomatically essential rather than in need of any kind of evaluation. Most people would accept this in the abstract absolute sense but unfortunately the cost of these activities is now such that it is unrealistic to try to live in a world of absolute values.

The scale of the university system requires that we have somehow to match values to costs and here we are on very shaky ground both externally and internally. Externally it is not clear how to decide how much the taxpayer should contribute to the national university system. Correspondingly, internally it is not clear how a university should determine its own policies; everything that seems desirable cannot be done. There has to be a scale of priorities but there can be little evidence to support it. Given these featureless decision situations, pragmatic policies develop based roughly on carrying on doing what has been done before with some minor shifts in the force of new circumstances. This could be a recipe for disaster; it is certainly a recipe for inertia.

Thus at the present time the collective mind of an English university moves along in the creative mode described for individual minds in earlier volumes in this series by Miller (1978), Lawson (1978), Branton (1979) and Hedge and Lawson (1979). Neither ends nor means can be described *ab initio* but the total situation is reacted to as it develops so that the more immediate objectives are modified as the available means become known within some overall general direction which is accepted without being defined.

Academic skills

As for all skilled performance, it is difficult to separate the manifestation of academic skill into neat compartments. Some years ago the University Grants Committee were unwise enough to ask university staff to take part in a survey aimed at separating their personal time allocation into three categories: administration, teaching and research. This proved impossible even for those pedantic academics who enjoy formalizing all their activities. One professor replied that he spent 100% of his time on administration, 100% on teaching and 100% on research. He exaggerated but he was making a valid point: all these categories overlap extensively. It is obvious that research experience, results and particularly thinking are rapidly fed back into teaching; this is one *raison d'être* for the university system. There is equal fertilization in the opposite direction; every lecturer knows the feeling of new doubts and innovations arising in his mind as he expounds what he meant to be the orthodox view in a standard lecture. A valuable first step in developing a new research interest is to deliberately commit oneself to a series of lectures on the topic. Long administrative-committee meetings have the advantage that the participant cannot suffer external interruptions by the telephone or visitors to his office and he can switch off attention to the debate and allow his mind to wander over other issues to do with research or teaching. The switch away from the meeting is not complete; this illustrates a widespread skill manifestation, which is the ability to stay in contact with a situation whilst devoting most of one's attention to something else. It seems to be possible, as it were, to say to the situation, 'don't call me unless you are really convinced that I would be interested.' There are at least two strategies which make this feasible. For example, in the committee the bored participant can sample what is being said either at given time intervals, which can be variable or can be triggered by external events such as a change of speaker in the debate. Alternatively he can rely on other triggers for his attention, such as raised voices, which indicate a change of tempo in the debate.

However, while accepting that administrative, teaching and research tasks overlap, the skills should be more easily separable. Research skills have already been described in earlier volumes in this series; teaching skills are predominantly social and will, no doubt, appear in the later volume but this chapter is focussed on the administrative or management skills.

The organization

The main variable which affects the organization of a department is size. Small departments of two or three staff obviously need little formal structure internally and externally. Since their consumption of resources is small, no very active work is needed to maintain their competitive position in relation to other departments. To survive they need either friends outside, such as the vice-chancellor or the appropriate dean, or they may rely on the seniority or academic status of their own members. At the other extreme there are some very large departments, a few with more than a hundred permanent staff. They have special characteristics and problems but their variety and uniqueness make generalizations difficult; the key variable as in all departments is the style and personality of the head. The vast majority of departments are in the middle range with between ten and thirty tenured academic staff. These are not small organizations. In an active department there will be roughly the same number in each of three other categories;

research staff, clerical and technical support staff and research students who are regarded as members of the department. Thus, a permanent academic staff of twenty may well imply a complete group of full-time workers of about eighty and a student population of several hundred, the whole occupying quite a large building and with a financial turnover equivalent to that of a medium-sized business.

In these departments the required tasks seem to change little between subjects and between universities. The responsibility for management, and indeed for almost everything else, rests with the head of the department. In his executive role, as distinct from his academic role as a teacher and research worker, he is the link between the university system and the departmental system and the role separates into two parts which take roughly equal amounts of time, one outside and one inside the department.

MANAGEMENT SKILLS OUTSIDE THE DEPARTMENT

The organization and functions of each university is based on a charter and statutes which have considerable uniformity; they are all endorsed by one national body (the Privy Council). They are currently quite democratic organizations although much depends on the particular head – usually called the Vice-chancellor or Principal.

The structure

There are invariably two parallel streams of decision-making. There is a democratically elected hierarchy of committees from the Senate to the departmental staff/student committees and there is an executive structure which centres on the relationship between academic and administrative departments. This relationship is dominated by one person, the vice-chancellor, who is the head of both academic and administrative activities.

The politics

The relationship between a vice-chancellor and the departmental heads is the same as that in any other high-level policy and executive group such as a cabinet or board of directors. On a specialist matter the views of those with the greatest expertise are accepted. On a matter of general policy the view of the vice-chancellor will prevail over that of any one head but sometimes he has to accede to the will of a group who get together with a common cause. At any one time there are many causes and many overlapping groups of related interests. Some heads of departments have a taste for elaborate intrigue, others are mainly spectators unless their departmental interests are directly affected. Whatever the level of interest in university politics a head of department cannot avoid involvement to the point where he has some understanding of what is happening and why.

Without this understanding the behaviour of individuals on committees and in personal contacts is incomprehensible; it takes a new head of department several years to obtain an adequate grasp of the maze of interactions in the total university political power game. The situation changes continuously; after a sabbatical year away, he has to relearn the position and get some insight into the main events during his absence which might have changed the balance of power or created social debits or credits which have still to be met.

The skills

When the position is described in this way it might appear that the required skills are at a very high level and are only attainable by individuals with unusual gifts. This is not so. A university is not very different from any other closely knit community; the personal interactions are analogous to those in large families or small villages. The main requirements are time and attention to gossip. This is evidenced by the fact that those who devote effort and emotions to these matters achieve no greater success than those with a minimal involvement. There are a number of reasons for this. A devious operator is quickly identified as such and others build appropriate obstacles in reaction to his efforts. For example, one experienced head of a finance department claimed that he had a personal equation for each head of an academic department which he used to modulate every request for funds. He knew that some heads stated their needs parsimoniously while others automatically asked for double what was needed on the assumption that there would be a cut; in these latter cases there invariably was a cut. In this way each side had its predictions verified and the game could continue with a stable equity. A second parameter in the equation was that some heads treated each transaction separately, while others had long memories and would bring up strings of precedents to argue new cases – again the reaction can be made adaptive to compensate for such effects. A third parameter was the overall reputation of the department for quality which includes many variables such as academic status, administrative competence, seniority and so on. Junior heads do not fare too badly, partly because the others know they are still acquiring skills and partly because there is an altruistic tendency to give the new men a good start. The level of skill is extraordinarily difficult to assess because of all the adaptive features of the system and because it is not closely related to insight and calculation. Some heads spend almost all their time analysing moves and anticipating future moves; others react intuitively to every situation as it appears. This would indicate that there is a total impact which results from a mixture of capacity or natural ability and learned ability; those who are strong on the former need less of the latter and they may indeed impede effective initiative if they try to do too much introspective analysis. There are individual differences also in the preferred level of detail; some like a very broad picture, others are unhappy unless all the minutiae are provided, usually in the form of tables of numbers. Again each approach has its advantages and limitations.

The cognitive model must take the form of an elaborate dynamic process with many related streams, some for key events, some for key individuals and some for key capacities to do with resources. For some individuals this map may be university based, with his own department seen within the total network. For others the department may habitually be the base with all other parts of the university related to it. For the analytical individual it will be a pictorial map with symbolic detail; for the intuitive individual it will be an empathic body-image extension map with pictorial and symbolic detail. Some individuals carry extensive detail in their heads, while others rely more on files. Externally supplied information, e.g. by administrators in relation to an academic issue, is invariably challenged on several grounds: that it is inaccurate (this almost always turns out to be invalid − university administrators are meticulous), that it only relates to some of the relevant factors, or that it is wrongly structured. The fact that the data are never comprehensive in relation to the issue ought to be self-evident, but academics, particularly scientists and engineers, are uncomfortable when faced with the need for decisions in situations of uncertainty. Objections about structure are revealing in terms of the differences between academics and administrators; one of the skills of the latter is in appreciating how to present data in ways which will make sense to those responsible for the decision. This is inextricably mixed up with the skill of presenting data which will orientate the users towards a particular decision, and herein lies the power of university administrators. Much of the general suspicion about data would be better directed towards whether it is comprehensive and how it is presented rather than to the data itself. It ought to be part of the responsibility of the academic chairmen of committees to direct what evidence is needed and also how it should be presented but such skills are not well developed in most chairmen.

Experienced academic committee men do seem to develop skills of timing and phasing. They know when to raise an issue, when to push it, when to delay it and when to let it go by default. They find it difficult to describe and analyse their own mental processes in arriving at these finely tuned decisions. It is largely inaccessible to introspection but it must be skilled because it does depend on continuous practice. A vice-chancellor or dean who has ten or more committees per week is much better at timing and phasing of issues than a professor of equivalent capacity who may well be an ex-dean but who now has many fewer committees. This activity is subtly demanding, as evidenced by the fact that the quality of committee activity diminishes appreciably in the second hour of a meeting and usually is approaching incompetence by the fourth hour. This can be used by experienced chairmen and members who can time their efforts when others are getting tired and by locating matters within agendas so that they will get maximum or minimum discussion as desired. All this relates specifically to the business of getting the desired decision and not to the validity of the decision. The ability to select the most appropriate decision in the face of uncertainty as justified by consequent events, perhaps over many years, is a much more stable attribute of individuals which might be called wisdom. This seems to be related to knowledge and experience but not necessarily to intellect. There are many very intelligent academics who are totally incapable of arriving at sensible decisions on policy matters. This is not a serious liability to a closely knit community; the specific ineptitude of an individual is recognized and can be compensated for.

The larger policy matters – where the university is going, what it is trying to do and how well it is succeeding – are matters about which the evidence is verbal and anecdotal rather than numerical. The spirit of the enterprise is not something which can be expressed using the techniques of accountancy or operational research. This is probably true of all organizations but it is more readily recognized in a university where market forces are less direct and where there is time and inclination to consider basic philosophical issues. The primary task of senior management is to express this spirit as coherently as possible and to relate it to the totally different facets of the organization such as budgets and student numbers. This requires a manifestation of the skilled individual met before in other contexts, that is to build bridges between logically entirely unrelated domains of descriptors. This can only be done on the foundations of human needs, aspirations and resources.

At the intellectual level – as distinct from the values level – the university system is a praiseworthy attempt to approach the ideal of the collective mind. A set of individuals has together so much more knowledge and experience than any one individual can possibly accumulate; the inhibiting factor on the expression of this joint power is in the difficulty of intercommunication. The secondary task of senior management is to facilitate this inter-communication. Unfortunately the only ways we know of doing this in organizational terms are groups, working parties and committees. The skills involved in these activities have already been described as far as is possible without going too deeply into social skills. They are needed both outside and inside the department.

MANAGEMENT SKILLS INSIDE THE DEPARTMENT

In some respects, communication within a department is easier than communication across departments within a university; academics in a department have common values because of their common objectives, interests, education and experience. However, these can be so unified and self-justified as to make it difficult for those who work mostly in the department to understand the reasons behind edicts and limitations set by the university as a whole.

Thus, there are a group of management skills to do with communicating needs and values between the department and the university; these are the skills of the delegate, the representative or the ambassador. The demands are greatest in communicating back to the group which has been represented. It is relatively easy, as a member of a group, to understand its needs and aspirations and to represent them at the higher level. During discussion at the higher level the delegate comes to understand the competing needs and aspirations of other departments and so he agrees to all manner of compromises. Then he has the serious problem of explaining to his own group why he did not get everything they all agreed was essential and why he accepted decisions and compromises not entirely in the interests of the department in isolation. To achieve this requires considerable care in developing trust and acceptable leadership on a long term basis.

Leadership is also required in achieving cohesion in the work of the department where some of the demands are short-term and obvious, e.g. the routine needs of the students met by lectures, laboratories, seminars and tutorials and the longer-term demands of research and development, which may require extensive travelling as well as laboratory work. The alternation of terms and vacations is of some help in that teaching can be given priority in term time and research in vacations but the practical situation is much less tidy than this might suggest. It is appropriate that some teaching aid preparation, apparatus design and other development is done in vacations, and field research in particular has to meet the timing requirements of the outside organization as well as the department.

Leadership rather than rules and planning is required because of the tradition of academic autonomy and freedom: control has to be by consensus rather than by edict. This requires extensive personal and group discussion as well as mutual trust and respect engendered over long time scales.

One feature of these management skills in operation is the long time scale. The academic manager is always thinking in terms of years. This is partly because his own performance can only be assessed and appreciated over such a period and partly because the system has a very high inertia. It takes about five years for a change in an undergraduate course to work through – one or two years to get it through the department and university decision-making structure and at least three years through the cycle of the course. (A change cannot be made in one year without effects in the previous and succeeding years.) Similarly a research programme takes several years to develop through its stages of concept, acquisition of funds, operational and report phases. As in many other fields, the management art is to know enough detail of each teaching or research activity to assess and communicate, and yet not to allow the detail to confuse the balanced picture of all the on-going activities.

Creative research workers and research groups are not easy to manage because all the effective individuals have some obsessional characteristics. They honestly believe that their topic of study is much more interesting and important than any other topic. Inevitably they do not take kindly to someone who has to balance their requirements and priorities against those of other research workers. There are skills here in implementing appropriate decisions without antagonizing the active individual research workers who need to feel that they are properly supported and therefore need not divert their own attention to logistic matters. The decisions themselves can be very difficult. All research work proceeds erratically; there are periods of progression interspersed with periods of dormancy. It is difficult to discriminate between work which is going through a normal dormant phase and work which has permanently run out of steam so that the research workers should be encouraged to change direction; so difficult that it would be best left to the individual concerned to make this decision, except that he may be taking up space or equipment or other resources which could be usefully redeployed. This is typically the kind of high level decision which depends on intimate knowledge of the history of the work. It requires consultations about the state of the art with other relevant specialists in other places as well as extensive discussions with those involved about what they are doing and how they feel about what they are doing. The decision then emerges, sometimes suddenly without prompting and sometimes because of the pressure of events; but in all cases it appears first as a feeling rather than a logical or convergent conclusion. The decision is subsequently reinforced by rationalization.

In addition to these systems-type skills the academic manager must also have more person-oriented skills to do with the career development of individuals. A disillusioned research director once commented that the only way to achieve a smoothly running group was to select gifted involved individuals, each with a large private income and no personal ambition. As a consequence of the rapid academic expansion over the past twenty years there has been a shortage throughout this period of competent research group directors. Those who emerged were quickly promoted to more senior posts and this has probably held back research progress in many fields where progress depends on effective team work by a small group. To describe these skills we have to resort again to descriptions such as visionary leadership combined with sensitivity to individual differences in personality and an ability to select from the heterogeneous mass of techniques and bits of evidence those which are of most consequence for the next step forward.

CONCLUSION

Academic management demands an unusual combination of intellectual sensitivity and toughness. Academics are like prima donnas; the manager has to tolerate and cope with tiresome personalities of both strength and weakness because they happen to be combined with unusual intellectual gifts. The stress is accentuated by the highly democratic ethos wherein implementing decisions is as difficult as arriving at them. So much so that, in arriving at decisions, what can be done is as important as what ideally ought to be done.

At least three different kinds of mental models are involved. Some are of a systems type to do with logistics, the matching of long-term and short-term demands to the available resources of staff, space, equipment and money. Some are of a person-oriented type to do with maintaining a dynamic model of each individual, his capacities, skills and aspirations and how self-development can be facilitated or at least not impeded for each colleague as well as for each student. Some are of a socio-political type to do with personal interactions which involve credits and debits and power balances as well as communication skills and an understanding of the formal and informal decision-making systems. The first manifestation of all these skills is the mixed feeling of unease and surprise when something is happening which is unexpected. All the activities being monitored are subject to continuous change and to random variation within limits which are comprehended rather than perceived. The greater the skill of the manager the earlier he will detect something happening which needs closer attention with a view to correction. Finally there is the elusive business of leadership which might be considered part of all the other skills but might also be considered as a separate interaction phenomenon with a strong emotional and sometimes irrational content which evokes terms such as charm and charisma. The central demand on a leader is that he must detect, define and articulate both the objectives the organization is seeking and the most appropriate means of achieving those objectives.

Obviously not all senior academics can develop all these attributes. There are also secondary skills of self-appraisal of weaknesses and strengths which affect the individual's choice of strategies. All these skills are additional to teaching and research abilities which are essential. This is not just a matter of credibility, although credibility based on respect from others is important. Many of the required decisions are to do with teaching and research assessments and it seems that such assessments cannot be made without the experience of being a practitioner in the present as well as in the past. Hence the time stress on the academic manager. He has not enough time to be a good research worker and teacher as well as being a manager, but he must be both in order to be a competent manager. Thus, there is an overall executive programme type of skill which also is essential; the prudent allocation of his own time in the context of a great variety of competing demands for it. This is rarely a static logical allocation made at a given time in relation to a given period in the future. Rather it is a process which is continuously modified by the stream of events monitored in terms of criticality and immediacy. At any one time there is a range of commitments extending for two or three years into the future; comprehension of the likely demands determines what new commitments can be accepted in which period and also the priorities of established commitments in terms of eliciting current attention. There is a queue of demands for attention, each tagged with priorities in several dimensions. Some of the priorities are from external events and some arise from the individual's duties, interests, moods and aspirations. To use an analogy, this self-control skill is like that of a Chinese juggler spinning a row of plates on bamboo sticks. It might be measured in terms of the number of plates (commitments) which can be kept in the air, except that each has its own variable time constant in terms of how long it can be left alone before it collapses. New ones are always being presented; some are ignored and some are picked up and manipulated at the expense of old ones which are being accidentally dropped or deliberately thrown away or passed to others or completed and tidied away. This self-management is sometimes consciously exercised and the total situation is reappraised, and sometimes it is unconscious and feelings arise about things going awry which cannot be traced to specific information inputs but which nevertheless trigger switches of attention.

In summary the academic in common with many other kinds of manager has technical skills connected with teaching and research, social skills including political skills, and planning skills which include self-appraisal and self-management.

References

Branton, P. (1979). The research scientist. In W. T. Singleton (ed.) *The Study of Real Skills II.* (Lancaster: MTP Press)

Hedge, A. and Lawson, B. R. (1979). Creative Thinking. In W. T. Singleton (ed.) *The Study of Real Skills II.* (Lancaster: MTP Press)

Lawson, B. R. (1978). The architect as a designer. In W. T. Singleton (ed.) *The Study of Real Skills I.* (Lancaster: MTP Press)

Miller, R. B. (1978). The Information system designer. In W. T. Singleton (ed.) *The Study of Real Skills I.* (Lancaster: MTP Press)

Newman, J. H. (1873). *Idea of a University Defined.* Reprinted: 1960 (New York: Holt, Rinehart & Winston)

Trotter, W. (1916). *Instincts of the Herd in Peace and War.* (London: Fisher Unwin)

5 The National Health Service

B. L. RICHARDSON

INTRODUCTION

The NHS is the largest organization in the country with a staff of nearly 1 000 000 people. It consumes nearly six percent of the gross domestic product. The relationship with Government, which provides virtually all the finance required, is different in England, Scotland, Wales and Northern Ireland and the structures in each of these parts of the United Kingdom are, as a result, also somewhat different. In England, the NHS is divided into fourteen Regions comprising something in excess of one hundred Areas, many of which are further divided into Districts. Regions and Areas are statutory bodies, each with a controlling body of members, whilst Districts are subordinate. Ultimately the various Secretaries of State remain responsible to Parliament for the operation of the National Health Service, although the Officers and Members of each Area Authority are empowered to lay down local policies within nationally or regionally agreed guidelines. The cost of running the Health Service is currently in the region of £7500 million per annum. There are over 5000 hospitals in the United Kingdom.

Management arrangements are well documented as a result of various changes in legislation and the comments of working parties, committees, Royal Commissions etc. It is a well researched organization: there are centres throughout the country whose livelihood is based upon examining the entrails of the NHS. Following its setting up in 1948, there remained three separate and distinct arms through which health care was delivered to the population. These were: (a) the hospitals – formerly supported by local authorities and by voluntary aid; (b) the community health services – formerly these were administered by the local authorities and had responsibility for providing care in the home or to children of school age in clinics related to the education service; and (c) the general practitioners – medical, dental and optical together with the chemists contracted to dispense drugs etc. for the NHS.

Following the reorganization of 1974, the three arms of the Service were brought together under what was intended to be common management. The local authority community services and the hospital service were merged, and management units were set up which shared common boundaries with the local authorities which had themselves been reorganized earlier in the '70's. Where the local authority was too large to facilitate control of health services as one unit, the Areas were divided into Districts with clearly defined geographical boundaries. Family Practitioner Committees were set up in each Area to administer arrangements for general practitioners in the service. Actually the arrangements were not as tidy as this brief summary would indicate and in many cases hospitals, geographically within the Area of one authority, have remained under the management of another because traditionally they have been managed jointly with another Unit.

The avowed objective of this reorganization was to produce for each Health District a reasonable degree of self-sufficiency so that the population living within its boundaries could look to a District General Hospital for the complete normal range of treatment; the community services were to be managed by the same body which managed the hospitals and were designed to provide preventive care and to continue to look after the patient after discharge from hospital; and general practitioners were expected to relate most closely to the Area in which their Committee was set up. In this manner the care provided would become more comprehensive and at the same time more economical.

This chapter deals mainly with the hospital services and its complex management relationships with the community service. The general practitioners operate as independent contractors.

There is one fundamental concept, perhaps peculiar to the NHS, which needs to be grasped before discussion of managerial skills can be entered upon – this is that management is based upon consensus. To put it more graphically, each management group meets as a Security Council and not a General Assembly. The importance of consensus in so complex an organization is clear and by now generally accepted; it cannot however provide an excuse for individual managers to abrogate their responsibility to colleagues and each must remain personally responsible for his own actions or those of his subordinates. Conversely each is individually accountable to his superiors. The other side of the coin is that any manager can have his aspirations frustrated by lack of agreement with one or more of his colleagues.

Further constraints upon the NHS manager arise from its accountable status within the public sector. Money once voted to the Secretary of State is divided, on his/her authority, down through the various levels of statutory body and ultimately to the District. It is finally allocated to individual managers as budget holders. This money should be spent in the year of receipt on the purpose for which it was voted. There is no profit motive within the Service and some would allege therefore no incentive to save costs and reduce expenditure. Managers are said to be influenced by a suspicion that an underspending will be perpetuated into next year's allocations. That this is far from the truth does not prevent the myth itself being perpetuated. Managers have a duty both to themselves and to the patients whom they ultimately serve to ensure that they consume all the necessary resources which are within their disposal. From this proposition stems the need for consensus – for it is no good doctors deciding that there is spare capacity and that they will therefore treat or diagnose additional patients if, to use the simplest link, the nurses are then unable to staff either the beds or the clinic sessions which would be required. Further, if the catering manager cannot afford to feed the additional patients and the laundry cannot deal with the additional linen, the whole delicate balance will be disturbed and money wasted. The need therefore is to manage in the context of an overall provision of service (which may on occasion involve decisions of a life-or-death nature) in concert with colleagues.

KINDS AND LEVELS OF MANAGEMENT

Most managers will start their careers at a level very close to that at which patients are seen and treated and such is the nature of the organization that as they become more senior they will become more remote from the patient. Whether this is either necessary or desirable is another matter but within this present system attitudes inevitably change as the individual manager progresses. Initially his demands are for more resources to enable the same job to be done better for a greater number of patients. When eventually he reaches the more senior echelons of management he will be seeking to change the use of buildings and the role of many staff who are subordinate to him in order to provide for a different type of patient or for the same patients in a different way. There is a natural conflict between those whose job is to deal with the immediate problems of the day and those whose role is to provide for a better future.

The largest single group of staff is the nurses and within their profession there is a well structured and discernable management hierarchy. The skills of management start to be employed whenever a nurse is left in charge of a ward even though at that stage she may not have aspired to the lowest grade of management recognized by normal tests – that of Ward Sister. The structure set up following the report of the Salmon Committee defines the lowest tier of management as being Nursing Officer, which is the grade immediately above that of Ward Sister. This does not invalidate the contention set out in the previous sentence unless management is very narrowly defined. That management skills may be subordinated to practical matters does not discount their existence. It is customary for the nursing function to be split into divisions relating to particular types of nursing. Examples would be Midwifery Division comprising all those units or wards concerned with Obstetrics and Gynaecology, Mental Illness Division dealing with Psychiatric Hospitals, Units or Clinics, and General Division dealing with all the general medical and surgical beds, clinics, etc. within the District. Each of these divisions would comprise the nursing staffs both within the hospitals and in the community and would be headed by a Divisional Nursing Officer. Next in line would be an appropriate number of Senior Nursing Officers according to the style of management of the Division. For example, in a Mental Illness Division, the Senior Nursing Officers might have responsibility separately for days and nights, whereas in a General or Midwifery Division the Senior Nursing Officers might be responsible for Hospital Services and Community Services, respectively. These arrangements are locally made according to the circumstances of the particular District. Below each Senior Nursing Officer will be an appropriate number of Nursing Officers, who are given responsibility for groups of activities and the staff working in them: it is difficult to specify particular examples since the circumstances of each District will be very different. In parallel with the Senior Nursing Officers and Nursing Officers respectively will be the Nurse Teaching Staffs – Senior Tutors and Tutors – who have responsibility for the academic and practical content of nurses' training. Immediately above the Divisional Nursing Officers will be the District Nursing Officer (except in a single-district Area) and above her the Area Nursing Officer. The responsibilities of these persons are total for the District or Area to which they are appointed since the structure is fully hierarchical. Assisting the Area Nursing Officer are a number of Area Nurses, who have no line management responsibilities but perform as specialist advisors in particular aspects of nursing. It is often the practice for administrators to employ a similar divisional structure and this can, of itself, facilitate consensus. The nursing profession, whose training is extremely practical, complain that as they obtain more senior posts, they have geometrically less contact with patients. They spend a lot of time in 'administration' when they should be 'managing'; that is, anticipating problems of the future rather than coping with the problems of the present. It is arguable that this situation has arisen because of the uncertainties which have surrounded the Health Service since 1974. The resources available for deployment have been constrained by a considerable shortage of funds; it is also extremely difficult to recruit the appropriate calibre of staff.

The real consumers of resources are the doctors working either within or for the NHS. It is however arguable that they are not managers of the Health Service, although the General Practitioner does in fact manage his own business either alone or in a small partnership. There is a particular concept very dear to doctors which will be familiar to those working in education. In

Universities it is called 'academic freedom', in Hospitals 'clinical freedom'. These concepts are not just about a set of values; they also contain the implication that no one outside the profession concerned can be allowed to question these values. For example, the doctors consider that their prime objective is the best available care or cure for the patient who presents himself and they find it difficult to accept the constraint of shortage of resources.

There is, however, a growing awareness amongst doctors that resources cannot grow forever in parallel with the continuing advances of technology. There has often been a scarcity of resources and patients have frequently had to wait for treatment. Sometimes they have died before they could be treated but rarely has it been necessary to *decide* not to treat potentially fatal disease because of scarcity of resources. Indeed, it can be argued that some, occasionally very costly, treatment has been provided without discernible effect upon the original prognosis. With an increase in potential for cure or alleviation but without the corresponding increase in the overall availability of resources it is becoming apparent that choices will have to be made. The clinicians are becoming aware that, if they are to influence the rationing process, they must take part in it and accept, since each doctor cannot separately be heard, a representative role in management on behalf of their professional colleagues. This was the intention of the management arrangements proposed for the reorganized NHS in 1974. Medical representation on Area and District management teams and consultation with medical professional interests through their various representative bodies facilitated the medical influence on management. The weakness has been that it is extremely difficult to obtain within the medical profession a common view of the most advantageous form of action which could be undertaken in any particular set of circumstances; in addition many doctors have felt themselves unable to accept or work within decisions arrived at on a representative basis.

MEDICAL AND MANAGEMENT INTERACTIONS

The services which are directly related to caring for patients are divided into three major groups; the Direct Treatment, the Diagnostic and the Therapeutic.

There are clear management interactions within the Direct Treatment services, in that, for instance, the number of beds which can be staffed by nurses will dictate the number of patients who can be treated, whilst the availability of theatre sessions will also be a critical factor in the number of surgical cases dealt with. Unless there is a fairly good match between the medical and surgical throughput, capabilities of doctors and the number of patients who can be looked after by the nurses there will be waste of resources. But equally managers of the Pharmaceutical Service can be placed under very considerable pressure if there is a change in the type of patient or treatment offered or should the efforts of the doctors and nurses succeed in increasing the number of patients treated without increasing the beds available by, for instance, reducing the length of each patient's stay. Indeed the very fact of reducing the length of a patient's stay may mean that the drug regime has to be more intensive than would be the case if a longer stay could be accommodated. In the diagnostic and therapeutic professions there are several grades recognized as managerial and responsible for matching the demand created on behalf of patients by the medical staff with the resources at their disposal.

The diagnostic departments are generally headed by a specialist member of the medical staff, for instance, a radiologist, pathologist etc., though the scientific staff of these departments will almost certainly accept and be expected to accept responsibility for the day to day management of the demands which are placed upon them. It is however these medical heads of departments who should ultimately negotiate with their professional colleagues if the burdens placed upon their departments become excessive and shortage of funds or skilled manpower prevents expansion of the service.

The therapeutic departments – radiotherapy, physiotherapy, occupational therapy, to mention but three – all receive their patients on the referral of a doctor and do not themselves dictate or control workloads for which nevertheless they are expected to accept responsibility. It is for the professional head of the department, as manager, to advise the referring medical officers at any time when demand is seen materially to exceed supply. A typical pattern might be that a patient will be referred, by a general practitioner, to an orthopaedic surgeon, who will need to see an X-ray as a diagnostic aid before deciding that there is no bone damage and that the appropriate treatment should take place in the physiotherapy department to relieve the symptoms or eradicate the cause of the complaint – the complex relationships are apparent in this simple example. If admission to hospital were to be required the complications increase many times over.

The remainder of the services are grouped into those facilities within a hospital which would be provided in a hotel; those which look after the equipment and the buildings and other physical resources (conveniently grouped under the general heading of 'Administration'). There is little doubt that those activities which would be appropriate to hotels would be sufficient to tax management of such an organization; that the organization has also to cope with the movement, admission and discharge of patients who come to be treated is an added complexity in its own right, since the patient cannot be the source of such information, as is a hotel guest. It must be remembered that hospitals are open 24 hours a day, 7 days a week, 52 weeks of the year and that many of the devices open to industry and commerce, which commonly work less than half the day, five days only in a week and equally commonly close down completely for the main holiday periods are not available to hospital managers. Thus, essential maintenance must result in the closure, either wholly or partly, of certain sorely pressed facilities within the hospital. This is never done easily and even though managers will press for engineering or building repairs and maintenance to be carried out they are equally reluctant to permit their departments to be closed down for the week or fortnight, which would normally be required to enable this to be done. As a result it is frequently necessary to employ large volumes of contract labour and to work round the clock, so minimizing the disruption in the hospital. This is, of course, very expensive.

The activities of three of the hotel service departments do have a particular impact upon patient care: these are the catering, domestic and portering services. To a lesser extent the laundry and linen service must also be considered. The porters not only have to move everyday items around the hospital but are also involved in the delivery of food and the movement of non-ambulant patients. There must therefore be very close liaison between the patient-care managers and those who organize the portering service. Many members of the domestic staff are involved both directly and indirectly at ward level with patients and there is therefore a clear need to coordinate their activities with those of the direct treatment services. Whilst patients are in hospital they need to be fed, sometimes with special diets which are dictated by their medical condition. The problems of providing three meals a day for patients, 365 days a year are complex enough but the necessity to provide special diets at short notice again requires a deal of interaction between those caring for the patient and those responsible for feeding him. It must not be forgotten that many staff in a hospital are resident or at least partly resident and also need to be fed at appointed times of the day and night. Sometimes the hospital's efforts are not successful, and amongst the staff and needing to fulfil a role which might well be seen to include an element of management are the Chaplains who comfort the sick and bereaved. In each of these groupings there are managers whose skills are deployed, at most levels, on a day-to-day basis but who need to become more innovative as greater seniority is attained.

The process of euphemism is one of the features of the special language of the NHS. For example politicians and those working in the service often talk about 'reducing Waiting Lists'. The real objective is to treat more patients but there is a reluctance to express it in these blunt terms. The use of euphemism may be seen also in one of the major statistics of hospital activity – 'deaths and discharges' – without any distinction being made between the two. The greatest danger of the continual use of euphemism (even the title of the NHS really disguises its dominant current role as a service for the treatment of illness as opposed to one for the positive creation of good health) is that management is conditioned always to be defensive. To investigate this further and to hypothesize on how it affects management attitudes one needs to accept that there are certain peculiar human characteristics amongst which is the belief that illness, in common with all other misfortunes, is likely to occur anywhere except to the person who is contemplating it at the moment.

This is the cause of the paucity of funds for the NHS; it is the cause of much self-induced health abuse and it creates an attitude amongst the public where, if illness is cured through the activities of any branch of the Service, that is no more than was to be expected but should it result in permanent injury or death, they have been let down. Staff attitudes have created defence mechanisms against this heads-you-win-tails-I-lose situation: these tend to be negative. The NHS was created by Aneurin Bevan on the hypothesis that an improvement and short-term investment in health would pay dividends to such an extent that within a decade it would be possible to close most of the hospitals in the country.

From the foregoing it will be observed that the skills of management in the NHS are those very largely of negotiation, conciliation and persuasion. In particular it is difficult to reconcile the policies of administrators arrived at within the constraints of regulations and resources with those of medical staff whose views are dominated by immediate issues of care of patients. This might seem to be a recipe for stagnation. However, there has been greater change in the NHS over the last 25 years than in any other organization of like size. There is a very strong emphasis in the reorganized service upon planning. There is no doubt that in many plans the emphasis upon 'the best' has been at the expense of 'the good' but steps are being taken to simplify the approach with this in mind. At the higher levels of NHS management where District Management Teams work together there is no doubt that the need to carry conviction with one's colleagues has produced plans and decisions that are better worked through than if they had had to be imposed in the traditional hierarchical mode. The greatest management failing in this situation is to seek to go it alone and there is little doubt that those administrators who had experience of the previous Health Service structure under Hospital Management Committees did find working in the consensus mode extremely difficult. The result was almost invariably that effective progress ceased since decisions made outside the consensus were unenforceable.

It has been a practice in the more enlighted Areas to seek to reproduce the multidisciplinary consensus management which exists at District or Area level within the operational units, both the hospitals and the community services. It has not always proved as easy to achieve this at the operational level as it has at the planning level; one reason for this is that the medical profession has sought to achieve parity of voting power in a situation where the vote as such is rarely resorted to and, as mentioned in the introduction, the right of veto lies with any individual member of the team. The problem with having more than one medical representative is, of course, the disparity of view which is brought forward, which means that, far from seeking to obtain consensus between the disciplines, it is necessary first of all to obtain consensus within one major discipline. It is perhaps amongst this group that the greatest demonstration of lack of skill in consensus-forming is found. It is frequently characterized by implying that if any view other than the doctors' is upheld their patients will suffer. In its extreme form this approach, known as 'shroud waving', can be used in an unfair and unprincipled way to enforce a point of view. As a last resort the mass media can be brought in since they can always be relied upon to dramatize such a conflict.

MANAGEMENT TASKS

To appreciate the essential tasks of management it is necessary to understand the background against which all levels of management have to work. This is essentially one where resources are constrained: there are limits to the amount of finance which government is willing to put into the service, even though it has grown in real terms. The more which can be done and the more which is seen to be done, the more the public will, quite rightly, demand of the service. There is an observed phenomenon in the behaviour of 'Waiting Lists' following an increase in resources which illustrate this. There will, on occasion, come a point at which it is possible by putting in more resources to start to make inroads on a List, which may well have stood at a high level for some years. This high level is often fairly consistent and is not the result of conscious manipulation. Within a few months of the introduction of the increased facility the List will drop quite dramatically to less than half of its previous level and may on occasion be eliminated altogether. However, within twelve to eighteen months Lists are just as large as they ever were. This arises because many people who had not been aware that the condition from which they suffered was treatable had never come forward for treatment. The general practitioners, knowing that the length of the List implied a waiting time of years before treatment could be commenced, in many cases did not bother to refer patients to the consultant and finally consultants, when they saw patients, would often decide that there was no point in adding them to a List when they were not likely to be treated in the foreseeable future. Once each of these constraints is removed and the unconscious rationing which has taken place is no longer required a greater measure of need as opposed to demand will emerge. On a crude analysis it will be seen that the effort and resources put into reducing Lists has had no effect; what needs to be observed is that whereas before only so many patients were being treated in a year there is now a proportional increase related to the increase in resources.

It is clear that the requirements from management are a high ability to communicate and motivate staff inside and outside the discipline of the manager and an ability to negotiate on an informed basis with all those who are concerned with the care of patients, directly or indirectly. It is furthermore important for managers to realize that the solution to one problem may very well create the next and conversely that striving to achieve the very best may well prevent an interim solution being adopted which would not only be perfectly acceptable in its own right but would not preclude the optimum solution being achieved in due course.

For many years the Service has responded to demand which has emerged from the population. This has arisen in the majority of cases by the self-referral of patients to their general practitioners and their subsequent transfer to the care of either the primary (that is the community) or secondary (that is the hospital) services of the NHS. One of the objectives of reorganization was to provide in each District sufficient staff to enable the future provision of the services to the population of the District to be planned on a more precise statistical basis and to relate reasonably accurately to the measured means which were likely to emerge. This has involved the study of morbidity; the incidence of illness amongst various types of the population generally divided into the very simple matrix of age and sex. The developing demographic pattern of the population is best considered in terms of age and sex because the requirements of the very young and the very old which represent major but not dominant numerical proportions of the population are so much greater than those of normal working age (i.e. between 16 and 65). An increase in the number of school and pre-school children or retired persons in a population over a period can require the construction of major additional facilities. This same demographic analysis can of course produce what should be reasonably accurate predictions of the number of maternity cases likely to come forward related to the number of women in the child-bearing age groups. The use of demographic studies is probably limited to small populations, that is those below a quarter of a million, and may well lead to incorrect conclusions if within that population there is a high degree of mobility as is found for instance in the prosperous outer suburbs of the major cities. There is little doubt that these studies form useful guides to the most senior levels of management when plans are being prepared for developments which will reach fruition probably as much as 10 years after the decision as to what is required has been made. It is unfortunate that they generate a large degree of suspicion, not to mention frustration, amongst those who are coping with the day-to-day problems when they are confronted perpetually with a 'jam tomorrow' prospect.

Despite the effort put into studying demographic patterns there are often unpredicted variations in observed trends. For example, there was a steady and apparently continuing long-term decline in the birth rate observable through the 1970's but there has recently been, throughout the country, nearly a 25% increase in deliveries at a time when the last publicly declared guidelines, from the Department of Health, asked for a continuing, year-on-year, 2% reduction in expenditure on Maternity Services. Clearly it is not possible to plan to fine limits when dealing with as unpredictable a product as people.

Not all managers perceive problems in the same way and there is often a surprising lack of awareness of the reaction on other functions for an action taken by one. There has been a considerable and very successful effort made over the past few years to reduce the length of a patient's stay in hospital. This enables more patients to be treated in the same number of beds. It has been achieved by dealing with many of the diagnostic processes on an outpatient basis and admitting the patient very shortly before the surgical procedure required. Equally, with improved techniques and drugs it is possible to guard against the risks of post-operative infection and cross-infection to a high degree and to discharge patients at a date which would have seemed inconceivable a generation ago. However, this has meant that many patients being nursed on ordinary wards are in fact fairly ill almost up to the date of discharge and place a greater burden upon the nursing staff than used to be the case. In these circumstances the nurses have rightly demanded that as many as possible of the non-nursing duties they undertake in the way of domestic and clerical chores should be taken off them and made the responsibility of other staff. This has led to the creation of what is called a 'ward team'. However, this creates problems of communication within the ward between the patient, the doctor, the nurse, the domestic and the ward clerk and the results have not always been wholly beneficial. It is also demonstrable that the intensity of the nursing care required in these circumstances is found to be very onerous and may well contribute to a higher incidence of nurses' absence through sickness.

MANAGEMENT SKILLS

It is possible to divide the long and varied management hierarchy of NHS personnel into three levels: the patient contact manager, the middle manager and the senior manager.

The patient contact manager

The popular image of a hospital with ambulances dashing up to the door, sirens howling and lights flashing is an exaggeration but in the management context it is not that far from the truth. It is in coping with these situations that the leaders in managers first emerge from the various staff groupings. Many emergencies occur every day in the running of a hospital and matters which might be regarded as irritants in a commercial setting become emergencies when they have an effect on the health and welfare of patients in the hospital, who, by definition, are already sick. The NHS generally recruits its managers at all levels from within its own ranks and takes responsibility for training. During the formative years most of its managers will have learnt their practical management techniques in coping with emergencies. All those who philosophize on this subject deplore what they call 'crisis management' but if managers were unable to respond adequately and on many occasions superbly to crises of all the varying magnitudes as they arise, the public outcry would be loud and long. Managers at the sharp end will always complain that those higher up the hierarchy do not understand the day-to-day problems and pressures from which they suffer. It is possible to argue that the reverse is the case and that many more senior managers are, from their own early experiences, over-responsive to crises and unable to see that there is in the regularly recurring crisis situation a type of stability which can in fact be planned for and managed reasonably effectively. After all the Accident and Emergency Services are set up on this very premise.

The essence of patient contact management is to cope with the daily flow of events, to anticipate (when this is possible) but also to accept that there will be many unpredicted emergencies.

The middle manager

This group is the most difficult to define – they are those who have responsibilities which either encompass a whole unit, where it is such a large entity that individual departments have their own managers at a lower level in contact with the patient, or it may cover more than one unit. If the group itself is fairly fluid it is true to say that the responsibilities are even more so: many middle managers will, on occasion, have to pick up crises whose dimensions exceed the capabilities of the patient contact manager directly involved. They may also have to advise, assist and eliminate from the spectrum of available choices many potential options before the senior manager is able to concentrate upon his or her task. Almost all middle managers will have emerged from the ranks of the patient contact managers though some of them will have done their stint at the lower level following a period of fairly intensive training in one of the training schemes which the NHS has set up to develop its own managers of the future. Both groups will in the process leave behind many of their contemporaries who will continue to operate throughout their careers at the lower levels of management. Some of the middle managers will develop in such a way that they will aspire to and achieve senior management positions but others will remain essentially patient contact managers with broader ranges of responsibility either in terms of numbers of staff managed or number of units managed.

The task of the middle manager towards which he or she has to develop skills is concerned with matching the demands and aspirations of individual patient contact managers (who are themselves impelled onwards either by patient demand or professional aspiration) with the overall capacity of the system to cope with the required work flows. Historically the most difficult patient contact manager to deal with has been the doctor but increasingly the paramedical professions are seeking greater status within the NHS hierarchies and expecting to be heard by the middle managers: it is thus possible to find therapeutic and diagnostic departments at least as large as a ward and certainly with as many staff as one would find in that situation; and whilst it is possible and indeed customary to group wards very simply according to the main stream of their activity, e.g. the surgical wards, the medical wards, etc. it isn't really possible to join together the therapeutic or diagnostic departments. Their individual characteristics are widely variable and they have separate managers responsible for the many streams of their day-to-day operation.

In general, middle managers are located on the site on which most of the patients are treated whereas the senior managers and their subordinate staffs may be located more remotely. This very physical separation tends to divide the middle management from senior management more positively than their separation from the patient-contact level. Middle managers, by using a combination of data to do with available financial resources, manpower resources and equipment and materials, should be able to devise solutions and ways forward in patient care which are not within the abilities of the patient-contact managers. The minutiae of the sometimes subtle distinctions between the various types of patient and the various treatments which can be afforded to them are correctly dealt with at this level which is not so far detached from the real situation as to prevent the middle manager from applying practical knowledge acquired at a fairly recent date to a set of data accumulated probably across his desk rather than by personal inspection or knowledge. Thus, when reaching middle management he becomes adept at integrating evidence, some acquired in the abstract format and some acquired in more practical terms at an earlier stage in his career.

The senior manager

In common with his counterparts in other facets of the public sector and in commerce and industry the senior manager is called upon to exercise corporate planning skills: in particular he seeks to match in the medium to long term the demands which will be made for health care with the resources he expects to have available so as to create the maximum in the way of facilities for the population he serves. This role is frequently carried out in the consensus mode, that is, true corporate planning. This requires some considerable insight into, and ability to interpret, trends in the population, the economy and social expectations of the population, some understanding of epidemiology and the morbidity factors which are likely to influence demand for health care in the future, coupled with some means of estimating the impact of technology upon the medical scene. Each senior manager will have a particular expertise which he is expected to bring to bear on the decision-making process. However, the final decision must find support from senior managers in all disciplines: failing this, those who have to implement the decisions will not find the leadership they seek. There are so many imponderables that it becomes impossible to lay them out in a precise equation and the skill of the senior manager becomes that of making progress on as many fronts as possible without committing too much in the way of resources, particularly of capital, to established current needs to the detriment of the requirement a decade or two ahead.

Inevitably many of the decisions to which the senior manager is party will, with hindsight, prove to have been wrong. It is, on the other hand, an established fact that the existence of a facility for health care will very rarely fail to produce sufficient patients willing to come forward and make use of it. It is therefore possible to claim, with some justification, that there is no black and white, right or wrong decision but that all lie within the penumbra in varying shades of grey. It is possible to regard many of the senior management failings since the inception of the NHS in 1948 as stemming from seeking the best solution to the manifestly complex problems as if it were the only one. In many cases the problems which have been solved were those of ten or fifteen years ago and the amount of physical alteration which is required to premises and accommodation only recently built is a manifestation of this unhappy situation. There is emerging a school of thought amongst senior managers which takes as its motto 'the best is the enemy of the good' and from this flows a philosophy that it is better to do something and do it quickly, even if one is reasonably confident that the solution will not be perfect, than to wait and seek additional information and guidance in the hope that this will improve the quality of the decision. If there is one thing that is certain in the last quarter of the twentieth century and has really been certain in the last half of that century it is that technological change, exemplified by the development of new drugs and new surgical techniques, coupled with social change in the expectations of the population, will rènder any buildings or policy plans for their operation outmoded before they can be implemented.

CONCLUSION

Hospitals were traditionally run by the Matron with assistance from the Hospital Secretary and perhaps a Medical Superintendent. This is satisfactory where the intention is to maintain the status quo. Many attempts were made between 1948, when the NHS was first set up, and 1974, when it was reorganized, to produce a management climate in which there was scope for innovation and change. As a result it became easier to alter the pattern to the needs of the public as they varied over the years. The virtual elimination of the scourge of tuberculosis, and more enlightened attitudes, assisted by the availability of modern drugs, in the management of both mental illness and mental handicap hospitals are illustrations of the more obvious changes which have taken place during this period. Before 1974 it was the practice to run the hospitals through bodies known as Hospital Management Committees where the larger institutions, of around eight hundred to a thousand beds, would have their own committee and small hospitals would be grouped together to produce a total complement of something of this order. This did encourage a tendency towards parochialism.

There was recognition in the 1960's of the need to modernize the hospital stock of the country, which largely predated the 1914–18 War, and the opportunity was taken to construct what are now referred to as District General Hospitals on a number of sites throughout the country. Most of these sites were already owned by the NHS and were not necessarily ideally situated in relation to the population they were designed to serve.

The reorganization of 1974 set out with high aims but these were not implemented before the energy crisis and inflationary trends made funds extremely short. The laudible intention was to recognize that the Local Government Units set up under the reorganization of the '70's were to provide services complementary to the NHS and that it would be sensible therefore that the management authority should also match. This would result in each Local Government Unit having an appropriate degree of self-sufficiency in health care. In broad terms this would mean that a member of the public would only have to cross his local government boundary to obtain some specialized type of service which it would be uneconomic to provide in every single hospital of District calibre throughout the country.

This desirable aspiration which resulted in a great deal of planning and management effort in seeking its achievement, is unlikely to be fulfilled before the end of the century and the constraints on public expenditure, when combined with the demographic changes and increased public expectation, have produced the current pressures. In comparing the situation today with that which existed prior to reorganization it is fair to say that there is a much greater emphasis upon planning to meet the needs of the population which each Area has to serve and that there is a greater realization on the part of managers in the NHS of the extent to which we fail to meet even our own aspirations. Hanging over the Service is the possibility of restructuring in 1981/2, the prime objective of which appears to be to place more management responsibility on those who are involved in running the hospitals. However, it is clear that the simplistic view being expressed in some quarters that a return to the situation which existed prior to 1974 would produce a better and more economically run and more responsive service is no longer tenable. It seems likely that the predicted turn-round in the economy in the middle of the decade will at last enable the Health Service to build 'up to specification' rather than 'down to price', to staff to the level which is desirable rather than that which is marginally safe and to cope with the massive increase in the numbers of elderly in the population who generate a very large proportion of the work load. It also seems likely that a great deal of the routine of administration (as opposed to management) which consumes such a large proportion of skilled professional time at the moment will be reduced by the arrival of cheap and easily accessible computing facilities. Certainly many conditions which at the present moment are not subject to amelioration will, within the decade, be treatable. Medical technology advances continually but, in the end, we are treating people not patients or cases and they are being treated by people and not by machines: it is the interaction of the various levels of management in the different skills and disciplines which is instrumental in producing a successful outcome.

6
The Social Services

S. CUMELLA

SOCIAL SERVICES DEPARTMENTS

In most industrialized societies, the last two decades have seen a major growth in personal social services provided to citizens by the state. In England, over a quarter of a million people now work for local authority social services: about the same number work for the National Coal Board. Local authority social services in England accommodate, feed, and have legal care over considerable numbers of people. For instance, over 139 000 old and handicapped people live in local authority homes; 41 million meals are provided each year by meals-on-wheels services or in local daycentres; and local authorities have 96 000 children in care (DHSS, 1978a). Local authority social services are remarkable not just for their size, but also for the variety of their provision for different groups in the community. For the elderly and handicapped, they may provide not only homes and meals, but also home helps, adaptations to homes, a wide range of aids for daily living, daycentres and social clubs, holidays, telephones, and television licenses. For the mentally and physically handicapped, local authority social services may provide workplaces and training centres. For children, there may be nurseries, playgroups, community homes (including former approved schools), remand centres, foster-parents, adoption services, and child-minders. Local authority social services may also give cash grants or loans to parents as a means of preventing children coming into care. Apart from all these services, local authorities provide a network of advice centres open to all members of the public, but dealing particularly with people experiencing emotional stress or material shortages. In all, local authority social services spent some £1192 million in 1976/7, making this the second most costly item in county and metropolitan borough budgets.

This array of resources, services, and expenditure is provided in England by 108 separate social services departments. The average department has about 2,500 employees. Departments of this size, combining such a wide range of functions are a comparatively recent phenomenon, dating from two administrative reforms in the 1970's. The first of these was the merging in 1971 of the former local authority children's and welfare departments, as well as some of the services provided by the former public health department. The resulting social services departments were greatly reduced in number three years later as part of the reorganization of local government. For many workers in the social services, these changes probably had only a limited impact on their day-to-day activities. But major changes in the organization of work did take place in two respects. These were the creation of a new role and profession of 'social worker', and the elaboration of social services management. We shall look at these in turn.

In the new social services departments, 'social worker' was initially a common noun for the three separate occupations of child care officer, welfare officer and mental welfare officer. What these roles had in common was the enforcement and monitoring of laws for the protection of vulnerable members of the community (e.g. children at risk, the mentally ill), and the power to assess the need for and to refer individual clients to a wide range of welfare services (e.g. admission to old people's homes, assessment of people as adoptive parents). These three occupations were similar also in that they were usually based in offices and advice centres rather than in residences or day-care centres. As soon as the new social services departments were in operation, it became standard practice to merge the roles and working conditions of child care officers, welfare officers and mental welfare officers, so that each social worker became responsible for covering the work of what previously had been three quite separate occupations. This process to 'generic' social work was confirmed by common training as social workers after 1971. The great majority of people currently employed as social workers are either trained or experienced only in generic social work.

Although forming less than 10% of social services employees, social workers have been of quite disproportionate importance in the departments. This is because of features of their role, the manner of their recruitment, and their prospects for promotion. When members of the public come to social services departments for help, the first procedure is usually an interview with a social worker. In the process of this interview, the social worker defines the needs and problems of the client in terms of practicable services (Rees, 1978). These services may involve further interviews with the social worker, or they may be merely a redirection of the client to a more appropriate agency. In many cases, however, the social worker will refer the client to other services provided by other groups of staff in the department. This makes the social worker the gatekeeper between the clientele and the various services provided by the department. Even when clients are referred to other groups of staff in the department, it is often the practice for a social worker to retain an overall responsibility for the client. In other words, social workers are seen as dealing with the full range of needs and problems presented to the department by the individual clients, whereas such staff as home helps or care officers in children's homes are seen as either providing specific and limited services, or as having responsibility for the client for a limited period within plans for the client defined by the social worker. Because social workers often have *de facto* a monopoly of information about their clientele, they possess rather more legitimacy than others (including departmental management) in determining what needs to be done for individual clients. Indeed, social workers may come to interpret their role as being that of broker between the clientele and the rest of the department.

Social workers' articulacy in defending their role has been accentuated by their manner of recruitment. The great majority of social workers are graduates, and the majority now have had postgraduate training in social work. Given the wide span of work carried out by social services departments, many social workers may be attracted to the work by general social aims rather than a desire to help a particular group of clients. Social workers therefore form a block of professionally qualified or experienced graduates in departments where the majority of employees are low-paid manual workers. It is not surprising to find that management in social services departments tend to be drawn more from social work staff than from residential or daycare staff. This trend has also been promoted by the insistence of central government that social services management requires professional qualification in social work.

The second major change in the organization of social services that resulted from the creation of the large unified departments was the elaboration of management structures and personnel (Jordan, 1974). Departments follow a traditional pyramidial hierarchy, with the Director of Social Services at the apex. The Director reports on the operation of the Department to a Social Services Committee of local councillors. Below the Director, management is specialized according to geographical subdivisions and/or type of 'service'. 'Service' here means kind of workplace rather than type of client. Thus children's homes and old people's homes are usually grouped under an Assistant Director for Residential Services. The department's local offices and advice centres (and hence the great majority of its social workers) are termed 'fieldwork services' and are usually grouped under a further assistant director. Figure 6.1 shows a typical pattern of departmental organization. This kind of organization typically presents problems to senior management in both planning and monitoring the delivery of services. In the first place, large centralized organizations tend to depend for information about their performance on relatively standardized measures of the activities of their operational units. Yet there is a marked lack of aggregate data in the social services by which current performance and future need for services can be estimated. In

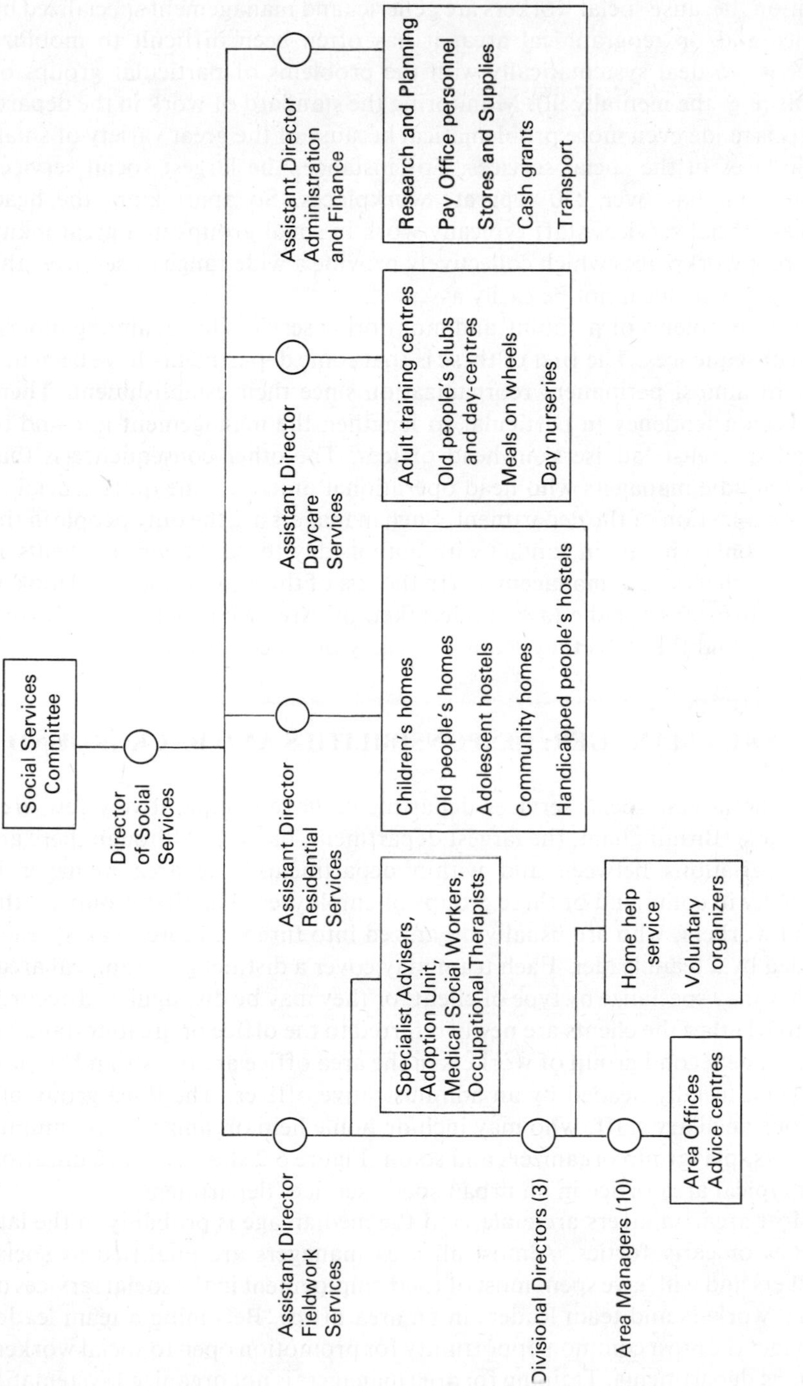

Figure 6.1 Outline of typical Social Services Department

addition, because social workers are generic, and management specialized by service and/or geographical area, it has often been difficult to mobilize expertise to deal systematically with the problems of particular groups of clients (e.g. the mentally ill). Monitoring the standard of work in the departments is made even more problematical because of the great variety of small workplaces in the social services. For instance, the largest social services department has over 250 separate workplaces. So apart from the head offices, social services staff typically work in small groups in a great many different workplaces which collectively provide a wide range of services, the quality of which cannot be easily assessed.

These problems of planning and monitoring services have, among others, two consequences. The first of these is that some departments have been in a state of almost permanent reorganization since their establishment. There has been a tendency in particular to lengthen the management line and to install specialist 'advisers' in head offices. The other consequence is that those middle managers who head operational units become quite crucial in the organization of the department. Such managers are the only people in the departments who are in contact with both its day-to-day service to clients as well as with its senior management. In the rest of this chapter, we shall look at what this means for the tasks undertaken by Area Managers in Fieldwork Services, and the skills they require to carry out these tasks.

THE AREA MANAGER: RESPONSIBILITIES AND BACKGROUND

Even the largest social services departments have comparatively few area managers (Birmingham, the largest department, has 13). Although there are wide variations between and within departments, the area manager is normally in command of three groups of employees. The first group are the social workers, who are usually organized into three or more 'teams', each headed by a team leader. Each team may cover a distinct geographical area, or they may specialize by type of client, or they may be distinguished according to whether the clients are newly referred to the office or are longstanding cases. The second group of workers in the area office are typists and clerical workers, usually headed by an administrative officer. The third group are various ancillary staff, who may include home help organizers, community workers, playgroup organizers and so on. Figure 6.2 shows the organization of a typical area office in an urban social services department.

Most area managers are male, and the median age is probably in the late thirties or early forties. Almost all area managers are qualified as social workers and will have spent most of their employment in the social services as social workers and team leaders in an area office. Becoming a team leader is in fact the most common opportunity for promotion open to social workers in most departments. Training for area managers is not organized systematic-

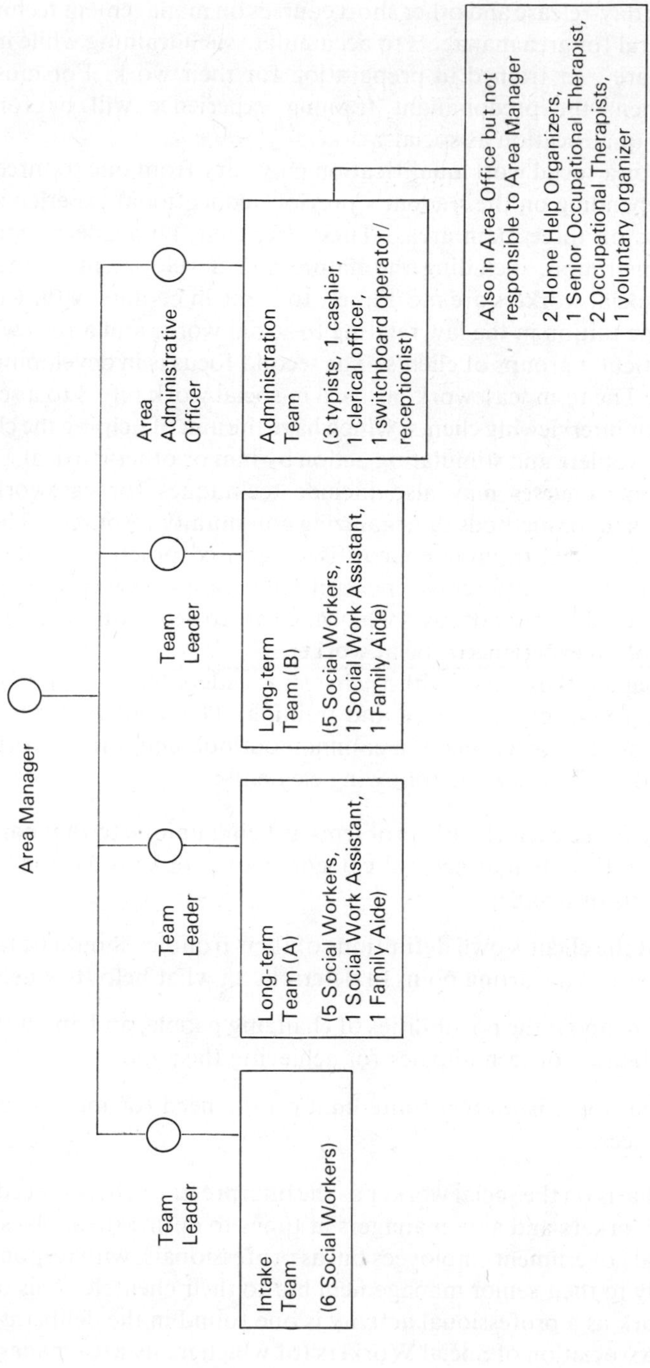

Figure 6.2 Outline of typical Social Services Area Office

ally, and varies between individuals and departments. Many area managers have been on day-release and other short courses on management techniques, but it is general for area managers to accumulate such training while in post. Few indeed are ever trained in preparation for their work. For most area managers then, the predominant training experience will be for their professional qualification as social workers.

Training for a social work qualification may vary from one to three years in length, depending on the student's previous educational experience. The courses focus on three main areas. These are, first, an academic study of social administration, including the nature and development of the main institutions social workers are most likely to come in contact with. Coupled to this is some tuition in the law relating to social work, and a review of the needs of particular groups of clients. The second focus is in developing skills in casework. The term 'casework' as used in social work refers to a series of techniques for interviewing clients, which have the aim of helping the client to redefine his problem and stimulating action by him or others to deal with the problem. Some courses may also include techniques for casework with groups of clients, or methods of organizing community resources. The third focus of professional training courses is supervised practice. Students are allocated to a range of different agencies in which casework is conducted, and are given a limited amount of cases which they are to deal with under the close supervision of an experienced social worker.

Area managers thus share with their team leaders and social workers a similar background of experience and training. This contributes to giving staff in area offices something of a common outlook about their work. This common outlook includes the following elements:

a tendency to see each client's problems as being unique to that particular individual rather than as general categories of problems associated with certain kinds of people;

a view that the client's own definitions of their troubles should be taken at the very least as a starting point in determining what help they need;

an optimism about the possibilities of changing people, and about the ultimate availability of technologies for achieving this; and

a belief that there is no real finite limit on the need for more and better social services.

This emphasis on the social worker as the interpreter of clients' needs leads both social workers and area managers at times to define themselves not so much as local government employees but as professionals, with responsibility not primarily to their senior management but to their clientele. This outlook on social work as a professional activity is one found in the deliberations of the British Association of Social Workers (of which many area managers are members), in the textbooks used for social work training, and in the social work journals. The professional outlook thus has something of a hegemony in the way social workers and area managers interpret their role. Many area managers, as a result, tend to define themselves more as 'social workers' than as 'managers' or 'administrators'. Their activities in supervising staff or in developing policy are seen then as being extensions of the same basic social work task, involving a similar array of skills to those used by social workers in dealing with their clientele.

THE AREA MANAGER: TASKS AND SKILLS

We can divide the various tasks that form the role of the area manager into five main groups. These are arranged in Table 6.1 from those which involve skills closest to casework, to those which require distinctive management skills. We shall look at each of these tasks in more detail, and try to determine which skills are required to perform them successfully.

Table 6.1 Tasks of the area manager in a social services department

Social work	*Hierarchy of tasks*
↓	Making decisions about individual cases
	Maintaining the standard of service provided by the area office
	Maintaining the staffing of the area office
	Transmission and liaison
	Developing social service policy for the area.
Management	

Making decisions about individual cases

It is rare for area managers to have their own cases, in the sense of being responsible for interviewing and casework with clientele. But it is common for area managers to make decisions about cases in a variety of circumstances. These include particularly the following:

(1) where the consequences of failure may be great, either for the client or for the reputation of the department. For instance, area managers usually make the final decision within the department about what action should be taken in the cases of children who may have suffered non-accidental injury;

(2) where the social worker believes that a cash grant or loan to a client may be justified as a means of keeping a child out of care. Area managers normally have authority to make such grants, and hence usually make this decision on receiving a report from the social worker;

(3) where there is a disagreement between team leader and social worker about the conduct of a case. This shades into circumstances where a social worker may use the area manager as a kind of consultant; and

(4) where the team leader is unable to find staffing resources to deal with a particular case. The area manager here is usually called upon to ratify a decision either to postpone any work on the case or to notify the client or those responsible for referring him to the department that no help can be given.

The skills needed to make decisions of this kind are similar in some respects to those required for casework in general. That is to say, they include the ability to make correct judgments about how clients are likely to behave, based on diverse and incomplete information. This information can include reports of how the client has reacted to his problem in the past, of how clients in similar circumstances have reacted, of the range of resources and social work techniques that might be employed, and of the legal powers and obligations of the department. Judgment on the basis of this information will often focus on key variables such as the motives of the client, his ability to make or accept changes to his way of life, and the range of practicable alternatives open to him. Skill in making decisions about individual cases is often manifested in two particular ways of reaching conclusions. Firstly, the conclusion is based on a range of considerations rather than just on one outstanding piece of data. Secondly, conclusions are based on information about the individual client rather than on seeing the case as just an example of a general category.

However, the skills needed by the area manager in deciding on individual cases differ from the skills required generally for casework in one important respect. This is because usually the area manager has not interviewed the client himself, and thus has his information secondhand from the social worker. Conclusions about the case therefore require the area manager to make a judgment not only about the client but also about the competence of the social worker. The skill here comes in knowing the right questions to ask the social worker to see if he has himself considered the full range of alternatives, or has sufficient and accurate information about the case. Clearly, such a skill is likely to be the outcome of prior experience as a social worker dealing with cases of a similar kind. These skills in making judgments about cases at one remove, and assessing the competence of the social worker are part of the skills associated with what in social work is called 'supervision'. Supervision is probably the bulk of the work of team leaders, who are responsible for allocating cases to social workers and maintaining the standard of work on a case-by-case basis. Area managers have almost always spent some years as a team leader, and hence are familiar with the techniques and expectations associated with supervision.

Maintaining the standard of service provided by the area office

We noted earlier the difficulty experienced by senior management in monitoring the quality of service provided by the department. Even in area offices, where the area manager is in daily face-to-face contact with his social workers, he may find that the quality of work done by them is anything but readily apparent. This is in part because of the nature of casework, and in part because of the setting in which it is conducted. As typically performed in social services departments, casework does not involve any specifications of clear objectives. Even though there has been some trend towards the setting of 'tasks' to be achieved as the result of casework, such 'tasks' may still be insufficiently clear for an outsider to determine with certainty whether a particular case had been a success or a failure. This problem is compounded by the intractability of the problems which social workers are called upon to resolve. Many clients may be seeing the social worker involuntarily or as a last stage before despair. They may be people whom other agencies have tried to help without success. Clearly, it would be unrealistic to expect even the most competent social worker to succeed in all cases, where so many have failed before. This all means, however, that many reasons can be presented for failure other than the incompetence of the social worker. Nor can the area manager assess the quality of service by observing progress rather than results. Casework always takes place between the social worker and client(s) in private, and usually away from the area office.

One common way of dealing with the problem of monitoring the quality of service is for the area manager to monitor ephemera or the things that he can actually observe. These include case-records, reports for other agencies, and letters. The area manager may also conduct spot checks on cases he has heard about or which have been the subject of complaint. The problem with this approach is that it is essentially negative, and is concerned with identifying failure rather than facilitating success. Probably the most important skill of an area manager in monitoring the service provided by the area office is a recognition of how success can be facilitated for the staff as a whole. There are three main ways in which this is usually done. These are: promotion of a good morale in the office; the recognition of particular areas of competence among individual members of staff; and developing systems for allocating cases appropriately.

As might perhaps be expected in a setting where people work in small groups dealing with an unpredictable flow of cases and where success cannot be counted upon, morale in area offices can fluctuate considerably. At times of low morale, the amount of work done by social workers can decline drastically even though the hours of work may not change. At times, there may even be bouts of near hysteria among social workers and even senior management (for instance, some bad publicity about the work of the department may lead to a stream of inappropriate emergency measures). There may also be personal disputes arising between individual members of staff. In small and often overcrowded offices these may become particularly stressful. There are temptations here for an area manager to concentrate on trying to maintain a happy atmosphere, whilst largely reacting to events. Such tactics invariably seem to produce discontent. The alternative approach to maintaining morale is to give the staff a sense of direction, which in social services departments means the development of projects which reflect the special interests of individual social workers. Projects of this kind might include new ways of working with particular kinds of clients (e.g. group casework with depressed mothers of children at risk), or an extension of existing services to a new location (e.g. setting up an advice centre in a local surgery). Projects are usually first proposed by individual social workers as a form of job-enrichment. By committing the area office to the project, the area manager can give all his staff a sense that the area office is moving forward. Unfortunately, proposing such projects usually proves much easier than actually maintaining them in being. Indeed, some area offices have a history of always being about to start some project or other (DHSS, 1978b).

To maintain projects beyond the initial burst of enthusiasm requires particular management skills. These are first, the ability to judge subordinates' self-confidence, in order to give the right amount of encouragement while still leaving the social worker with a sense of personal responsibility for his project. Secondly, the area manager needs an ability to understand the work of his office as a whole, rather than seeing it simply as a set of individuals. This is important because the kinds of work social workers prefer to do and the projects they propose will usually not coincide with the type of work that has to be done by the area office. As the latter takes priority, the interests and projects of individual social workers may become squeezed out. This inevitably produces a state of despondency among staff, with accusations of bad faith against the area manager. The area manager therefore needs to develop some system of organizing the work of the area office so that each social worker has some 'protected' time in which to undertake his special projects or interests. The normal means of doing this is to develop a system of estimating the work involved in each case and ensuring that the total caseload of each social worker does not exceed a given proportion of their time. The skilled area manager will normally contract openly with the social workers the extent of protected time, and also draw up clear guidelines for assessing the implementation of any projects.

Systems for determining and monitoring social workers' caseloads are now quite numerous. The area manager needs to be able to assess which of these is most appropriate to his own office and what adaptations need to be made to render it suitable. The skills required to do this successfully are quite complex. In the first place, there needs to be an ability to estimate how a proposed system would work in practice, particularly in the least favourable circumstances. This is related to being able to spot possible hitches before they arise. One such hitch in many area offices may be staff suspicion. Social workers are notoriously reluctant to keep paperwork up to date, and thus for any system to be successful, it must be comparatively simple to operate. It must also offer some clear reward to staff in terms of a reduced caseload.

This in turn requires commitment from the area manager to accept the consequences of caseload monitoring systems in the sense of being prepared to recognize that from time to time some of the work coming into the office can no longer be allocated to a social worker.

Maintaining the staffing of the area office

A major concern of area managers in most departments, at least until the recent past, has been that of simply filling vacancies in their establishment. With a high proportion of social workers being young, women, geographically mobile, and/or with good prospects of promotion, a high rate of turnover is common. But filling vacancies is more than simply a question of finding some person with a suitable qualification. In the intense relationships within the small group of people working in many area offices, an ill-chosen newcomer may prove disruptive, or may not fit into the existing pattern of special interests. The area manager normally plays an important part (in some cases the *only* part) in interviewing applicants. He therefore requires skill in interviewing and assessing the competence of prospective employees. An area manager with this skill will tend to prefer to be selective even if this means a vacancy unfilled for a longer time. He will also be honest to the applicant about his prospects for pursuing special projects or interests in the area office. This may avoid the disillusion that is all too common among newly-appointed staff when they come to realize (after about six months in post) that promises given to them at the interview are not being kept. Skilled area managers also realize that a further answer to the problem of filling the establishment lies not so much in frantic efforts to recruit as in preventing staff from wanting to leave. An unstated reason for a proportion of staff leaving is almost certainly disillusion with their work. This often relates to the contrast between on the one hand their educational qualifications and the high hopes of their social work training, and, on the other hand, their limited control over their caseload and their low status in the department hierarchy. Offices which develop successful schemes for managing caseloads and which promote the special projects of social workers do seem to hold their staff longer.

Aside from problems of filling vacant posts, area officers may also be concerned with increasing their establishment or, more recently, in preventing cuts. Both require similar skills, which are essentially those of advocacy. These include the ability to marshal information so that the area can be seen as a 'special case'. Such advocacy is necessary because social services departments rarely have any formula for calculating the appropriate size of area establishments according to the characteristics of its population and 'social need'. Area managers therefore normally rely on changes in local circumstances (such as an increase in population), or the need to develop or maintain particular projects. It helps particularly if the latter are in line with departmental policy or with fashionable concern (such as a project to help black adolescents in inner city areas).

Transmission and liaison

Much of the time of many area managers is taken up by meetings concerned with views and transmitting information within the department. As in most command hierarchies, the predominant flow of information in social services departments is top–bottom. This pattern presents a major problem for a welfare organization. This is because in such organizations professional staff see their role as one of marshalling services to meet the individual needs of clients. Where such services prove insufficient or of the wrong kind, professional staff may make demands for changes on senior management. They are, in other words, attempting to reverse the predominant information flow in the organization. In social services departments, social workers may view administrators as properly being the facilitators for the professional staff, and pressure may be applied via the usual staff meetings in area offices or, in the recent past, by means of trade union action. This may all place the area manager in a difficult intermediary role as both the transmitter of departmental instructions and the representative of the opinion of his staff to senior management. This problem is not helped by the inappropriateness of some departmental instructions, based as they may be at some distance from the day-to-day work of the department with its clients.

Placed in an intermediary position between his staff and the senior management, it clearly requires some skill on the part of the area manager to avoid being seen as either simply a mouthpiece or as untrustworthy. The skill involved here amounts to an ability to construct his own role. By this is meant a specification by the area manager of his tasks and responsibilities in a way that is consistent and can be communicated to others in the department, as a means of modifying their expectations. Construction of a role is circumscribed by departmental rules and by what is broadly acceptable to colleagues. But if successful, it may, for instance, lead area staff to see the area manager as someone who will honestly convey staff opinion to senior management but who has responsibilities beyond being simply a delegate of his staff. Similarly senior management may come to see the area manager as more than a means of enacting policy-statements, but also as having a responsibility to test their practicability and report back.

Developing social services policy for the area

Of all the five groups of tasks discussed here, the development of policy for social services in the area is probably that performed least adequately by area managers. More area managers will tend to define their role primarily as facilitating casework by individual social workers or as implementing general departmental policy. Where an attempt is made to develop a policy specifically for an area, it will most often be concerned with the relationship between the area office and the local offices of other agencies, such as social security, the housing department, the police, or various voluntary welfare organizations. This is because most of social workers' clients will have been in recent contact with officers from such agencies, or may be seeking help in dealing with problems relating to these agencies. As a result, social workers become aware of how changes in the procedures and policies of other agencies may have an impact on their own caseload. For instance, a policy by one of the power boards to charge a deposit before reconnecting supply may result almost immediately in an increase in the number of clients coming to a social worker for financial help. This problem can be intensified by a growing tendency of other agencies to administer a routinized and impersonal service, disposing of their difficult customers or clients to the social services. Social services departments can therefore become involved in an endless series of boundary disputes with other agencies.

Area managers normally attend a series of liaison meetings with their equivalent heads of the local offices of external agencies. At the same time, the social workers will tend to make informal links (often just because of frequent telephone contact) with their equivalents in these agencies. From these links, both sides can develop some mutual understanding about the division of responsibilities between them. There is a danger that if the formal liaison meeting takes over the consideration of too many individual cases, then the informal links between the agencies will lapse, and decisions about each case may be unduly prolonged. Formal liaison meetings may be more usefully concerned therefore, with general policy questions as exemplified in cases that have not been resolved at a lower level of liaison. Once again, there appears to be a skill in identifying the general implications of a number of individual cases. A few area managers have developed systems for reviewing social workers' caseloads in order to discover where the policy of other agencies or a lack of resources in the area may be hindering a successful resolution of cases. An attempt may then be made to fill the gaps in local services by promoting voluntary groups to carry out such activities as organizing social clubs for the disabled. A policy of this kind would seem to require a vision of social work as something rather more than just trying to help individual clients as they come through the door.

Tasks and skills as a whole

We have reviewed five groups of tasks that make up the role of area manager, and have tried to determine which skills are required to perform these tasks satisfactorily. Not all of these tasks are performed by all area managers, and individual area managers may assign quite distinctive priorities to them. There may be rather more uniformity in terms of the allocation of time between different tasks. The most time-consuming of all the five groups of tasks listed above is probably that of transmission and liaison. Second is probably the time spent making decisions about individual cases. Problems of maintaining the staffing level will in most offices be an intensive effort to fill one or two vacancies rather than a regular and predictable use of time. The time which area managers spend on monitoring the standard of work in their office, or in developing area social services policy may have a low priority. Many area managers do not in any real sense ever develop a social services policy for their area.

DISCUSSION

Many of the skills required by area managers clearly correspond to those needed for the management of people in general. These skills include an ability to judge people, their capacities and reliability; to be able to delegate; to understand the working of an organization as a whole; and to be able to assess the impact of new systems of work upon its performance. Like managers in other settings, the social services area manager also needs a knowledge of the kind of activities which are performed by his subordinates. In social services departments, this is ensured by appointing area managers (and much of senior management) from people who have worked in the past as social workers and team leaders.

Yet in a number of respects, management in the social services would seem to pose quite distinctive problems and conflicts. Chief among these is the lack of clear objective throughout the organization, and the absence of any aggregate data by which to judge the quality and, in fieldwork, even the quantity of service. This problem is made all the more acute because social services departments dispense a wide range of different services, to a most diverse clientele, from a multiplicity of small workplaces. This all makes for many difficulties in monitoring and planning services on a central basis within departments, and gives an important role and a certain amount of latitude to area managers. Indeed, we have argued that an ability to construct a suitable role is an important skill needed to do the job. In some respects, it is an indispensable skill. This is because area managers receive little prior training for their work and will find few texts which discuss what area managers should make of their job. They may face quite contradictory expectations within the department about what they should be doing and to whom they owe their first loyalty. Also the very skills and habits of mind that make for success in casework (especially the ability to focus on the particular rather than the general) may prove disadvantageous in management.

If area managers indeed have this latitude to define their own role, is it possible to distinguish a skilled from an unskilled area manager? To do so, we would need to look in some detail at the day-to-day work of the area office rather than pick on a few aggregate statistics such as rates of case closures. If we looked at day-to-day work, we might find that skilled area managers have a staff turnover somewhat lower than the average for the authority and that fewer staff than elsewhere talk frequently of moving on; that some system is in operation for monitoring and fixing maximum caseloads per social worker, and that this is adhered to even when the pressure of work is great; that the area manager is seen by staff as having a set of loyalties distinct in some respects from those of his social workers, but that he can be relied upon to honestly convey their professional concern to senior management; that there will be some system for involving area office staff in developing area social services policy from the experiences of individual cases; and, finally, that the area office will have a number of special interests and projects under way rather than always being about to start them.

If it is indeed difficult to distinguish skill from its opposite in the work of area managers, then we might expect to find that skilled area managers may often go unnoticed and unrewarded. A further consequence might be that the importance of skill itself may receive little attention. This has certainly been the case in academic research into social services management, which has focussed mainly on the formal structure of departments rather than on the skills needed to manage them (e.g. Rowbottom *et al.*, 1974). Some change can be expected as a spin-off from the increase in the amount of in-service training for social services management. But until then, the best hope for improved skill in practice is perhaps from accumulated experience as the departments settle down after the turmoil of reorganization.

Acknowledgements

The author is indebted to several area managers, area officers, and area directors who gave their help. In particular, he wishes to thank Derick Wood of Hereford and Worcester Social Services Department.

References

DHSS (1978a). *Health and Personal Social Services Statistics for England.* (London: HMSO)
DHSS (1978b). *Social Service Teams: The Practitioners View.* (London: HMSO)
Jordan, B. (1974). *Poor Parents: Social Policy and the Cycle of Deprivation.* (London: RICP)
Rees, S. (1978). *Social Work Face to Face: Clients' and social workers' perceptions of the content and outcomes of their meetings.* (London: Edward Arnold)
Rowbottom, R., Hay, A. and Billis, D. (1974). *Social Services Departments: Developing Pattern of Work and Organisation.* (London: Heinemann)

7
The Town Planner

A. HEDGE and N. PENDLETON

INTRODUCTION

Planning is a general term denoting a wide variety of human activities. We may speak of someone planning a career, a holiday, a family; of a company planning new products, expansion, redundancies; of a local authority planning new housing, roads, shops; or of Government planning for defence or the economy. Yet clearly there are vast differences between the size, scope and complexity of these various undertakings even though they are all commonly described as planning.

To clarify the confusion which frequently surrounds this term Bruton (1974) argues for a distinction between two kinds of planning – general or generic planning and physical planning. General planning comprises procedures whereby a desirable future situation is defined and attempts are made to organize events in such a way that this endpoint is realized. This form of planning basically involves 'deciding in advance what to do, how to do it, where to do it, and who is to do it' (Koontz and O'Donnell, 1974), and as such can usefully be thought of as a continuous process comprising a logical sequence of operations (see Figure 7.1), which may be applied to problems of differing levels of complexity (see Table 7.1).

Physical planning may be thought of as a subset of general planning which is specifically concerned with determining the use of land and buildings and the scale and form of development. Town planning* is founded in the activity of physical planning and is traditionally associated with the production of plans for the development of areas and with the operation of the statutory

*Town planning is here also used as a term synonymous with town and country planning, environmental planning, and land use planning, and from now on the term planning itself and *vice versa*.

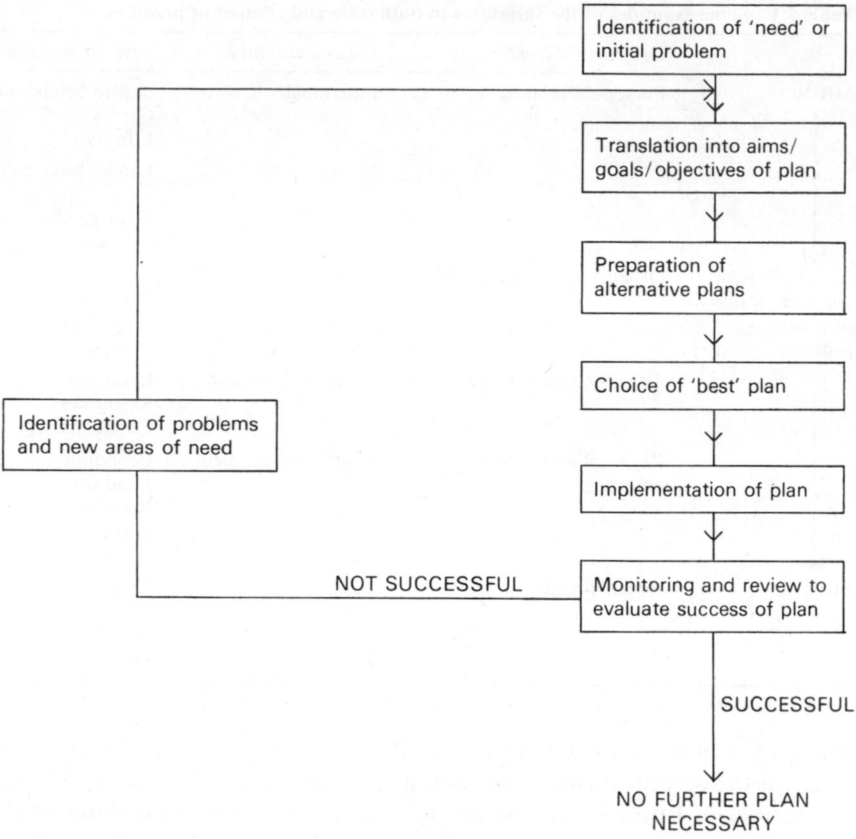

Figure 7.1 The cyclical nature of general planning

system of development control. However, it also makes use of the methods and procedures of general planning.

Because of this emphasis on physical planning it is difficult to compare the professional skills of town planners with those of planners in other settings. However, it is possible to draw parallels between the managerial skills of senior staff in a planning department and those in other organizations. Before attempting this, two points in particular must be strongly emphasized. Firstly, unlike many kinds of work, much of the work of the town planner may be prescribed by statute since there is a statutory requirement for local authorities to undertake town planning, and in addition to this the Government also provide considerable guidance on how this work should be conducted. Secondly, as a consequence of the former, town planning is basically an operational activity which is conducted within and through organizations. Thus the work of particular staff may to a greater or lesser degree be constrained by both the statutory requirements and the organizational climate. To convey some appreciation of these constraints and of the

Table 7.1 Some examples of the variations in both scale and content of planning

	Operational level	*Organizational level*	*Area of concern*
MICRO	Personal Planning	Individual	Skilled behaviour Career Life style
↓		Group	Family budget, size, holiday Team tactics, functions
Increasing scale and complexity of planning procedures and problems tackled	Organizational planning	Company	Products Markets Resources Manpower
	Town and country planning	Local government	Land use Resources Public need
↓	Regional and national planning	Central government	Economic Land use Resources Manpower Social
MACRO	International planning	EEC, OPEC, NATO	Economic Resources Manpower Defence

complexity of much planning work we shall briefly outline both the development of the current formal town planning system and the structure of local authorities in England and Wales, as well as describing something of the actual nature of the work done by planners. Only with such insight into town planning can one fully appreciate the intricacies of managing in a planning department.

THE FORMAL TOWN PLANNING SYSTEM IN ENGLAND AND WALES

The origins of the present town planning system in England and Wales (which differs in various ways from town planning organization in Scotland and Northern Ireland) can be traced back to the town planning movement of the 19th century when, appalled by the poor amenities and living conditions in cities, many prominent social reformers suggested that solutions to these problems could only be achieved through the systematic planning of towns and countryside (Hall, 1975). This early approach to town planning reflected a comprehensive concern for improving conditions in towns and cities. Moulded by the professions of architecture and engineering this concern eventually resulted in the establishment of the Town Planning Institute in

1914 and by the 1930's town planning was firmly established as a profession.

In addition to professional ideals, the practice of town planning has been largely shaped through the legislation and statutory instruments which have been introduced by successive Governments since 1909 (for a more detailed account of this legislation see, for example, Cullingworth, 1976; Ratcliffe, 1974). Although town planning is concerned with guiding and coordinating the way in which land is developed, early legislation (pre-1947) did not provide any statutory powers for this. As a result the uncoordinated patterns of urban growth in the inter-war years resulted in many problems. In particular those of urban sprawl (reckless consumption of rural/agricultural land regardless of quality and food-producing capacity) and ribbon development (private development along main arterial roads which leads to inefficient provision of essential services, e.g. water, gas, elecricity, and which was considered unaesthetic) highlighted the need for a comprehensive planning system.

The 1947 Town and Country Planning Act provided a framework for such a system. Local planning authorities were given powers of development control whereby all developers were required to apply to them for planning permission prior to initiating development. The development over which planning authorities were given control was, and still is, defined as 'the carrying out of building, engineering, mining or other operations in, on, over or under the land, or the making of any material change in the use of any building or other land'. Furthermore, local planning authorities were each required to prepare a development plan (basically a physical plan defining patterns of present and future land use), which, after receiving Government approval, would provide the framework for exercising the authority's powers of development control.

Because the 1947 system was apparently a much more positive planning system planners in the immediate post-war years assumed a much greater degree of confidence and certainty in their work. Planning was defined as 'the art and science of ordering the use of land and siting of buildings and communication routes so as to secure the maximum practicable degree of economy, convenience and beauty' (Keeble, 1969). Planners held commonly shared though implicitly assumed objectives, e.g. ensuring equality of opportunity, prosperity and standards throughout the whole country, getting the urban areas into shape, etc. (Buchanan, 1972). As a consequence throughout the 1950's and early 1960's the planning profession generally operated as an enlightened elite and many townscapes were radically changed with little regard being paid to the views of the people affected.

However, the breadth and rate of post-war social and economic changes soon outstripped the capacity of the 1947 system, and its success was limited because of its 'inability to produce a satisfactory integration of land use planning and social and economic policies' (Bruton, 1974).

The current system is based on the Town and Country Planning Act, 1968, which extensively revised the 1947 approach. The most significant effect of this legislation has been the replacement of the old-style development plan system. The new system operates at two levels – structure planning and local planning. The relationship between these and the various types of plans which may be produced is summarized in Figure 7.2.

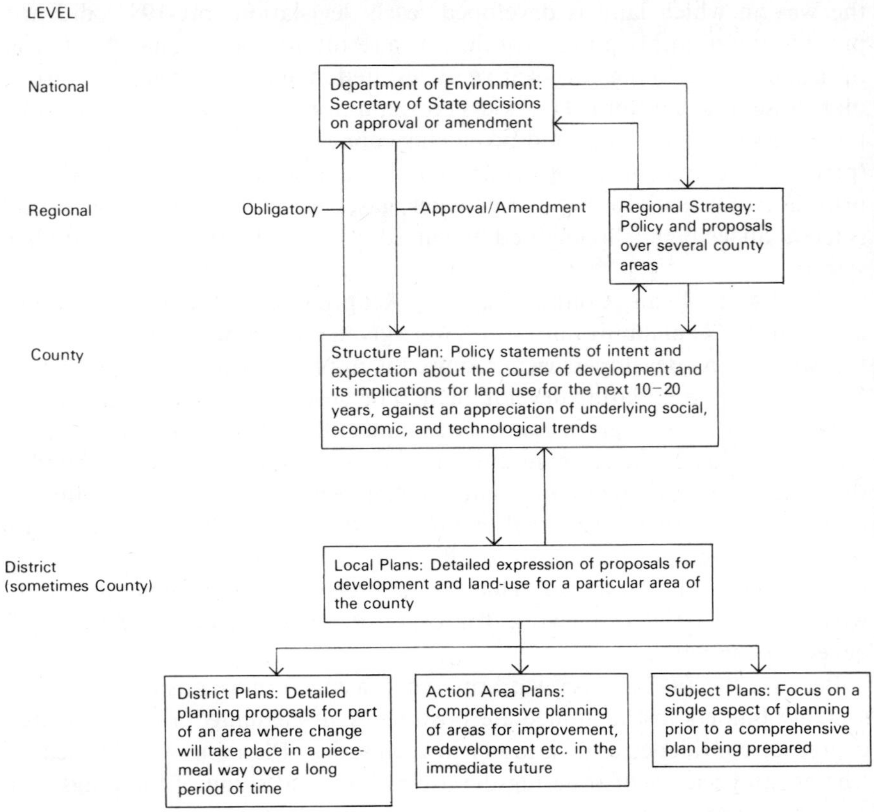

Figure 7.2 The 1968 Development Plan system in England and Wales

The aim of structure planning is to facilitate 'a broad and open consideration of planning problems by taking account of physical, economic, and social aspects' (D.o.E Circular 4/79) and emphasis is placed on the need to integrate and coordinate policy. In addition to this change to the development plan system, local authorities are also encouraged – indeed required – to engage in public participation and to demonstrate to the Secretary of State that this has been done in a satisfactory way. This attempt to foster greater public involvement in planning signifies a fundamental change in thinking with the public now seen as playing a positive role in defining planning objectives (Sewell and Coppock, 1977). Thus, unlike the previous system where decisions on planning objectives were typically the prerogative of the planners and politicians, the current approach favours the derivation of these from the planning process itself in which the public have played a part. The significance of this point should not be lost for the town planner is no longer seen as an expert whose opinions are unchallengeable but is seen more as a servant of the community capable of translating its wishes into policy.

To summarize, the current statutory system aims to provide a framework for planning which allows a more integrative, coordinated, flexible and participative approach to planning problems than has previously existed. This change in emphasis is in keeping with current planning ideology which holds that 'there is no finite or static conception of an optimum or ideal environment; ideas of urban settlement are no longer concerned with a social or physical ideal state; rather with understanding the process of change' (Rose, 1974), and which views planning as 'the means by which the public interest is brought to bear on the process of developing land' (Eddison, 1979).

THE ORGANIZATIONAL CONTEXT OF TOWN PLANNING

As we have seen the present development plan system operates at two levels – structure and local planning. Similarly, since the Local Government Act, 1972, local authorities are also organized into a two-tier system – the county authorities responsible for structure planning and the district authorities responsible for local planning (see Figure 7.3).

Other than the unique Greater London Council there are two different types of county and district local authorities. The major conurbations, e.g. West Midlands, Greater Manchester, are serviced by Metropolitan County Councils (responsible for strategic land use and transportation planning and management along with limited development control and certain aspects of environmental and recreational management) and Metropolitan District Councils (responsible for education, personal social services, housing, local planning and development control, etc.). For other areas of the country, shire/county rather than district authorities assume responsibility for education and personal social services. Thus the precise nature of the work being undertaken by town planners can vary enormously depending on the kind of authority in which they are employed.

Apart from these differences in the functions of local authorities there are also wide variations in internal organizational structure. Although many authorities are still organized along traditional lines, i.e. an aggregate of relatively autonomous departments, others have reorganized themselves along the lines suggested by both the Maud Report (1967) and the Bains Report (1972) and introduced some form of Corporate Management (Planning) system. Ideally this represents an attempt to create a better integrated authority in which the various kinds of departmental planning are united so that all

ENGLAND

London

Greater London Council

City of London

32 London Boroughs

England outside London

6 Metropolitan County Councils	39 Shire County Councils
35 Metropolitan District Councils	296 District Councils

WALES

8 County Councils

37 District Councils

Figure 7.3 The new local government structure in England and Wales (Town and Country Planning in Britain, 1975)

departments work in a complementary way towards the achievement of compatible objectives.

THE WORK OF PLANNING DEPARTMENTS

So far, we have briefly described how town planning developed as a service provided by local government, what the main characteristics of the present planning system are, and how local authorities are organized. Unfortunately such a discussion of the formal planning system does not really give much of a flavour of what planners actually do. To do this we must briefly outline some of the main types of work undertaken in the planning departments in local authorities. In particular we shall concentrate on the non-development control activities which, although very varied, can be grouped under the heading of forward planning.

All planning departments are organized into sections, usually one of which is solely concerned with development control. Planners involved in development control are responsible for the processing of planning applications through to a decision of approval or refusal. The job is essentially reactive because the workload is determined by the number of applications submitted by private concerns, public bodies and the general public. There is a statutory time limit of eight weeks for dealing with applications and after this period the applicant can appeal against non-determination. This time limit is often reinforced by political pressure, particularly when Government is concerned that the planning system causes excessive delay to the development process. The job of the development control planner is thus quite well defined, since it is a process controlled by statute with the workload governed by external forces, with clear expectations concerning the speed of performance, and with immediate feedback on performance.

By way of contrast the job of forward planning is far more complex and uncertain. Most departments possess a separate forward planning section which deals with all matters other than development control (in the larger Districts and County Councils these other matters may actually be split between two or three sections). Such a section is typically concerned with four main areas of work and we shall briefly describe each of these.

The policy context for development

The main forward planning activity which is undertaken in most planning departments is work involved in the provision of an adequate policy framework to guide development in an area. This work is traditionally associated with the preparation of statutory plans, and in some authorities considerable staff resources are devoted to these exercises. However, many planners are critical of the statutory system for preparing plans, particularly the time required to go through the complex statutory processes and the tendency to retain a relatively narrow emphasis on physical and land use matters. Thus, in many authorities a large amount of the policy context for development is actually established through non-statutory plans approved only by the council concerned. Plans may vary enormously in their nature, and a particularly important distinction is between those plans which are primarily intended to provide a framework for development control decisions, and those intended to stimulate coordinated action using more than just the regulatory powers of development control. The former provide guidance, through policy statements and allocations of land for particular uses, on the considerations to be taken into account when individual planning applications are being assessed. The latter type of plan is often aimed at attracting investment to a declining area and so the emphasis is on resource expenditure in such fields as industrial development, environmental schemes, and improved road access, to try and catalyse new development. Since planning departments do not normally manage budgets with which to finance these sorts of proposals the success of plans of this nature ultimately depends on the active cooperation of other local authority departments and agencies outside the local authority.

In addition, to this general policy guidance there is often a need for specific guidance on the way in which individual sites or small areas should be developed. This is provided by much more specific plans, e.g. pedestrianization schemes, or by planning briefs which aim to ensure that the developer is aware, in advance of scheme preparation, of the particular constraints and requirements affecting the development of a site. Planning briefs should also ensure that the requirements of the local authority are properly fulfilled, and that the developer does not waste time preparing an abortive scheme. In some departments, particularly in the more urban authorities, the preparation of such plans and briefs constitutes a major area of work.

General policy and research work

As well as preparing policy guidance for development, planners often become heavily involved in other policy work both within and outside the authority. Two main sorts of involvement can be distinguished. Firstly, there are many agencies which may be drawing up plans for land use, and comments on these on behalf of the local authority may be required. In particular the split of town planning functions between County and District Councils, with each authority having an interest in the plans of the other, means that a large amount of time can be devoted to this kind of consultation. Secondly, the forward planning section is likely to become involved in general policy work within the authority where the cooperative action of different departments on such matters as the authority's housing or industrial strategy may be needed. This involvement arises not only because of the department's interest in any land use implications, but also because of the contribution it can make in terms of research and information and through the generic nature of the skills required in the plan preparation process. The work in relation to research and information is particularly notable because planners are more likely to be equipped with skills and knowledge in this area than staff in other departments in local authorities.

Implementation

In some authorities, the planning department is only really concerned with using the statutory powers to regulate the development initiatives of others, principally from the private sector. In other authorities, the planning department plays a much more positive role in implementation and is directly involved in undertaking or catalysing development and improvement in the area. The forward planning section may perform this latter work in either of two main ways. Firstly, on behalf of the department, it may either control or be corporately involved in programmes to carry out schemes for say, environmental improvement, or industrial development and improvement, etc. Secondly, and probably in conjunction with these sorts of schemes, effort may be made to draw in other departments and outside agencies with resources which can be used for the benefit of an area.

The rational view of the general planning process emphasizes the importance of close links between plan-making and implementation activities, with the latter being based on and following on from a well worked out planning framework. In practice, however, implementation activities often take place fairly independently of this because it may be more practical to achieve successful implementation by responding to opportunities rather than being strictly tied to a policy framework. This divorce is reinforced whenever forward planning work and implementation activities are managed in separate sections within a planning department.

Ad hoc land use exercises

While the preparation of policy guidance represents the more long-term work of the forward planning section, there are many *ad hoc* tasks which arise where guidance or decisions are needed on specific land use and development questions, e.g. a specific proposal is put forward which must be evaluated in terms of council policy, or a request is received to identify a site or sites for a particular use. These sorts of tasks sometimes involve the interpretation of existing policy guidance but frequently have to be undertaken in the absence of an adequate or up-to-date policy framework. What is more these tasks may actually occupy a large part of the section's work capacity.

Thus there is clearly a wide range of activities which may be undertaken by a forward planning section within a planning department. But before concluding this outline of town planning in practice, it is worth noting an important difference between the nature of forward planning activities in different authorities. At one extreme, in some authorities there are many well established functions such as the preparation of briefs, day-to-day participation in housing improvement work, and consultation on other authority plans, which employ most of the staff resources available, and this may mean, particularly in small planning departments, that there is little scope for getting beyond reactive work. In other authorities there may be much more scope for deciding where forward planning work is needed and deploying staff resources towards the achievements of a longer term work programme.

MANAGEMENT SKILLS IN TOWN PLANNING

At the start of this chapter we pointed out how general planning was an integral part of all management, but that these activities are not synonymous. Koontz and O'Donnell (1974) define management as 'the creation and maintenance of an internal environment in an enterprise where individuals, working together in groups, can perform efficiently and effectively toward the attainment of group goals . . . Essentially, managing is the art of doing, and management is the body of organized knowledge which underlies the art'. Within this framework effective managers are seen as those best able to efficiently mobilize the human, financial, and material resources at their disposal. Thus the job of managing demands diverse skills and personal attributes, for a manager must be able to set goals and objectives, devise strategies for realizing these, effectively deploy resources, and shoulder full responsibility for his decisions.

One problem which quickly emerges when trying to analyse the management skills of senior staff in a planning department, is that these staff seldom work just as managers. They typically spend much of their time working in their capacity as professional planners, and it is sometimes difficult to distinguish between professional and managerial roles. Another problem of discussing management in planning is that the management skills (and the professional skills) needed to operate effectively in a planning department depend on the purpose and approach to planning. As already shown this can vary considerably between local authorities especially since there is no single conception of what 'good' planning is, either in terms of ends or means.

To help overcome these problems we have chosen to focus our discussion on the skills needed by a manager of a forward planning section and to examine only those activities which, in our opinion, incorporate a reasonable degree of managerial involvement and require some form of skilful response. The picture which we present has been derived both from interviews with senior staff in planning departments in Metropolitan County, Metropolitan District, and Shire District authorities, and from the personal experience of one of the authors. However we have not ventured to examine how such skills have been acquired by these staff.

From the information which we have gathered it is clearly impossible to neatly compartmentalize the work of senior planning staff heading forward planning sections into separate sets of management and planning tasks. However it is possible to describe their work in terms of four managerial roles – planning, representation, work control, and staff management. Because these roles are inextricably linked to the professional planning roles of these staff we have decided to refer to the latter as planner-managers rather than either planners or managers. So, having described the context of the work of the planner-manager, let us now examine the skills associated with each of his managerial roles.

The planning role

At the macro-level this relates to the complex task of defining the overall role and purpose of the forward planning section within both the planning department, the local authority, and the community as a whole, while at the micro-level it involves determining what specific jobs need to be done, how they should be approached, and how staff resources should be deployed. In relation to this planning role the planner-manager's professional skill is in the preparation of policies and plans to guide development in an area; in other words he is skilled in the *management of land and building resources*. However, since he leads a group of staff who also possess similar professional skills to a greater or lesser degree he must extend his own professional skills to embrace a broader range of tasks. In particular he is responsible for making decisions on three major tasks – strategy, organization and implementation, and monitoring and review.

Strategy

This is the planner-manager's most basic task. Quite simply, he is responsible for deciding on a strategy for what his section is trying to achieve and how best to do this. Since there is no consensus view on what constitutes 'good' planning, and since the forward planning function can be performed in many different ways this is a very complex undertaking. The planner-manager's decisions on strategy may also be constrained by the amount of time which may need to be spent on *ad hoc* tasks, as previously described. Since most of this reactive workload concerns land use issues he will have little alternative but to accept this and fit it into the section's workload as and when it arises. Notwithstanding these constraints, the planner-manager's decisions on strategy will also be significantly affected by the views of his chief officer, the councillors, other departments and the views of his own staff. This means that a major challenge for the planner-manager is to arrive at a view on strategy which he sees as both desirable and feasible, and which he believes will gain the agreement and commitment of those whose support he needs both within and outside his section.

Organization and implementation

Many problems face the planner-manager when trying to organize the work activities of a forward planning section. Firstly, it is simply not possible to programme the reactive workload since much of this is unpredictable. Secondly, planning is a time-consuming process and planning exercises may take anything from six months to five years or more before completion. Thirdly, the almost inevitable delays which occur in many exercises lead most planner-managers to show reluctance to set out any firm work programmes for consumption outside the section. Finally the planner-manager may have to overcome inertia and conservatism which sometimes exists concerning established ways of working and expectations about who should do what sort of work. In deciding on his strategy the planner-manager will need to have considered the numbers and capabilities of the staff resources available to him, and when it comes to organizing work activities he must be able to get the right staff working on the right projects at the right time, even if this means changing established patterns of working. He also needs to have a very clear view of priorities based on his strategy and he must be able to apply these priorities in decisions on how to handle work so that, for example, those involved in essential work are not disrupted by *ad hoc* tasks and thus some continuity of effort is maintained. He must also be able to maintain momentum in the progressing of work even though it may not be practical to adopt a firm timetable. Deadlines may have to be set as work progresses through various stages rather than at the outset. Thus, in order to give realistic guidance, the planner-manager must have an appreciation of what is involved in a planning exercise and in any other jobs an individual is handling in order to know what is a reasonable length of time to complete a task.

Monitoring and review

Within the context of the planning role this refers to the monitoring of the success or failure of the section strategy rather than progress on individual work items. As we have seen, monitoring and review is the final stage in the rational planning process prior to initiating a new planning cycle. However, even though the planner-manager may have a very clear and coherent picture of strategy the task of evaluating the degree of success is extremely difficult. The product of the forward planning process for any one exercise is normally one or more written reports containing policies, proposals or advice on the use of land. Of these, the major reports are submitted to the relevant council committees for resolution, and in special cases, like structure plans, they also require Government approval by the Secretary of State for the Environment. However, it is not possible to assess performance solely in terms of the quantity of output. Reports are intended to provide a sound basis for policies and a framework for decision making, and thus it is quality which determines the value of the work. Many factors usually operate to influence this, e.g. the nature of the problems, time pressure, and in the absence of objective standards it is frequently very much a matter of subjective judgment to decide how to approach an exercise and equally, when it is completed, to decide whether or not the work was well done. In particular it is likely to be difficult to assess whether the right amount and type of work was done in relation to the importance of the exercise and the recommendations that were made.

A second problem of evaluation exists because it is often difficult to assess how useful a planning exercise has been in actually helping decision making. This is partly a reflection of the fact that the policies and proposals contained in a planning document will be intended to guide decision making over a number of years. It is also because many factors influence decision making in local government, including political values and beliefs, public opinion and pressure from developers, and ultimately it may not be very clear just what contribution the planning guidance has provided.

A third and perhaps most fundamental problem of evaluation is the long term and indirect nature of the relationship between a planning exercise and development, redevelopment, or improvement activity on the ground. Plans are prepared for periods of up to 20 years in the future and so there will often be a long timespan between plan preparation and implementation. During this time, planning guidance and controls will be just one factor influencing the development processes in an area. Thus the degree to which things happen or do not happen because of planners and their plans is inevitably difficult to assess. As there are no objective standards or indicators which on their own provide an adequate guide to performance, and because of the intrinsic difficulties of assessing so much of planning work, the planner-manager needs to develop his own internal standards. To do this he will need to ask two basic questions of both individual exercises and the general work of the section: 'are we doing the right sort of forward planning work, and are we doing it well?' He may then be able to work out certain criteria to help answer these questions, but by far the most important step he can take is to ensure that he receives the opinion of the recipients of the service, be they the development control section, other departments, the councillors, or the general public.

To summarize, for the planner-manager to successfully perform his planning role he must exercise both a high degree of personal/professional ability, and a political awareness of what is feasible given the views of the councillors and other interested parties. In addition to this he needs to possess persuasive skills which will assist him in gaining the agreement and commitment of all parties essential to the eventual implementation of plans, i.e. his chief officer, the councillors, other departments, and outside agencies. He must also be capable of evaluating the staff resources at his disposal and making the optimum use of them in persuance of the section's strategy. Finally, he needs a clear mind and a strong sense of purpose to establish priorities and apply them in the organization of work activities.

The representative role

This is basically a function of the planner-manager's position as a senior member of staff responsible for a large and fairly coherent area of activity within a local authority department. He performs this representative role in two senses. Firstly he is directly accountable to his chief officer and to the councillors for what is produced or not produced by his section. Secondly, his seniority means he is often the most suitable person to talk authoritatively whenever there are important discussions which concern the functions and work activities of his section, e.g. council committees, public hearings, etc. The extent to which the planner-manager represents the planning department at meetings such as council committees will depend on the attitude of his chief officer. In most authorities the planner-manager will normally be expected to appear at the regular council committees either on his own or in a supporting role to the chief officer, since all important decisions concerning the strategy of the section and individual planning exercises require approval by the councillors. At these meetings the planner-manager will have to introduce reports, justify their recommendations, and answer any questions on their contents and related issues. The extent to which appearing at committees proves a demanding task varies from authority to authority because sometimes planning is treated as a professional technical matter and committees are normally willing to follow the guidance of the officers, while in other authorities the objectives and operation of planning are subject to a much greater degree of political control and the role of the officers is a more limited advisory one.

There are also numerous other situations where the planner-manager may appear as the representative of his section and these can be grouped into three categories. Firstly, there will be occasions where the planner-manager is keen to get the support and cooperation of other departments and outside agencies to facilitate the work of his section. Secondly, the planner-manager will need to appear at meetings where the interests and concerns of his section, the department, or the authority as a whole must be presented and either defended or promoted as necessary; e.g. the planner-manager with a District Council may appear at the examination in public of the County Structure Plan with a brief to speak for the amendment or rejection of a range of policies contained in this. Finally, there will be occasions where the planner-manager must represent the section to explain, justify or instruct other parties in relation to a planning exercise undertaken by or in preparation within the section; e.g. during public participation on a local plan he is the person most likely to represent the department at public meetings and other important discussions concerning the exercise.

To summarize, all of these situations require the planner-manager to be capable of communicating effectively. However, the precise skills necessary will vary. In some situations the emphasis will be on diplomacy, with the planner-manager trying to enlist support and cooperation and create good working relationships, e.g. with councillors. In other cases a more aggressive approach may be called for with the planner-manager fighting to win arguments in the face of critical questioning, or the forceful presentation of alternative points of view. It is not just a matter of his possessing the skills necessary for the fluent presentation of ideas and arguments; it is also necessary that he possesses the insight and the character to judge which manner of presentation best fits the situation.

The work-control role

The control of specific planning exercises is the 'bread and butter' of management in a planning department. The planner-manager in his work-control role is concerned with ensuring that work is done to an acceptable standard and in a reasonable time. The nature of this role will obviously vary according to the size of the section. The larger the section, the more likely there are to be senior staff under the planner-manager's control with managerial responsibility for the day-to-day progress of work. Although a different approach is called for in large and small sections, the basic problem for the planner-manager in both cases is to decide just how far he should become involved in detailed planning work. There are many reasons for such involvement, including the fact that he is responsible for the output of the section and is accountable to his chief officer and in turn to a council committee which has general control of the planning department. Furthermore, since planning exercises are often characterized by a complex intermingling of technical and political considerations, the planner-manager may decide to become involved in detailed planning work because he needs a good understanding of what is contained in any report produced by his section and what lies behind this to enable him to feel confident of his position at council committee meetings. Finally, the planner-manager may also get involved in detailed planning work because he recognizes that it is politically sensitive or has important ramifications and therefore must be handled in a particular way. Also if he is not very confident in the abilities of the staff available, or alternatively if he is short of staff, he may consider it simpler and quicker to do the work himself rather than provide very detailed supervision.

Underlying these pressures for involvement is the fact that, as we have previously emphasized, the planner-manager is usually somebody with a professional training in town planning. He will typically have achieved his present position largely because of his interest and capability for detailed planning work, and he may therefore find it very difficult to concentrate on managing other people rather than doing planning work himself; indeed he may even be inept at man-management.

Thus the challenge facing the planner-manager is how best to strike a good balance between two conflicting forces. On the one hand he must have sufficient involvement in planning exercises to bring the benefits of his own knowledge and experience to bear, to ensure that the exercise is being handled expeditiously and to have sufficient understanding of what has been done to be able to represent the work to other parties. On the other hand he must try to make full and efficient use of the staff resources at his disposal and allow his staff the job satisfaction and motivation which comes from having responsibility for an area of work. The skills required to find this balance are basically the skills of delegation, and to do this successfully he needs a good understanding of what is likely to be involved in the work and a reasonable knowledge of the staff at his disposal. He must also be able to judge what sort of guidance is needed in each case and to communicate that guidance in a clear and concise manner. When problems and queries arise he needs the intellectual capability to disentangle the important from the unimportant so that unnecessary work is not done and time is not wasted discussing work which could or should be sorted out by other staff.

Once a task has been delegated the planner-manager needs to rely on experience to have a reasonable idea of how long work should take, and he needs to establish some method of monitoring progress regularly to ensure that all is well. In a small section he may be able to rely on informal daily contact with staff to monitor whether or not good progress is being made, whereas in a larger section he is more likely to rely on some formal system of verbal or written reports from senior staff or group meetings at regular intervals. A wide variety of approaches to monitoring are possible and his managerial skill comes in devising the most appropriate method given the particular environment.

Finally, when a piece of work has been completed the planner-manager must assess its quality. He also needs to skilfully question his staff so that he is satisfied the work has been done properly, and so that he can extract the information he requires to adequately fulfil his representative role. Skilful questioning is related to both the planner-manager's ability to perceive the essentials, and his knowing from experience what is likely to be of importance.

To summarize, for successful performance of his work control role the planner-manager needs to judge how far he should become involved in detailed planning work and how far he should 'manage' his staff and delegate responsibility. This decision will be influenced by many pressures including his own inclination as a professional planner, his confidence in the abilities of his staff, his own ability to give sound guidance, and his intellectual ability to skilfully question staff on work and to disentangle important from irrelevant information.

The staff management role

Because of the professional nature of town planning the planner-manager is usually dealing with staff of a high calibre who are likely to be reasonably articulate, capable of presenting well reasoned views, from a diverse background and with a wide range of beliefs, and who tend to expect an informal and participative style of working. The job of managing such staff is further complicated by the nature of forward planning work and by the traditional procedures of local government. Many factors operate to make planning a frustrating job, e.g. the lack of agreed objectives and therefore lack of criteria of success, the long time delays between the initiation and completion of plans and between this and implementation, the possession of only crude powers which usually have only limited impact on the problems and so on. The resulting feelings engendered in many planning staff of being divorced from the action, i.e. from actual on-the-ground changes, are usually exacerbated by traditional practices in many authorities, e.g. the fact that only the most senior staff report to council committees and that senior staff in departments tend to talk only to staff of equal seniority in other departments. In addition, planning often requires a large amount of routine and undemanding work.

Because of these problems, maintaining staff motivation and morale is often a difficult task. It would certainly be wrong to assume that planners are self-motivated just because they are usually professionally qualified and have received a graduate level of education. The planner-manager must be able to recognize these problems and have the ability to engender and maintain enthusiasm and commitment amongst his staff. This means attending to basic principles of management such as ensuring that staff understand why they are doing pieces of work, responding quickly and constructively to work produced or queries made, and providing a variety of jobs so that staff do not become bored on one piece of work. It is also useful to have the social skills needed to form good working relationships with staff because, without any real sanctions at his disposal, the planner-manager needs to win the active support and cooperation of his staff. However, because the job does not provide tangible results which make it easy for staff to gain feedback on performance, the planner-manager must be prepared to go further and try to ensure that his staff feel they are making a worthwhile contribution to the planning department and the community as a whole. In order to do this the planner-manager must constantly be able to create opportunities for staff involvement in decision making and for delegating his responsibilities, even though this may mean delaying work progress, taking some calculated risks (when delegating responsibilities), and going against traditional local authority practices.

To summarize, the planner-manager needs to be sensitive to the skills, abilities and weaknesses of his staff. This knowledge is valuable to him when recruiting new staff, since he needs to have a clear view of what abilities are required for the job itself in relation to the pool of abilities in the section; when allocating tasks, since he needs to match the abilities of his staff with the skills required for each piece of work; when supervising work, since he needs to assess the amount of guidance necessary in relation to individual staff and act accordingly; and when monitoring work progress, since he needs to take account of the motivation and reliability of individual staff. Above all he must be conscious that job satisfaction can be a major problem, that he has some responsibility for this and that he must consider appropriate means of maintaining self-motivation in his staff.

CONCLUSIONS

In the brief space of this chapter we have tried to convey something of the nature and complexity of town planning, of the managerial problems facing senior staff in planning departments, and of the skills needed for successful managerial performance. In an attempt to systematically describe the planner-manager's job we have suggested that the diverse tasks which he performs can usefully be grouped into four roles. It has not been our intention to suggest that these roles are either well defined or performed independently of each other, for such is not the case – there are many overlaps. Furthermore these roles tend to be implicitly assumed rather than explicitly stated, as indeed is the very notion of 'managers' in a planning department.

There are clearly many similarities between the roles performed and skills required by planner-managers and by managers in a variety of situations. However, there are two main characteristics of the situation facing the planner-manager which uniquely shape the nature of the skills required and create the need for a particular mix of these. Firstly, forward planning encompasses a diverse range of activities where there are many different professional and political views about the role, purpose, and general approach to the job; where much of the work can be handled in a variety of ways; where political and technical considerations intermingle in a complex way; where quality of the product and not quantity is important; and where evaluation of the product can be a very difficult task. Secondly, town planning is subject to democratic control by local councillors and consequently many decisions about what the forward planning section does, how it does it, and what the final product should be are ultimately taken by a locally elected 'board of managers'.

It is these circumstances which make a number of skills and abilities stand out as being particularly important and often difficult to apply – the ability to form a professionally desirable and politically feasible view on everything from strategy to the conclusions to be drawn from each piece of work; to communicate with a variety of audiences in a style appropriate and effective for each situation; to organize resources so that work priorities are achieved; to find the right balance of personal involvement in detailed planning work; to engender and maintain staff enthusiasm and commitment; and to establish standards of 'good' planning and review performance accordingly.

Yet in spite of this need for a diverse range of managerial skills amongst senior staff, the planning profession which successfully develops skills for managing land to date pays little attention to developing those required for managing the planning service in local government.

References

Bains Report (1972). *The New Local Authorities – Management and Structure.* (London: HMSO)

Buchanan, C. D. (1972). *The State of Britain.* (London: Faber)
Bruton, M. J. (1974) (ed.) *The Spirit and Purpose of Planning.* (London: Hutchinson)
Cullingworth, J. B. (1976). *Town and Country Planning in Britain.* 6th Edn, The New Local Government Series No. 8. (London: Allen and Unwin)
D.o.E. Circular No. 4/79. *Memorandum on Structure and Local Plans.* (London: Department of the Environment)
Eddison, T. (Chairman) (1979). Making Planning more effective: a discussion document. In *Report of the Implementation in Planning Working Party.* (London: The Royal Town Planning Institute)
Hall, P. (1975). *Urban and Regional Planning: Problems in Modern Geography.* (Newton Abott: David & Charles)
Keeble, L. (1969). Principles and Practice of Town and Country Planning. *Estates Gazette.*
Koontz, H. and O'Donnell, C. (1974). *Essentials of Management.* (New York: McGraw–Hill)
Maud Report (1967). *Management of Local Government.* (London: HMSO)
Ratcliffe, J. (1974). *An introduction to Town and Country Planning.* (London: Hutchinson)
Rose, E. A. (1974). Philosophy and purpose of planning. In Bruton, M. J. (ed.) *The Spirit and Purpose of Planning*, Chapter 2. (London: Hutchinson)
Sewell, W. R. D. and Coppock, J. T. (1977) (eds.) *Public Participation in Planning.* (London: Wiley)
Town and Country Planning in Britain (1975). Central Office of Information Reference Pamphlet No. 9, (6th Edn.). (London: HMSO)

8
The Civil Service

E. B. McGINNIS

SIMILARITIES AND DIFFERENCES

There are few respects in which management roles in the Civil Service are essentially different from management roles in other organizations, and the great diversity of Civil Service management roles is at least as marked as their common identity. The Civil Service itself is not sharply differentiated from other parts of the public service, and the public service in turn has an ill-defined or shifting philosophical and economic borderline with the private sector. Functions which could be discharged by a Government Department are hived off from time to time to public bodies which may or may not be staffed by civil servants, and functions may be discharged within or outside the public service according to the philosophy of the government of the day. The recent high mortality among QUANGOS* has emphasized the arbitrariness of dividing lines (as well as sharpening debate as to whether leaving things undone is the sin of indifference or the virtue of discrimination). Against this background, it would be surprising if Civil Service management did differ markedly in essentials from management elsewhere.

In non-essentials, that is in features which are of the form rather than of the essence, there are some distinctive features. First, thanks to the central role of the Civil Service Department in terms of recruitment, training and staff relations, there is wide dissemination of ideas, insights, policies and fads throughout the vast network of organizations of all shapes, sizes and functions that make up Her Majesty's Civil Service. Second, accountability has a

*'quasi-autonomous national government organizations' — non-departmental public bodies with executive, advisory or adjudicative functions, e.g. a committee of outsiders which advises government department.

special importance and a fairly specific form in the Civil Service. Civil servants are in general accountable to Ministers and Ministers to Parliament; and the great diversity of 'personal' statutory responsibilities (e.g. as adjudicators or inspectors) does not undermine the overall effect of this particular form of public accountability. Within this accountability, civil servants and their organization are probably much more geared to caution and less to risk than is the case in other organizations large or small. Third, it may well be that management of words has an importance even in today's increasingly technological Civil Service which is almost unknown in other sectors – academic and educational ones apart.

This distinction between form and essence is an important one; but it is not a distinction between what matters and what does not. The form matters less than the essence; it still matters. Lovers of Ezekiel Chapter 37 will recall that before dry bones were brought to life they were clothed in sinews and flesh; the form an essential accompaniment to the essence. The accountability of Her Majesty's Civil Service to Her Majesty's ministers and through them to the Queen in Parliament is in a sense only one form of the accountability to which all managers are subject, but it has a considerable influence both on what we do and on how we do it. The businessman who seeks to use his business skills within the Civil Service and the civil servant who moves into business must both be wary of assuming that transplanting is all that is required. For example, the manager of a retail outlet may legitimately, if not honestly, sell only a new fashion line and persuade his customers and himself this is what they want. The Civil Service manager has no right and little opportunity to manipulate his 'market' in this way. Similarly, words are a matter of how something is presented; not of what it is. Yet words have considerable importance because words link the public whose Service it is with the Service; and there are no commercial limits to the need for good communication if you are the monopoly supplier of essential commodities.

MANAGERS AND OTHERS

This narrative has so far evaded the question of what management is – the insider's definition, as opposed (if opposition there be) to the editor's definition. Where, if anywhere, does management diverge from administration? Why are some civil servants well content to be called managers, while others insist that they are administrators, or, apparently at a further remove from management, policy makers? (The Fulton Report commented that 'administrators' preferred to look up with advice rather than down with guidance.) As this writer sees it, management is the art or science of getting things done (your particular things and the wider things of your particular organization) by identification, evaluation and then planned deployment and use of manpower and non-manpower resources. On the basis of this definition, the manager needs to know what his job is and what his resources are, to have in mind the constraints on both his scope for success and his choice of methods, and to be able/be allowed to plan and deploy. While reconciling demands and resources in order to attain objectives, the manager has to be ready to question and revise each and every one of these. It could be argued, plausibly, if not compellingly, that in ordinary unselfconscious usage 'management' tends to refer to the use of people and 'administration' to the use of paper. Since this distinction is not a rigid one, and since paper and people are hardly separable outside the realm of the archivists, I am inclined to argue that it is reasonable to ask the question how does administration differ from management, but that it is not necessary to answer the question.

With such a broad definition of management, very few civil servants are not managers, whether they recognize the fact or not. At the same time, many are managers by virtue of the calls they make on human and material resources which are not theirs in a 'line management' sense. They lay claim, for example, to typing and computing resources by virtue of the fact that the line manager of those resources has the supplying of their needs as part of his management remit. Traditionally, the support function has been undervalued. Line managers have tended to think that, given more hours in the day, they could arrange their own personnel and accommodation work quite as well as those who specialize in those areas. There may have been some element of self defence in the personnel or supplies manager who dons the cloak of professionalism – an attempt to show that he has specific skills which the 'amateurs' who try to pursue their own personnel policy lack. In a large organization, and most Civil Service 'units' are large, there is a point of balance – a point at which the wide skills of the line manager, including personnel insights, complement but do not conflict with the more specific skills of the personnel manager. There is, however, a more recent threat to the line manager, which could tend to devalue his generalist skills. This arises when support functions become primary functions – most obviously when supply of pencils and paper becomes supply of computer hardware and software. As cost and complexity and time scale increase, so the manager may find that he is no longer able to define the task and demand the tools. Those who understand the tools ask the manager to shape his requirements to what he can have, when he can have it. Fortunately for the manager, the broadening of management skills and the microchip revolution are combining to bring technological concepts and the technology itself back within (or at least more nearly within) his grasp.

As with other organizations, both the extent and the formality of management training have increased in recent years; and some senior positions are occupied by older men and women who have had little or no management training and little experience of personal responsibility for handling large blocks of work, and who see their role primarily as the exercise of the personal, intellectual, literary and political skills they have acquired in small, relatively unstructured units handling 'policy' work. Career development does something to blur those lines, but the system itself recognizes that some jobs require 'a manager' (this usually means a staff manager), while others require a person with different skills who will spend relatively little time telling others what to do and seeing that they do it although his influence on tasks to be done is considerable.

There is, of course, a danger of creating and subsequently reinforcing stereotypes. On the one hand, the manager may be seen as the unimaginative but resourceful person who successfully controls a large number of staff in the movement of substantial blocks of work along predetermined lines, and whose career progression is in terms of increasingly large units of command. On the other hand the 'policy man' may be seen as someone who enters the Service at a more senior level, and progresses more rapidly, and whose skill with ideas and political flair absolve him from the need to immerse himself in practicalities and operational matters. His are the loaves, the fishes and the belief that they will go round; others can resolve the details. There are those whose marked private virtues compensate for their relative dearth of managerial virtues; and, equally, there are those whose sense of direction falters when the guide book ends although they set a cracking pace while the route, albeit very uneven, is clearly marked. (In the matter of guide books, it should be said that such are best seen as providing suggestions as to what to look for, rather than instructions as to what to see.) An efficient organization does not depend on everyone being able (or wanting) to do everyone else's job. Teamwork means pooled talents not common talents. Where stereotypes are in line with reality and the reality is fairly static, all is well. What is not well is stereotyping running ahead of reality. Management types, like management styles, are best seen as an appropriate response to a specific need at a particular time. Outside these boundaries, they are helpful neither to the individual nor the organization.

A number of factors have converged to blur the sort of distinction sketched above. One is greater staff/union activity, as a permanent feature of the Civil Service scene – within and without the traditional Whitley machinery which brings staff and official sides together at national, departmental, regional, and local levels. Anyone who has staff, however few in number, now has to be aware both of the network of employment legislation which bears on his relations with those staff (as well as governing his Department's relations with its staff), and of the unions which keep a watchful eye on that legislation and on the much wider ranging house rules superimposed on it. Moreover, the union membership of his staff is less significant than the role of unions and staff side in his Department and in the Civil Service as a whole. Policy cannot be implemented without detailed consultation, and if it cannot be implemented there is little point in initiating it. A Headquarters unit has to think in terms of the staffing implications centrally, regionally, and locally, and of staff reactions. I say unto this man, go and do this; and he consults his local representative and they ask me why. This process is like a cold bath healthy, but initially disconcerting; and just occasionally fatal. It is required of a manager in these circumstances that he is circumspect and patient and realistic, not least because staff reactions to proposals and events will be influenced by wider current considerations such as pay and staffing levels quite as much as by the inherent merits or demerits of a particular management objective. There is even less sense in banging your head against a brick wall if the wall is built by another and can only be demolished by another. In the local resolution of national issues local Whitley Councils often have an important role, as the local manager has an important role within the Whitley machinery. Size and solidarity are important aspects of this.

As well as the realities of individual and collective man-management, the policy maker/manager has to contend with the rigidities of machines. Electronics have given him marvellous tools, but the tool is not simply mightier than the hand; it is different from it, and it is less adaptable. You can ask a colleague to do what he is doing in another way, or to do something else; and you can issue an instruction to lots of colleagues which, if acceptable, comes into effect immediately everyone has read it. A computer programme cannot be so easily changed; and some changes which staff could cope with, at a price, may require such substantial rewriting of computer programmes or additional hardware that they cannot be made at all. The civil servant whose tasks are of such a nature that a computer solution must be found may feel like the respiratory cripple whose breathing is done for him by an artificial ventilator – uncomfortably vulnerable because totally dependent; or the army commander who knows that highly mobile cavalry are no more, but whose big guns are all pointing in the same direction, which may be the wrong one. Microchips will shape the application of technology to new areas; they will be slow to replace main frame computers in the control of massive operations which would be impossible without the computery of the '60's and '70's developed into the '80's and '90's.

Finally, operations and policy merge the one with the other because policy making has become increasingly complex and interdependent. In part this is no more than a growing awareness, enhanced by statistical and economist expertise, of what has always been true. In part, the range of Government activity and the political pressure for complexity while demanding simplicity have turned those ever popular Civil Service chimeras, the repercussions, into very real animals which require expert handling. The simplest of social security benefits is likely to require 200 pages of instructions – involving a concentration of expertise as well as paper. (Those tempted to condemn the civil servant for his self-inflicted burden may care to ponder the difference between a flat-rate 10/- a week for all those reaching a certain age, and a benefit related to revalued earnings over a prescribed period, adjusted to take account of occupational pension scheme entitlement, increased to cover dependants, enhanced in respect of postponed retirement, reflecting residual rights from the schemes of earlier governments, possibly adjusted for the earnings record of the spouse. Soup kitchens are simple; modern benefits – private as well as state – are not. But nobody believes in soup kitchens any more, and it is pointless to lament a lost innocence which was deliberately abandoned.)

In his new world of unions and machines and repercussions which are 'for real', the Civil Servant sits with the doors and windows of his ivory tower fairly wide open. His constitutional accountability remains as it was, but much more than in the past he is required to explain himself to pressure groups (professional and incidental), to Parliament, to Government-sponsored bodies such as the Equal Opportunities Commission and the Parliamentary Commissioner, and, by no means least important, to individual members of the public. Letters which began 'Dear Sir, I am directed . . .' and finished, with more regard to resonance than to truth, 'I am, Sir, your humble and obedient servant', have been replaced by phone calls using Christian names. No longer remote, inaccessible, 'hid from our eyes', the wise ones of Whitehall at times feel like that proverbial man in the strange hotel who has lost his dressing gown and cannot find the bathroom – and his name is boldly printed on his pyjamas. Whether this makes him more or less like his counterpart in any commercial organization could be debated at length. More of those that customers meet across the commercial counter wear labels giving their names; and yet it often seems that with larger units and more remote senior management (at the apex of a complex structure that only the accountants and the tax man understand) the label wearer uses his label to set himself aside from the system, not to identify with it.

SKILLS: SINGLE AND GROUPED

It will already be clear that in a vast organization where the individual units are often large even at the level where a sense of belonging is possible, survival is itself a necessary skill, while something more positive and less self-centred than survival requires skills of the highest order. Skills can be brought together in a distinctive package which might be called a style of management. Style is a visible thing, and the stylist is recognizable by the way he marshals his skills. It may be in part unconscious – a matter of personality – but the trained manager will develop his style to a large extent quite deliberately. Some of the visible features are familiar: clear or cluttered desk, air of calm or excitement. Styles of Civil Service management vary from location to location, and from time to time. They also – which is a source of encouragement for the believer in the individual in a world of systems – vary from person to person. There is always a potential conflict between style, which implies discretion for the stylist, and organizational theories which emphasize the demands of the situation. The organizational emphasis is on three key features: trained management, accountable management and participative management. Those three imply a fourth, which at times has seemed to stand on its own but might equally be said to stem from the three: management by objectives.

Training helps the manager to see what he is doing, why he is doing it, and what effect it has. Once through the naming process, which tends at first to make the familiar look alien, the trained manager is in a position to carry on training himself – which is the end result of all good training – to work out his own solutions to his own problems with his own staff in his own office. The process of training is first one of eliciting questions; the answers come later. (There is nothing sadder than answers in search of questions – if the question comes first, there is hope; if the answers come first, there is indifference.)

Accountable management requires definition of task, disposal of resources, a time of reckoning, an instrument by which to measure achievement, and a person or persons to whom the reckoning can be rendered. It also requires others to be aware of and to respect that accountability, and to know how their accountability relates to management. Civil Service staff reports begin with a section which describes the job of the person being reported on, and which has to be agreed between the reporting officer and the individual. It is not unknown for there to be disagreement, and it is not unknown for the reporting officer to leave completion entirely to the person being reported on because he himself could not describe the job. There have even been instances where the reporting officer has completed this section without agreeing it with the person concerned. All these lapses – which are of course exceptions to the normal – make accountable management unreal, and evaluation like marking blank examination papers on an unknown subject. This is not to say that any job can be pre-described in every detail, and every aspect of performance precisely measured against a calibrated scale; it is to say that both fairness for the individual and efficiency for the system require a considerable measure of agreement in advance on what it is the manager is supposed to do.

The manager who is to define his task, marshal his resources, measure his own achievement, and render an account of his stewardship in due time, requires not only the technical understanding that training helps to give him, but also basic qualities of integrity, endurance and equability. He must be ready to identify what is important and discard what is not, and he must have that combination of modesty and confidence which enables him to see his own job in perspective but not undervalue it. It is not perhaps the most appealing of comments to suggest that civil servants need a sense of their own importance. But if they lack this, they will see no importance in their job and will correspondingly undervalue (or at least give poor value to) those whose servants they are.

Participation seems on the face of it the irreconcilable opposite of accountability; and it has seemed so to many of the managers faced by it. But, in Civil

Service terms at any rate, participation makes sense in a way that no other system does. For his local office staff side, the local office manager is, for many purposes, 'management'. The same manager may be active in the affairs of his own union, and pressing at regional or national level for a management-side response to his staff-side point of view. A Director of Establishments may well have come up through the ranks and served as a staff-side representative in his earlier days. Management is a function not a status in life; and participative management means that within a given unit a group of managers achieves greater involvement by collective discussion of individual responsibilities. It is not consensus management in the sense that nothing can be done without unanimity; that would indeed confuse accountability. When the accountable manager in a participative unit takes a decision, he does so in the knowledge that those affected have contributed their expertise and have the facts on which the decision is based and have shared in the conclusions drawn from those facts.

The word 'fads' was used earlier in this chapter, in connection with the dissemination of ideas (or something firmer than ideas) by the Civil Service Department. Management is not exempt from the vulnerability of all systems of thought and practice to the confusion of new insights and transitory fads. The management theorist discovers a new name for an old heresy, packages and markets it with enthusiasm, and is aided and abetted by the trainer. For a time Finkenstein's theory of critical intervention holds sway, and then the thorns and briars of the real world spring up and do a much needed choking job. It is the saving grace of management theories that if even their best practitioners cannot make them work they will not survive – management being an essentially practical task, the satisfactions of which lie in the end product rather than the process. Sometimes it is the emphasis rather than the whole theory that is wrong; so with management by objectives, the more useful (and more obvious) aspects have been retained, and the name itself is now relatively little used.

ESSENTIAL SKILLS

What then are the essential skills of the good Civil Service manager? The answer to that question will never be an entirely objective one. Management means linking your own personal resources to those that the job itself gives you, in order to achieve with others the objectives that your job and theirs are set. The significance of the personal dimension as well as the variety of jobs causes the variety of answers. The answer attempted here relates to a variety of jobs, and parts of it are more true for some jobs at some times than for other jobs at other times. As a highest common factor type of answer it is less likely to be uniquely true for the Civil Service.

There is an intervening question, what is a skill? It has already been suggested that management style is the application of a range of management skills. The package of skills that constitutes a style is shaped by personal qualities; indeed the stylist will deploy his skills in order to suit his personality to his situation. That deployment is itself skill as well as intuition. A skill has to be something that is capable of being taught and acquired, even if this is only possible where there are certain innate qualities already present. It must require a certain discipline, because, certainly for the apprentice, it is more than doing what comes naturally. From all this, it follows that some managers will be more skilled, in certain respects or generally, than others; and, equally, that any manager can reasonably hope to enhance his existing skills. Perhaps the difference between quality and skill is not in reality very great: qualities you have, skills you exercise. Basically then, a skill is the purposeful exercise of a particular quality appropriate to a given situation. Style is, as already noted, often highly visible – the empty desk or the empty room; skill may be like the wind, visible in the long term by its effects and not immediately by its essence.

First, the skill of *awareness* – or, in quality terms, sensitivity – of people and of circumstances. For most of us, this is a matter of discipline as well as instinct, and in more trying circumstances, of discipline rather than of instinct. In either case it requires listening and observing before answering and deciding. It is an uncomfortable posture because it will from time to time, or, in very difficult situations, for much of the time, mean uncertainty. The new unit manager who answers with ready made answers will make a more immediate impact, and he will feel himself less vulnerable (remonstrating with a tank is unattractive to many). He may even 'succeed', at least if the task in hand is a relatively simple one. Sensitivity, on the other hand, respects the established conventions of the job until they can be seen and be shown to be a hindrance rather than an asset; and it respects the other people involved in the job consistently and permanently, for so long as they stay involved. Awareness is a balancing skill, which enables the manager to maintain his poise because he is concerned about the poise of others and not just about the issues divorced from the people, and about the whole truth and not just certain aspects of it. There are parallels with Advanced Driving. Many drivers could achieve Advanced standards in a particular test; but to wear the triangle requires consistent maintenance of those high standards under all the stresses of everyday all-weather driving conditions.

Second, the skill of *flexibility*, underpinned by integrity. Civil servants tend to change jobs quite frequently. Sometimes the changes are dramatic in terms of subject matter, size of unit, lines of communication, range of contacts, and character of the objectives. The manager of a local office with 300 staff may become head of a policy section with three staff. The backroom planner may become a prime mover with outside industry. Flexibility is the essential companion of sensitivity. To be sensitive and inflexible is to listen to all questions and give the same answer to all questions. Procrustes carefully observed his guests, but then ruthlessly fitted them all to the same bed. The underpinning of integrity is necessary to the public servant, involving loyalty to himself and to the standards of behaviour required of the civil servant. It may be thought an old-fashioned virtue, but virtues do not become out-of-date as fashions do; and those who are most suspicious of echoes of Kipling and the playing fields of Eton would be most irate at a civil servant whose flexibility took him from the paths of virtue.

Third, the skill of *maintaining direction* with patient consistency. This runs with flexibility. If it does not, then the manager becomes a tacking boat which has lost its original course. In some circumstances, the direction will have been laid down by others and it will be clear to all whether the manager is going where he was meant to go. In other circumstances, this is not true. There may be political/policy objectives to achieve, but the development of an organization capable of meeting those objectives may be for the manager to determine – by discussion, consultation, persuasion and perseverance. Or, the broad policy objectives may have been determined, but the detail of the policy and the timetable for its implementation may be within the manager's control, to the extent that he has to develop a rational programme, sustain it against the powerful forces of irrationality (external and internal) and seek the approval of Ministers and, in support of Ministers, Parliament. Inherent in all this is the need to know and use the totality of the 'system': efficiency may require reorganization; effectiveness requires only use of the organization already to hand.

It must also be said that the civil servant can be very much involved in the creation from scratch of major policy which has to be followed through under successive Governments. Sometimes, with constitutional proprieties in mind, the civil servant's role is presented in purely responsive terms: the Minister saying what he wants to do, the civil servant telling him he can do it, and how much it will cost, and on occasions pointing out the objections. This is not entirely valid. It may be the civil servant who sees the policy need, identifies the policy options, and pinpoints the most appropriate policy choice, and who thereafter has to hold his torch aloft and get it to the Olympic stadium over many weary miles of wet and windy weather. The point in a democracy is not that this is to be avoided – that would be to waste the money spent on highly paid civil servants – but that it is only to happen if Ministers, and thence Parliament, have been persuaded by a full and fair deployment of the problem, the range of possible solutions, the wider implications, and the costs. Half-truths will not do. Once agreed, it is entirely legitimate for the civil servant to fight hard to ensure that later half-truths do not prevail. In the end, of course, the civil servant may have to accept and implement a policy decision with which he disagrees; and so he should, if it is not a moral issue which obliges him to resign. That is no excuse for giving up before the argument has been deployed; nothing could be more unfair to a busy Minister who has to take quick decisions on unfamiliar topics.

Fourth, the skill of *getting information and deploying it*. The Civil Service manager's operational aims are much like those of any manager – using minimum resources to maximum effect. Like any manager, he needs data about the work and personal knowledge of the staff. His ultimate objectives may well be different from those of many managers outside the public service. In general, he is not concerned with profit (though he is certainly concerned with cost). He has, in a crude but real sense, more masters than most managers: his Ministers; Parliament and individual MPs; those members of the public to whom he provides a benefit or service or from whom he requires a duty; the wider public who pay his salary; the interest groups, representative or otherwise, which seek to influence him or call him to account; the news media, etc. He needs to be well informed about his own subject matter; he may be the only person who is able to be well informed about it. He also needs to be well informed about what others are thinking and saying on his subject matter. Public opinion is a sea of silence with islands of noise: the noises may be contradictory, and they may or may not speak for the silence. It is not, incidentally, the civil servant's role simply to listen to 'public opinion'; he ought to seek to influence it by informing it. At times a shortage of relevant information may be the problem. More often, it is the selection of relevant facts from that great sea of facts in which there is more danger of drowning than of going thirsty. Information skills require, at the decision-making end of the process, a selection based exclusively on relevance; even if at the publicizing end of the process some selection is apparently based on convenience. (Integrity again.)

Fifth, the skill of *motivating* – of self and others. Nothing does more damage to the morale of a work unit than a manager who is bored with his job and makes no effort to hide the fact. Motivation is not necessarily going to come, consistently, from the work. For a lot of people much of their work for much of the time is going to be inherently uninteresting, and no amount of job enrichment will entirely prevent this. It is up to the manager to persuade them that it matters, because the people for whom it is done matter, and that they themselves matter. The manager's own job may be much more inherently interesting (as well as better paid) than those of his staff; as has been said in the context of absence attributed to sickness, it is with some jobs more surprising that people usually go to work than that they sometimes stay away. To be given a dull job, no clear indication of its purpose, no discretion in discharging it, no encouragement to believe that it matters, and no say in the running of the wider unit of which it is part, is the ultimate insult. He who sits on someone's face should not be surprised that eventually they stop breathing. Given managerial commitment and provided that the commitment carries with it sensitivity, flexibility and awareness, even those who do not share the distant vision may share the satisfaction of shorter-term progress towards it.

COAL FACES

These skills, and the need for them, are not peculiar to the Civil Service. Within the Civil Service, they are not peculiar to one group or function. They are basic skills on which the individual manager can build up his own individual job and from which he can evolve his own individual management style. One manager in his time, even the time-span of one job, plays many parts. The local office manager who on day one is contending with the domestic repercussions of a breakdown in the heating system, is on day two dealing with a Member of Parliament whose constituent has run foul of the system, and on day three representing the 'field' on a Headquarters Working Party.

The civil servant's business is the business of government, which means that its range is as wide as the needs of the population or the concerns of those who look after their affairs – needs and concerns which should, in a democracy, coincide. Civil servants manufacture, and advertise, and sell; they underpin our military preparedness, husband our forests, watch over our interests abroad, keep a watchful eye on the education of our children, concern themselves with those who are in our prisons and those who ought to be, plan for our financial and service needs from birth to death, and much else. Within any one Department, subject matter will be more narrowly (though still widely) defined; but functions can be almost infinitely varied within a single Department and can vary widely within a single command. The more senior the manager, the greater the element of choice among claims on his time; and the greater the responsibility for choosing in a way fair to his colleagues and his job, and not just fair to himself. Within the range of basic skills outlined above, the manager can both respond to the challenge of his job and shape the job itself – wherein lie some of the greatest satisfactions.

GETTING IN AND GETTING ON

For a large number of its male members, the administration group of the Civil Service (clerical, executive and administrative, to use an earlier terminology), as distinct from, for example, the scientific and professional Civil Service, is – war and other accidents apart – a lifetime career. They enter it when their formal education ends – at 'O' Level, 'A' Level or university level – and leave it when they reach age 60. The same is true for single or childless women; and married women with families may pursue an interrupted career. It is big enough and varied enough, geographically and otherwise, to provide a lifetime career to suit most needs. There are, of course, many exceptions to the whole-working-life pattern. The more junior the grade and the more youthful the civil servant, the greater the likelihood of early leaving; and at all stages there is some fall-out as people for personal, domestic, financial or career reasons look elsewhere. Late entry in the most junior grades is not uncommon; and there are attractions for a Department in a mature clerical recruit in terms of likely stability. Late entry in the higher grades, however, is very rare, and it tends to be opposed by the staff side because it reduces the promotion prospects of aspirants to those grades. Negligible numbers enter the administration group from outside the Civil Service at Principal level or above.

Clerical recruitment may, because of its scale, be delegated by the Civil Service Commission to individual Departments, subject to detailed guidelines and to final approval of candidates by the Commission. For executive officers and above, all recruitment is conducted by the Civil Service Commission, centrally in London or through regional centres. The emphasis is on freedom from political or other bias or influence, so that the right people with the right talents are selected to give efficient and impartial service to Her Majesty's ministers, and through them the public. If a Prime Minister's child, or indeed a Monarch's child, wanted to become an established civil servant, he would no doubt have certain advantages because of his upbringing and his awareness of current affairs, but he would have to go through the same selection process as anyone else, achieve the prescribed standard and, where there was competition for places, come sufficiently high in the merit list. He could well fail – certainly there is nothing at all in the system to guarantee his success. We tend to take this for granted – it is sufficiently unusual in the world to merit rather more attention. That the Civil Service Commission rather than the Civil Service Department is in charge ensures that, to some extent, the recruitment process is independent of the bureaucracy too. The value judgements involved in selection are at least tested and approved, and to some extent applied, by non-Civil Servants.

The selectors are looking for literacy, numeracy (to a lesser extent), basic intelligence, and a personality which will not conflict with Civil Service standards of behaviour or with the need to work as a team. Literacy, numeracy and intelligence may be vouched for by examination results, though for executive officers and above more is required. Personality is checked, as far as this is possible, by personal interview and by following up referees named by the applicant. There have been occasions when rapid expansion of vacancies or short-fall in applicants of precisely the level required has led to some relaxation of standards for the consideration of applicants. This has been accepted only with reluctance. Normal selection procedures and standards are not a guarantee of ideal results; but setting them aside certainly increases the risk of poor results, and mistakes which are discovered much later are hard or impossible to remedy. If it is true that the job creates the man, and that a person whose suitability is initially suspect may in the event become very good, it is also true that the man creates the job and that appointing the apparently unsuitable is therefore hazardous.

For aspirants to higher posts, for example those seeking entry through the administration trainee scheme – which is designed to enable the best graduate entrants to rise rapidly to top posts – the selection process is particularly thorough. Being particularly thorough, it well illustrates the basic principles, although it is *atypical*. The thoroughness of the administration trainee selection, training and career development process represents in a sense what the Civil Service would like to do for all its recruits in appropriate form if it could afford to. (It can afford *not* to, but only in so far as some of the gilt from the gold-plated scheme rubs off on other arrangements.) Superimposed on degree papers (and the requirement, for external candidates, of a good honours degree) are a written test of use of English, use of ideas, and use of data; group exercises designed to test ability to live with and contribute creatively and consistently to a group's attainment of its objectives; and a series of interviews. The interviewers are a psychologist, a current member of the Civil Service, and a chairman who may be a retired civil servant or someone from right outside the Civil Service. The interviewers already have a profile of the candidate, built up from his application form, his referees and his written work. They are looking for the candidate's ability to handle words and the ideas those words encapsulate, and for what the candidate says about himself, whether explicitly or implicitly.

Nobody pretends that an examination or interview of this sort (or the less intensive interviews required for other entry competitions) is a natural situation; but most situations that challenge people are not experienced as natural, and certainly they are not often freely chosen. The question is how well the candidate can use what he knows to complement what the interviewer seems to know, and how well he can match his personality with that of the interviewer, so that the two participants move more or less in step to a destination they are both content to arrive at. Intellectual fireworks are not the main requirement – fireworks tend to emphasize the surrounding darkness and are a spectator not a participative sport. Nor is verbal felicity enough, though it helps. The person who says nothing beautifully will get as much credit as the car salesman who so dwells on the high gloss paint that the customer begins to suspect the engine. It is a virtue of the three person interview team used in administration trainee recruitment that the need to bring together, from separate interviews, their separate impressions and judgements allows for the possibility of one of the interviewers being unduly influenced, for good or ill, by a personality or a foible or a single splendid remark.

Sensitivity, flexibility, maintenance of direction, deployment of information can be tested in interview and in group exercises, albeit fairly superficially. The skill of motivating others can be tested quite effectively in group work, where the opportunity is provided to be chairman on one occasion and member on another. Not the least testing aspect of the group work, although it is played down in the literature, is the fact that each participant is anxious to shine – or, to put it less kindly, to score points. The person who can keep a sense of proportion, and thereby occupy the driving seat when required without seeking to grab it when not required, deserves to succeed and is likely to succeed.

The administration trainee scheme, and the method of recruitment to it, have both been under attack, and there has been a good deal of study of them in Parliament, in Whitehall and in academic and other circles. Staff side are suspicious of a scheme that chooses 'special' people at a time when many able graduates are now recruited as executive officers and do not get such a ready chance to progress rapidly through a series of specially selected, predominantly Headquarters posts. (The opportunity to progress rapidly includes, it should be said, the opportunity not to sparkle under the bright lights, which in turn will mean a move from the special category into the ordinary category; and many do make this transition, most of them successfully.) Some politicians and others are suspicious of a system which, for all its apparently rigorous fairness, consistently recruits a substantial proportion of Oxford and Cambridge graduates, and ex-public school pupils; though it should be said that these critics do not allege political bias so much as educational and social bias. Whether the Oxbridge success owes more to traditions of applying for posts, to traditions of applying to Universities, or to a coincidence of particular educations and particular selection procedures, is, for the purposes of the discussion in this chapter, irrelevant. The criticism of bias is not mainly a criticism that the system fails to select the right people, but that the right people are the wrong people. The particular selection process is not, of course, designed to select *all* the right people. In fact it does not select most of them; and even at the very highest levels in the Civil Service it is evident that some of the best people had a much more ordinary start in their Civil Service careers.

More serious, because more relevant to this chapter, is the criticism, from within the Civil Service, that the Civil Service Selection Board procedure is better geared to picking the administrators of the past than the managers of the present and future. There are at least three good responses to this crticism. First, the selectors are well aware of the importance of resource management in the Civil Service and are under no illusions that 'resources' means only personal resources. Second, as already noted, very few people, compared even with the total number of graduate recruits each year, enter by this particular door. Third, given the success, testified to in the abstract by independent observers and in practice by the long-term results, in selecting people with the basic Civil Service skills, it is arguable that any subsequent shortcoming stems not from the selection process but from the training – including training by experience. What can be validly argued is that external graduate selection (and internal Civil Service candidates can also try this door – though they have not been as successful as had originally been hoped) should be as well matched as possible by career development for those who enter by a less special door.

Getting on in the Civil Service depends in some part on the jobs you do and the people you do them for – in other words, there is inevitably some element of luck or chance. Over time, it is improbable that luck or chance will run consistently either for or against you; and in the longer term the official system therefore tends to achieve the results it is intended to achieve, albeit the results are orientated to the good of the organization rather than to the good of the individual. Even in the shorter term there are, in fact, checks which modify any incipient unfairness. Career development is the responsibility of Establishment Sections which, however hesitatingly, stand a little aside from line management. Jobs are not allocated primarily with the interests of the civil servant in mind, but it is recognized that there tends to be good for the job in the job being good for the man. The Establishments Section is in a position to take account not only of the man and the job, but of the personalities and talents of those with whom the man will have to work. The civil servant unhappy with his job can go to his Personnel Officer – which, even if nothing else is achieved, ensures that there is an independent awareness of any management shortcomings, real or imagined. There is moreover a formal system of 'trawling' vacancies – which puts a range of jobs on offer and gives people the opportunity to make their own mistakes; and in many 'groups' there is an informal network of information about jobs and people which can be used to good effect by those with the energy and will.

The reporting system itself secures, in the short term as well as the long term, a balance of views. The annual written report has at least two, and sometimes three signatories: the reporting officer, the second signatory (*his* reporting officer), and the second signatory's reporting officer. The second signatory is required to say whether he agrees with the report, and, if he does not, to discuss it with the reporting officer. In the three years or so of a posting, there is the balance between those three signatories; the strong possibility that one at least of the three will change; and, more recently, the requirement that the person being reported on is to be told much of the report's contents on request. In the early years in a new grade, formal job appraisal interviews by the second signatory ensure that he is briefed on the officer and his job and that the officer in turn is told formally how he is doing. The Establishments Section checks that the report is properly completed and is not internally inconsistent; and it also looks for consistency with earlier reports. Any paper reporting system simplifies and may thus over-simplify; and it can only be as good as the people doing the reporting, and may not be as good as the people being reported on. (A bad report will tell you a lot about the person who wrote it and not much about the person it purports to describe.)

The annual report is not a substitute for day-to-day communication to staff of what they are supposed to do and how well they are doing it. But it focuses the less formal business of the reporting year. The current form requires the reporting officer to define the job, and to agree his description with the person being reported on – including the priorities within that job in terms of scale of values and, separately, time consumed; to evaluate job performance for each of the key elements in the job; to identify the extent to which the job requires various listed qualities and how far the officer provides them; to assess overall performance level and list training needs; and to look to the future in terms of promotability and/or the need for a change of job. There are remarks spaces to qualify the ordinal assessments, and space for a pen picture to balance the parts with the whole. The qualities section runs easily with the identified key skills, though the wording is different – picking up the symptoms rather more than the underlying condition. The new report form, to appear shortly, moves a little away from evaluation of each job element separately towards a general evaluation with comments on particularly strong, or weak, points.

Advancement is not determined by reports alone, though these are given considerable weight. From these reports are derived merit lists, lists for promotion boards, or schedules of promotable officers, according to the circumstances. This process brings to bear additional views – independent of line management and of Establishments – and collective views. Promotion boards set the experience of reporting officers over a period against the interview impression made on those who may be complete strangers. The Board look at the man aside from his job, and judge him as a person on his ability to handle data and ideas and people. Boards are, like the Civil Service Selection Board, three man boards (I use 'man' consistently in a sex-neutral sense), and the differences in experience and personality of three members bring a breadth to the interview even though all three are usually from the Department of the man being interviewed. The Boards have career details in front of them and have seen previous annual reports, and they tend to look closely at skill areas where there seems to be a weakness which casts doubt on promotability. The boarding session structure consists of a short initial warming up or cooling down period, to establish some measure of rapport and ease the nerves of Board and candidate; the main central section with a balance of questions which are job-related and questions which go much wider; and a final opportunity for the candidate to say those things he had hoped to be able to say but which have until that point gone unsaid. (He may of course also say those things that in retrospect he wishes he had left unsaid.)

Where there is no interview board and promotion depends on a paper board or on a sifting process based on panel judgements, the same principles apply. With panel sifting for very senior posts, the emphasis is on peer judgement, through the person's 'senior peers'; and the system has the advantage that those being sifted are known to those doing the sifting. This is the collective application of shared values, as an added element in a process which depends primarily on how the man is seen to have done a succession of jobs by the succession of people to whom he has been accountable. Throughout, the system maintains a juxtaposition of formal and informal expression of values, which allows for change but avoids perversity. In the same way, it helps to keep to the fore the need for a range of skills rather than the single solitary virtue.

9
Management in International Organizations

P. F. C. CASTLE

INTRODUCTION

The present chapter discusses the tasks and skills of management in international organizations of the United Nations family. There are many such organizations outside the UN, but the UN together with its specialized agencies, ILO, WHO, UNESCO, etc. is large enough and diverse enough to merit study on its own. The bare statistics give an idea of the populations we are discussing. The staffs comprise some 44 000 people, who include nationals of 150 countries, and who work in about 640 different places scattered around the globe. They are drawn from 300 or more different occupational groups, from which, we may note in passing, the profession of applied psychologist is almost totally absent. All these people are employed, not by national governments, but by the international organizations themselves. They are known as international civil servants. Their loyalty is to the international community, not to their own national government; at least that is the theory, the ideal on which the concept of an international civil service is based.

Published writing on the international civil service generally falls within one of two categories. Much consists of analysis, often of a legal or legalistic nature, of conditions of service, obligations, conduct, personnel policy, rules and regulations. Generally the word 'management' does not appear in these texts. The second type of writing is of a more popular kind. Essentially it deals with scandal, espionage, 'the merry-go-round of high salaries and allowances, abused immunities, incessant parties and earth-girdling trips' (Hazzard, 1973). This literature is much more fun, but is barely more helpful.

We can all regret that management in the international civil service has been so neglected. Many of us, especially those of the older generation, had pinned our hopes for a better world on a vision of a new world order founded on international organizations and based on international law. This dream has now faded. Yet the potential for international cooperation has never been greater, and this potential is necessarily based on the quality of the management conducting international affairs. There is no doubt, therefore, that the subject has a possible significance for us all and may even ultimately prove vital in determining the future of mankind.

TASK ANALYSIS

The manager's job

There is a great diversity of tasks carried out by managers in the international organizations. It may be useful first to divide these operations into two main categories. One of these consists of work in the large headquarters secretariats, situated in New York, Geneva, and certain capital cities of Western Europe and North America, as well as in a number of large regional offices mostly in the developing countries. The second comprises what used to be known as technical assistance and is now euphemistically referred to as technical co-operation: here the task of management is normally to direct a team of international 'experts' working in a given country helping the authorities of that country to develop their institutions, set up training schemes, build educational services and so on. For the purposes of this chapter, we shall limit ourselves to the first of these, namely headquarters work, not because it is any more important as quite evidently it is not, but essentially for the sake of restricting diversity.

As in any national organization, the management jobs in the secretariats are widely diversified. Clearly every managerial position is unique. Some of these jobs are very much like those found in a national context: the manager of a computer operation, a systems manager or a senior librarian, for example, performs much the same function wherever he works. Others are less comparable. Some of the jobs may be primarily technical, some financial, some political, some linguistic, some more purely managerial. Some of the jobs are essentially sedentary, backroom paper-pushing jobs, often of a regulatory nature, whereas others may be much more active, concerned with emergency operations or the relief of disaster in a distant country. In general one can say that most of them involve: directing work; ensuring compliance with directives received from the executive head or the governing organs; determining policies, or giving advice on policy to the executive head or the governing organs; representing the organization at meetings; and negotiating with governments, or with intergovernmental or other bodies.

One common element is no doubt getting the work done through people, though in many cases the manager, however senior he may be in the hierarchy up to and including the executive head, may in fact have to do the work himself. He cannot delegate it, even if he so wishes.

Another phenomenon often found is that of collegiate decision-making. Sometimes this occurs through formally constituted committees, sometimes not. The reason for this process is not necessarily that the manager is avoiding responsibility, since often for political or cultural reasons he needs to associate others with the decision. One result, however, is that seldom is any individual fully responsible for anything. Whatever the finished product may be, whether it is a written report, a plan for a project or the conduct of a meeting, there are generally half a dozen people who have shared some of the responsibility. If anything goes wrong, nobody is responsible for the blunder. Nobody can be blamed. Analysis of such mistakes thus rarely throws much light on the deficiencies of the managers implicated. Yet many of the individual grievances, complaints and faults undoubtedly stem from weaknesses in management, where the manager fails to play an adequate role. This is certainly a potential area for research, if the organizations ever wish to improve in a systematic way the quality of their management.

National cultures and subsystems

When considering the role of a manager in an international organization, one becomes immediately aware of the pervading problem of supervising staff of varied cultural origins and values. Again this problem is in no way particular to international organizations, and indeed in the most homogeneous national group there will always be substantial differences of this nature between one person and another. But no doubt there is an additional dimension to supervising a group comprising a Finn, a Greek, a Pole, a Swede, a Thai, a Turk and an Uruguayan, rather than a group of seven Englishmen, however disparate the latter may be. It is a common mistake to exaggerate the importance of these social and cultural factors. The international manager soon learns that each foreign person is an individual with a distinctive personality, whose uniqueness is not explained by stereotyped generalities about national character. Moreover the group of individuals supervised have in common the fact that they are all working as international civil servants, and, just as many other occupational groups may have their own characteristic values and habitual modes of thinking and behaving, so international civil servants soon tend to adopt such ways regardless of their personal origins.

Lists have been made of some of the many social and cultural factors which nevertheless affect management. One such list (ILO, 1966), which is too lengthy to be quoted here in detail, mentions, for example, varying attitudes to authority and responsibility, educational and intellectual traditions, status, concepts of justice, attitudes to work, to property, to women, to government, and so on. Certainly language, customs and attitudes can all give rise to obstacles to effective communication.

It is not only in supervising a multinational staff that difficulties arise. Less evidently they occur in the national sub-systems on which international organizations often draw. For example, the notion of a career service appears to be a Western or a Japanese concept not appreciated or understood by the Soviets; the notion of classification of positions, or rank-in-the-job rather than rank-in-the-man, appears to be a North American concept not appreciated or understood by the French; and there may even be a conflict between a career service and the classification of positions, as the two systems have different origins. Another example is the cabinet system (using the French pronunciation as in 'cabinet-de-toilette', not as in 'cabinet-maker') whereby the executive head is supported by a private staff of his own, who not only act as a filter between him and his managers, but who also watch over the implementation of the policies he has laid down. The cabinet system is essentially French and is often resented or misunderstood by those whose experience is Anglo-Saxon. These national subsystems are adapted by international organizations to their own needs, and are then adopted as their own. Often they complicate the task of the manager, who rarely recognizes them as the source of his problems. Another hidden influence is that of the informal organization. This is important in any organization, whether international or not, but in the international civil service, because of the common bonds of nationality, language and culture which hold together groups of individuals on the staff, it may assume an especial significance. Again this may complicate the task of the manager who may or may not be aware of the forces operating.

The executive head

In any large group the chief executive sets the tone and determines the direction which the organization will take. In the UN family this remains true in some respects but not in others. The limits to the power of the Secretary-General of the United Nations are self-evident: the Directors-General of the specialized agencies are subject to similar constraints.

The role of the executive head has been compared to the monarchies of 15th century Europe (Cox and Jacobson, 1973). The king is the central, most powerful figure, but his power has limits. He must retain support among the barons since, as they represent interests on which his own position depends, he has not the power to crush them. He can strengthen his position by enlarging his own court. Courtiers are dependent on him for favour, but he must always be watchful of courtly intrigue, of barons quarrelling amongst themselves and nourishing rival ambitions, but united in their loyalty if not to the king, then at least to the crown (i.e. the institution).

The executive head, if not actually crowned, is in this special position by virtue of the legal arrangements whereby he is responsible for the secretariat according to the 'constitution'. In practice he is forced to take the ultimate decision on all major issues. Staff regulations, which have the force of law because national laws do not apply to the staff, confer on him the power of decision on a whole range of questions, sometimes minor but sometimes affecting the vital interests of individuals. All appointments, for example, are his responsibility.

The executive head, therefore, whether he so wishes or not, imprints his style of management on the organization. The differences between Hammarskjöld and U Thant were well known. Similarly in the ILO, which in its early years was headed successively by Albert Thomas, a French socialist intellectual who centralized everything in his own hands; by Sir Harold Butler, a British civil servant who decentralized everything so that questions were referred up to him rather than coming down from him; by John Winant, an American who adopted a more personal type of administration than an institutional one; and then by Edward Phelan, an Irishman, an excellent diplomat, who never came to work before noon, when he promptly called a staff meeting until 2.00 or 2.30, thus making everyone a little late for lunch.

Managers lower in the hierarchy are thus necessarily affected by the management style of the current executive head. In the UN system where there are now a dozen or more executive heads, there are correspondingly an equal number of management styles, the task of the manager will vary accordingly.

SKILLS ANALYSIS

The criterion problem

As psychologists have so often found in other contexts, there exists no readily accessible criterion of skilled performance of managers in international organizations. In this respect, social and management skills differ from physical skills. In the latter the level of skill can be determined by reference to some objective standard which can be treated as fixed. For example the skilled operative may produce 1000 units a day, or the skilled golfer may do a round in 72.

In social and management skills however, the criteria are those of value, goodness, fittingness, qualities which have to be defined by reference to social conventions which may well be transient. The manager who is skilled in the eyes of one executive head may prove quite unable to function with another. The successful manager in one cultural setting may be less so in another. The individual who is skilled in participative decentralized management may be ineffective in an organization which stresses centralized controls. Alas, we shall never be able to say that the best managers are those who go round in under 72.

There is indeed no means of deciding objectively who the skilled managers are, because the criterion of skilled performance is a judgement of value. Perhaps this is why, in the international organizations, management selection has been unsystematic and management development programmes have rarely taken root. The selection of managers is generally based on little more than a superficial statement of duties and responsibilities, together with an arbitrary listing of qualifications required. All too often, therefore, an individual may be promoted to a management position because he has shown himself competent in a subordinate role: certainly this phenomenon is not unique to the international civil service.

Alternatively a manager may be selected from outside the organization. Here too the criterion for selection has generally been expertise in the technical field concerned, although on occasions the decision to recruit has simply been a response to ruthless pressures from governments or other interested groups. In such cases the ability to manage, whatever that may involve, is often a minor or negligible consideration.

The same kind of problems arise with management development. It is not possible to persuade managers to change their behaviour if you cannot agree in which direction you wish them to change. Of course it must be added that management development is concerned not only with the development of skills; it is conventional to express management objectives also in terms of knowledge required, of attitudes, as well as of performance and results. The manager in an international organization certainly requires knowledge in his technical area and he requires certain attitudes especially those reflecting freedom from prejudices. Objectives can be set concerning his performance, the results of which can be specified in terms of the output of his programme. All of this can be done, and is done.

Discrete skills

Although one of the characteristics of physical skills is that skilled behaviour 'cannot be analysed by separation into discrete units along either space or time axes' (Singleton, 1978), it appears nevertheless possible to differentiate various skills which constitute management.

One obvious example of this is language skills, for the manager who can speak fluently and understand the language of his subordinates is undoubtedly better placed in an international setting than his monolingual colleague. The language skills which are commonly found in international organizations are a source of constant wonder to those with schoolboy French, or the equivalent in other languages. Alas, the managers are often not those with the most developed skills.

Another discrete skill, the need for which pervades international work, is skill in communication, both written and oral. The main product of the UN family is paperwork, tons of it every day. The written word, if it is to be useful, has to be understood. Often the written word is a report of a meeting, where the spoken word is used. The manager is the more competent if he is skilled in both.

Social skills are desirable too, as in any supervisory position. The manager is more effective if he has learnt how to listen, to curb his tongue, to respect the feelings of others and to promote group cohesion. Often he needs an ability to negotiate with a view to reaching agreed solutions between apparently irreconcilable positions. In motivating subordinate staff he needs to be able to adopt their differing cultural values. Above all he needs to show a sense of humour, particularly difficult in an international organization the feelings of others, to promote group cohesion, to show a sense of humour, particularly difficult in an international organization where improbable misunderstandings are commonplace, where a joke in one language can be a disaster in another.

Another special skill which is particularly useful in an international organization is the ability to get support from higher up in the hierarchy of management. The skilled manager succeeds in provoking positive reactions from his superiors. He must therefore be free from any tendency to show excessive deference or anxiety in relationships with his own boss, and indeed he often has to exhibit genuine courage when dealing with individuals who, prior to becoming international civil servants, may well have been government ministers or other top people in their own countries and who all too often are treated with VSOV (a service abbreviation for 'Very Senior Officer Veneration', a well known phenomenon in the international civil service).

Undoubtedly certain work skills are also needed. In some jobs this skill may be essentially bureaucratic: an ability to operate in a bureaucratic setting, to plan the work, to manipulate the machine for the purposes of the programme or the organization. In other jobs the skill needed may be entrepreneurial: so in new fields of work, when new programmes are being developed and more is needed than simple empire-building.

Qualities required in a manager

The importance of effective leadership in the international civil service has never been underrated, particularly since in the 1920's Albert Thomas left his mark on the ILO as a man of action and courage. Writing in 1943 Jenks observed that qualities of leadership would determine the effectiveness of a future UNO: the desirable attributes were 'integrity, conviction, courage, imagination, drive, and technical grasp, in that order' (Jenks, 1943). A similar list was given by the International Civil Service Advisory Board in 1954: integrity, international outlook, independence, impartiality (ICSAB, 1954). More recently Hoggart (1978), analysing the qualities ideally needed by a Director-General of UNESCO, suggested three: great intellectual distinction, great diplomatic abilities and high competence in complex administration. Clearly all these attributes and qualities overlap with skills. Some may be learned, whereas others depend more on native abilities.

It is tempting in conclusion to try to identify some successful and some unsuccessful managers and then to compare their attributes. Alas the result is entirely predictable and totally unenlightening. We find first that we cannot get much agreement in identifying the superior and the ineffective managers, essentially because of the criterion problem discussed earlier. So all we can do is to give our own opinions. We find, if we agree with Jenks, that the better ones have integrity, show courage, hold an international outlook. No doubt they are highly intelligent and have verbal skills. They also have well-developed social and supervisory skills.

Beyond this there is little we can say. Independent research, free of cultural bias if that is possible, is urgently needed if management in the international civil service is to be improved. Let us hope that this book may provide the stimulus.

Note: The author expresses only personal views, not those of the International Labour Office or the United Nations.

References

Cox, R. W. and Jacobson, H. K. (1973). *The Anatomy of Influence.* (New Haven: Yale University Press)

Hazzard, S. (1973). *Defeat of an Ideal: the Self-Destruction of the UN.* (London: Macmillan)

Hoggart, R. (1978). *An Idea and its Servants: UNESCO from Within.* (London: Chatto and Windus)

International Civil Service Advisory Board (1954). *Report on Standards of Conduct in the International Civil Service.* (New York: United Nations)

International Labour Office (1966). *Social and Cultural Factors in Management Development.* (Geneva: ILO)

Jenks, C. W. (1943). Some Problems of an International Civil Service. *Public Admin. Rev.*, III(2)

Singleton, W. T. (1978) (ed.) *'The Analysis of Practical Skills'.* (Lancaster: MTP Press)

10
Production Management

P. MOORHOUSE

PREFACE

This chapter reports some empirical studies of the skills of managers associated with industrial production. Although modern industrial production comprises many facets, for example work measurement, production planning and quality control, Thurston (1963) identifies product/process design and material flow as the basic elements of any productive operation. These elements are reflected in the choice of data presented in the chapter which concerns three managers: two holding responsibilities for the process of material transformation at different levels of seniority and the third holding overall responsibility for product/process design. In each case there is a brief description of the job as a whole in which the main tasks are identified. One task in particular is then considered in some detail and this is followed by a discussion of the skills associated with the task. In order to provide a contextual background to the research findings, the introductory section considers the nature of production in general terms. This is followed by a section presenting a description of the research approach highlighting both theoretical and practical issues.

INTRODUCTION

It is possible to distinguish various types of production in industry. Drucker (1968), for example, identifies four main categories: unique product production, 'old style' mass production (where uniform products are produced), 'new style' mass production (where production is of uniform parts that are assembled into diversified products) and process production. The classifica tion relates to the degree of replication in product manufacture; at one extreme each product is different whilst at the other extreme all products are identical. It is difficult to provide examples of these categories in 'pure' form and most production operations lie somewhere between the two extremes. 'Batch production' is a term often used to describe product manufacture towards the unique end of the scale; 'mass production' refers to a repetitive output of similar products. One important feature associated with the type of production is the layout of the production facility and the degree of specialization in plant layout is the classificatory dimension used by Wild (1972). In the least specialized layout the product remains stationary forming the focal point of activity, whereas in the most specialized layout products move along a relatively inflexible path between fixed operations. Again it is unlikely that an organization would rely exclusively upon any one type of layout. Organizations heavily reliant upon mass production, for example, still have need to produce certain items such as tools and equipment in small quantities or batches.

Although there is a variation in type of production, each has a common objective, namely to increase material value through some conversion procedure. Typically, materials will pass through several stages of transformation eventually to become finished goods stock whereupon they will be allocated and despatched to customers. It is convenient to regard the productive operation as a 'system' and Berrien (1976) defines a 'system' in general terms as '. . . a set of components (also systems) interacting with each other, "enclosed" by a boundary which selects both kind and rate of flow of inputs and outputs to and from the system' (p. 43). The boundaries of the system will be determined by the objectives of the system which may be (arbitrarily) assigned by an observer. Following the distinction made by Singleton (1974) that all systems comprise a control part, dealing essentially with information, and an operating part, dealing essentially with power and physical entities, it is possible to represent a production system in very general terms as in Figure 10.1. The objectives of the operating part of the system are to convert the various inputs into products through man–machine operating procedures. However, there is a need for control in order to ensure that the conversion activities satisfactorily attain the overall requirement. At a corporate level this control is the responsibility of management. The production system is itself part of the wider business system. This comprises a range of subsystems, each contributing towards the overall business goals. The importance and size of each subsystem will vary according to the nature and size of the organization, but some important subsystems with a very generalized statement of their functions are shown in Figure 10.2.

Each subsystem will include its own management team, the whole management hierarchy usually being depicted by an organizational 'tree structure' where the horizontal distinction denotes specialism and the level of responsibility/authority is represented vertically. The tree structure associated with

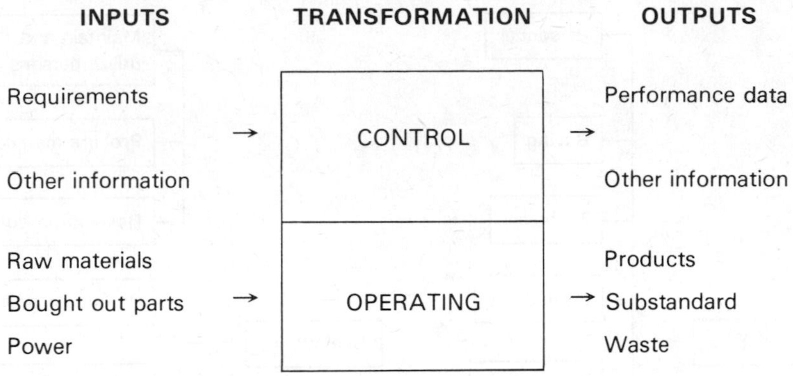

Figure 10.1 Block diagram depicting production system (after Singleton, 1974)

production might typically have a production director at the apex with other hierarchical levels comprising, in diminishing levels of responsibility; works managers, production managers, and departmental managers. However, tree structures are of limited value in representing organizational functioning because there is little recognition of both the formal and informal information flow across specialism boundaries. Competent managers will obtain information from whatever sources may improve the quality of decision making, thus minimizing the difficulties at interfaces between subsystems.

In any 'sociotechnical' system the human participant remains the key to the functioning of the system because he has the responbility for attaining whatever purpose stimulated the system design and because of his adaptability to internal and external unpredictability (Singleton, 1974). Since the manager holds responsibility for the production system (or some inherent subsystem) he clearly has a central role. His function is essentially to facilitate the efficient flow of material through the conversion process. An important related management function is product and process design/development. This involves setting up the production system and is usually the responsibility of technical/research and development personnel. The responsibilities of production managers are more often associated with on-line system control, but the setting-up function is included here in order to provide a wider perspective.

The specific tasks of managers will be dependent upon the demands created by the nature of the production system and parent system. Hence managerial problem-solving and decision-making are context specific. In contrast, when considering skills rather than tasks, the supposition is that there will be skills relatively independent of context. This is because, by definition, skills are more general than tasks and it is further assumed that, notwithstanding the great variety of skills, there will be some fundamental skills associated with the tasks of management. The objective of this research was to make a modest contribution towards understanding such skills.

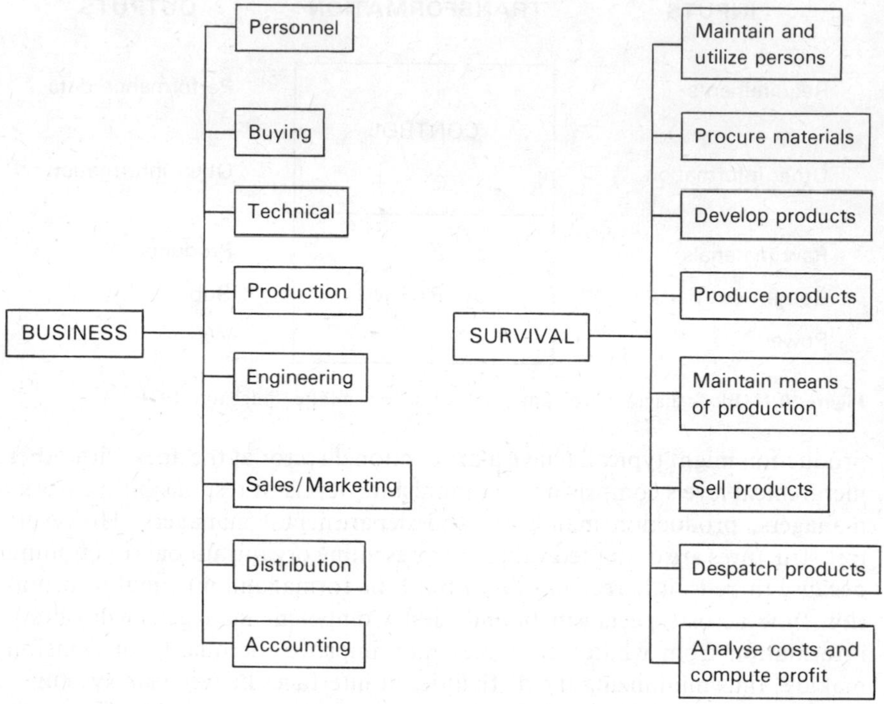

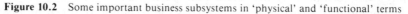

Figure 10.2 Some important business subsystems in 'physical' and 'functional' terms

THE RESEARCH APPROACH

Theoretical considerations

'Management' as an activity is often popularly defined as 'getting things done through other people'. As Glover (1977) remarks, another potentially popular definition might be that management is 'what managers do', which is sufficiently expansive to include work irrespective of whether or not it is done through (or in spite of) other people. Having thus passed the conceptual buck, the problem now becomes one of defining the nature of managerial activity. Although much has been published on this subject, authors continue to express the view that too little is known. A somewhat idealistic section of literature inculcates an uncritical acceptance of the nature of managerial work, and as something of a reaction against this there are more research-oriented writings dating back to the 1950's. In the more empirical literature, a major concern has been to measure time-sharing amongst various categories. The categories employed have involved a number of perspectives at various levels of description (such as reading, writing etc., planning, coordinating etc., personnel, sales, etc., etc.) but generally they remain open to criticisms of unreliability and ambiguity. In addition the basic unit of measure has often been the 'episode' (some incident terminated by a change in one or more of the categories of interest to the researcher) and this has enabled only limited meaning to be given to managerial activity since it has been difficult to identify explicit relationships between episodes and objectives. Finally as Glover (1977) points out (in an excellent but so far as I know unpublished review) the emphasis has been much more upon work relationships than upon a comprehensive description of the output of managerial work.

The view adopted here is that it is useful to begin with the responsibilities held by the manager and that these may be described in functional terms, that is with regard to their purposes. Some examples might be 'to determine a pricing policy', 'to set a business strategy', 'to maintain and control a works agreement' and so on. As a result of holding these responsibilities, managers engage in activities geared to achieve the desired ends which will include, for example, dealing with people, writing reports, etc., but, important though these activities are, they rarely provide the rationale for the existence of the job; they are the means to certain ends. Since it is possible to describe behaviour with varying degrees of specificity, from the molar to the molecular, managerial work and tasks may be represented hierarchically and concomitantly, and so may managerial skills. In general terms, higher level skills will be supported by 'means-type' skills, that is skills underlying interpersonal interaction, written communications and so on. It is possible that a manager may hold a high degree of competence in means-type skills and yet fail to achieve the output requirements of his job simply because the necessary *gestalt* is missing. The overall objectives that the manager is trying to attain may well be established by others at higher levels in the organization, but the formulation of sub-objectives or the steps to be made towards attaining objectives will be dependent upon the skills of the individual manager. Similarly the manner in which the manager makes progress towards his objectives will reflect his skills and, finally, skills will be evident in the way in which the most feasible decisions are implemented.

One crude classification of skills is in terms of dominant function within stages of information processing and hence skills are said to be of an input, output or cognitive nature (Singleton, 1978). Accordingly, managerial skills are essentially cognitive, that is intellectual functioning or 'thinking' is the key feature around which the other skill components are structured. Bartlett (1958) characterized thinking as a process not of recalling or perceiving something that already existed, but rather of using information about something present to get somewhere else. Thinking is about filling transitionary gaps in evidence to make progress towards some terminal goal, and in this context it is useful to regard the skilled operator as a 'model builder'. Models are inner representations of the outside world that might be manipulated to predict the results of certain decisions and thus influence the making of these decisions (Singleton, 1967) and on the assumption that the manager does construct inner models the skills might be focused as: 'What kind of model does the manager hold and manipulate?'. An important parameter in model building is that of learning, and this is the process through which skills are acquired. Differences in skill between individuals or over time for one individual stem from differential prior experiences.

Practical considerations

It seems clear from the previous volumes of *Real Skills* that an analysis of skills might be conducted via discussion between the analyst and practitioner. The principal sources of evidence are the performance of the practitioner and his thoughts on what he is doing and how he is doing it. Unless the analyst is very familiar with the job in question it is necessary first of all to find out what the manager is trying to achieve, that is the objectives that he holds. This means conducting a task analysis to separate and describe the main tasks within the job. As the best qualified to describe the job, the manager himself can impose the overall structure. It is possible to move to more general levels of description through asking 'Why?' type questions and the analysis can become more detailed by posing 'What?' type questions. Having identified the range of tasks, one or more can then be selected for more detailed analysis with the aim of discovering precisely what the manager does. This involves a progressive clarification of the goals that the manager is trying to attain and inevitably it seems that there is a key decision that is the hallmark of the task. Although the discussion may become detailed, the task – that is *what* the manager does – is still of prime concern and at some stage it becomes necessary to make that transition into the skills domain to say something as to *how* the manager is accomplishing his objectives.

The data reported in this chapter were obtained primarily through tape recorded interviews structured around the ideas already mentioned. The findings are part of a wider study that was undertaken with the objective of contributing towards better understanding of skills to assist in management development activities. In addition to the more formal interviews, some participants were observed at work and there was considerable informal discussion concerning the aims and content of the study. The data are a revision of an earlier account that was presented to each manager for additional comment. The description is somewhat abbreviated and is of a general nature to protect the anonymity of the participants.

THE PRODUCTION DIRECTOR

Job overview

The Production Director has held his post for about eighteen months following a reorganization of the business. He reports to a General Manager and is ultimately responsible for about eleven hundred employees in several factories. He distinguished two broad classes of decisions in his job, namely decisions with shorter and longer term impact, although it was clear that the boundary between the classes often became blurred. For those decisions concerned primarily with the future, the manager is closely linked with senior colleagues in contributing to a group decision process with the aim of setting a corporate strategy which will influence and be influenced by production factors. The task is to plot an optimal path through a decision tree where nodes include technology specification, equipment options, choices in operating methods and support systems. It is also necessary to determine the personnel requirement and the timing and locaton of the production facility. There are many factors to take into account such as costs, efficiencies, legislative changes and so on.

As for decision-making with a relatively shorter term impact, two responsibilities predominate – what the manager termed 'making enough' and 'making it at the right cost'. In order to meet the sufficiency requirement it is necessary to ensure that there is the available capacity to satisfy the market demand. The orthodox view of production is that factory capacity (plant and people) is laid down to meet the forecast sales levels. If it transpires that the actual sales levels temporarily exceed planned levels, overtime working is the likely option, whereas if the increased requirement is permanent, consideration is given to securing additional production facilities. Should actual sales fall below expectations there is a situation of excess capacity and the tendency is for acceptable cost levels to come under threat. In practice, the task becomes one of planning the utilization of equipment and people which is made more complicated by a number of factors including temporal variation in product demand. What tends to happen is that resources are geared to specific commitments and allowances are made for the remainder. A basic plan is set annually and is regularly updated according to specific circumstances. Although the manager retains the ultimate responsibility for the task his level of involvement will vary. For example there will be a high level of participation in the installation of a new piece of equipment to manufacture a new product, whereas minor product alterations will not be of undue concern. However, it is the case that, on a day-to-day basis, volume problems caused by 'industrial relations' issues, process difficulties and so on will remain of major importance in the job.

Whilst there are other important responsibilities (notably to ensure that there is compliance with Health and Safety legislative requirements) the second of the manager's more immediate responsibilities, namely the financial control of the factory operation, will now be considered.

Task description

The production operation was expected to make a positive contribution towards profit through judicious cost control. On the assumption that selling prices remain constant in the short term, profit is dependent upon levels of production volume and costs. It has already been noted that production volume is a major concern for the manager and so is cost control. His task is to recover actual costs despite variation in volume and there is an additional aim that the factory should become increasingly more efficient. 'Recovery' may be construed as the piece-rate through which costs are refunded from the standard system which will determine standard (or allowable) direct labour, material and overhead costs for a unit of production. The difference between the actual costs and the standard costs that should be incurred are termed 'variances'. To improve standards and increase efficiency, the manager holds an objective to meet a positive target for total factory variance (against standard costs). This gross target is divided into individual factory targets and subsequently into departmental targets (whereupon this manager's involvement ceases, otherwise the detail would become overwhelming). Targets may be altered.

The prime source of information concerning factory variances is the monthly operating report which provides a detailed analysis by factory and department in terms of materials, waste and substandard, labour and variable overheads. However, this is not the only information source. A weekly report comprising less detail is also received and in the event of a marked change in the ongoing operation the manager would expect to be informed immediately and cost effects would be quickly, albeit crudely, calculated.

The overall task comprises a number of components. Firstly, although the factory variances presented in the operating report inform over the profit/loss situation, the manager must decide upon the validity of figures. This means interpreting the figures against a personal knowledge of actual production events and descriptively this shades into the manager's skill. Having understood the variance position, the manager must make a decision over its acceptability. *Ceteris paribus*, criteria of acceptability concern the overall planned variance target, individual factory targets and standard costs (for if the manager is satisfied that production performance is optimal, perhaps the standards will need amending). Should the variance position be unacceptable it will be necessary to initiate a programme of improvement. This will mean either changing the system in some way because of inadequacies or ensuring that the existing system functions properly in the future. Any programme that is implemented will, of course, be monitored.

Skills analysis

On the basis of the preceding analysis it may be possible to define a skilful manager as one who, through his understanding of the production operation and its representation in financial terms, is able to phase his actions to deal with the precipitating situation such that he will move ever nearer to his ultimate objective of increased efficiency. However, it is difficult to provide a firm criterion of skilful performance (c.f. Drasdo (1979), for example, assessing skill in a different context). The mere use of 'increased efficiency' as a yardstick fails to account for the interaction between the practitioner and the prevailing 'states of nature'. In general, whether or not task objectives are attained is a function of managers' skills and the external environment. In order to overcome this difficulty it becomes advantageous to consider performance over an extensive time scale where, it might be supposed, the interaction effects would iron themselves out. Any management assessment will take account of both the longer term and the strength of the prevailing situation.

Returning now to this particular manager, it is worth remarking that the relationship between the manager and the information sources is a dynamic and reciprocal process. As a result of initiating action the manager will look for cost effects, which will, in turn, guide him in his actions. Hence the cost information provides both feedback and a stimulus to action. Whilst compiling and interpreting the cost figures may be regarded as 'keeping the score' rather than 'playing the game', it is important to note that the manager is not merely a scorer; he reacts to the situation that the figures represent.

Developing expectations

In order to make sense of incoming data, there must be some pre-existing model to which the information can relate. Firstly, the manager must have an understanding of the costing system to enable some fundamental meaning to be attached to the cost information. He appears to hold some body of knowledge that is organized in accordance with the rules of the knowledge domain, namely cost accounting. Secondly, a more complicated model concerns the reality of the production operation. A process of cross reference between the two allows the manager to switch between them, relating changes in the production operation to changes in costs.

The understanding of events crystallizes in some expected value so that, broadly speaking, the manager knows the nature of the cost information that he will receive. He holds expectations for all departments along each cost dimension and there are a number of factors contributing to expectations. Firstly, since annual targets for savings against standard costs have already been established, the manager can anticipate a proportionate amount relative to the year to date. Secondly, there are a number of non-financial information sources (e.g. output levels, waste levels, etc.) that will contribute to an expectation in cash terms. If, for example, a particular department was short of volume because of diminished market demand, the manager would expect this to show in the figures. Thirdly, there is a whole range of miscellaneous factors that seem important, for instance a strike situation or, more subtly, certain costs (such as heating or lighting) that are not adjusted seasonally but which nonetheless vary with ambient temperature so that allowances ought to be made for this. Hence it might be postulated that the manager holds some hybrid model (partly pictorial, partly symbolic), structured around the key features of the situation facing him. In short, the cost information is being read against a fairly detailed knowledge of what is actually occurring within the production departments. Since the competent manager knows what is happening his working knowledge enables him to discern the unexpected signal from the data he receives. If, for example, there was a certain percentage shortfall in volume he would know the kind of impact this would have upon the financial data and if the figures appeared out of sorts it would be spotted quickly. The manager is freed, therefore, from routine analysis and attention may be directed to those problem areas that have not conformed to expectation and need further investigation. It would seem that there are probably three types of decision – at one extreme the expectation and inputs coincide whilst at the other there is such a wide discrepancy between the two that the manager knows that it must be inaccurate. Between the extremes there is incomplete understanding, when the information does not conform to expectation, and the problem is to find out why. This would invoke some analytical process, beginning with the unexpected evidence and guided by the need for a terminal solution through a series of interconnected steps. This may require a search through existing records, discussing the matter with others or observing machine performance with its operator. It is worth remarking that if there was a large unexpected gain that could not be quickly substantiated, the manager would ask for its suspension but, on the other hand, an unexpected loss would always be recognized.

In order to avoid any erroneous expectation the competent manager will try to keep his model up to date. This means ensuring that relevant information is continually received. There is, of course, a time lag between production and receipt of the monthly report – indeed the weekly report is received some days after the week ending – and as a result, in order to keep up to date the manager ensures that he talks with his subordinates continually. Having understood a variance figure (whether or not it conforms to expectation) the manager then determines whether or not the figure is acceptable. In this context 'unacceptable' would mean that there is room for improvement, reflecting a value judgement that the manager makes. It is possible to indicate several factors influencing the decision and these will now be discussed.

Exercising judgement

The manager holds a firm objective, the plan target, and, if this is not being attained, action is required. Moving down from the aggregate position, a variance that does not jeopardize the aggregate target but nonetheless falls short of expected recovery may be construed as unacceptable; it all depends upon the nature of the discrepancy. Firstly, if too great a sum is being incurred in the materials cost of a product, this is unacceptable. Materials, waste and substandard aggregate to provide the materials cost of any good product. The highest net yield is required from raw materials and if one product cannot be made without incurring a loss in material costs, making more only exacerbates the situation. Secondly, whilst negative labour and variable overhead variances are partially related to waste, they are primarily volume related. Thus, for example, if money is being lost simply because people are short of work, an increase in sales will improve the situation. Where production volume is the problem a number of issues relate to the making of a decision, and once more the manager appears to hold a classification scheme.

Between the extremes where a situation is either obviously acceptable or unacceptable, there is a range of situations requiring a more subtle assessment where nothing may be done because the manager may elect to wait and see what happens or because in trying to maximize his pay-offs, reacting to one figure will seem less important than reacting to another. With the passage of time, and, perhaps, the emergence of additional evidence, there is a stage when it is felt that something ought to be done. At this stage there are additional parameters to consider; essentially the issue concerns the possibilities that might be accomplished.

An important issue relates to seeing each individual department against the background of the whole operation. Through holding the overall picture the decision to act is a balanced judgement that might be made inter-departmentally or intra-departmentally (along cost dimensions). For example, consider the latter method, where it is the case that material costs are rapidly escalating. Each unit amount of materials that may be recovered is worth increasingly more and a decision has to be taken to 'overspend' on labour to recover 'scrap' products because of the cost benefits. Turning now to the consideration of one department against another, the manager is out to maximize his gain and the actual decision hinges on the comparison of relationships linking estimated probabilities with anticipated outcomes. Whatever has created the variance figure will influence the assessment of likelihood; i.e. if the manager understands why a particular variance has arisen he will try and gauge whether or not any remedial action will be easily implemented. The decision is further influenced by a time factor and the manager may find himself in the difficult position where not to act may incur short term costs but acting may jeopardize a long term gain.

Summary of skills of the Production Director

The hallmark of this kind of skill is that the manager is very clear about his objectives and the criteria that inform over their attainment. These vary from the shorter to the longer term and comprise a whole series of feedback mechanisms. The manager holds a model relating to the costing system that allows 'immediate' meaning to be given to cost data, and a further model concerning the production operation. The latter appears complex, representing the key features of the production operation. How the financial data will be affected by manipulation of the production operation is also understood.

When the cost data is received it is compared with expected values. At one extreme, data and expectation match whilst at the other extreme the mismatch is so great that the manager recognizes there must be an error in the paperwork. Between these extremes the reason for any discrepancy has to be determined. If the accounts are in order so that the manager is not chasing myths, attention will be directed to the factory to determine the anomaly. Once the variance is understood there is a further decision over its acceptability. Although there is a firm overall target, particular circumstances provide a series of moving targets. Again the manager classifies the situation he faces; on the one hand there is a clear indication to act, while on the other hand the manager may be satisfied that costs are as low as possible. Additional parameters are relevant between the two extremes. Since there is some flexibility as to how the aggregate target might be attained, there is an opportunity to balance different factors and reaching a decision seems close to a process of comparing anticipated likelihood and utility combinations, although assigning probabilities may not be easy.

THE DEPARTMENTAL MANAGER

Job overview

The Departmental Manager has the responsibility for the operation of a department within the production function; he reports to the production manager. Before taking up his current level of responsibilities he was a departmental supervisor. His prime job objective may be simply put, namely to participate in ensuring that the required production output is attained each week. In order to meet this objective several major duties were identified. The first is that of resolving 'low key' industrial relations issues, primarily through relatively informal discussion with union representatives. Secondly, the manager must liaise with technical/maintenance personnel, partly because of problems that have occurred (e.g. quality problems) and partly in order to accommodate project work or maintenance work that technical or engineering departments may wish to implement. The third major duty is to ensure that the department is kept in a tidy condition and does not contravene Health and Safety regulations. The manager will also try to resolve issues that erode employee morale and he will generally seek to enhance performance. Finally there is a whole miscellany of more minor duties, for example resolving wage queries, taking responsibility for the fire register, visiting suppliers and so on. However, attention will now turn to a main objective that was considered in some detail, namely the deployment of available resources to maintain the flow of work through the department.

Task description

The manager must ensure that there is sufficient work to keep each section throughout the department operating effectively. Putting this another way, decisions must be made to facilitate an adequate flow of work through the department by means of the appropriate deployment of resources. By way of background information, the production system is one of flow production where similar products are machined and assembled in a prescribed order. There are a number of stages each comprising a particular working cycle, with operations at each being conducted on a piecework basis mostly demanding specialist skills.

If there are no machine breakdowns, absenteeism, raw material supply problems, etc. then the feeling is that the inherent logic of the production process and the adaptability of the human operators would produce the required output. The manager must, however, resolve those problems that disrupt the ordinary functioning of the process. The stimuli that provoke the manager's response predominantly concern operator absenteeism, machine breakdowns (and rare instances where a machine may be out of commission for a few days), and other situations where there are inadequate stocks for some section (because, for instance, operations have exceeded the usual time cycle or certain of the work has been defective through human, machine or material faults). When faced with such problems the manager must determine what to do in order to ensure that the output requirements are met as well as possible and this is dependent upon his skill. The deployment of labour is considerably enhanced through the availability of 'multiskilled' operators who can perform any job in the factory operation and remain permanently on call, and 'utility' operators who have developed the necessary skills to work in more than one section.

In general terms, therefore, this manager is at the 'sharp end' of the production operation, controlling the flow of work through the department and ensuring that there is sufficient work to meet the demands of each section in producing the requisite output through deploying the available resources – particularly people – that are at his disposal. He is the key adaptive element in the system ensuring that it functions effectively through his intervention in resolving difficulties.

Skills analysis

The manager's basic objective is to deploy his resources in a manner that enables the system to continue functioning in the face of unexpected events;

the nature of the internal mental operations that appear to be a necessary concomitant for competent performance will be considered.

Understanding the departmental operation

As a basis for any deployment of resources the manager must understand the nature of the departmental operation. Firstly it is necessary to know the production target which is broken down into a daily requirement – hence the overall objectives are represented symbolically. Secondly the work in process stocks that should be maintained at each section must be known. The manager also knows the machines that will need to be operated and the numbers of operatives (at standard performance) that are required to run the machines in order to maintain the necessary stock levels. Finally there is understanding of how the production system functions in real time, that is how long it takes for products to be processed at different stages throughout the system. As a result the manager is able to predict the consequences of particular events. To take a simple illustration, the manager knows that, as 24 hours must elapse between operations at one particular stage and those of the next stage, any work produced in the former section on any one day will not be ready for further processing until the next day. This situation is reflected throughout the production process so that it is not possible to increase output in any one section without increasing output in previous sections. In sum, the manager holds a model organized in a manner consistent with the external operation of the production process. The solution to any problem concerning the disruption of work flow is intimately bound up with this knowledge.

Problem-solving

If the manager is faced with a problem that calls for his intervention he will seek to restore equilibrium to the operation of the departmental system. One of the most persistent problems is that of absenteeism and the manager must offset the reduction in personnel in order to maintain the output requirement. His overall approach might be summed up as 'looking before leaping', not merely to find people to fill vacant spaces on the production line, but rather to establish the best way of meeting the required output. The competent manager will consider any problem in the context of the entire departmental operation, taking a broad rather than a narrow view of the issue. Within this framework it is then a matter of looking for suitable solutions to the problem. There are a number of options such as moving people between sections, utilizing multiskilled labour, persuading people to work overtime, etc. and the manager must determine a course of action dependent upon the consequences of that action. In this context it seems appropriate to say that the manager holds a number of precepts or 'rules of thumb'. He is not operating upon the world directly at this stage, but upon a collection of notions he holds about the problem facing him. Each problem that the manager faces will vary in detail concerning numbers of persons, sections, shifts, current pressures, etc. and so the following examples are necessarily simplifications.

Taking an extreme example, if there was an absentee in the 'milling and mixing' section where there are only three people working ordinary daytime hours, the manager would, virtually without hesitation, call in a multiskilled operator because the output loss would be felt all the way along the line. In this case the manager is very limited in what he might do. In the case of the assembly section, no specialist skills are required and virtually any non-handicapped person could be employed in the work, thus there is less of a constraint upon a solution and the rule of thumb is to utilize any likely individual. For other sections the manager would adjudge whether or not there would be fairly normal functioning despite the absenteeism. He knows, for example, that other operatives could compensate through higher performances and this approach could be tried while the manager closely monitors output levels. If stock levels are low – the manager knows what this means – the options would be to deploy utility operators, that is those operators with the necessary skills in another section, and to instigate overtime working. Hence the manager appears to run through the available options that have been learned through experience, almost checking them off along a path of least resistance.

Decision implementation

Having devised a proposal, the requirement is then that it should be implemented. Since any decision is implemented through the efforts of other people, the manager will take into account the likely reactions of his subordinates to that decision. The situation may be regarded as one of salesmanship, where the manager has to 'sell' his decision to individuals who may turn out to be less than sympathetic. Like any good salesman the manager will want to understand the needs of the 'customer' and he must be open to developing his model through internalizing those held by other individuals. Subsequently, the process will be reversed as the manager seeks to influence the same individuals through mapping his model onto their representations of events. In this context it will be an advantage to 'know' the individuals concerned since this will facilitate predicting their responses and this kind of knowledge is acquired by experience. In actually dealing with the people concerned the domain is that of interpersonal skills, the meeting of two adaptive systems, a situation of mutual construing. The 'lower level' skills involved will concern face to face communication, selecting the appropriate behaviour, listening, questioning, proposing, etc. consistent with the overall purpose.

Summary of skills of the Departmental Manager

In exercising his skill the manager is clear about his objective, namely to meet the production target, and he receives prompt and efficient feedback as to whether or not the objectives are being attained from the actual output levels. Indeed information concerning stock levels is of prime importance and this is part of a more complete model organized in a manner consistent with the departmental operation. In response to problem situations, the manager takes account of broad constraints by viewing the problem in its wider context and appears to follow certain rules of thumb in devising a course of action. Finally, the implementation of any decision will depend upon interpersonal skills, the overall strategy being one of persuading, with lower level skills focusing upon the adaptive situation of face-to-face communication.

THE TECHNICAL DIRECTOR

Job overview

The Technical Director is responsible for research and development work with a staff of forty or so people in total. He reports to the General Manager and is a member of the management committee with corporate responsibility for running the business. He has held this post for about eight years, having joined the Company some thirty years ago when the commercial application of the fundamental technology supporting the business was at its inception. The importance of the technology ensures that the technical function occupies a central position in the business with obligations to both marketing and production functions, its objective being to provide the necessary means for the successful manufacture of products to meet the market need.

During the interviews, the manager outlined a number of principal responsibilities. Firstly there is the responsibility of optimizing current product manufacture by applying appropriate technology, providing necessary departmental facilities, and advising on raw material procurement strategy. The overall requirement is to manufacture products without incurring unnecessary costs and without compromising upon quality. The manager is also looking to extend the business operation through the development of new products and processes; this second responsibility is considered below. Thirdly there is the responsibility of participating in setting the overall business strategy. A fourth objective concerns the earning of revenue through technology transfer. This includes technical aid fees, the manager being chairman of an international technical policy committee where he provides relevant technical information to various overseas companies. In addition, there is the selling of patents, licences, plant and equipment as a result of technical innovation. Finally there are wider responsibilities for the whole industry where the basic objective has been to establish an approach to issues faced by the industry as a whole. This involves liaising with various expert bodies – for example, university departments.

Task description

As mentioned previously, one of the manager's main tasks is to develop new products and processes, to extend current capabilities through innovation. In practice the role is to direct the departmental effort in research and development work, taking projects from their inception to a satisfactory commercial conclusion. The manager may deploy resources (people and equipment) in support of some project and equally resources may be withdrawn. In either instance a wrong decision may be made at any time; that is a project that might have succeeded may be curtailed or one that will ultimately fail may be encouraged. Whether or not to lend support to developmental work is the key decision that is the hallmark of this task. The decision remains ubiquitous throughout the course of the project.

Initially the manager must decide whether or not to actually begin any development work, although this sometimes will not be his sole responsibility. Descriptively this blends into his skill, for even at this stage a judgement over the likely success of any proposal must be made. In addition there are opportunity costs to consider; the requisite resources could be employed elsewhere.

When resources have been allocated and the project gets under way, it is continually under review and the task is to monitor progress. If the work is markedly innovative it is likely that there will be significant problems to overcome. If the continuing belief is that the project is worthwhile and success attainable, the need will be to provide a safeguard during difficult times, often in the face of negative attitudes. This will require a careful analysis and evaluation of research findings. These circumstances are particularly apparent when the developmental work is near completion and production proper is about to begin. The task is now to ensure that there will be a satisfactory transition and translation to the larger scale. In the ordinary production situation the process will not be so carefully controlled and monitored by a strong technical presence. Furthermore the generally supportive atmosphere of the laboratory where there is familiarity with experimental failure will give way to the more relentless pressures of production where the requirement is for relatively prompt success. Once production personnel have taken over the manager will continue to monitor events particularly in the early days, and he will resolve miscellaneous problems. This final stage may be reached several years after the decision of inauguration.

Skills analysis

For any research project the manager will know, albeit in general terms at times, his objectives, even if he is unsure as to how he might achieve them. His skill lies in being able to decide on the basis of evidence available at a particular point in time whether or not the objective will be attained. Equally, however, he must be able to recognize the potential of a particular idea where it is not formally linked to any objective. Putting this another way, when the unexpected occurs its potential worth to a possibly vague objective outside the existing scheme of things must be discerned. In practice this would be the starting point for further development work and, if its potential was confirmed, the project would become established.

To reiterate, associated with any research project there is some representation of an ideal concluding state. For the manager a fundamental process is one of measuring how close the development work is to attaining this ideal. Since he is never absolutely certain that the project will be successful, he is making a judgement under uncertain conditions. The following discussion will focus upon the nature of the modelling that, it is inferred, allows the manager to interpret any evidence and to manipulate key parameters in anticipating the ultimate outcome. As a basis for action the manager appears to reflexively pose the question: 'Is my model sufficiently integrated such that I can anticipate a pattern of events, devoid of unsurmountable problems, that will allow progress to be made from the laboratory to the market place?'

A preoccupation with technology

In order to exercise his judgement skills the manager must have a mastery of the technology of the business; the plethora of technical information that is received must be competently interpreted. Through his technological understanding the manager will be able to view any new proposal against existing accomplishments. He will know something of the interrelationships between key parameters, and the likely difficulties that will occur. Suppose, for instance, that someone within the department is working on a problem that the manager failed to resolve in the past. This will not prejudice the issue but his knowledge will provide an early warning signal – the first negative feature in this instance – that alerts the manager as to the future course of events. Putting this another way, it enables the manager to be 'one step ahead' in anticipating the outcome of the empirical work and also in establishing an approach towards attaining the objectives, that is the means to the ends.

Beginning with limited evidence

Essentially the initial state of the thinking process is one devoid of any experimental evidence provided by ongoing laboratory work; there is merely some idea in embryo. If the idea satisfies a criterion of commercial viability (which will be determined by a group decision process), a second important criterion, which is the prime concern of the technical manager, is whether or not the project is technically feasible.

The manager appears to make a number of decisions, once more organized around various categories. On the one hand it would seem that on the basis of his experience and knowledge he may be able to label a project as feasible without recourse to experimental work. He knows that by proceeding along well established and well understood technical/scientific lines progress will be made. It is recognized that problems will occur but the feeling is that these will not prove insoluble. Perhaps the best example is where the research work has already been undertaken by technologists elsewhere; the reliance is upon the reliability of science, i.e. what has occurred once may be repeated. On the other hand, some desideratum may be classified as being outside the bounds of feasibility. Between these extremes, the position is more uncertain and the decision to proceed clearly depends upon being able to see *how* to proceed. Where it is difficult to see a way forward one heuristic device is to look for even remotely similar work that has been undertaken previously. The inference is then that through competence in his field the manager can perceive subject matter in a distinctive manner; he is able to evaluate notions along a continuum shading from high to low feasibility. In the extreme case it seems that it is possible to know that something is possible before knowing how it is feasible, but in other cases ways of making progress dominate the decision to start.

Progressing with increasing evidence

Once the developmental work is underway and as the evidence begins to build up, the odds on success may be revised. There is no substitute for empirical work; notwithstanding his preliminary notions the manager will wish to collect hard evidence on an issue. It is recognized that preconceived ideas can be misleading and, as Branton (1979) points out in a discussion of pure research scientists, it is also possible to regard this affirmation of empiricism as a constraint upon more fanciful theorizing.

The mere accumulation of hard data is only part of the story, however. The manager uses the additional evidence to indicate the appropriateness of direction; it is a further contribution to a developing predictive base. The process is one of tagging each piece of evidence with some weighted value set against the objective. There is a comparison with what is known, the evidence being set against a framework built upon experience. Thus the manager may recognize, for example, that some negative issues may be easily corrected whilst others may lead into a 'box' wherein the solution will probably remain elusive. The integration of evidence with the existing model will push the manager closer to the critical choice point where the prediction is that the project will succeed or that the next experiment will solve nothing. This is the important decision, the judgement being determined by the balance of the weighted evidence – which is put together to yield some whole – and clearly made that much more difficult by changeable evidence.

There is a further dimension in the progression towards an objective, namely the practical limit upon resource allocation. Clearly a constraint upon the manager's thinking is that the development work should not become prohibitively expensive. Furthermore, since resources are limited the need is to set priorities. One important factor in addition to technical considerations is the urgency of the situation in a business sense.

The transition to production presents its own set of problems where the position is much less one of speculation because so much more is known, and where concern rests upon practical difficulties created through changes in scale. Typically problems will be presented in terms of symptoms – for example, that there is a high number of substandard products – from which the manager might diagnose the fault. There is a broad distinction between operating faults and process faults, where the cause of the former tends to be human error and that of the latter some inherent technical weakness. As a general heuristic if there is a radical departure from expectations the implication is that it is human error; a more subtle problem may well be a process fault. The application of a range of widely recognized analytical methods will assist in establishing causal connections.

Accommodating new ideas

Throughout the whole decision process the manager must remain sufficiently flexible to perceive any new insights or opportunities that are presented. Even if the need is to develop a particular type of product to meet a known market demand, unexpected properties may also be exploited. What is required is an ability to connect quite disparate elements, a process of accommodation where the existing model is restructured to accord with the new information (c.f. Hedge and Lawson, 1979). A sudden realization of the potential of hitherto unconnected elements may also prove useful in making progress towards known objectives.

Summary of the skills of the Technical Director

In the context of limited resources, the manager must determine whether or not to lend support to project work on the basis of incomplete evidence. His skill lies in the development of a predictive model founded upon the dynamic relationship between previous learning (expectations) and cumulative data, but there appear to be several fundamental processes underlying the manager's use of that data including *analysis* where evidence is broken down into more basic elements that are differentially weighted, *synthesis* where evidence is compiled into a wholeness and *synergy* where pieces of evidence of somewhat limited independent value, in perhaps unlikely combination, yield something of greater value. Hence the manager must be prepared to update his model, sometimes from subtle sources, and at times the model may be restructured as new information is accommodated.

DISCUSSION

A synopsis

This chapter has provided a description of some of the skills exercised by managers associated with production in manufacturing industry. The skills information was extracted from interviews which were of several hours duration with each manager and which were transcribed verbatim. Whilst the interviews were the main data source, additional 'informal' discussion and observation provided supplementary information. There is also a dialectic value in discussing ideas with other analysts/practitioners and the empathy between analyst and practitioner also plays a part in skills studies (see Singleton, 1978 and 1979 respectively).

Consistent with most aspects of organizational work, managerial work may be regarded as comprising more fundamental units or activities. When describing their work managers readily talk in terms of such activities which may be progressively described in greater detail or aggregated into broader units of description. This is a task description which defines the objectives that a manager seeks to accomplish. On the other hand a skills analysis concerns how such objectives are attained, that is the strategies and tactics that the manager uses to make progress towards his objectives.

The skills of the Production Director lie partly in combining perceptions of the real (production) situation with the associated numerical (cost) evidence. The ability to process cost information in relation to the production events to which the costs relate would be most likely to distinguish the production manager from the accountant. Furthermore, comparing the process to mere 'number crunching' gives some indication of the superiority of the skilled man over both the unskilled man and the computer. The Production Director must also remain sensitive to events that do not conform to expectations. In terms of the overall system, this procedure enables him to cope with the complexity of the system, by reducing the amount of information concerning the system state and allowing a highly pertinent response. In a study concerning managers apparently holding similar positions to that of the Production Director, Brewer and Tomlinson (1964) also found that their sample operated via the 'exception principle' in cost control tasks. The authors added that, since the managers spent considerable time in acquiring and systematizing the requisite information, this need not be a simple and straightforward matter. The Production Director is managing a number of production events proceeding in parallel, each providing intermittent signals that contribute to the existing model. Since there are also a number of objectives relating to the events, presumably in order to facilitate some kind of cognitive order, the manager holds categories for both inputs and outputs. It seems likely that category systems mentioned here are not based upon one uniform property varying across each category. Rather the categories appear to be of a 'polythetic' nature (see Sokal, 1977) sharing a large number of properties but not necessarily agreeing in any particular property. Putting this another way, the manager is operating from a shifting multidimensional base, and, interestingly enough, there is a sense in which the definition of actual dimensions is less important than the existence of some dimensions, for dimensions will not be of a 'standard' format. In addition there are high level skill mechanisms concerning input manipulation and output execution. On the input side, the manager must be able to allocate information to the appropriate model of events otherwise the tendency would be towards some kind of cognitive entropy. A further mechanism appears to enable him to know whether his models are inadequate or whether it is the data that are in error (and this is the basis of one categorization). On the output side, the manager is able to monitor the success of any action against the overall purpose, namely the positive variance target(s).

One higher level skill mechanism of the Technical Director is reflected in his first feeling that a project is possible, the reasons as to why it is possible being adduced later. This is the reported introspection and it is only possible to speculate why this is the case. Certainly the process is dependent upon some experience/knowledge base and the notion of a 'frame' proposed by Minsky (1977) may be of descriptive value here. When facing some new situation it might be supposed that a 'frame' or stereotype is recalled which may be adapted to square with reality by altering details as necessary. The frame or data structure comprises a network of hierarchically organized information slots and in the absence of specific values for these slots the stereotype allows the insertion of some typical or ideal value. Hence, given that certain critical slot values remain invariant, in the case of the Technical Director, it is possible that the decision over some product/process development may be specified by default. As for a further part of his skill, the Technical Director may be regarded somewhat analogously to the Production Director in that he is gathering information (on some project) and the question is: 'Does the evidence fit my expectation?' In Branton's terms the critical decision concerns a 'rendezvous with a stranger', a paradoxical recognition that the research answer has arrived. This decision will be supported by analytic, synthetic and synergetic processes operating with a developing empirical data base. The synergetic processes are of an inductive nature, extending beyond the current scheme of things and unchecked by criteria of validity. Only later will the resultant hypotheses be more formally put to the test.

At least some of the decisions of senior management will be implemented by people at other organizational levels. Indeed the manager's most important resource is that of personal skills including his own and those of his subordinates. Moving down the organizational hierarchy, the skill of the Departmental Manager in resource allocation is founded upon his knowledge of the departmental operation. This is not lexical knowledge, rather it is some experientially influenced understanding that appears to be organized through fidelity to the departmental operation. The solution of any problem is bound up with this knowledge and may be executed through applying certain 'rules of thumb'. Brewer and Tomlinson (1964) point out that supervisory problem solving may be conducted by means of stored 'programmes', but it is worth exploring the 'rule/programme' concept further to avoid misunderstanding.

The 'rules' or 'programmes' of the competent manager are the result of learning via a 'productive' model (Miller, 1968). This learning has built upon previous learning thus facilitating information storage, and has provided a framework within which the manager has been able to develop his own sub-routines or rules of thumb in problem-solving. Furthermore, each successive response and its effect will change the existing stored model in some way, allowing a flexibility that is prohibited with mere rote learning. As a result of this productive learning the manager is able to think more broadly about the operation; he has the broad picture to which he can relate the details that confront him at any one time. In implementing his decision, the Departmental Manager is dependent upon his subordinates and the suggestion was that it was advantageous to know the individuals concerned. This is worth exploring a little further since one theoretical perspective is that the manager, as an order-taker and order-giver and monitor, will, from a 'legitimate' authority base, incur problems only as a result of 'insubordination' or a breakdown in communication. Sayles (1964) directly challenges this viewpoint, his research results demonstrating that this is too simple a picture of organizational relationships. Rather, the manager lies in a network of relationships that will impose various patterns of initiation and response, and will change for a number of reasons; for example, fluctuations in manufacturing requirements concerning entities such as costs, quality and so on. Hence the competent manager must shift his behaviour accordingly and this will be underpinned by an attempt to construct and maintain what Sayles has termed '. . . a predictable, reciprocating system of relationships, the behavioural patterns of which stay within reasonable physical limits' (pp. 258–259).

Differences in skill

Contrasting the managers by level, it may be seen that, not surprisingly, the more senior managers are exercising their skills over a wider perspective both temporally and organizationally. The importance of being able to maintain diffuse developing models or schema is implicit in the discussion by Marples (1967) of managerial behaviour. In regard to the manager as a problem solver and decision maker, he compared the managerial job to a stranded rope comprising fibres of different length (where length = time), each fibre coming to the surface at one or more times in observable episodes representing a single issue. The higher the managerial position the greater the average fibre length and the more intertwined the issues become. The suggestion was that 'a prime managerial skill may be the capacity to keep a number of issues in play over a large number of episodes and long periods of time' (p. 287).

Whilst most managerial decisions will comprise on-line and off-line inputs, it would seem that the latter assume a greater importance with increase in organizational seniority. Whilst senior managers certainly require information concerning the current state of the system for which they hold responsibility, they remain particularly aware of the more superordinate organizational goals and policies. The decision making at lower levels appears to concern relatively more sensory experiences, whilst the more senior managers will need increasingly more abstract models in order to cope with the increase in complexity of inputs. Simon (1965) proposed a continuum anchored at the poles by programmed and non-programmed decisions; the tendency is for decision-making lower in the hierarchy to lean towards the programmed pole because of the relatively more routinized problem presentation.

Contrasting production and technical managers, it may be seen that each manager operates from a fundamental base allied to the function within which the job lies. The foundation of the technical manager's skill is his experience with a technology that has resulted in a mastery of his field. Whilst it is possible that another technical manager may have a different base and may operate successfully, it is difficult to imagine a similar base resulting from anything but protracted learning. Broadly speaking, for comparable levels in seniority, the technical manager will require more abstract models and greater competence in processing abstract information than the production manager. Because of his prime concern with the concrete demands of the production operation, it is possible that the production man will deal with information of lesser abstraction and may place greater reliance upon experiential learning. However, the more complex the product, the greater is the need for someone to hold a composite model linking technology, process and product and it is possible that this may be a manager within the production function.

Managerial skills: common threads

In terms of the overall system, it would appear that each manager is active at a number of systemic levels and in a number of systemic functions (although the importance of such functions, for example policy setting, will vary). Generally speaking, within the system each manager is managing a process, that is some pattern of events proceeding in time. Hence he is aware of the background to any event and is not merely operating with the 'here and now' (and the higher the position in the hierarchy, the more extensive the time scale may need to be). Part of the manager's skill will concern picking up information; in general terms the more skilled a person, the more he will perceive. From a complex environment, managers may well extract key features which feed into some inner representation of the external world. To be consistent with a number of authors it may be useful here to distinguish different aspects of information throughput. Miller *et al.* (1960), for example, talk of the 'image', i.e. all the accumulated knowledge that the individual has of himself and his world, and the 'plan', a hierarchical process controlling a sequence of operations, and Pounds (1969) distinguishes problem-finding, the difference between existing and desired situations, and problem-solving, the process of reducing such differences. Hence in 'primary' processing the manager relates the current experiences to what has occurred before and to his expectations, plans, ideals, objectives, etc. In later processing there is a decision invoking some 'programme'/'plan'/'operator' that will operationalize the cognitive/perceptual 'conclusions' of the earlier phase. It should be noted that there is a close relationship between these aspects, and one would be of only limited value without the other. For example, for the child memorizing the rules of how to calculate the area of a triangle, in the absence of the appropriate understanding of geometrical relationships, it would be more difficult to identify mistakes and nearly impossible to correct them (Miller, 1968). For the manager with an absenteeism problem, merely to fill gaps in the production line without understanding the whole line functioning may well lead to a suboptimal use of resources.

It is worth separating out an information storage function from throughput aspects and, following computer systems terminology, stores of information/experience/models may be labelled 'files'. Some files will remain relatively invariant, for example learned procedures, whilst others will record a changing situation, for example an ongoing research project. There will be individual methods for the gross organization of the filing system and the records within files, and there need be no uniformity in speed of access to files either between or within individuals. Furthermore strategies of access will vary, although it seems likely that there will be least structure in inductive-type processes. In any analysis, however, care must be exercised to avoid losing the whole essence of the skilled performance which is an integrated *gestalt*. Indeed it is open to speculation that for the skilled manager, at times the context surrounding an event will define the choice of action with quasi-automaticity and that the decision will be reflected upon and checked out later.

Acknowledgements

I would like to express my warm appreciation to Norman Chell who has contributed many helpful ideas and no little encouragement during the course of the project from which the data have been extracted. My thanks are also due to Professor Singleton and Peter Spurgeon for their insightful comments throughout the project and to the managers who gave generously of their time.

References

Bartlett, F. C. (1958). *Thinking.* (London: George, Allen & Unwin)

Berrien, K. F. (1976). A general systems approach to organisations. In Dunnette, M. D. (ed.) *Handbook of Industrial and Organisational Psychology.* (Chicago: Rand McNally)

Branton, P. (1979). The research scientist. In Singleton, W. T. (ed.) *The Study of Real Skills, Volume 2: Compliance and Excellence.* (Lancaster: MTP)

Brewer, E. and Tomlinson, J. W. C. (1964). The manager's working day. *J. Ind. Econ.*, **12**, 191

Drasdo, H. (1979). The rock climber. In Singleton, W. T. (ed.) *The Study of Real Skills, Volume 2: Compliance and Excellence.* (Lancaster: MTP)

Drucker, P. F. (1968). *The practice of management.* (London: Pan)

Glover, I. A. (1977). Managerial work: A review of the evidence. *Dept. of Industry.* (Unpublished paper)

Hedge, A. and Lawson, B. R. (1979). Creative thinking. In Singleton, W. T. (ed.) *The Study of Real Skills, Volume 2: Compliance and Excellence.* (Lancaster: MTP)

Marples, D. L. (1967). Studies of managers – a fresh start? *J. Management Stud.*, **4**, 282

Miller, G. A. (1968). *The Psychology of Communication.* (Harmondsworth: Penguin)

Miller, G. A., Galanter, E. and Pribram, K. H. (1960). *Plans and the structure of behaviour.* (New York: Holt, Rinehart & Winston)

Minsky, M. (1977). Frame System Theory. In Johnson-Laird, P. N. and Wason, P. C. (eds.) *Thinking.* (Cambridge: University Press)

Pounds, W. F. (1969). The process of problem finding. *Ind. Management Rev.*, **11**, 1

Sayles, L. R. (1964). *Managerial Behaviour.* (New York: McGraw–Hill)

Simon, H. A. (1965). *The shape of automation for men and management.* (New York: Harper & Row)

Singleton, W. T. (1967). Acquisition of skills – the theory behind training design. In Robinson, J. and Barnes, N. (eds.) *New Media and Methods in Industrial Training.* (London: BBC)

Singleton, W. T. (1974). *Man Machine Systems.* (Harmondsworth: Penguin)

Singleton, W. T. (1978). Introduction. In Singleton W. T. (ed.) *The Study of Real Skills, Volume 1: The Analysis of Practical Skills.* (Lancaster: MTP)

Singleton, W. T. (1979). Conclusion. In Singleton W. T. (ed.) *The Study of Real Skills, Volume 2: Compliance and Excellence.* (Lancaster: MTP)

Sokal, R. R. (1977). Classification: purposes, principles, progress, prospects. In Johnson-Laird, P. N. and Wason, P. C. (eds.) *Thinking.* (Cambridge: University Press)

Thurston, P. H. (1963). The concept of a production system. *Harvard Business Review*, **70**, 75

Wild, R. (1972). *Management & Production.* (Harmondsworth: Penguin)

11
The Personnel Manager

B. WILSON

INTRODUCTION

This chapter is concerned with the complex interrelationships and with the particular contributions and skills required of the effective personnel manager. It will explore the critical importance of senior managements' beliefs about people and the style of management which they themselves practise and propagate. It will examine the 'processes' which need to be established to gain managers' commitment to some of the necessary longer-term people developments. It will look at the complex management development process, and at the development of an effective personnel team.

Superficially personnel management is about recruitment, pay, management development, employee relations and so on. But is it so simple? Is personnel management no more than running a number of systems, or is it, in reality, about achieving results through people? And, if this is so, how does it overlap with line management? Such questions help to outline the complexities of the personnel task. Unlike other functional areas, the boundary between line manager and the personnel specialist is extremely grey. There is no way in which responsibility for people and their utilization and development can be delegated to a specialist. Equally, there is no way in which the task can be done by the management unaided.

MANPOWER PLANNING

No organization can achieve its results other than through people; it is important that the right people are available with appropriate skills, whenever and wherever they are required and that, when they are in position, they perform well. It is also important that their skills should continue to be developed to meet the future needs of the organization and so that they do not become obsolescent in due course. To achieve these linked objectives is the central thrust of creative personnel work.

The future needs for people, the 'demand side' of the manpower planning equation, stem from the corporate plan which, within environmental pressures and constraints, is establishing the future patterns of growth, diversification, divestment, rationalization, geographic dispersion, reorganization, new technology, etc. for the company. Each one of these will have a profound impact on the numbers and sorts of people required, and on the particular kinds of skill which will be needed. Manpower planning is about establishing these needs and about developing and implementing plans which will ensure both that shorter-term needs are met and also that appropriate actions are being initiated to ensure a continuity in the supply of the right kinds of people. The supply side of the equation breaks down conveniently into five aspects; acquisition, conservation, utilization, development and wastage.

Acquisition

This is concerned with making up any shortfalls which cannot be met by the growth and development of existing employees. It raises such policy questions as the proportions to be developed rather than recruited, the extent to which vacancies should be publicized and internal transfer encouraged and it raises issues such as: how do we ensure that we select the right people to avoid subsequent problems and wastage?

Conservation

Once we have the people we need, how do we keep them and avoid unnecessary wastage? Again, personnel policies are important. What should our pay stance be opposite the market to ensure that we attract and keep the people we need? Do we have a rational rewards structure? At what level should we set our working conditions and fringe benefits? What should our employee relations policies be to maintain harmony? What style of management is most appropriate to business success?

Utilization

It is not enough to have the numbers of people we need; we must also stimulate their performance. Are the company, unit and individual objectives clear? Do our structures and systems encourage performance or

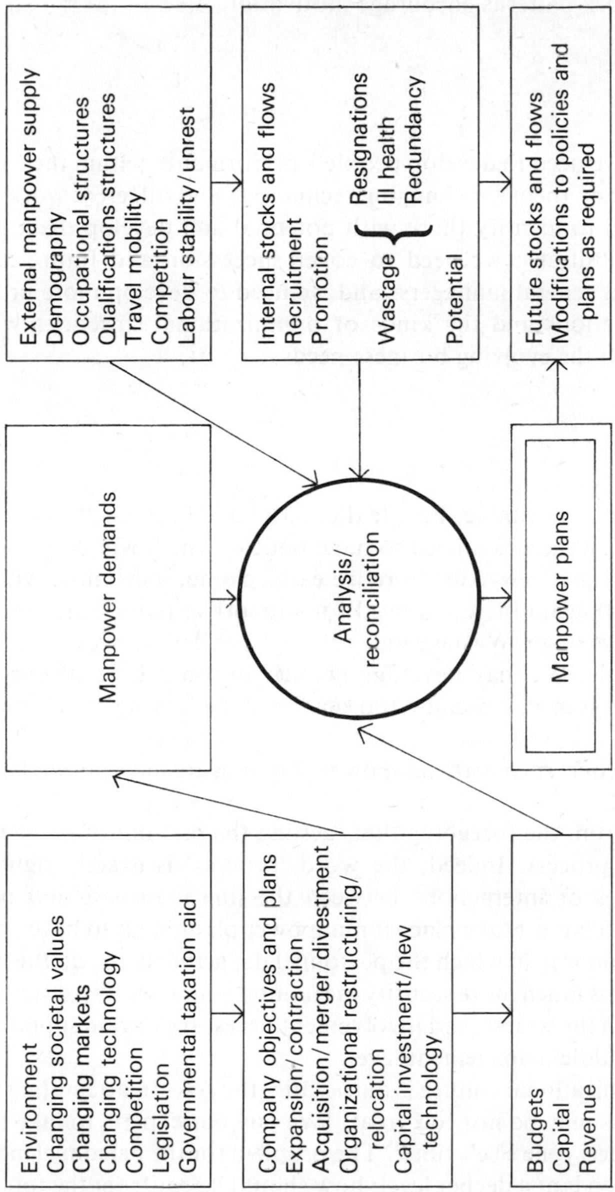

Figure 11.1 Manpower planning: the process

are they road blocks to be got around? Do we have an effective appraisal system for improving people's performance? Have we got/do we need a bonus for improving productivity? Should everyone be included? Do the shop floor work patterns encourage motivation, etc?

Development

Not only do we need to develop people's performance within their jobs, but we need to equip them for changing technology and different working practices; we need to identify those with potential and develop them for more responsible positions; we need to cover succession and future needs for managers and general managers; and we need to develop more progressive industrial relations and the kinds of organizational structures which are appropriate to the evolving business needs.

Wastage

Some wastage is inevitable. People die, retire and become ill. Some become obsolescent and there is a need to have policies which will encourage those who will not learn new skills to retire early. Some, inevitably, will become redundant and again there is a need for supportive redundancy policies for those who have to go. Wastage may reflect other deficiencies in our employment of people. We may have age profiles in some areas of our business which can put it at risk because too many will be leaving at about the same time.

The issues concerned with manpower planning are incorporated in Figures 11.1 and 11.2.

It is clear from the foregoing that 'getting the best out of people' is a far from simple process. Indeed, the word 'process' is exactly right for the complex series of interactions between the line managers and personnel specialists which must take place if manpower planning is to have any meaning. There is no way in which the personnel department can do this by itself, and yet, there is much more security in running your own tidy systems than in setting in train the widespread involvement necessary to gain support at both senior and middle management level.

If the organizational culture is autocratic, the risks in attempting to set up such a process may be just too great: 'We pay our experts to take decisions not to waste everyone else's time!' The problem for the personnel manager in such a situation is at a deeper level; how should he confront the top management team with the adverse effects of a highly autocratic style on the morale and motivation of employees and on overall business effectiveness? If he can get some acceptance that this may be so and some experimentation with a

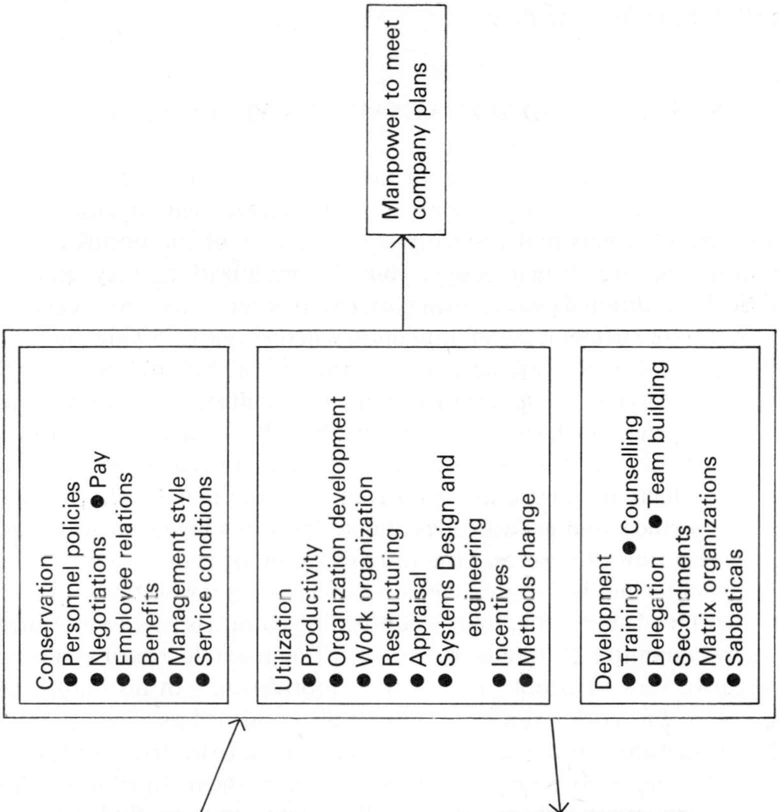

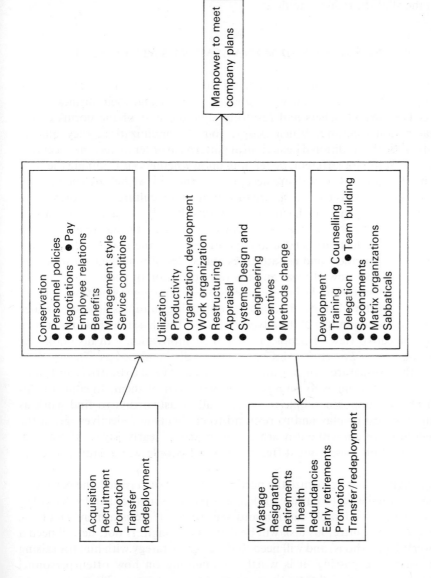

Figure 11.2 Manpower supply: stocks and flows

style which allows more delegation and which seeks to gain support for policies and action rather than to impose them, he is beginning to make real progress. However, to do this requires considerable skill and courage.

The next section explores the problems facing the personnel manager who is attempting to open up these deep issues of management values and style and the skills he requires to do it.

PERSONNEL SKILLS AND MANAGEMENT VALUES/STYLE

Few executive committees ever debate their beliefs about people and the implications of these for the ways in which they manage their business activities. The current beliefs and resulting style are part of the norms of the organizational culture. When people join an organization, they quickly conform to the traditional behavioural patterns in order to become accepted. These patterns are different, depending upon whether one is joining the staff or the shop floor, but both are accepted as 'the way we behave round here' and are perceived as part of the organization's total culture. It is a brave man indeed who challenges such values and norms; it is all too easy to be rejected. And yet, there is a great deal of evidence to show that negative attitudes to work, low productivity, and uncompetitiveness in the market place, are a direct result of 'them and us' attitudes and styles of management which do not encourage a flow of ideas and the full utilization of people's potentials.

The problem facing the progressive personnel manager who finds himself operating within an autocratic, tightly controlling culture is how to convince his executive committee of the adverse effects of such a style, based as it is on a very negative view of people and of their motivations. In his book *The Human Side of Enterprise* McGregor (1960) distinguished as 'Theory X', a belief that people are basically untrustworthy and need to be driven or bribed or controlled if one is to get any useful work out of them. In contrast, his 'Theory Y' supposed people to be basically trustworthy, to find work as natural as rest or play and to respond to challenging objectives, given the freedom to get on without overbearing control. Clearly, styles of management based on these quite different views of people will, in turn, be quite different.

Though he may recognize the need to confront such issues, the personnel manager will be acutely aware of the personal risks involved and will need to move with considerable caution and sensitivity. If he is a member of the executive committee, his task will be difficult enough. If not, he will need a powerful ally who is, and will need to develop a strategy with him for raising the issues. (In passing, it is worth commenting on how often personnel managers are excluded from their top management teams. This is perhaps a sad reflection of the way in which they are perceived as not contributing to total business effectiveness. It should be the aim of anyone in this position to demonstrate the critical contribution which he can make to business results and, in due course, to gain a seat.) Apart from having the advantage accruing from a seat on the top management team, the opportunity for confronting the way in which the business is run will be further enhanced if the organization is facing a painful situation – loss of market share, decreased competitiveness, impossible industrial relations, inability to recruit and retain the necessary staff, low morale, etc. An exploration of the issues involved will provide data which begins to expose some of the nonsenses resulting from the current ways of doing things and from the style of management which is being practised.

A case drawn from personal experience will illustrate these points. I was fortunate in both having a seat on the executive committee of a big division of a multinational company and having joined at a time when its middle managers were becoming alienated at the constant pressure for results and little apparent concern for them as individuals. Senior management had been shocked by the strength of feeling expressed at the annual middle-and-above management conference and were aware that something had gone wrong and that changes would need to be made – but what? In opening up issues, I had already shown the power of data feedback, if handled in the right way. How data are handled is critical. If someone were to be open with you and you were to feed back data straight to his manager, any trust which you had established would be immediately destroyed and there would be no way in which anyone would risk being open with you again in that organization! Thus it is important, before collecting any data, to establish a number of contracts: firstly, with the top management team, that any sources of data will be kept confidential and that positive as well as negative data will be collected; and secondly, with each individual, that anonymity is guaranteed. Further, to build up trust, (without this the data will be only partial and carefully filtered at that) it is important to check understanding from time to time, both to ensure that the ideas are being correctly recorded and also to demonstrate that one's own constructions are not being put on what has been said. Once the data from a cross-section of employees has been obtained, it is possible to collate the ideas and concerns under appropriate headings. It is easy, at this stage, to be seduced into diagnosing the problems and presenting them to the management team.

It is better to feed back the raw data under collated headings using people's own words. In this way it is possible to hold up a kind of mirror to the organization and then there is no evading the issues, whereas someone else's diagnosis and constructions can easily be rejected. Faced with such powerful data, there is no pretending that the problems do not exist or that they will go away. It is then a relatively easy next step to encourage the management team itself to diagnose the underlying problems. Around the kinds of issues mentioned earlier, these would almost certainly be in the area of style of management; over-tight control, low creativity, under-utilization, slow decision-taking, low risk-taking, poor productivity, poor management development, etc. These were certainly the kinds of concerns which I picked up. There was no pretending that these were not serious issues and that they were not contributing to reduced organizational effectiveness.

However, though the problems were accepted, there was, as is usual in such cases, a feeling of helplessness and a natural inclination to look to me, the personnel expert, and say, 'You tell us what to do!' In such cases, temptation has to be resisted. It is only by encouraging managers to accept that they themselves are contributing to the problems and that changes in the ways in which they manage will be necessary, that any significant steps forward can be made. It is all too easy, if someone else produces a plan, for managers to shelter behind the fact that something is now being done. The upshot of a lot of hard and painful facing of issues and development of appropriate plans was the production of a 'Statement of Management Philosophy', expressing management's beliefs about people in relation to the business and an exposition of the much more open, more involving, less controlling, style of management which was thought to be appropriate in future. It led to a considerable amount of training in team-working and group problem-solving, to the establishment of an effective management development approach, built on a 'work plan' based appraisal system and to carefully thought out succession-planning. It also led to the establishment of a fully representative joint consultative system, to a thorough overhaul of the salary structure and to complete openness about the salary policy. Interestingly, it also led to the opportunity to bring about a major shift in the role of the personnel department towards change facilitating and problem-solving with a future orientation.

I was lucky, in this case, to have been recruited to help deal with a problem and to be a member of the executive committee. But how is it possible to open up such issues in less propitious circumstances?

As a personnel manager one is privy to a large number of confidences and it is relatively easy, by tuning in and complementing what is proferred by appropriate research, to identify the key issues which are around. The need to feed back the data in people's own words, appropriately collated, is even more acute when one is not a member of the management team, since the risk of rejection is so much greater. Whether, if the data is sensitive, one will be allowed to be involved oneself in the problem definition stage, is problematical. If a powerful friend can be encouraged to clear this, this could be an enormous step forward, handled properly, and lead to enhanced credibility, a quite different perception of the role of personnel and ultimately, one would hope, to a reappraisal of the need for personnel to be represented on the management team.

To confront issues in the way suggested is far from easy and full of personal risks, but the alternative – to soldier on, putting out fires which should never have started and somehow keeping the vessel on an even keel – is an even less attractive prospect. Once one has made the breakthrough, then a much more creative and satisfying personnel and personal contribution becomes possible.

THE MANPOWER PLANNING PROCESS

Once the organization has begun to realize the significance of 'people values' for business success and how they affect every aspect of organizational life, the development of a more meaningful manpower planning process is made so much easier. It is a sad fact of life that so many organizations are littered with well intentioned plans which have never been realized. It is often forgotten by planners that not only must their plans be soundly based, but also that the key people in the organization must believe this to be so. Furthermore, they must have credibility in the eyes of those who, in due course, will have to implement them. If the key people do not trust the judgments, the plans will be rejected out of hand. If the implementers do not believe in them, the rejection will not be as spectacular, but will be just as effective. They will find ways of ignoring, subverting or getting round them and carrying on doing their own thing.

The foregoing is true of plans in general, but what of manpower planning in particular? As already said in the second section, this has two important aspects, demand and supply-side considerations which need to be reconciled. The supply-side statistics are relatively straight forward for the personnel manager, or, in the bigger organization, for his manpower planning expert to produce. Wastage rates, age profiles, skill inventories, etc. can be extracted from personnel records and are readily available to computerization. Indeed, when companies talk of manpower planning, all too often they are talking about their computerized supply statistics.

The real problems occur when one is trying to develop the estimates of future manpower demands. These are almost entirely based on judgments related to the corporate plans and the answers to questions such as:

'If we do diversify/move into an area of new technology, what kinds of skills shall we need? Can we develop our own people, or should we recruit?'

'If we do decentralize our operations and run down the size of our headquarters unit, what will be the effect on numbers? How many will have the skills needed to work in the regions? Down to what level are we prepared to carry the costs of relocation? How many redundancies shall we have to deal with?'

'If we continue to lose market share with this particular product line, as predicted, should we be thinking in terms of rationalizing our manufacturing base?'

'We are just not competitive in terms of manning levels with the Germans and Japanese. How do we achieve the necessary 25% reduction in numbers over the next three years?'

'We must take account of word processors, and trends towards office automation in general, in thinking through our future staff requirements. What kinds of reductions should we plan for?'

'Even if we make our policies clear, how can we get our various managers to face the issues and come up with realistic estimates for the future manning requirements in their units?'

Senior managers often expect, somewhat optimistically, that their specialists will somehow be able to do their various manipulations and produce the desired plans without too much effort or involvement on their own part. Sadly, the real world is not like this. As already mentioned, manpower plans are only worth the paper on which they are written if they: (a) are based on well thought out policies and judgments provided by the top managers in relation to corporate plans; (b) are based on the detailed knowledge, insights and judgments of the various operating and specialist managers, taken within the policy guidelines; and (c) are understood by those who, at the end of the day, will be required to implement them. If the plans are not seen as credible, they have little chance of being successfully achieved. The task of the personnel manager is to help his manpower planner (if he has one; if not, he will have to do it himself) to get a complex and interactive process under way which, at the end of the day, will produce plans which are accepted as realistic and which do influence the ways in which people behave.

In setting up a manpower planning process, the personnel manager will face many problems. There is likely to be an expectation, if it is now accepted that manpower planning should be done, that he and his team will just get on with the job. There is unlikely to be much understanding of the need for a process or for the commitment of a great deal of time and energy on the part of managers at all levels. Further, he will lack credibility in the role. In the shorter term 'if he wastes our time in involving us all' instead of getting on with the job, his perceived credibility will be low. Alternatively, if he gets on with the job himself and the plans are then rejected as being out of touch with reality, his credibility will be even lower. There is no instant solution to this dilemma; credibility can only develop with time as people begin to see the value of what is being done.

The innovative personnel manager will also face a great deal of resistance to any suggestion that things should be done in different ways. People are always much more comfortable in behaving in their well established patterns. If he tries to force through change using his 'expert' power, the resisting forces will be likely to become even bigger. The only way of getting people to move is to involve them to the extent that they become co-inventors of the plan and committed to it as a consequence. To operate in such a way, he requires great sensitivity to how people are feeling. His work could also be hindered by having to use inadequate corporate plans as his starting point. They are unlikely to have been much influenced by 'people' considerations, either at the environmental level – legislation, changing norms, expectations and social values, etc. – or indeed by supply considerations, which might, for example, mean that a particular new product line cannot be introduced quickly for lack of appropriate resources. Finally, the size of the real task is unlikely to be recognized in the early stages. Until the need for a 'process' and the demands on time are accepted, provision of appropriate resources could be a problem, and it is more than likely that he will find that he is having to put in long hours and a great deal of energy himself to build up the necessary momentum for the whole process to get under way.

These problems will be overcome only by dint of great personal energy and as a result of a great deal of intellectual effort and careful planning. Firstly he has to decide on the information required as a basis for deciding which are the issues, in particular, which need to be taken into account in developing meaningful demand estimates. Table 11.1 illustrates the breadth of the necessary coverage. There will probably be numerous gaps in the information required

Table 11.1 Manpower planning: estimating demands

Growth, contraction, diversification, divestment, relocation, new technology, new products, new services, organizational changes	Source of information – corporate plan. What are the implications? What gaps are there?
Need for productivity increases – staff and hourly paid	Does productivity need to be increased to regain/maintain competitiveness? How much?
Wastage rates	Are too many people being lost and why?
Salary/wage stance opposite market fringe benefits, bonuses, etc.	Can you attract and retain the people you need?
Age distribution	Do you have bulges which will cause replacement or career development problems?
Legislation	If planning closures, what are the implications?
Changing social norms and expectations	Is there an intention to move towards shorter working weeks/years, dual jobs, more involvement, etc? What are the implications?
Style of management	Is it changing? Should it? What are the implications for control, e.g. more self control, less supervision? Numbers implications?
Staff development	What is the policy on internal development *versus* recruitment?
Unit size	What is the policy? Should there be a move towards smaller units?
Planning time frames, etc.	What do these need to be? 1, 5, 10 years, or what?

and the personnel manager needs to decide which he can fill himself and where he needs help. He then needs to plan how to get it – to cajole, to get a power figure to commission it, or what? Once he has the data, he needs to identify what is likely to be of significance in relation to the numbers and kinds of people who will be required in the future. The trap is to try to be too sophisticated and cover everything. It has to be remembered that the perfect plan is an impossibility and that if the process becomes too complex the demands on the time of the people who need to contribute will become too great and the final result will be much worse than if the sights were set lower.

Once the key issues have been identified, he can then develop the policies or guidelines which will be necessary. However, he must recognize that these cannot emanate from himself. He can only be the catalyst and he must decide how best to approach the executive committee. If he is a member, this presents no problem. If not, he needs to plan how to get a member to introduce the draft proposals and how best to brief him so that the debate is conducted in the right way and the appropriate decisions are taken.

If this is the first attempt to get an interactive process underway, he must also decide when will be the best time to introduce his proposals on this as well. It might be appropriate to use the policy/guidelines debate to register the thought that he will be asking the executive committee to consider such proposals at its next meeting. He needs to have great sensitivity to where people are and not to ask for too much at once and risk having the whole initiative rejected. Once the need for a process has been recognized as contributing to better plans and their smoother implementation, this will not be a problem. From experience, this is not so the first time or two around.

In developing proposals for the process, he will need to decide what information he wishes to collect, the timescales and accuracies of estimates, and the format which should be used. He will also need to think about timing so that, in due course, the one year projection can be built into the annual budgeting process. He will need to think about who to involve, who has the necessary information and who will be critical at the implementation phase. And, finally, he will need to develop proposals for the process, which will attempt to balance the demands on people's time with the need to reconcile different viewpoints, create understanding of how the different decisions within the consolidated plans have been arrived at and develop the general belief that, give and take a bit, the final plans make a lot of sense.

There is no formula for achieving all of this. Each company has different structures, systems, traditions, etc. It is important to link into as much as possible of what has gone on before and not to set up a whole new set of meetings. It is important to show the greatest sensitivity to the demands which are being made on people and to make sure that, through communications, meetings, or whatever, there is wide understanding of how and why the plans have developed into their final shape. If the process can be arranged in the right way, gone will be the days of the old games – building in slack in anticipation that there would be arbitrary decisions on an x% cut, or whatever, working hard to achieve comfortable manning levels and so on. It will lead to people having to face painful issues and, within the carefully constructed guidelines, producing realistic estimates and becoming committed to the changes necessary for the future health, vitality and competitiveness of the organization.

THE MANAGEMENT DEVELOPMENT SYSTEM

This is the third main area in which the personnel manager has a critical part to play. Apart from his contribution to personnel policy-making, as required, in the other personnel areas, he will be able to delegate much of the actual work to his specialists, within appropriate guidelines. Of course, he will still need to give help and support from time to time but most of the day-to-day work should be well within the capacities of his subordinates. This is not true of management development. Most systems fail because they are delegated to a personnel specialist who is able to operate paper work systems to his heart's content, but who has no authority to arrange any staff moves on his own initiative. Moves involve one manager agreeing to give up a subordinate, usually an able one, who is contributing to the unit's success – and his own kudos – and another manager being prepared to take him on someone else's assessment of his capability when, in all probability, he has a good candidate, whom he knows well, ready for promotion. In any case, how can he be sure that someone else is not trying to palm off some deadwood?

It is hardly surprising, given these dynamics, that management development systems which attempt to delegate responsibility to a third party have little chance of working effectively. The responsibility for the utilization, growth and development of a subordinate is quite clearly the responsibility of the manager himself and there is no way in which he can opt out of this. He may need help, and this is the personnel specialist's role, but in the final analysis it is his own clear and undivided responsibility to develop his own subordinates.

Thus, management development systems will only work if the managers are actively involved themselves. This is an issue which can only be confronted at the most senior level. Unless the executive committee accepts its own responsibilities in this respect, there is little chance of an effective system operating at lower levels.

The only man who can raise the issue and stimulate the necessary debate is the personnel manager. Before he does so, however, he needs to be clear himself about what is involved in the term 'management development'. Developing every manager regardless? Developing, say, 20% with real potential? Developing for what? For succession and defined future needs, or a kind of grape shot, casting-bread-on-the-water approach? Again, he needs to be sensitive to the time demands he is likely to put on his colleagues. He will probably be wiser to concentrate on the prime needs first, i.e. covering succession and future defined needs, where there are gaps. And succession at what level? Should the top management team be considering all cases of succession or should some of the task be delegated to lower level management teams? And then there is the question of how it should be done. How much of the weight can be taken off the senior managers without taking the real decision-taking away from them?

I should like to illustrate the kinds of issues which arise, from a particular experience. The top management team had been confronted with the wide dissatisfaction with management development in a working party report on the topic. It was looked upon as a 'cattle market' and 'blue-eyed boys' were felt to be at a premium. The current system was run by a management development specialist who beavered away but who seemed to have little impact on what happened. The top management turned to me, as the new personnel manager, to ask what I was going to do about it and were shocked when I said, 'Nothing; it isn't my problem!' That led to an interesting debate about where the responsibility lay and in the end my colleagues admitted that the responsibility was theirs but that they needed help, to which request, of course, I agreed. We discussed how we should tackle the problem and I agreed to provide a list of names extracted from the previous year's appraisal forms of those who were felt to have potential and a list of the key positions. The managers would put names, individually, of likely successors against each of the latter for debate at the next meeting. At this meeting, there was considerable surprise expressed at some of the names which had appeared. One senior manager waved one of his own appraisals and said, 'This is a load of rubbish'. When asked why, he said, 'In the past, filling in the appraisals was just a chore; nothing was ever done with them, so we did not take the exercise seriously. What we want now is a much more honest appraisal process!' And that was exactly what happened. A management working party was set up and developed a 'work plan based' appraisal system, which began to produce much better data for the management development process. The question of management development became a biannual, major agenda item for the top management team, and they began to plan moves to broaden people's experience, cover gaps and ensure that the general managers of the future would be coming forward. The only mistake was in trying to do too much. The task had been limited to succession, but they were covering succession at too low levels, a task which should have been delegated to lower level management teams.

Thus the personnel manager is the only one who can confront the fundamental issues involved in effective management development and help his colleagues invent a process to which they will be committed and which is thus likely to succeed. He needs to be acutely conscious of the demands on people's time that this will make and should aim to make the process as simple as possible, restrict it in its scope to management development to meet clearly defined needs (at least in the early stages) and should provide as much support as possible from amongst his own specialist resources. Finally, he should endeavour to set up a phased sequence of discussions, starting at the lowest level management teams charged with dealing with all the developments which fall within their own areas of discretion and only putting forward the names of individuals who need wider moves to the next higher management team. And so on, until the top management team deals with all the moves and other developments necessary to ensure trained successors for their own jobs.

One other aspect of which he needs to be acutely aware is the individual's own aspirations. One could surmise, from what has been written, that these are unimportant. This is increasingly less so in this age of the autonomous individual. Management's own thinking about suitable candidates for succession need to be checked out with the individuals against their own aspirations. If there are good fits, then those particular bits of development can sensibly go ahead. But even then, it is important not to raise expectations. All that one can say is: 'we believe that development to fit you for a move in this or that general direction would be sensible. What do you think?' To name specific jobs until the vacancies occurred would be to put up real hostages to fortune.

Thus the personnel manager has a key contribution to make in persuading his colleagues to set up and contribute to the kind of process which is likely to produce the managers of the future in relation to the identified needs. It is not something which he, any more than his line management colleagues, can leave to his management development expert. He has his own unique and critical contribution to make.

THE SKILLS OF THE PERSONNEL TEAM

So far this paper has dealt with the particular contribution of the personnel manager as an individual. Much of the personnel work, however, is done by his team and the way they perceive their task and perform is critical in relation to the effectiveness and credibility of the department.

Personnel departments, all too often, do not have a very high reputation. There are many reasons for this. In the past, the personnel department was often seen as somewhere where the 'failed other professionals' could be moved without creating too much damage. Unfortunately, such individuals meet their own security needs by becoming expert runners of bureaucratic systems; not only do these systems provide the desired security, they also give power to the systems experts through their ability to force people to conform to the requirements of the systems. These, then, tend to become the ends themselves instead of the means towards much broader ends. Personnel department can all too easily become the defender of the status quo.

Another problem is the piecemeal development of the people activities in most organizations. Frequently there are separate personnel and labour/manpower service departments, separate management and craft/operator/supervisor training establishments and so on. Each tends to work to its own value system. Personnel departments and management training centres tend to have a Theory Y view of people. Often the others have a strong Theory X view. Does this make sense? Do the different behavioural patterns of 'white' and 'blue' collar workers spring from different views of people and the different treatments which result? Perhaps there is a need to develop a cohesive set of values which applies to all employees?

A third problem is the short time-focus of most personnel departments. How often are they involved in putting out brush fires, reacting to this or that problem, to such an extent that they never have the time or energy to think ahead, anticipate problems and avoid them?

How many departments have thought through what they are really about? Are they the runners of systems and sorters-out of the short-term problems, or should they be concerned about the growth, development, motivation, commitment and utilization of people to make a real contribution to business success? And if changes in the way things are done – the structures, systems, roles, work organization and methods, the approach to industrial relations, etc. – are necessary to achieve better utilization of people's energies and potentials, should not personnel people have skills in diagnosing the needs for change and in helping to develop strategies for bringing them about? And if so, should not the systems be modified as necessary to support the kinds of changes felt to be necessary? These are fundamental questions, springing from a different perception of the personnel role, a creative and change-orientated one rather than the more traditional, stabilizing, status quo role. The answers and decisions taken will have a profound impact on the role, structure and focus of personnel work, on the kinds of staff who are required and on the kinds of skills needed.

It is my belief that the more creative, change-oriented role is the right one and that the personnel manager should ensure that his people have a diagnostic/problem solving skill as well as the ability to run systems professionally and well. However, it must never be forgotten that the reputation of personnel will always depend upon systems which operate smoothly and to time, but at the same time that they must never be allowed to become ends in themselves.

What does this mean for the development of the personnel staff? First of all it is necessary to develop a view of the changed roles which the department should be performing and to check these with the other departments and with the executive committee for confirmation. It is then necessary to translate these into role descriptions for each individual. Some will have the kinds of temperaments which make a more creative, open-ended and less well clearly defined role an impossibility. However, the department will always need its professional systems, but those charged with running them must accept that they are to help managers, not to put road blocks in the way of sensible action and that this will require more sensitivity and flexibility in their operation. For the others, training aimed at increasing diagnostic and problem-solving skills and sensitivity towards people in their many interactions might well be appropriate. There is a need to develop skill in confronting issues in the right way, in saying 'No' when expected to deal with problems or things which the manager should be doing himself. The personnel man needs to be able to act as conscience, counsellor, confronter, supporter or in whatever role is most appropriate in the particular situation and he needs the credibility to become a valued member of the management team and to be seen to be making a real contribution to the better achievement of business goals.

This reorientation in roles of both department and individuals cannot take place overnight and the ability to make a deeper and wider contribution will become possible only as the credibility of the department and its staff increases. But it will only happen at all if the departmental manager has a clear idea of the kind of department he wants and is prepared to invest a good deal of time and energy in the development of his team and their perception of their own roles.

THE EFFECTIVE PERSONNEL MANAGER

The personnel job described in this chapter is far removed from the more traditional one still practised in the majority of companies. Nevertheless, in the rapidly changing and highly competitive world in which we live, companies will increasingly recognize the need for incumbents who can operate in the less systemized, more flexible way described. Such an approach makes great demands on the individual. He needs to have a high tolerance for uncertainty, an inner self-confidence and personal security which will allow him to take the risks inherent in challenging many of the assumptions behind current ways of doing things and in sometimes forcing his colleagues to confront painful issues which need to be tackled if the organization is to maintain its competitive edge. He needs skills in diagnosis and in designing change strategies which take account of people's sensitivities.

His concern should be primarily in the development of ways of doing things which minimize the waste of human energy and which maximize the utilization of potential towards competitive business operation. He will try to detect nonsenses in goals, structures, systems, roles or work organization and methods, whenever these cause frustration, conflict, or low morale. He will be concerned that reward structures reward the kinds of behavioural patterns which the organization needs and will see his personnel systems in general not as ends in themselves but as lubricants for the complex organizational processes.

12
The Marketing Manager

K. G. BURNETT

MARKETING IN CONCEPT

The emergence of marketing

Marketing is one of the newest specializations to appear on the organization structure. It showed first in the late fifties; currently in the UK there are about 20 000 individuals who take the function of marketing seriously enough to belong to the Institute of Marketing. Of that number there are approximately 360 Fellows and 12 500 full members although the criteria for entry are based more on experience and current status rather than qualification. The only measurement of academic level known is that more than 8000 Diplomas of Marketing have been issued up to 1980 and the Institute embraces more than 18 000 students worldwide. The majority of these students are under 25.

Of course, marketing has been around for longer than twenty years. Hotten's Slang Dictionary of 1874 defined a marketeer as 'a betting man who devotes himself by means of special information to the study of favourites and the diseases incident to that condition . . . The Marketeer is the principle agent in all milking and knocking-out arrangements!' Hotten's definition may not seem inappropriate even today despite its original equine connotation. Marketing has always been an integral part of the commercial scene; almost every commercial transaction involves some facet of marketing common sense. The shaping of this common-sense into an organized activity started probably with the development of the retail trade in the late 19th century, in particular the Cooperative movement. Most of those marketing activities were, however, concerned with the consumer market. The real volume of business activity centres around the many industrial transactions which take place between the companies associated with the intermediate processes. Every consumer purchase is the end of a series of industrial transactions between buyers and sellers, the value of which will be considerably more than the final consumer deal.

In this century, there have been three phases of business development in most industrialized nations. In the beginning, disposal of output presented little difficulty and the main management effort went into production efficiency and extension of capacity. The early industrial giants were engineers dedicated to the task of finding new ways to improve manufacturing. The fact that there was a huge market willing to purchase a low-priced car was incidental to Henry Ford's passion to implement his revolutionary ideas for mass production. 'Any colour you want as long as it is black' is no marketeer's slogan. In this production-orientated phase, the engineers were ousted gradually by the financiers who sought to benefit productivity (and themselves) by the advantages of volume. In addition to creating the multinational industrial empires so familiar today, unwittingly they sowed the seeds of 'business portfolios' which, in such companies, are a key aspect of the marketing function as it is practised today.

The second phase started when disposal of output began to present difficulties. In the United States, this was evident from the 1920's, but two major wars postponed the impact in Europe until the 1950's. Production and technical prowess were still the backbone of management. Companies strived to become 'sales-orientated' and, in many companies, sales techniques were imported from the USA. Advertising and promotion were developed as a support to selling which was still essentially a distributive function to allocate production.

In the late 1950's, for the first time in the Western world, supply overtook demand. In that simple statement are implications of change in the concepts of pricing, selling, research, advertising and distribution. These were the early chores of the marketing man. To these chores have been added the complications of a changing business world in which companies cannot disassociate themselves from the consequences of government, political pressure, world recession, third world emergence, consumer and environmental groups. All these factors add new dimensions, and problems, to the trading process. A more fundamental shift in attitude in management outlook was necessary by the early sixties in order to cope with the problems created by the new supply/demand imbalance. The aggression in selling was proving no real answer to the problems of supply exceeding demand – problems exacerbated by the accelerated pace of world economic development, technological advance and political change.

These changes meant that manufacturers could no longer produce subjectively what suited them; they needed to be sensitive to consumer reactions and competitive strategy. The customer had a choice; markets were more extensive than ever before and more suppliers, worldwide, were looking for a share. The new rate of economic change signalled the need for management to determine business policy with respect to both short- and long-term market considerations. The incidence and implications of product commercial failure were becoming more acute. Mr Gillette had 50 years to get his safety razor blade right and enjoy a financial payback. Since 1960, the wetshaver may have changed his 'system' no less than six times as he progressed from the stainless blade to the disposable razor. By the 1970s some consumer hair-shampoos would enjoy only 6 weeks brand leadership in which to recover enormous 'launch' expenditure.

These new management problems and needs of the 1960's led to the conception of the Marketing organization that could combine all those activities involved in identification, stimulation and satisfaction of market needs in an integrated fashion to achieve company objectives profitably (Kotler, 1975).

Marketing orientation

In the early days, the Marketing organization consisted of a number of well defined functions – notably market research, market forecasting, product planning, advertising and promotion – under one executive reporting to the Chief Executive. The other business functions including sales, distribution, finance, production, personnel etc. each had an executive reporting directly to the Chief Executive.

The particular pressures of the last 20 years have, in most companies, induced a final shift in management attitudes to marketing-orientation. In organization terms this is exhibited by a unification of all marketing functions – including selling and distribution – under one single coordinating executive. In attitude terms, there is acceptance by all functional managers that the objectives of the business are determined by market considerations and that the priorities demanded by the marketing function may conflict with criteria by which their own job performance is measured.

This ultimate commitment to marketing-orientation is reflected in the attitude of the Chief Executive who, faced with the problems of shorter product and business life-cycles, accelerating technology and the pressure of inflation, is increasingly encouraged to take a portfolio approach to his job to cope with the complexity of decision making. In this approach the strategy options to be considered are determined by the stage of development of the product or business. These stages and strategies are well documented and call for management actions which may, for example, demand the 'killing-off' of a business or the optimum exploitation of market dominance (usually to finance another less prosperous part of the portfolio). The social and moral implications of such decisions will colour the choice of executive necessary to perform effectively in the business 'culture' which prevails in that company. Market considerations will determine not only the tasks and skills of management, but also the style.

The organization of marketing

The extent to which companies have made the final attitude shift to market-orientation is directly related to the degree of complexity experienced in dealing with their markets and their competitors. The regrouping of particular activities as the company moves towards market-orientation is shown in Figure 12.1 which sets out the four principle types of organization structure. The activities which are regrouped are pricing, advertising, forecasting, credit control, sales recruitment and training, product planning, packaging, distribution and, sometimes, public relations.

Surveys indicate that the integrated marketing concept is twice as likely to be found in a large company as a small company which will tend to be geared to the sales oriented structure. However, definitions may distort; small companies may be more integrated than surveys suggest in that the individual managers are less physically separated and the span of markets served and implications of market share may be less significant.

The total activities of marketing embrace such a wide range of tasks and skills that it is unlikely that the individual practitioner has work experience of all facets. In practice, the nature of the business determines the key activity areas and the necessary task experience and skill: for example, contracting businesses may place emphasis on financial skills, industrial equipment on personal selling, consumer goods on advertising and promotion. Interestingly, these are three of the major generic skills in the marketing job.

The career path for the marketeer is not well defined. In the small business with either a small market share or whose products are aimed at a specific segment of the market, the attributes sought will be geared to a particular marketing activity and the practitioner will have a participating 'up-front' role in the day-to-day detail. This background will almost certainly have been in the same market but with a different company as, perhaps, Product Manager, Area Sales Manager or Advertising Executive. Market knowledge is regarded as significant and what the practitioner has gained in ridding himself of the bureaucratic culture is discounted by the limitation on available resources in his new smaller employer.

In the large business, the Marketing Manager is more likely to be part of an integrated marketing organization structure headed by a marketing-orientated Chief Executive. At one time, his responsibilities might have been defined by a group of products, but nowadays he is more likely to be in charge of a business-orientated group whose function it is to serve a defined market with a range of products some of which may have been manufactured by another part of the company or even factored from another manufacturer. For example, a team responsible for marketing dictation equipment in the early 1970's is now more likely to have lost its product identity, and to be part of an 'office-systems' group selling word-processors, typewriters, filing or anything that their defined customer cluster might require. In this group

Diagram 1 PRODUCTION-ORIENTATED ORGANIZATION STRUCTURE

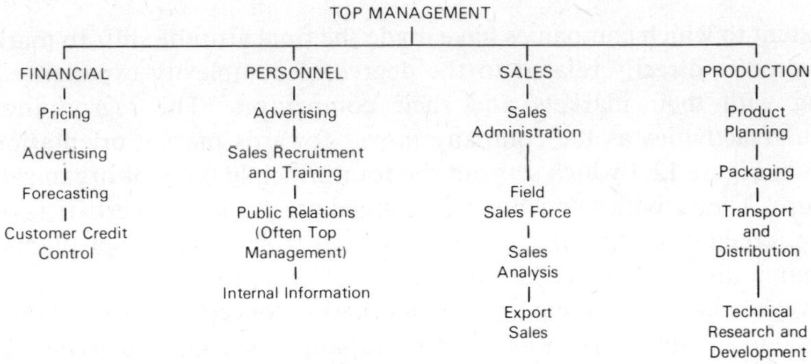

Diagram 2 SALES-ORIENTATED ORGANIZATION STRUCTURE

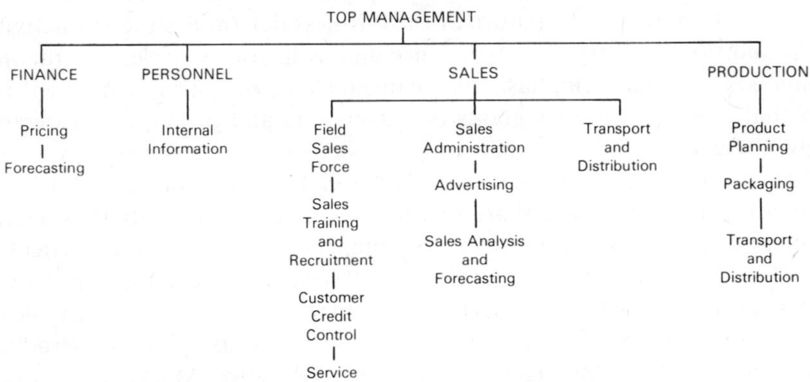

Diagram 3 SPLIT MARKETING ORGANIZATION STRUCTURE

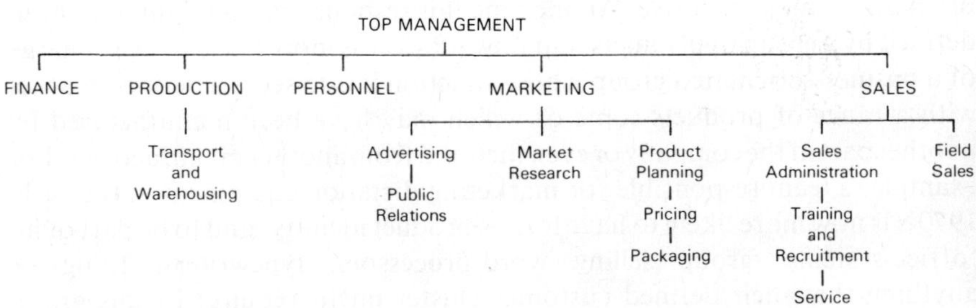

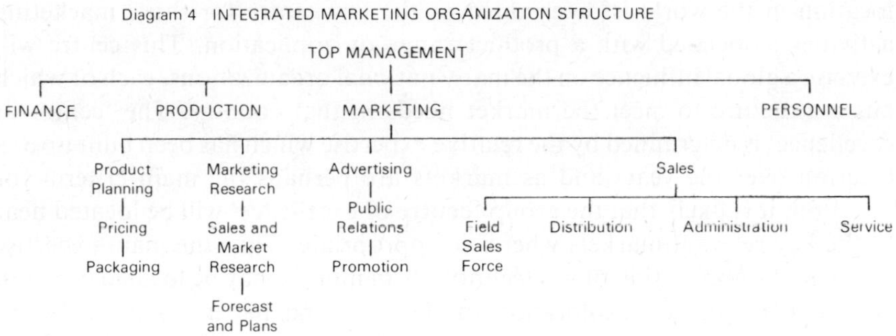

Figure 12.1 The evolution of the organization structure towards integrated marketing

there is likely to be a 'portfolio' of products to be managed (as discussed later in this chapter), and the emphasis is on anticipating complete solutions to customers' problems rather than simply pushing individual products. It is a total 'package' approach with well defined target customers and the realization of optimal added-value potential as a business objective. The larger company wrestles with the problem of establishing individual accountability usually by adopting a 'matrix' organization structure. In a service-based company it is likely that profit will be monitored on a local geographic unit while the marketing function is centrally based and, to some extent, 'competes' for the attention of the local geographic unit.

Some of the complexities of maintaining accountability whilst benefiting from good central marketing strategy are demonstrated by examining part of the organization structure for a major UK industrial Company – British Oxygen. British Oxygen in the UK is essentially a service and technology based company supplying gas and welding gear to nearly 200 000 'drop points'. These are serviced by some 40 branches each run by a profit-responsible Branch Manager who responds through a line organization to one of four Regional Controllers. Marketing is essentially a central staff function exerting influence on profit-responsible geographical units. Whilst having a localized marketing substructure providing necessary liaison between R & D, technical support and the local branch, the centralized marketing think-tank is geared more to the organization of group resources, the advancement of technology and the monitoring of the financial implications of the portfolio of company products and activities. The emphasis is research, pricing and promotion.

The acquisition of a substantial American company – Airco – greatly extended the international scope of BOC and at the same time duplicated resources in the R & D and other marketing functions. BOC's approach to this overnight growth in portfolio resources has been to develop the idea of 'centres of excellence'. This is an analysis and selection process whereby one location in the world is determined as the key centre for those marketing activities associated with a product range or application. This centre will exercise a global influence on the many national organizations, each of which has a structure to meet the market needs in that country. The 'centre of excellence' is determined by the relative expertise which has been built up at a location over the years and as markets are perhaps the main criteria for selection, it is likely that the group 'centre of excellence' will be located near to the key relevant markets wherever appropriate. Thus the main expertise group in the application of gas technology in mining may be located in South Africa, off-shore oil exploration in the UK, and papermaking in North America.

In this way, an intricate matrix organization structure extends through the BOC group internationally. The 'weave' of the structure is profit-responsibility extending from the local branch or manufacturing centre to the International Chief Executive. The 'weft' of the organization is essentially marketing where the generic skills associated with products, pricing, distribution and promotion create the corporate synergy which is the raison d'être of a world-wide group. There is theoretically a two-fold accountability and a built-in 'fail safe' mechanism to ensure the organization will succeed.

Philips, the Dutch electrical giant, uses a multi-dimensional organization matrix. Eindhoven is the geographical heart of the matrix and, for instance, directs the R & D programme for the Group. These policies are derived from feedback by the individual national organizations who, in turn, choose whether to market the product technology generated by Eindhoven. Eindhoven decides where the product should be manufactured. Thus the British Audio Division Marketing Manager will 'cherry-pick' specific hi-fi units which are appropriate to the UK market from the considerably larger range of styles and specifications available through Eindhoven.

In a unified organizational structure, the marketing function is an appropriate path to General Manager or Chief Executive status. At this level, one is managing a portfolio of businesses rather than products and the emphasis moves to strategy and positioning of the business in the short and long term. In this area of decision, marketing has taken impressive strides in the past decade assisted by the tremendous growth in the information storage and analysis facilities afforded by computers.

The implications of marketing strategy

Two popular conceptual aids to strategic marketing are the Boston Grid and the PIMS programme. These concepts are concerned with market share and business life-cycles and have significant implications as to the permutation of skills and management styles appropriate to different businesses at various stages of development.

The Boston Grid

This concept was developed in America by Bruce Henderson of the Boston Consultancy Group (BCG). Though dating from the late 1960's, it was adopted in the middle 1970's by multinationals as an aid to the classification of businesses or products in the portfolio. The basic idea is that there is a correlation between market share and return on investment (ROI); the higher the market share, the better the ROI is likely to be. This correlation derives from the measurable fact that the cumulative experience acquired in manufacturing a product will result in a gradual reduction in controllable costs. It has been suggested that every time aggregate production is doubled, controllable costs reduce by approximately 20%. This is known as the 'experience curve' effect. The advantages of lower costs in a competitive market place are self-evident.

It is however, when the overall market ceases to grow or begins to decline that the real implications of these ideas become more significant. When the total market begins to plateau, the relative market shares are stabilized because: (a) no additional market is available to secure; (b) market share growth is only possible at the expense of others; and (c) no new competition enters a static or declining market.

At this stage, the market leader can harvest the payoff from his market position because he is less vulnerable to competitors' activities. When the market declines, he will be tempted to use his pricing muscle against competitors to maintain his volume . . . unless his spare capacity is to be filled by another product that he is developing in a growth market elsewhere.

These implications are classically displayed in the Boston Grid (Figure 12.2) which labels the four strategic positions on a matrix which correlates market share with overall market growth. The four classifications are as follows.

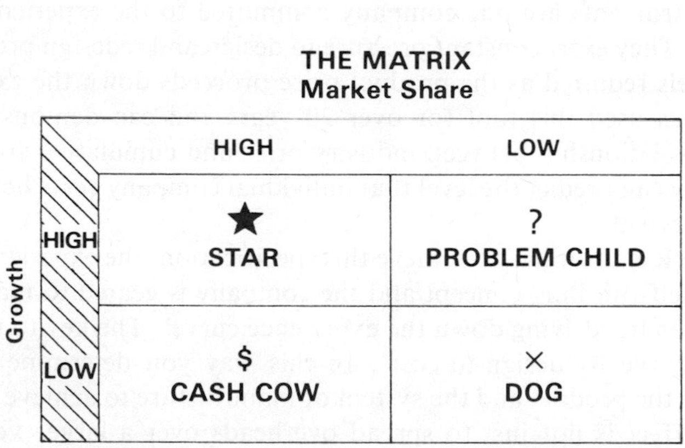

THE MATRIX
Market Share
HIGH
LOW
Growth
HIGH
LOW
?
STAR
PROBLEM CHILD
$
×
CASH COW
DOG

Figure 12.2 The Boston Grid. Source: The Boston Consulting Group Ltd., New Zealand House, Haymarket, London SW1

The Cash Cow
(High market share/static or declining market) which by harvesting the payoff will finance other parts of the Group portfolio.

The Star
(High market share/high market growth) which by doing well in a dynamic market will become the Cash Cow of the future when the market stabilizes. For the moment, however, it absorbs as much money as it generates to protect its market share.

The Problem Child
(Low market share/high market growth) which having failed to win market share in a dynamic market needs either a substantial cash injection to turn it into a Star (see above) or a firm decision to kill off.

The Dog
(Low market share/static or declining market) which having failed to win share in what is now a stabilized market should be realistically killed off.

These ideas may be applied to products or companies. A company may have a portfolio of products which will be classified as described. There will be some 'bread and butter' products (Cash Cows) which will be generating the cash to fund the Stars and Problem Children that may become the Cash Cows of the future. The Dogs are shed or, at best, heavily monitored to avoid resource-drain if it is decided that they are strategically significant (e.g. to complete the product range).

Some companies identify so strongly the experience curve effect that it becomes the keystone of their management philosophy. By forecasting the 'effect' for, say, 5 years ahead, they essentially are targeting themselves on product development.

Texas Instruments are one company committed to the experience curve philosophy. They exert constant pressure to design and redesign products to the cost levels required as the product price proceeds down the experience curve. TI has used this tool for over 20 years and can demonstrate the predictable relationship between industry price and cumulative volume. In this way they can predict the level that individual company costs have to fall to ensure survival.

By setting R & D targets to achieve this specification, the experience curve becomes a self-fulfilling concept and the company is geared to making the future happen by 'driving down the experience curve'. The key to using the experience curve is 'design-to-cost'. In this way you determine the cost required for the product and the system of manufacture to achieve that cost goal. The effect is not just to spread overheads over a larger volume of product produced; it also involves constantly forcing manufacturing costs down through design improvements of the product and the production processes.

Table 12.1 The evolution of organization culture as the business life cycle develops*

	Stage in business life-cycle			
	Introduction	*Fast growth*	*Maturity*	*Decline*
Type of leadership	Entrepreneur Innovator	Skilled analyst Risk taker	Critical administrator Caretaker	Hard nosed operator Undertaker
Management style	Participation	Leadership	Guidance	Loyalty
Organization	Free-forming task force	Semipermanent task force Product or market divisions	Business divisions	Cut back to essentials
Corporate emphasis	Market research New product development	Operation research Organization development	Value analysis Data processing	Purchasing
Industry/market	High growth Low share	High growth High share	Low growth High share	Low growth Low share
Communications	Informal Customized	Formal Customized	Formal Standard	None Command system
Reward	High variable Low fixed Individual	Balanced Individual + Group	Low variable High fixed Group	Fixed only
Reporting	Qualitative Marketing Unwritten	Qualitative and quantitative All functions	Quantitative Written Production	Numerical Written Accounting

Maturity curve

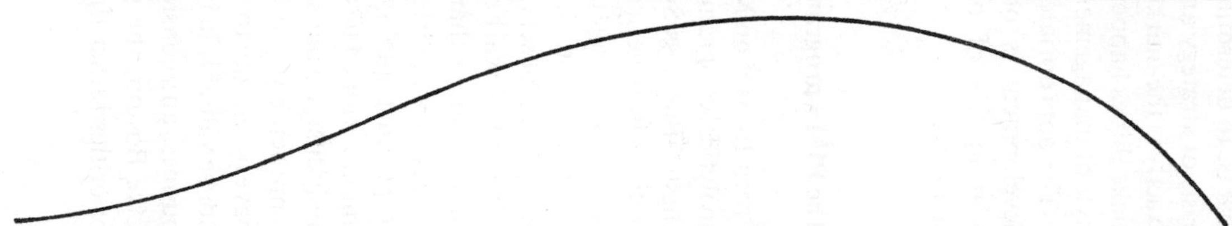

*Source: R. V. L. Wright (1974). *Strategy Centres*, 9. (Cambridge, Mass.: Arthur D. Little)

The real value of the Boston Grid is that it helps to position the business: that is, to determine exactly where you *are* and where you *want to be.* It is a basis of strategy and the fact that there are pitfalls in the concept (e.g. what exactly is the market?) is incidental. It is a device for stimulating action – to make things happen – and its relevance in this chapter lies in the fact that the style of management action required must reflect the position of the business.

The appropriate management style for businesses in different stages of development is obviously different. Table 12.1 demonstrates the inter-relationships of organizational aspects and the stages of business cycle maturity.

The PIMS programme

Profit Impact on Marketing Strategy (PIMS) is the full title of an ambitious analytical programme, administered by The Strategic Planning Centre, Manchester Business School, which systematically scans more than 2000 organizations in America and Europe for activities which appear to correlate with success. Once again, success is defined as 'return on investment' (ROI), and like the Boston Grid, the graphics use a two-dimensional matrix to demonstrate their observations. However, where Boston sticks to market growth and relative market share as the coordinates, PIMS scans the inter-relationships of more than 28 aspects of the business. Market growth and market share (though differently defined to Boston) are included, but the list extends to product quality, value added, investment intensity and even degree of unionization. The purpose of the scan is to generate a performance norm for an industry against which contributors can monitor their business. Perhaps more acutely, it tries to assess the degree of sensitivity the business is likely to have in relation to the aspects specified. This wealth of cross-related data may not be valuable in itself but it does permit a starting point for positioning your business and considering the many strategic options that are available to you. Like Boston, the programme serves to clarify information and emphasize priorities rather than make decisions on your behalf.

Organization ideologies

Handy (1976) classifies these ideologies into four principal cultures. These cultures are concerned with the organizational styles of the business: the degree of formality; the depth and scope of planning; obedience and initiative; work hours; dress; eccentricity; and whether committees or individuals are in control. The culture is evident in the type of premises and the kind of people employed.

The power culture

The power culture is found in small entrepreneurial organizations and demands a strong central individual (or power) which is the source of activity and influence. The organization works on following or anticipating the wishes and decisions of the central power source. It has the ability to move and react quickly without bureaucracy or necessarily logic. Individuals employed will be power orientated, risk-taking, politically minded and have little desire for security. They judge by results and are tolerant of means. The problems for power culture is size. The web of power can break as it extends. Morale can suffer as individuals in middle management fail or opt out of the competitive atmosphere.

The task culture

The task culture is job or project orientated, often reflected in a matrix form of organization structure. The emphasis is getting the job done by getting together the right resources. Influence is based on *expert* power rather than individual authority or influence. By identifying the individual with the objective of the organization, the task culture develops the unifying power of the group to improve efficiency. The group is adaptable and task forces are formed, reformed, continued or abandoned. Each group contains its own decision-making power and individuals enjoy a high degree of control over their work, judgment by results, and easy working relationships with mutual respect based upon ability. The task culture is appropriate where flexibility and sensitivity to the market or environment is important. It is particularly important in the early fast growth stages of the product/business cycle where speed of reaction, integration, sensitivity and creativity are more important than depth of specialization. At this stage of the product/business life-cycle, control is difficult and has extended perhaps beyond the aegis of the entrepreneur who has conducted the project through the introductory lift-off period. Parts of the project are delegated to good people with modest constraints on resources. In this way, top management concentrates on resource allocation decisions and the hiring and placing of key people.

The role culture

The role culture works by logic, rationality and procedures. It is the bureaucracy resting on the strengths of its functions and specialists which are well established when the organization is in the maturity stage of the business life-cycle. It is the culture of a stable environment where the market is negotiable or controllable with perhaps a good few years of product life still available. It is a culture characterized by job descriptions, authority definitions, copy memoranda and compromise. It is populated by interchangeable individuals selected for satisfactory performance of the role. Performance over and above the role is not required. The role culture thrives where the economics of scale, technical expertise and depth of specialization are more important than product innovation or product cost (assuming that the experience curve benefits are being realized). It is found where there is a sellers' market or where the State is the sole customer. The role culture is not necessarily inefficient – it is the right culture for a market situation where there is a high premium on product reliability and few penalties for cost or lack of product innovation.

The person culture
The person (or existentialist) culture is an oddball in which the individual is the central point. The structure exists to serve the individual within it. It is a cluster of individual stars, all doing their own things, without any subordinate objective, and examples include barristers, architects, and hippy communes. It is populated by a fee-earning rather than wages mentality: the individuals do what they are good at and are listened to on appropriate topics. Although it is rare to find an organization where the person culture predominates, it is not uncommon to encounter individuals who favour this culture operating within a more typical organization. It is likely that the marketing function embraces more than an average share of this self-centred breed who indulge themselves in perhaps sales or advertising or even the more extreme forms of 'gobble-de-gook' found sometimes in market research or high technology.

In summary, each stage of the business life-cycle may require a different culture, a different style, which may be determined more by market forces than anything else. The role of marketing manager will probably be looked to in order to reflect the appropriate culture at any one time. The right culture – power, task or role – is determined by the life cycle stage being experienced by the product or business. The fourth culture – person – which lends itself to the ideologies of the individual, might well conceal itself within the marketing function especially, at any stage of its evolution. Of course, most organizations consist of a portfolio of businesses or products at different stages of development. They may require a portfolio of cultures which may not coexist amiably within the same overall organization.

Computer software companies are interesting examples of hybrid organizations embracing all four cultures with frequently all too evident personal stress to the individuals employed. There are always new products, services and facilities generated daily by the technology explosion. These demand high creativity in the early stages to screen out and develop commercially viable applications which are then realized by the skills of the *individual entrepreneur*. He launches the project (often on the chicken-and-egg self-financing basis) with a *power culture* organization. Once on a growth trajectory, the project is limited only by the attitude of the entrepreneur who may be ousted by the delegating, coordinating manager who develops a *task culture*. When the project matures, having achieved dominant market share in a now static market, the management priority moves towards administrative efficiency, the replacement of red tape with procedures, standard specifications and authority limits. In this way, the *role culture* emerges to reap the harvest of the project's *cash cow* status. At all times, the nature of computer software science is that it attracts a significant number of individuals who do not recognize anything but the *person culture*.

In theory, the organization should have a stable of marketing managers ready to conduct each project through the stages of its culture journey, each bringing to bear their specialist skills at the appropriate time. It will be seen that as organizations grow to maturity each phase carries the seeds of its own destruction. The reasons for growth lie somewhere between minimizing vulnerability, and gaining material benefits of dominant share when the overall market stabilizes. The satisfaction of the objectives of most commercial organizations hinges upon the management of its position in the market place. The marketing manager is in the eye of the storm and more than any other manager his style is determined by market position at any one time.

MARKETING IN PRACTICE

So far this chapter has laid emphasis on how the organization structure of business and the style of marketing management reflects clearly the position of the business in the market place measured in terms of market share and progress through the business life-cycle. The relevant style of marketing management is likely to determine the 'culture' in which the executive team will have to operate. Each culture demands a different emphasis in terms of skill and effort; varying attributes and experiences are necessary to achieve the objectives towards which the organization is addressed.

Tasks and skills

The main objective of marketing managers is to maintain the equilibrium of the business by matching those pressures exerted in the business by outside *uncontrollable* forces with the *controllable* resources contained within the business. The outside 'uncontrollable' elements may include: market demand; governmental actions; environmental pressures; legal decisions; consumer wishes; competition; and raw material availability or prices.

In practice there are six task areas to the job. They are: market research; market forecasting; product planning (including pricing); distribution planning; sales (including administration); and advertising and promotion.

The task priorities will vary according to the business and to clarify this it will be useful to refer to a basic definition of marketing. Marketing, in practice, consists of two functions: (1) determining and defining the most suitable market or markets in relation to the company's resources; (2) ensuring that these resources are used to design, produce, and sell a product or range of products in such a way as to win the maximum number of favourable buying decisions from the prospective customers in the defined market at an economic cost.

In reality, the instances when one is starting in business from scratch are rare: it is usually a going concern with existing products and customers. The overall marketing objective will be one of the following:

Market penetration (existing products into existing markets);
Product development (new products into existing markets);
Market development (existing products into new markets); and
Diversification (new products into new markets).

In the final analysis, your success will be determined in terms of winning the planned number of favourable buying decisions from your target market. Therefore your effort and budget will be directed towards the factors which influence those decisions. The first stage is to evaluate this criteria in order that the appropriate skills are available and that management has a clear idea of priorities. The factors which influence your customers' decisions are complex and multidimensional. The broad areas for consideration are listed in Table 12.2. If one can establish the most important aspects in your customer's mind, you have a lead into your task and skill priorities.

Marketing consumer goods

By definition, your product is a consumable and might well be a rod for welding purposes or an industrial glue just as much as a grocery item in the local supermarket. However, with most consumer goods – biscuits, beer, cigarettes, screws – your main concern is likely to be *distribution*. Your consumer is likely to buy the product as he requires and if it is not available at that point of sale, he will buy another product. If the product is cigarettes, your aim is to get your brand into every newsagent, canteen and kiosk in the land. Unless you do, most other marketing effort is wasted. If your product is biscuits, you are aiming to get as many as possible of your brands listed by the great supermarkets.

Your success is measured in listings, outers per sale, getting more space on fixtures than competition, keeping the shelves stocked by local part-time merchandisers. Advertising and promotion may be a significant element, particularly if you are trying to secure a premium price for your product.

The role of the salesman is purely as part of the distribution function and you will have a training machine to ensure a constant supply of young, inexpensive, conscientious, reliable men and women who can give a good day's effort and deliver the sales message accurately. The sales task at shop level does not demand sophisticated selling skills. Good experience, stamina,

Table 12.2 Inter-relationships of marketing tasks with factors influencing customer's buying decision

Factors	*Tasks*					
	Market research	*Market forecasting*	*Product planning*	*Distribution planning*	*Sales and administration*	*Advertising and promotion*
Purpose, suitability for	√	–	√	–	–	–
Design, perception of	–	–	√	–	–	√
Price	–	√	√	–	–	–
Availability	–	√	–	√	–	–
Quality	–	–	√	–	–	–
Reputation	–	–	–	–	–	√
Service	–	–	√	√	√	–
Credit	–	√	√	–	–	–
Advertising	√	–	–	–	–	√
Salesman, significance of	–	–	√	–	√	–

perpetual enthusiasm and good work-rate are the prime virtues. Initiative is applauded more than pure intelligence. Care in not crashing your vehicle is another valuable attribute. (But lest it be thought that the consumer salesman is being maligned, two years' apprenticeship in consumer goods gives an excellent understanding of the importance of *activity* in marketing. Remember also, it takes a lot more imagination to talk about a Cream Cracker for any length of time than about some complicated piece of technical equipment.)

Marketing FMCG (fast moving consumer goods) is about distribution, pricing, merchandising and promotion, as well as knowing about competition, short product life-cycles, new products, relaunching products, packaging and repackaging, and market shares. The uncontrollable factors which may threaten you may include: the purchasing strength of distributors and retailers who are getting fewer and larger; the dumping of products by foreign producers; changes in population and age distribution patterns; high cost of media and merchandising operations; tighter margins and cash flow; and own-brand policies by distributors and retailers.

Marketing industrial equipment

Purchasing decisions for industrial equipment involve a more complex scenario. In the first place, the decision is probably going to be made (or influenced) by a group of people each of whom will have a different criterion for decision. Secondly, the greater financial implications of the purchase may demand a more considered and less subjective decision. Thirdly, as most of the supplier proposals will meet the technical specification, decision-making may be difficult and depend upon some of the less tangible aspects of the deal – perhaps the credibility of the salesman.

In such a situation, the influence and skill exerted by the salesman may be the most meaningful part of your marketing strategy. Money and effort will be spent to ensure that the most skilful salesmen are employed and rewarded. Sales support systems will be marshalled, and considerable resources will be speculated in developing relationships with the purchasing team. The salesman is, in this instance, the fulcrum of the marketing function, not only because of his personal persuasive skills, but also because he stage-manages the multiple relationships – technical, commercial, financial – between the supplier and purchaser organizations.

Price might appear to be important but often pressure on price is generated more by your own salesman than by the customer. The customer is interested in a solution to his problem, and price is only important when he has a number of different options. Good industrial selling is about defining the problem for the customer, writing the specification around your product, and eliminating other options. That is why a first-class salesman is going to be more profitable than aggressive pricing. Marketing has to devise a total solution package to enable the skilled salesman to justify his price.

Industrial marketing, because more people are involved in the scenario, has to cater for more permutations of purchasing decision criteria. All the influencing factors will be important to somebody in the decision-making team. For this reason, one cannot ignore even marginal factors like design and appearance. It has been known for key decisions to be made, given equal specifications, on the basis of the colour of the demonstration machine. All factors will be important – but some will be more important than others.

As an industrial marketing manager you will be judged by your personal selling ability, your technical prowess, your experience in the industry, your contacts with key purchasing industries, how customized you can make your service appear, and by your justification of prices. Your skills may be highly personal and related to motivating both customers and your fellow executives. You will pursue a forward looking but realistic R & D programme. At the same time you will be highly sensitive to product life-cycles and be skilful enough to understand the strategic options available to you. As R & D is expensive, getting most out of existing products is important and you will incline more towards market penetration and development. Significant factors outside your control are likely to include: foreign manufacturers taking advantage of favourable experience curve costings and offering lower prices; acceleration of new technology, shorter product life-cycles and pay-off periods; the economic prospects of your customers; greater competition for resource allocation in your own group; and competitive pricing policies based on non-commercial objectives.

Marketing services

Services may mean everything from financial advice to making sure the towels in the washroom are changed at decent intervals. In both cases, what you are marketing is a release from hassle and headache for the customer.

The marketing of expertise

The service you are marketing may be your specialist expertise. The criteria for choice may be similar to that of industrial equipment, with the very real difference that the product is intangible. This complicates the task of the salesperson and makes even more significant his contribution to the customer's decision-making process. However, the more intangible the product, the less comparison is possible with competitive options, which makes for more permutations in pricing strategy. In the expertise field, the marketing task is geared to personal selling and company reputation building. To some extent there is likely to be high speculation of resources before screening out your ultimate customers. This must be controlled by careful definition of target-market segments and procedures for evaluating prospects before too much marketing resource is squandered. Your main resource will be people. You will be measured by the utilization of that resource, and the main problems will be maintaining your people resources in a business which, by definition, may not depend on capital assets.

The marketing of utilities

The service you are marketing may be utilitarian, e.g. hygiene services, office cleaning, etc. or a product with some 'mass' appeal, such as double glazing. Price will be an important influence on the customer's decision but only in so far as there are competitors trying to create differentiation in their proposals. The basis of your marketing strategy must be freedom from hassle, which probably means particular stress on: the company image of *reliability*; *designing* a standard service, which is perceived as a customized solution by the prospect; and *service*, in terms of quick, friendly response and elimination of delay and complications.

Image may be specially significant and measured in terms of vehicle, letter-heads, advertising and testimonials. The importance of the sales function to the marketing mix will depend upon the size of the target market and its accessibility. If you are selling encyclopaedias or double glazing to house-holders you may choose either a selective approach or a mass coverage tech-nique. Premium-priced, 'up market' products and services will call for higher levels of resource selling skills. Such a selective approach will have highly committed sales people following up leads generated by advertising and pro-motional activity. The mass coverage approach may well depend upon an army of modest calibre (perhaps part-time) agents knocking on doors to track down (and convert) the 1% of the population who need little persuasion to buy your product because of genuine, primary, self-generated interest.

These examples may not be readily recognized as services but it is a measure of the importance of 'influencing factors' analysis that more products are being marketed as total services or packages rather than simple products. It could be argued that in recent years individual products have tended to be less distinctive. Saloon cars look the same and have similar performances. The main distinction lies in the total supply package rather than the products – after sales service, guarantees, image, reliability and reputation.

Marketing fashion

Essentially, marketing fashion is the art of making money out of short life-cycle products or businesses. These range from the one-off hoolahoop or skateboard to permanent industries like dresswear or cosmetics which switch smoothly to cater for, or even change, market taste. Such marketing organ-izations may lean heavily on advertising and promotion since the shortness of the product life-cycle does not afford much time for other ways to the market. The business may be about a continuous series of product launches, repackaging, relaunches and brand names. Each project will be a carefully planned operation calling for creativity, timing and courage, but based upon carefully evaluated market volume and financial implications. Outlay may be substantial, pay-off may be quick. There may not be time for market research and indeed a major business in this field may actually create the market (e.g. in dress design, films or toys).

The marketing of fashion goes hand-in-hand with the 'power culture' type of organization. At the centre is the entrepreneur who has the talent and speed of response to capitalize on opportunity. The key marketing skill is to determine the parameters of expectation and to control the project within those limits. It is a sound marketing principle to stay with the winner and cut your losses on the losers. The temptation is to plough more money into a project to cover your mistakes.

The word 'fashion' must not be taken too literally. Management education is an industry with many cyclical fads and vogues. If your business is 'running courses', then your marketing organization must be geared to repackaging your resources to meet the requirements of a target market temporarily inspired by some fashionable guru. They are going to spend their money this year on 'Positional Dominance' or 'Dimensional Management' and there will be no money left for your once popular 'Finance for Non-accountants'. Once you have sorted the product, you will use your mail-shot facilities and membership file to make an immediate penetrating coverage of your target market. One highly reputed management education centre in Europe will mount a 'Famous Name' seminar and is in a position to mail 10 000 prospects initially. If the response exceeds expectation, a further 40 000 mailshots are released. A response rate of 1 : 1000 is calculated as viable on the basis of the fees charged.

Table 12.3 Some special marketing situations

Single-customer businesses:	such as supplies to Government or the National Health Service
Nationalized industries:	where social and political objectives complicate the issues
Monopoly or duopoly:	where the key corporate objective is to protect its position and keep others out
Critical resource businesses:	where a shortage of raw material (or even a foreign currency) may call for higher selectivity in marketing portfolio strategy
Prestige businesses:	such as newspapers where poor financial performance is tolerated in exchange for power

Special marketing situations

Every business is a unique permutation of factors which will influence acceptance in the market place. Sometimes there are very special factors which can distort priorities; these are summarized in Table 12.3.

CONCLUSIONS

In a small business the Marketing Manager (if he is called that) may fulfil all the functions of the marketing mix, perhaps assisted by his accountant, a salesman and the local advertising agency. A large business (which by definition may have a 'role culture') is more likely to boast departments manned by specialists responding to a marketing manager who may be a line-manager or staff manager depending on the extent to which the company is marketing-orientated (or practises unified marketing).

The specific marketing tasks are determined by a number of considerations including the 'culture' and the relative market position of the business. Whether markets are growing, static or in decline, the extent of controllable/uncontrollable factors which influence the enterprise adds further dimensions to the job.

The real essentials of the job however are determined by evaluation of the factors which make your target customer decide for or against you; this shapes your marketing strategy and establishes your priorities. The permutation of possible priorities makes it impossible to define the specific job skills of the marketing manager as a species. However, the marketing tasks and skills associated with a specific industry will cluster around four generic areas: data analysis (economic, statistical, financial); personal selling (including team motivation): advertising and promotion; business strategy and portfolio management. All marketing jobs will have these elements but in each industry there will be one area which will dominate and will determine the acceptance of new entrants to the job. The experience of the marketing manager is likely to be developed in one of these four areas and unless he makes a conscious effort to acquire the full range of skill experiences in his career, this will serve as a constraint in his working life.

References

Handy, C. B. (1976). *Understanding Organisations.* (Harmondsworth: Penguin)
Kotle, P. (1975). *Marketing Management.* (New York: Prentice Hall)
Wright, R. V. L. (1974). *Strategy Centres.* (Cambridge, Mass.: Arthur D. Little)

13 Line Management and Management Services

W. T. SINGLETON

INTRODUCTION

The line manager is always a generalist rather than a specialist. He is part of a hierarchy defined by the 'line' of responsibility. His role is to pursue the objectives of the organization at his particular level, to monitor and adjust activities at lower levels in the context of these objectives and to be sensitive to activities at higher levels which might imply an adjustment of objectives. He must be able to take a broad view and to cope with the great variety of unpredictable and sometimes intangible perturbations which disrupt the smooth running of the organization. Except at the lowest management levels a narrow expertise or interest is regarded as a liability because it will detract from a balanced perspective. He may develop new special skills of a broader kind such as an expertise in distribution or mass production or commerce.

Such men cannot run a large organization unaided. They need specialists and experts who can provide support at many levels of management. There are several kinds of these experts: those who can take decisions and action which laymen would not feel qualified to attempt; those who monitor the routines of the organization; and those who provide, code and structure information on a non-routine basis. The specialized decision and action men are from the physical sciences and the engineering and medical professions; for example the works chemist, the works engineer or the works doctor. The maintainers of routines also now regard themselves as professionals: accountants, lawyers, personnel officers and so on. Their claim to professionalism rests on longer-term non-routine functions to do with development plans or interpretations of policies. The third group have many titles; work study officers, operational researchers, ergonomists, training officers, work designers and, most recently, systems analysts. The term 'management services' could be used to encompass all three groups but it is commonly restricted to the third group. Their history is described in the second volume of this series, *Compliance and Excellence.* Their early aspiration was to 'scientific management' but, after a century or so of practice, they remain a service to line managers of the traditional generalist kind. They are regarded as useful but not as indispensable; when there are cuts in the offing it is always the management services which receive the first reappraisal. The exceptions to this now are the computer people: systems analysts, computer programmers and data processors. They have made remarkable inroads into all kinds of organizations over the past decade. They have established a position so entrenched that the organization could not function without them although the cynics would say that it does not function too well with them either. We have yet to grasp the full implications of this sudden and apparently irresistible change. The data-processing manager is now becoming one of the maintainers of routines. The technology is still developing rapidly and the roles will develop further as micro-computers take over new functions as well as some of the functions recently carried out by main-frame computers and their satellites.

THE MANAGEMENT SERVICE ROLE

Although there is considerable ambiguity in the use of the term, the management services (MS) specialist can be described generally with reasonable accuracy as a person of management status who carries out specialized tasks in support of line management but who does not have the responsibility for management decisions. He will be responsible for preparing a case that something should be done, and may even be responsible for doing it but he will not be responsible for the decision as to whether or not it should be done. This is the precise opposite of the line manager who is there essentially to decide what should be done although he may not have the expertise to either prepare the case or to do it himself. This is not, however, a partnership of equals. To use Churchill's phrase about scientists (who have a management services role in relation to a war-effort) these people must be 'on tap but not on top'. This universally accepted principle has many ramifications.

It confuses the key issue of lines of responsibility. Because he must await the decision of a line manager the MS specialist is effectively responsible to the particular line manager but that line manager may well be totally unqualified technically to assess or to supervise the work of the MS specialist. Nonetheless the line manager's criterion of whether or not the proposal will meet his objectives remains crucial. The orthodox solution to this difficulty is to specifically subordinate the MS specialist to two bosses. One, on a temporary basis, is the line manager for whom he is currently working, another, on a more permanent basis, is a senior person in the management services functions. This does not solve the problem of adequate technical guidance because, for example, the Head of Management Services in a company may have several specialists from quite different disciplines responsible to him. It creates all the standard difficulties about ambiguous responsibilities which have been acknowledged since biblical times. 'No man can serve two masters' (Matthew 6:24). The ambiguity does give the MS specialist some autonomy which, if he is competent, is highly desirable.

There will always be communication difficulties between line management and management services. These are partly due to lack of technical expertise in line management and absence of ultimate responsibility for the MS specialist. More fundamentally the impediment to communication is that the two have very different values; they attach different orders of importance to aspects of a situation. The MS specialist has a professional pride in his application of techniques and the emergence of elegant solutions; the line manager is interested only in feasibility and minimal disturbance of his precarious but functioning system. This last remains true even though the line manager has specifically asked for proposals for change. When the proposals arrive he will often be negative, possibly because having to face the consequences of taking actions is quite different from encouraging the development of a plan and, less honourably, because he never really intended to make any changes but he commissioned the investigation as an alibi which he could quote if pressed by his own seniors. However, the situation is not an impossible one. As the MS specialist gains experience his values will shift from pure discipline-based ones to solution-based ones. He will begin to take a pride in simple, effective strategies. Correspondingly the experienced line-manager will make allowances for the 'culture-gap' between him and the specialist. The MS specialist may be a colleague of certain line managers on a more or less permanent basis; he may be semiexternal in that he is an employee of the same company but functioning from some central service facility which the line manager actually has to pay for, or he may be external in that he moves from company to company as a Management Consultant.

MANAGEMENT SERVICE PROCEDURE

The MS specialist has three phases of activity: firstly he must execute an investigation which is within his technical competence, secondly he must communicate the results of this work to management and thirdly he may be required to implement whatever change is decided upon by the line managers.

Technical investigations

Any investigation implies that some evidence is to be selected, collated and structured within an orientation provided by an hypothesis, a model or a theory. The different MS specialists use different models (Singleton, 1979). The business analyst traces what happens to the money, the work-study practitioner traces what happens in time, the ergonomist looks at bodily and behavioural functions, the training specialist considers what can be done by changing skills, the work-restructuring specialist thinks in terms of attitudes and motivation, the systems analyst considers how new computer functions may be inserted in the system, and the operational researcher uses a mathematical approach to model some key parameters of a system – usually a procedure. It can be argued that the business analyst is the most fundamental because he deals in money which is the final common measure, but the operational researcher, as a quantifier of complex interactions, has the most generalized procedure; this is regarded as having the following phases:

(1) Study the context – the organization, the people and other constraints.

(2) Decide on the criteria of effectiveness which are measurable (productivity, efficiency, speed, cost, etc.)

(3) Set up a mathematical model to represent the system under study, e.g. linear programming, queueing theory, critical path analysis, etc.

(4) Collect data which can be fed into the model.

(5) Manipulate the model to check its validity and to generate some possible solutions in terms of the criteria.

(6) Communicate the new understanding of the situation to line management, including one or more possible solutions. Invite comments and a decision.

(7) Evaluate by monitoring the implementation in practice and examining the validity of predictions.

In fact all MS specialists follow this procedure but with their specific biases in terms of preferred models as indicated earlier. This is not the place to describe in detail the expertise of particular specialists. Descriptions of specialisms written without excessive jargon are available elsewhere: for example, business analysis (Horngren, 1977; van Horne, 1980); work study and related topics (Livy, 1975; ILO, 1979); ergonomics (Singleton, 1972; Grandjean, 1979); training (Barber, 1968; Stammers and Patrick, 1975); work-restructuring (Davis and Taylor, 1972; Sell and Shipley, 1979); systems analysis (Davis, 1974; Daniels and Yeates, 1979); and operational research (Ackoff and Sasieni, 1968; Littlechild, 1977). Technical competence is indicated by modelling ability in one or more of these fields but operational success is much more dependent on the ability to understand the constraints, to acquire valid data and to help managers make effective decisions – in short, on the ability to communicate.

COMMUNICATION

The MS specialist is, in social and cultural terms, functioning within other people's territory. This can be an advantage in the sense that the spectator sees most of the game but it seriously inhibits communication.

In his first phase of understanding the context he must talk to many people and, inevitably, they want to know why he wants to know. If he explains honestly that he is investigating the possibility of change he may easily come to be regarded as a threat. For most people even a *status quo* with many known liabilities and limitations is preferable to an unknown innovation designed by an outsider. His strategy to deal with this obstacle is a combination of two essentially opposite approaches: on the one hand he can imply, tactfully of course, that he is a professional in some esoteric expertise which ordinary workers can't be expected to understand but which will make their job easier if they cooperate, and on the other hand he can stress his unfamiliarity with the situation compared with those with years of experience and invite them to advise him on what needs to be done. He will imply that the management will listen to him and therefore he can get something done about deficiencies which are obvious to the workers, but unknown to the management. He will stress that anything said to him is confidential in the sense that its source will not be revealed to management. This is not a confidence trick; in any organization communication upwards is difficult and the MS specialist can be a very important channel in this communication.

In the case of data as distinct from opinions the MS specialist will be very cautious. He knows by experience that all data from real situations are contaminated by many fluctuating effects some of them can be identified but others are quite untraceable and unpredictable. However, he will find out what he can because this must be the basis of his recommendation; the line manager ought to be better than he is at the impressionistic approach. There will be some 'hard' data to do with physical dimensions – costs, ages and so on. There will be some ostensibly hard data which in fact need expert knowledge of norms such as that to do with environmental variables – light, heat, noise and vibration. There will be a plethora of 'soft' data which require considerable selection and interpretation to do with rates of action or production, quality standards, crises, failures, errors, absences and so on. Some of these data exist and need only be picked up, whereas others have to be generated by various survey techniques which can vary from production sampling to opinion studies. This is the first category of communication. All these data acquisition methods are dependent on effective cooperation between the data sources which are always people and the investigator.

The second category of communication is with line-management. The MS specialist needs to know what his objectives are, including allowable costs and time scale. Sometimes these can be formally stated in a memorandum or contract but even here there is ambiguity which usually takes the form of open-endedness. Often the statement of objectives is left to the investigator after discussions with line-management. Finally, on the basis of his directive, his model and evidence the MS specialist will have arrived at a new understanding of the situation and what might be done about it. Superficially this might appear to conclude his part of the proceedings but all this is mere preparation for the key phase which is to convey his picture of the situation back to line management. The orthodox procedure for doing this has three parts: a written report, a verbal presentation, and a discussion. All these have their own difficulties, the general underlying obstacle already mentioned is that the MS specialist and the line manager have different ways of thinking and different priorities.

The report is, from the MS specialist's point of view, a statement of an exercise within his professional expertise. He probably likes to explain his procedures for overcoming obstacles, the depth of his theory, the fittingness of his modelling and the elegance of his solutions. The line manager is not interested in difficulties or concepts, only in remedies. His attitude is summed up in the standard reaction to lengthy reports or presentations: 'Don't tell me how clever you are, or what the problem is, tell me what the answer is!' The report should contain the facts coded and presented in the context of the issue to be discussed. It forms the data store and the catalogue of relations between variables in the form of graphs and diagrams. To take account of the limited time and interest of the recipient it is common practice to have a brief text which surveys the situation and the proposals supported by extensive appendices containing the detail. The presentation should concentrate on the model and the remedies it generates with emphasis on the latter and the comparative pros and cons of different remedies if more than one is available.

If both parties are competent the discussion phase can be most interesting and satisfying. The line manager will seize upon a solution and examine its feasibility in terms of his priorities. He will have inexpressible intuitions about what is right or not right and he will question the MS specialist to clarify his own thinking. The MS specialist will respond by translating the vague objections or approvals into more rigorous if more limited terminology, and he will provide evidence which confirms some feelings and refutes others. There is a common trap here in that, when asked to explain his objections the line manager may generate reasons which the MS specialist can easily demonstrate are invalid but the objection itself may still be valid for reasons which the line manager feels intuitively but which he cannot express verbally. The line manager will look for compromises and will prefer procedures which are not too radical and which can be reversed without too much damage if too many unpredicted obstacles emerge. The MS specialist will agree, partly because he has no choice but partly also because he knows the line manager will be much more committed to something which he believes he has thought of himself.

The ideal solution is ultimately less important than any agreed solutions which everyone involved is really committed to. Nevertheless it is sometimes desirable to start with the ideal solution and compare this with the practicable solution to provide a check on the extent of the compromise being made. On the other hand too intensive a pursuit of the ideal can interfere with acceptance of the reasonable. There are two different approaches – one as just mentioned is to leap to the ideal and then retreat to the feasible; the other is to proceed step by step from the present to the possible future, stopping when reality intervenes too strongly. Both approaches rely ultimately on a cost/value criterion although costs and values are always multidimensional and many are unquantifiable.

IMPLEMENTATION

Successful implementation is again dependent on good communications with all those involved in the system more particularly those at the lower levels who will have to continue to keep the system running when the innovators have departed to make more innovations elsewhere. There is bound to be a difficult early phase because many of the participants are required to become accustomed to new routines and to abandon older ones. This is not so difficult providing that the basic skills remain the same or, at least, that new skills can be developed by modifications and supplements to those already existing. It can be very difficult if radical switches of skill have to be made as for example when a craftsman is invited to become a process operator or a filing clerk becomes a computer operator. There has to be adequate underlying constancies which enable workers to feel that their previous experience is still relevant. These constancies can take many forms; the same raw materials, either substances or information or perhaps the same people who either provide the inputs or accept the outputs. The version of Murphy's law which states that 'anything which can go wrong, will go wrong' is particularly applicable to innovatory phases. It is difficult enough to cope with the vagaries of physical systems but if the people involved are either negative or hostile this will confound the situation further. No new system will function unless the majority of the people involved are positively inclined to make it function. Effective implementation, in common with every other kind of work, depends entirely on the skills and attitudes of the participants. Thus, the MS specialist or line manager responsible for innovation will ensure that there are adequate resources of time and money to cope with the personnel aspects as well as the equipment and procedural aspects.

MANAGEMENT SERVICE SKILLS

These can be subdivided into technical, conceptual, practical and political.

Technical skills

These are acquired during the academic and professional training of the practitioner. They are necessary but not sufficient as the repertoire of a competent MS specialist. There is a danger that as he gains the obviously necessary practical and political skills he will tend to underestimate the importance of the technical skills and he will become, in effect, a charlatan operating on his wits and his experience. The knowledge and techniques within any discipline advance continuously and it is desirable that the practitioner stays up-to-date even though he may not see any use for the new methods in his current job. He might argue, with some justification, that the detailed practice of techniques is a sure indication of the novice. The experienced practitioner may still be relying on his expertise but may get to the right solution without going through the detailed exercise. Nonetheless the expertise must be there in the background. Professional societies' meetings and journals provide an essential service in keeping their members informed; it is not easy for them to function at the appropriate level. At the instigation of their members, they can become too practically orientated and degenerate into catalogues of case-studies; equally if the only speakers and writers are pure academics they can drift the other way into the development of esoteric concepts which have no practical relevance. Maintaining the right balance is difficult but essential for effective meetings or journals.

For all these reasons a proper education in a particular field is a crucial asset; a mere training in the application of current techniques will date very quickly. A good education in a particular field provides the enduring base on which the developing repertoire of techniques can be built throughout the working career.

The implication here is that technical skills form a hierarchy or concatenation from the general abstract theory to the specific applicatory technique. The whole forms a model of some aspects of reality, some ways of manipulating the model and some ways of acquiring reliable and valid evidence which can relate the model to a specific situation. This model is inevitably symbolic; it involves generalizations which are abstractions from many particular perceptions of reality but these abstractions are related both to a real situation under study and in so far as they prove to fit (that is they provide understanding and successful prediction) then the application advances but because they do not quite fit exactly then the model itself will advance and will in future incorporate the new knowledge. Although the MS specialist may never have comprehended what he is doing in these terms he nevertheless does it successfully. In short, he is and must remain a technologist, applying scientific models and scientific thinking to new situations.

Conceptual skills

These follow directly from the technology. The MS specialist is faced with a system which is not functioning satisfactorily from the point of view of the parent system of which he also is a part. In common with every other skilled observer he models this bit of reality but the model he uses is drawn from his own technology or professional expertise. He must have a higher level model or executive programme which guides his thinking in the making of choices such as that the problem is or is not within his expertise and if it is within his expertise then a particular theory or procedure is selected as the most fitting. This fit is not merely the matching of the model to the problem, it includes also the practical constraints of the available resources and the accessibility of necessary evidence. He goes through this apparently quite difficult intellectual exercise by a process of interaction and convergence. He begins by a very general scan of the total situation within the context of the external constraints: his budget, his time available, his terms of references and so on. He alternates between this gross perception of the whole and detailed perception of the minutiae which are considered in a sequential and systematic way by checking elements against a list which may be a formal written check-list or a less formal list internalized in his mind. This sampling of detail seems to be a procedure for reinforcing or refuting the overall impression he has already formed. The more skilled he is the less he needs these detailed sampling checks and the less he relies on formal techniques such as ticking off check-lists or preparing routinized charts. In a sense the more skilled he is the more he approaches the problem as a line manager would, except that he is still working within the formal modelling techniques of his particular profession. He has to bear in mind that arriving at the solution is not enough, he has to communicate this solution to others and he may need the detail as a vehicle for communications rather than as a necessary part of his own convergent thinking.

One difference between a highly skilled and a less skilled practitioner is that the former has a greater awareness of and sensitivity to the key bits of evidence which determine whether or not a particular hypothesis is worth following. These bits of evidence may come from the situations under study, from the balance of objectives or from the constraints. In common with every other skilled thinker the MS specialist is operating in an internalized multi-dimensional decision space with parameters from many different domains interacting in a manner which has meaning for him.

Practical skills

The MS specialist has some minor motor skills to do with preparation of specialized charts and diagrams and in interaction with computers but even at the practical level his skills are predominantly perceptual. They are similar to universal perceptual skills in that they involve identifying a useful signal when it appears within a welter of noise. This may occur visually when walking around a factory, an office or any other working environment and locating the cues which indicate symptoms of a problem or it may be in a conversation with an interested party when, out of all the redundancies and irrelevancies, there emerges a key phrase which again orientates the investigator towards the problem or even the solution to the problem.

To achieve this sensitivity as a recipient of information requires two conditions. Firstly he must be able to participate without disturbing the main action in a situation, whether they be workers working or individuals and groups involved in discussions. Secondly, he must know enough already to be able to pick up the cue when it becomes available. A single cue such as a chance remark or a key piece of behaviour may generate the solution. This is what Branton (1979) graphically described as the 'rendezvous with a stranger'. Alternatively, by selecting the essential cues and ignoring the mass of irrelevant detail he may recognize the form of the problem for which there is a known solution.

This assumes that the investigator arrives at his solution on the spot by creative thinking but there are, of course, other less dramatic and less inspired but still successful ways of proceeding. He may use the ability to selectively search the academic or technical literature to identify a piece of equipment or a procedure which will form an appropriate innovation.

When the solution is agreed he may become involved in the implementation which requires other practical skills. One way of establishing confidence is to demonstrate competence by doing the job personally under the new conditions and then gradually hand it back to the routine operators. This will perhaps apply more at the supervisor level than at the operator level, since operators and sometimes supervisors have special skills which the investigator relies upon for the success of his solution although he may not have these skills himself.

Political skills

Knowledge of the locus of power and the manipulation of power is an essential facet of the MS specialist's skills. Any innovation is bound to disturb the balance of power and influence within the organization. The innovator must be aware of what is happening in these terms. Sometimes line managers use innovations as strategies within their personal power struggles and although this is not necessarily undesirable it can have a fundamental influence on the success or failure of a particular project. The MS specialist is not adequately skilled if he only realizes afterwards why his innocent proposals were completely blocked at some management level. He gains knowledge of these situations not by interacting directly himself but by observing interactions between others and perhaps by deliberately provoking these interactions. Power rests not only with individuals but also with institutions such as trade unions and professional associations. A background knowledge of these matters is also essential.

LINE MANAGEMENT SKILLS

The contrasting roles of the MS specialist and the line-manager gives some indication of the skills of the latter. The essence of the line manager's job is that he must keep the system in operation and aligned with the requirements set by the parent system. He is a maintainer and a progress-chaser. In common with all other skilled performers he has perceptual skills, conceptual skills and implementation skills. His perceptual skills are the most specific and distinguish his particular job. Every system is subject to perturbations from its environment which are resisted by inertia and by negative feedback loops. The line-manager is like any other steersman; he monitors the behaviour of the system under his control and he continuously makes decisions as to whether the perceived perturbations are such that the system will put itself right or whether the disturbance is such that he must take positive action to correct it. He is most likely to be using an enactive model; the system is an extension of his body-image and basically he functions intuitively although his intuition may be reinforced or modified by pictorial or abstract data. He cannot be remote from the system he is controlling, he must be within it and reacting continuously to its behaviour including its reactions to his actions. Such skills are not easily accessible to introspection and this explains why the literature and theory on line management is so poor. The practitioners literally do not know how they do it. Their skill is not related to their ability to think about their jobs or to analyse their actions. These comments only apply to the on-line control function. If the manager is also responsible for generating his own objectives then he will need conceptualizing skills to do the planning.

The implementation skills also are more complex than those of a steersman of a physical system. The manager steers by acting through other people. To do this effectively he must be sensitive to their individual characteristics and limitations. In addition he must deal with groups and institutions; they in turn have characteristics and limitations which are not predictable from the attributes of the individual members. These social skills are quite different from the basic steering skills and there is more profit from analysis and conceptualization at the pictorial and symbolic level.

The line manager interacts also with other line managers above him, below him, and at his own level in the hierarchy. This is a competitive position; his personal interests intrude on his actions and they may not always coincide with the interests of the system he is there to control. These political aspects of the management role are extremely complex; they will reappear in Volume 4 of this series, on social skills.

The point at present is to contrast line management and management services. The line manager is more of an intuitionist and an artist; the MS specialist is more of a systematic thinker and a scientist. The line manager is usually a more ambitious and politically sensitive person, but the MS specialist also has these very human attributes which intrude on his work, sometimes beneficially and sometimes not.

MANAGEMENT SERVICE CAREERS

The MS specialist is inevitably in a position of some frustration. It is the nature of his work that he must wait upon decisions by another person who he may well consider to be his intellectual inferior (at least until he has enough experience to become aware of the subtle skills of line management). His promotion prospects within his specialism and within one organization are not usually very good. Even large companies are unlikely to have more than two or three management grades for one kind of specialist. Since many of the skills are dependent on experience in one company mobility is low and a MS specialist over about 40 years old is unlikely to be attractive to another company. Thus if he gets promotion he is likely to stay in the job and to block the promotion of others. There are some compensations. The day to day pressure is not so high as it is in line management and there is satisfaction in the creativity and innovation which is often required. Nevertheless there are fundamental problems for an energetic ambitious person. There are two orthodox remedies.

Firstly he can move into line management. This can be successful if he has the necessary attributes and if he moves rapidly enough. The combination of line management skills and a broad technical expertise in a management service discipline can be very formidable. A management service post with a series of assignments across a company is a valuable initial training phase for line management over a period of not more than five years. Beyond this time the individual is likely to be too closely identified with his particular discipline. Secondly he can shift into the educational world. This is a common solution which can be satisfactory to everyone concerned. The educational instititution gains a person with practical experience to supplement his academic expertise. The company gains in mobility and flexibility to adjust the range of skills within the management services and perhaps to make promotions.

The company can, of course, avoid the long-term problem by relying on external consultants in the MS role, either from specialist companies or from the educational world. In the current working world where obligations to every employee increase steadily with his time with the company, this can be a most economic strategy.

A CASE STUDY

Since this chapter has been highly generalized in order to comment across all MS roles and on general MS skill it seems appropriate to conclude by a case study of a specific project.

The problem

The company had changed, some years previously, from a set of warehouses scattered across the country to one central warehouse. The Sales Director complained that many salesmen's visits to customers were on a five-day cycle and often a second visit would be made before the order received on the previous visit had been delivered. The Distribution Manager considered whether to reverse the centralized policy and go back to area warehouses: he put the problem to Management Services.

The procedure

Three kinds of data were collected:

(1) The details and history of a sample of 2000 orders were computerized. The sample was random but a check was made that it covered the obvious strata.

(2) Salesmen were interviewed.

(3) Some information about competitors' performance, customers' attitudes and national trends was obtained.

The results

The time taken to process each order was separated into: order note → delivery note (average 2.9 days); assemble and despatch (93% sent on day delivery note received); despatch to carrier (average 11.4 days); and carrier delivery (average 2.9 days).

Frequency distributions were obtained for each part of the process and for the total process. The average delivery time was 7.2 days. 37% were delivered within 5 days and 95% were delivered within 11 days.

The consensus amongst the salesman was that it did not matter if they made a second visit before the previous order had been delivered provided the customer had been given an accurate delivery time.

Generally competitors performance seemed to be the same or worse, whether or not they had depots. Customers confirmed that reliability was usually more important than speed.

Delivery points are still dwindling. The trend is towards larger, fewer shops (there are 1.7 shops per 1000 population in the UK, 0.7 shops per 1000 population in the Netherlands), and small shops tend to buy more from local general warehousing centres.

The proposals

Firstly, in view of the long time taken to process an order, a detailed costing was made of various alternative methods of processing: salesmen phoning orders into clerks; salesmen keying orders directly into computers by telephone; salesmen entering forms read directly by computer, etc. The delivery time of all letters was analysed into a distribution (average 1.4 days). The time saving by phoning-in was examined in detail, and the choice was left to the Board.

Secondly, there was no evidence to justify returning to regional depots. The Sales Director queried this again but at another meeting his Sales Managers confirmed the MS view.

References

Ackoff, R. L. and Sasieni, M. W. (1968). *Fundamentals of Operations Research.* (New York: Wiley)

Barber, J. W. (1968). *Industrial Training Handbook.* (London: Iliffe)

Branton, P. (1979). The Research Scientist. In Singleton, W. T. (ed.) *Compliance and Excellence, Vol. 2 Real Skills*, Chapter 13. (Lancaster: MTP)

Daniels, A. and Yeates, D. (1979). *Basic Training in Systems Analysis.* (London: Pitman)

Davis, G. B. (1974). *Management Information Systems.* (New York: McGraw–Hill)

Davis, L. E. and Taylor, J. C. (1972). *Design of Jobs.* (Harmondsworth: Penguin)

Grandjean, E. (1979). *Ergonomics in Industry.* (London: Taylor & Francis)

Horngren, C. T. (1977). *Cost Accounting.* (London: Prentice-Hall International)

International Labour Office (1979). *Introduction to Work Study.* (Geneva: International Labour Office)

Livy, B. (1975). *Job Evaluation.* (London: George, Allen & Unwin)

Littlechild, S. C. (1977). *Operational Research for Managers.* (Oxford: Philip Allan)

Sell, R. G. and Shipley, P. (eds.) (1979). *Satisfaction in Work Design.* (London: Taylor & Francis)

Singleton, W. T. (1972). *Introduction to Ergonomics.* (Geneva: WHO)

Singleton, W. T. (1979). Some conceptual and operational doubts about job satisfaction. In Sell, R. G. and Shipley, P. (eds.) *Satisfaction in Work Design.* (London: Taylor & Francis)

Stammers, R. and Patrick, J. (1975). *The Psychology of Training.* (London: Methuen)

van Horne, J. (1980). *Financial Management Policy.* (London: Prentice-Hall International)

Warr, P. B. (1976). (ed.) *Personal Goals and Work Design.* (London: Wiley)

14

Management Education and Training

G. A. RANDELL

INTRODUCTION

By taking a skills approach to management some severe questions and practical implications arise for management education and training. These will be first set out in simple terms, then analysed in depth. The main problem is to define the nature of managerial skill. Like all skills, it can be approached in a broad way through defining objectives or standards of performance, i.e. the macro-level of definition. Alternatively, it can be defined narrowly when it is regarded as a sequential process, where timing of exact acts achieves a defined single purpose at a precise instant, i.e. the micro-level of definition. One of the main problems in all skills definition is integrating the macro-level descriptions with the micro-level, for skills when performed expertly are both superb totalities and exquisite individual acts. So how can this be achieved?

The next difficulty arises from the observation that managerial skill is a sensitive issue. Most managers would not be willing to own to lacking in it; 'How else would I have got my job?' would be a common retort to the implication that a manager had skills to learn. A lack of managerial knowledge may be grudgingly admitted, but not skill. As skills can only be learned by people who want to learn them, how can highly experienced and senior managers be encouraged to want to become more skilful?

The next problem is setting up the skills training. Skills can only be acquired from practice with feedback about the effects and effectiveness of performance. As has been implied many times elsewhere in this book, practice without feedback is sterile. Sadly, managers are still heard giving as evidence for their level of skill their twenty years experience, but without feedback. So how can training be established so that managers have the opportunity to do exercises and get feedback from tutors?

Another difficulty arises from the fact that it is not possible to become skilful at anything with just a few days or even a few weeks of skills training. Acquiring knowledge can be achieved through a flash of insight when sitting at a desk, or anywhere, even including lectures on management training courses! But a skill has to be built up laboriously and sometimes painfully, over a long period of time. No skill of any consequence is ever acquired easily, so how can the complex skills of management be established and extended through the occupational life of a manager?

THE NATURE OF MANAGERIAL SKILL

Managers are people who make things happen to individuals, in organizations and within society. By taking a systems approach to human society, from the viewpoint of the work that has to be done to maintain and develop society in relation to individual workers, a simple outline of management emerges (see Figure 14.1). The boxes represent the 'constants' in the system and the arrows the main 'interactions'. Three levels of management and eight main interactions can be seen, starting with individuals in relation to their tasks, then jobs, and working up to work groups and organizations and then to the relationships between societies and cultures and how they all interact back to produce the individuals that make up the world of work. These are the processes that lead both to stability and change in the world of work. Of course the interactions are taking place 'naturally' within the system; however, it could be hoped that the total system could be made more effective if the interactions were managed skilfully. This is the basic assumption that underlines all managerial activity.

Many people would argue that nature is a considerable force to beat, and that managers are more inclined to have a dysfunctional effect on the interactions! Evidence for this can be gained from the many examples of managers who have destroyed rather than enhanced the systems that they have attempted to manage. The question is, what exactly is skilful management that does result in a system being more effective? Unfortunately, this question is so broad that to answer it would require analysis at the economic, sociological, or even religious levels, incorporating the kinds of explanations and criteria for effectiveness that are applicable in such systems. This chapter is written at the psychological level and is concerned with managerial behaviour, and so the analysis will continue at the behavioural level. The systems and skills approach to management creates the need to identify the different kinds of interaction and the main problems arising from them. This is a necessary next step in understanding the nature of management, so that skills are built on explanations of the rules and processes that make up the system and on the awareness of what has to be achieved as a result of the interactions.

Figure 14.1 demonstrates a system in which all components can be said to

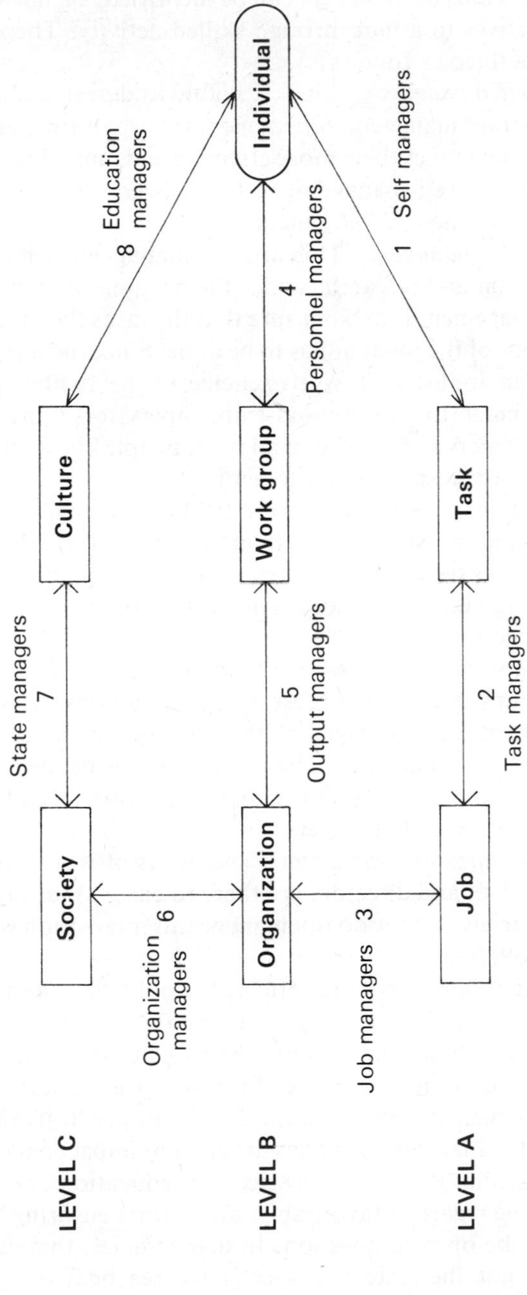

Figure 14.1 The system of management

interact, but the first analysis indicates eight main interactions. For the system to work effectively these interactions need to be managed skilfully. Consequently eight kinds of managers can be identified, each with decisions to make and objectives to attain through skilled activity. These groups of managers can be defined as follows.

Interaction 1 – Self-managers This is a highly underrated skill. Courses exist that claim to train managers to manage their use of time and personal resources in a way that makes them more effective and minimizes their stress. Nevertheless training in self-management is still a very sensitive and under-utilized area of management development.

Interaction 2 – Task managers This area of management has received a great deal of attention and research, under the heading of 'supervision'. A critical area of management is making sure that the tasks the individuals can perform fit the needs of the job that has to be done. Since the introduction of the Training Within Industry (T.W.I.) scheme in the 1940's considerable efforts have been made to educate and train supervisors, foremen, office managers, section leaders and in general all those people known as 'first-line' managers who have the responsibility to get jobs done.

Interaction 3 – Job managers This is the field of 'management services'. There are various kinds of 'staff' rather than 'line' managers whose function is to study and improve the effectiveness of jobs in relation to organizational needs. These would include practitioners in work study, in organization and methods, and in ergonomics.

Interaction 4 – Personnel managers The interaction between individuals and their work groups, e.g. their professions, trade unions, training boards and legal arrangements, are managed by the personnel managers.

Interaction 5 – Output managers The responsibility for meeting production targets and standards, or levels of service, is the province of the departmental heads and the general managers.

Interaction 6 – Organization managers The heads of work organizations such as chief executives and directors are there to ensure that organizations meet the needs of society. If they do not manage this interaction well enough, then bankruptcy follows.

Interaction 7 – State managers Hopefully, the politicians and senior civil servants in a society manage well enough to maintain and develop the culture required by the members of that society, their electorate. If the quality of legislation is high then the quality of life of the individuals, not only in terms of economic development but also in cultural well-being, will also be high. It is perhaps this area of management that has the greatest impact on most people. Although the effort that goes into the selection, education and training of civil servants must be regarded favourably, any efforts ensuring the abilities of politicians must be open to question. In democracies, there are ways to signal whether or not the state managers have reached the standard of management expected of them by means of the ballot box.

Interaction 8 – Education managers The final main interaction to be considered in this system occurs between a culture maintained by the society and the individuals within it. This interaction can be said to be managed by the academics of the culture, who by their study and teaching develop individuals in relation to their cultural heritage. There are examples both in history and many parts of the world today, where a change in culture is being brought about by the people who manage the educational activities of the state. The conditioning and indoctrination of children is one of the peaceful ways to change a culture. In higher levels of education the opportunities to teach radical ideas to students has been the springboard for many a revolution. Education managers in society bear a heavy responsibility, and how best they should be educated and trained is a practical problem of considerable importance.

Figure 14.1 also demonstrates three main levels of managerial responsibility. Each level has its own techniques, concepts and even theories to cope with the problems that arise at the particular levels. The activities and issues that dominate these levels can be set out as follows.

Level A – Work content This area of managerial activity makes much use of the techniques of work study. The problems for the manager include the introduction of new processes and equipment and present a possible conflict between how work is controlled and how workers are controlled. The more detailed techniques of method study are often used by managers to develop this segment of the system together with those of ergonomics. The possible source of conflict here is matching the needs of the organization by loading as much work as possible onto a worker, and the needs of workers to use adequately their abilities within the scope of the job that they are asked to do.

Level B – Work context Every organization develops, either explicitly or implicitly, certain policies concerning the treatment of workers. Many concepts concerned with working conditions and rewards exist. This level makes use of knowledge about motivation to work and theories of leadership. The problem of management here is whether or not the managerial procedures that are used by an organization can be changed so that they meet the expectations of the individual workers in a way which would add to the effectiveness of the organization to meet its objectives.

Level C – Work structure The techniques of organizational analysis throw some light on the managerial problems that arise from different work structures. Traditional ideas concerning such concepts as bureaucracy have relevance to the creation and distribution of wealth and power within the closed system of the management of worker behaviour. In such a system, wealth and power are as much a resource as raw materials, equipment, and capital. It is a useful and interesting academic exercise to speculate upon the 'ownership' of such commodities inside the system and to see how far such thinking leads to understanding about the more diffuse but key managerial issues such as job satisfaction, quality of life, pollution, and cultural survival.

One purpose of analysing Figure 14.1 in detail is to illustrate a very important point: this is the range of knowledge and expertise required of managers. This range is so wide that it is not expected to be found in an individual manager, nor in a single management education and training course. The particular system put forward above attempts to show the relationships between the various kinds and levels of management, so that any curriculum development for management education can be built upon an awareness of the differences that exist.

The systems approach to management set out in Figure 14.1 can be contrasted with other systems approaches to understanding and controlling the operations of work organizations. A managerial theory viewpoint, based on the functions of planning, organizing, controlling and communicating was taken by Johnson, Kast and Rosenzweig (1967). A more behavioural approach, emphasizing the constants, constraints and treatments inherent in a more 'open' system was taken by Randell (1966, 1978). A diagnostic approach was taken by Seiler (1967), who emphasized the organizational, technological and human forces that bring about choices and constraints within work organizations. All these systems approaches have in common the attempt to set out an overview of managerial activity in terms and in a form which aids understanding of a highly complex field. Like all systems approaches, the focus is on the main interactions of the essential operations within the system and the main points of contact of the system with the environment or outside world. The purpose of presenting such systems is to ensure that the main explanatory concepts which are required to understand the function of the system are placed in context.

SKILLS AND MANAGEMENT TRAINING

The above section illustrates the macro-level approach to defining managerial skills. Such broad overviews of the objectives of management can make attractive and stimulating reading. Unfortunately an understanding of any concept is necessary but not sufficient to be able to put into action the practical implications of the knowledge. This is the key to the difference between education and training. Management education is concerned with providing understanding about the nature and objectives of managerial activity. It starts, as this chapter has done, with broad concepts. Unfortunately, a great deal of management development stops there, built on the assumption that providing able people with an understanding of management, is all that is necessary to enable them to practise it. This assumption is a dangerous oversimplification. It requires considerable skill to bridge the gap between complex concepts and appropriate purposeful behaviour. The inculcation of this skill must be the objective of management training. Glaser (1962) puts the difference succinctly by saying that education is aimed at coping with behavioural endproducts that are difficult to specify, and the activity of training is applied to behaviour that can be precisely specified. Skilled people are able to bridge the chasm between concepts and behaviour; they can arrive at solutions to problems for which there is not a set formula. They achieve this by being able to perform all relevant and appropriate behaviours, and at the precise moment, being able to select the right action.

Consequently management training starts at the opposite end of the curriculum, the acquisition of the ability to perform exact acts. It is interesting to note the difference in emphasis in Britain between education and training in engineering and in management. In engineering, training usually starts with hours spent at the bench learning to file 'flat and square' and other basic acts; only later does the teaching of broad concepts appear in the process. In management the reverse is more apparent. After being appointed a manager, courses in a Training Centre or Business School based on the broad issues and concepts of management are experienced, and only later, if at all, comes training in the specific acts of management. It can be argued that the macro- and micro-approaches to becoming a skilled engineer or manager have become out of balance, but in opposite ways.

The problem is where to start with the training in the micro-processes of management. Management ability is extremely diverse and varies with the different functions that managers perform. The macro-approach to defining management, as the previous analysis displayed, is mainly concerned with organizational aspects. The micro-approach starts its analysis with the question; 'What does a manager actually do?' In a study of 66 middle managers in ten British firms, Horne and Lupton (1965) showed that 76% of a manager's time was used in interacting with other people for the purposes of getting work done or assessing the needs of subordinates or colleagues. Stewart (1967) showed in a study of two groups totalling 160 British Managers, one group spent on average 66%, and the other 80% of their time in direct oral communication with other people. Of this time, 47% of their time was spent with their staff and immediate colleagues, 41% with people outside their group and 12% of their time with their more senior managers. Mintzberg (1973) in a similar diary study of five American Chief Executives found that 78% of their time was spent in direct oral communication, of which 48% was with subordinates, 44% with people outside the organization and 7% with other directors and corporate trustees. As a result of these studies, and many more like them, it can be concluded that the essential activity of a manager is to get the work needed by an organization done through the people who work for and with the organization, and at the same time meet the needs of the people involved in doing it. The operational basis of managerial behaviour must be in making use of the human resources provided by the organization to meet the organization's ongoing and continuing objectives, and in so doing to meet also the ongoing and continuing needs of the staff. Starting from the assumption that the staff are able and willing in the first place to meet the organization's objectives (the selection process having been skilfully undertaken and industrial relations not being sour) then the essence of the manager's job is to use and develop the capacities of the staff, to maintain and perhaps create the conditions of growth and to orient the staff to apply their capacities to the tasks to be done. This sounds easy, but to achieve it requires the assembling of a considerable amount of information about the determinants and outcomes of an individual member of staff's job performance, to check this information with a member of staff concerned and finally to decide and hopefully agree upon a course of action. This foundation of managerial activity can be defined as data-based decision-making about human behaviour at work.

The starting point, therefore, for a skills approach to management, is the notion that the behaviour of an effective manager stems from a set of interlocking information gathering and using activities. This includes first the diagnosis of what subordinates have to do next to achieve or improve performance standards (use or add to ability), and second, the diagnosis of what the manager has to do next to maintain or add to subordinates' motivation to work at the task, and third, the main twist, the agreement of action plans that bring about the outcomes of the diagnoses, to which both subordinates and manager are committed.

To help the understanding and learning of this process, a diagrammatic model has been developed in Figure 14.2. This gives a descriptive account of the structure of the skill of managing the capacity and inclination of people to work. Obviously the total skill of managing is far more complex than this diagram indicates, but it is argued that any complex theoretical structure has to be built on firm conceptual foundations. This is used as the starting point from which students and managers can build their skills.

Figure 14.2 shows just how complicated is the apparently straightforward task of developing people in their jobs. Further, the point needs to be made that this rather simple notion is surrounded by all the complexities of the fundamental psychological theories of perception, learning, motivation, personality and even psychotherapy. The model shows that analysing and then developing a subordinate's capacity is the primary step (if an individual is basically incapable of doing the job the manager is thwarted from the outset). It displays how the management of motivation is concerned with the interactions that take place between what is 'inside' a person and 'in' a job. This is affected by individual differences and time, as well as the economic and organizational conditions of the task. Finally the question is asked; 'Are the individual's and organization's needs met?' If they are, then after an appropriate interval of time, the cycle starts again. If not, the individual may have to be transferred to another job, or if no needs are being met, then plans to restructure the organization will have to be made.

Figure 14.2 gives a conceptual model for managing the work of individuals. It still does not show how it should be done. To get to this level of

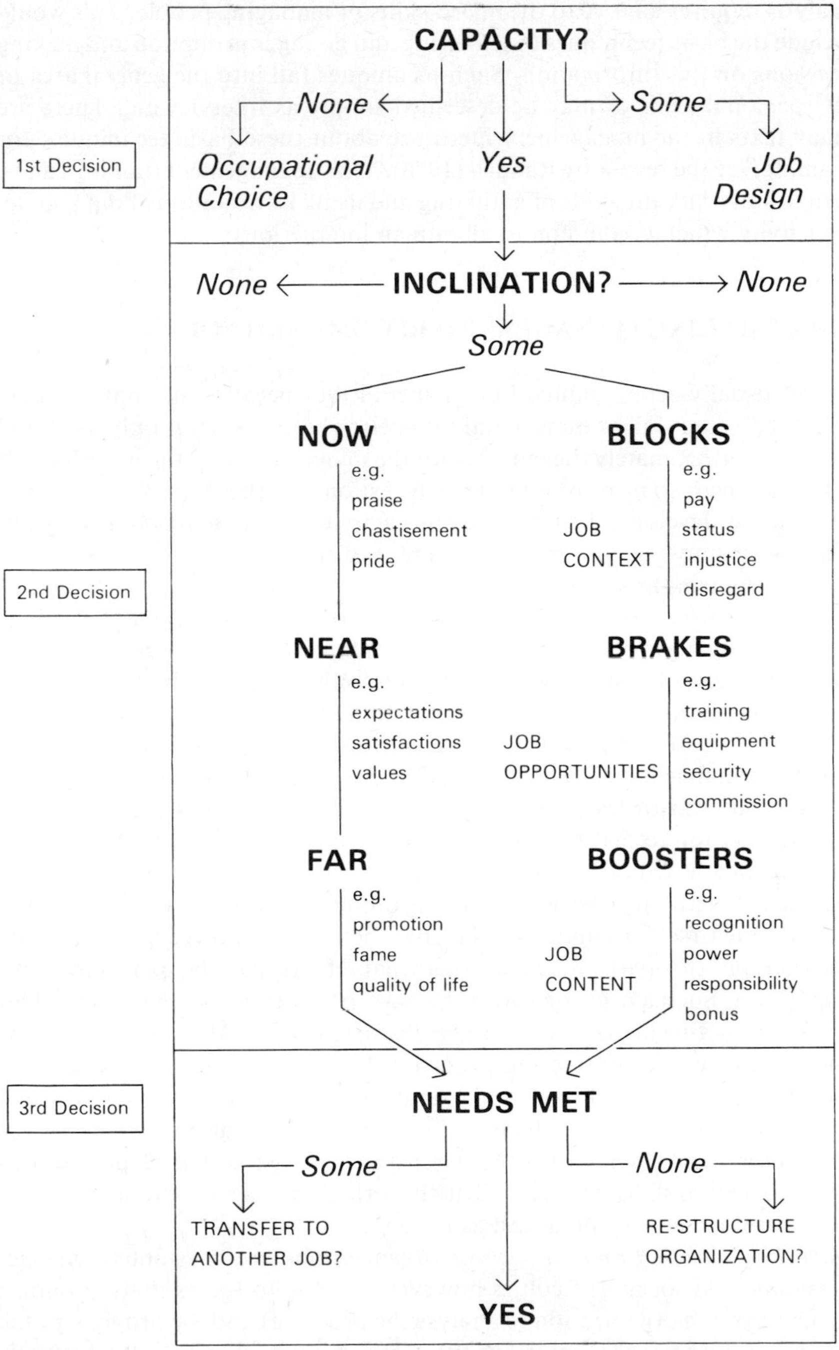

Figure 14.2 A conceptual model for people management

analysis requires a move to the micro-skills of managing people. This would include the basic techniques of gathering and giving information and making decisions on this information. Such techniques fall into the general area of interpersonal skills or may be described simply as interviewing. There are many texts in the management literature about these basic techniques; for example, see the review by Randell (1978). Thus management training can be seen to start with the skills of gathering and using information about people, an activity which is common to all human interactions.

ENCOURAGING MANAGERS TO BECOME SKILFUL

People usually get appointed to managerial jobs because they have already displayed some skill at managerial tasks elsewhere – even if only as school captain! Unfortunately the more senior the managerial job, the more likely it is for managers to be resistant to the suggestion that they have skills that still need to be developed. Of all learning activities, the acquisition of skills requires the most commitment on the part of the learner.

Two problems arise from this observation. The first is what are known as 'negative transfer' effects. A great deal of laboratory research has been done to investigate how previous learning, particularly of skills, can help or hinder the acquisition of new knowledge or skills. When the old ability helps, it is known as 'positive transfer'; when it hinders, it is 'negative transfer'. Negative transfer effects are very common in skills acquisition. Consequently, a manager may first have to decide to unlearn old ways of managing before going on to learn new ways, and this is sometimes a difficult and painful decision to make. The second problem is the selection of new skills that are worth acquiring. As skills learning is a mixture of cognitive and experiential activities, the understanding of the necessity for skills acquisition has to come first. This understanding has then to be followed by a deliberate decision on the part of the learner that effort will be put into skills acquisition. Such a decision forms the basis of the motivation to learn. This process of getting managers to want to change their old skills and acquire new ones is often called 'unfreezing'. It is a difficult process to bring about.

Although there is not likely to be a universally effective way for working with these motivational problems within work organizations, a pattern has been observed over ten years of research and experience of attempts to inculcate managerial skills into many British work organizations (Randell, 1980). This pattern can be summarized as follows.

Stage 1 – Cultural analysis Most organizations are resistant to change. Economic and social difficulties however give rise to forces that encourage members of the organization to analyse the processes and the progress of the internal culture towards achieving the organization's objectives, or even survival. From this analysis, pressures for 'unfreezing', and for time and effort to be put into management skills acquisition can emerge. Such pressures can come from the top of the organization, when a senior executive realizes that something should be done and makes proposals to the operating board or management committees. Pressures can also come from the lower reaches of an organization where a joint consultation committee or a trade union branch votes that the level of management skill is inadequate. Everyone at work has to be managed, and given the choice they would probably prefer to be managed skilfully rather than ineptly. These pressures are then picked up by the appropriate department of the organization, usually Personnel or Training and, hopefully, the next stage is entered upon.

Stage 2 – Conceptual analysis As this book demonstrates and the earlier sections of this chapter illustrate, managerial skills are many and varied. Precision is therefore required in identifying the exact area of skills that are needed to be applied to the particular problems identified within the sources of pressure in Stage 1; this is not easy. There are many pitfalls for the unwary, such as being influenced by the contemporary 'in' theory of management that prevails in business schools or in the mind of the Chief Executive. Being precise about a problem goes a long way towards solving it. If the resources of the personnel/training/planning departments of the organization are not adequate, outside help from a consultant or academic may be required. Even if the internal resources are adequate, outside help may be needed to sell the results of the conceptual analysis to the organization. (Prophets find it difficult to have their concepts accepted in their own country.) The conceptual analysis of managerial activity set out in the previous section of this chapter could form the starting point for the 'in company' analysis suggested by this section. As a result of the conceptual analysis being completed and accepted by the key decision makers the policy decision is then made to proceed with the managerial skills development. The resources implication of that decision must also be met by the organization, as skills training is probably the most expensive kind of management development in terms of time, money, facilities and effort involved.

Stage 3 – Skills analysis The conceptual analysis would lay down the basis for the cognitive – or educational – aspects of the management training. The precise actions to be taught would emerge from a skills analysis. The temptation here is to study skilled practitioners and use their previous actions as a model for others. Many senior managers would expect this to be done by their staff, and think that emulation is the best kind of learning for their subordinates. What is required is a micro-skills analysis, observing the basic components of the actions, isolating them, categorizing, and then defining their effects and how they should be carried out. Again, the skills analysis carried out above could form the basis of the 'in-company' analysis. The outcome of a skills analysis is a set of the basic components of the skill, presented in such a way that they can be understood cognitively by a learner, and exercises can be designed to allow their practice. The next problem is to design and administer the management training programme.

Stage 4 – Self-analysis All the attention on skills development that the previous three stages have brought about within the working environment of a manager should have the effect of making individual managers decide for themselves that they should accept skills training. Unfortunately it does not always happen. Management trainers often remark that the participants on their courses are those managers that need the training least. As a result of his research quoted earlier, Mintzberg (1975) made his 'first and foremost conclusion' that 'the manager's effectiveness is significantly influenced by his insight into his own work'.

If encouragement is not sufficient for a manager to decide to become more skilful, then more severe procedures are required. Various 'unfreezing' seminars and courses exist in the commercial management training field. They range from exposure to an impressive management thinker or 'guru', often at great expense. These lectures should have the ability to stimulate and change the thinking of even the most resistant manager through powerful presentations of their concepts. Then there are varieties of 2–3 day 'workshops' which, through the use of cleverly designed exercises, can help managers to analyse themselves in relation to their position in a notional 'grid' or other theoretical or normative scales of managerial activity. Finally, there are 2–3 week training courses which purport to make managers more sensitive to themselves and their relationships with others. It must be stressed that none of these experiences train managers in how to behave, although they may claim to do so. They can achieve a personal commitment by the manager to attempt to behave differently in the future. When this decision has been brought about, the manager is ready for training.

TRAINING IN MANAGEMENT SKILLS

The bridge between the unfreezing problem and the training problem can be helped or hindered by the name given to the training activity. A skills training workshop can be given various labels and such labels can be attractive or off-putting; they can raise expectations or suspicions. In some organizations a low-key name can be given, which makes the training sound less threatening to a manager; for example, it can be called 'Staff Appraisal' or 'Staff Development Skills'. In other organizations a more grandiose name may be necessary to get managers to justify their attendance at the workshops; for example, 'Leadership Skills' or 'Motivation Skills'.

As the previous analyses have shown, in the fundamentals of managerial activity, the skills are common to all types and level of management. The label has more relevance to motivational effects, rather than as a precise description of training events. No matter what the level, it must be remembered that as management skills have both macro- and micro-content and require both cognitive and practice components, their acquisition is not an easy experience, for either the learner or the tutor.

To achieve a high level in any complex skill obviously requires a great amount of training, but what is the minimum for making a start? Experience has shown (Randell *et al.*, 1974) that a two day training workshop is probably the minimum on which the foundations of the skill can be laid. The first day is needed for the unfreezing, unlearning, encouragement to learn and the cognitive macro-aspects of the skill. The second day is needed for the practice of the micro-aspects of the skill. There must also be time enough to achieve sufficient progress with the two main components of a skills course. The first is the provision of practice with feedback about the effects and results of the practice. The second is the opportunity to learn how to be effective in self-analysis.

The key to the success of such workshops lies with the tutors. Being able to train highly experienced and often still resistant managers is itself a very high level skill. Taylor (1976) has given a useful analysis of what is required of tutors in the field of staff development skills and has demonstrated that the main task of tutors is not to teach but to bring about learning by the trainees. A tutor is not expected to tell a learner how to behave. As has been frequently asserted, all skilled activity is made up of a sequence of decisions – and acts based on those decisions that are timed and graded to produce a specific result. It is not therefore possible for a tutor to prescribe decisions and associated acts because these depend on the other events in the sequence. In training for a skill, all possible decisions and acts can be taught but it is not possible to prescribe their sequence or timing. If it was possible then the task would become immediately deskilled; it would be an operation rather than a craft. Unfortunately many managers behave as operators rather than craftsmen at the skill of managing and many management training courses teach the process of managing as a mechanistic technique, which results in a deskilling rather than an enhancing of the activity. It is therefore necessary for the tutors to resist any request for a model performance, or even a demonstration on how to carry out the skill being acquired. Their task is to continually focus the trainees' attention on working out and practising the most appropriate behaviour for them within the conditions created by the exercise.

This approach to tutoring also leads to the managers learning how to acquire their own feedback. With such sensitive skills and with the minimum of training, the main hope for the long-term growth of the skill rests within the manager. A workshop can only lay the foundations.

EXTENDING SKILLS

Accepting that an essential feature of a workshop programme is to lay down the facility within managers for self-analysis and feedback, there remains the problem of how to encourage them to carry on developing their own skills by the use of this facility. The purpose of most follow-up studies of the effectiveness of any personnel or training procedure is for 'validation' purposes, i.e. to demonstrate that the procedure 'works', but a second and no less important factor in skills training is the pressure such studies can bring on managers to continue to develop their skill. The act of filling in a questionnaire, albeit to report on the skills training, can provide a useful reminder, both of the content and importance of the practice of the skill.

A great deal of the literature on the evaluation of management training (e.g. Warr *et al.*, 1970) reports only the use of follow-up studies to collect validation data, and more often than not points out how weak such data are. The use of follow-up studies to make training more effective is hardly touched upon. The point of training is to bring about changes in behaviour in a desired direction. Measuring behavioural change is a very difficult technical task and invariably produces disappointing results. In skills training the growth of skill within an individual is probably noticeable by that individual, even though such growth is not necessarily detectable by any measuring instruments. Therefore, follow-up studies based on self-reports are quite appropriate for validation studies of skills training. When managers report a growth in their skill it is both encouraging for them and the trainers. At the same time, such a self-report, if the report form is designed well, should highlight where growth is still needed, either through more effort on the part of the manager, or through more advanced, or refresher, skills training.

However, there are aspects of skilled performance that can only develop through a continuous interaction within the practitioner of the macro- and micro-components of the skill. One of the features that determine the elusive but superb totality in any skill is the existence of balance; all skills display this element. This is obvious in physical skills, such as gymnastics, and clearly noticed when absent. In musical skills again it can be readily heard, but what about in managerial skills? The most obvious balance is between meeting the needs of the organization and the needs of the individual. If the organization's needs are met without regard for the individual then exploitation is apprehended and eventually strikes will occur; if the individual's needs are met to the detriment of the organization's needs, then bankruptcy can soon follow. So obtaining a balance is essential. The balance between organizational and individual needs is a macro-level of balance; the concept applies all the way through the conduct of the skill. In the mid-range there is the application of balance to time and effort spent on different problems confronting the manager. Then at the micro-level there are the balances between explicitness and tone in giving certain information or instructions to a member of staff. To be too explicit may stifle initiative, but to be not explicit enough may lead to misunderstanding. To be too sharp in tone may sound too authoritarian and be resented; to be too soft may sound too casual and may not result in the desired action. As in walking a tightrope, balance is essential for effective and safe performance. The concept and achievement of balance must be at the limits of what can be currently taught to managers. Perhaps all that can be conveyed is an awareness for its need; the precise meaning of what that entails must be left to the individual manager.

This awareness of the need for even more skills development completes the loop in the management education and training system. It returns to the basic question asked at the opening of this chapter about the nature of managerial skills. As this area of study is extended it is probable that even higher and more complex skills involved in managing people and work organizations will be revealed, to make even more demands on managers and management trainers in the future.

References

Glaser, R. (1962). Psychology and instructional technology. In Glaser, R. (ed.) *Training Research and Education.* (New York: Wiley)

Horne, J. H. and Lupton, T. (1965). The work activities of middle managers. *J. Management Studies*, **1**, 14

Johnson, R. A., Kast, F. E. and Rosenzweig, J. E. (1967). *The Theory and Management of Systems.* (New York: McGraw–Hill)

Mintzberg, H. (1973). *The Nature of Managerial Work.* (New York: Harper & Row)

Mintzberg, H. (1975). The Manager's job: folklore and fact. *Harvard Business Review*, **53**, 49

Randell, G. A. (1966). A systems approach to industrial behaviour. *Occupational Psychol.*, **40**, 115

Randell, G. A. (1978). Interviewing at work. In Warr, P. B. (ed.) *Psychology at Work.* (Harmondsworth: Penguin)

Randell, G. A. (1980). The skills of staff development. In Singleton, W. T., Spurgeon, P. and Stammers, R. B. (eds.) *The Analysis of Social Skills.* (New York: Plenum)

Randell, G. A., Packard, P. M. A., Shaw, R. L. and Slater, A. J. (1974). *Staff Appraisal.* (London: Institute of Personnel Management)

Seiler, J. A. (1967). *Systems Analysis in Organizational Behavior.* (Homewood Ill.: Irwin–Dorsey)

Stewart, R. (1967). *Managers and Their Jobs.* (London: McMillan)

Taylor, D. S. (1976). *Performance Reviews: A Handbook for Tutors.* (London: Institute of Personnel Management)

Warr, P. B., Bird, M. W. and Rackham, N. H. (1970). *Evaluation of Management Training.* (London: Gower)

15 Management Development

H. N. CHELL

INTRODUCTION

Management development is one of the latest functions to emerge in our post-industrial society. Rooted firmly in a perceived need to manage change, and still in an embryo state, there is as yet no well defined group of tasks which collectively make up the job, nor is there any definition of where the job fits into the general organizational configuration.

The present state of management development, as well as the direction it takes in the future, depends largely on the assumptions made about the nature of managerial work, assumptions which frequently make reference to management skills. The word 'skill' in this context is used in such an arbitrary manner that it is impossible to attach a consistent meaning to the word. As an example, a well advertised programme, which purports to develop management skills, uses the word to mean 'knowing, understanding, achieving, deciding, evaluating' amongst many other meanings. Alternatively, the word is used to describe categories of skill such as communicating skills or problem-solving skills and so on. Although such ambiguous uses of the word 'skill' are no doubt satisfactory for general conversational purposes they are totally inadequate for the management development practitioner wishing to initiate skill-based programmes as an alternative to those based on knowledge of tasks.

When developing the operational model of skill proposed here the criterion was never 'Is the model right?', only 'Is the model useful?' While this in no way implies that the model is necessarily wrong it does mean that in this first attempt to develop a practical tool, rigorous criticism has taken second place to practical advantage.

The views expressed in this chapter arise from long personal experience both as a manager and management developer and represent a view which is not necessarily shared by anyone else.

THE BACKGROUND

The contents of most organizational jobs are such as to permit a reasonable level of definition and understanding. For example, the general range of tasks which make up the jobs of cost accountant and works manager would be known to most experienced industrial managers. The same cannot be said of the job content of the management developer. The truth is that even management development practitioners themselves are in some disarray when it comes to defining their work. One obvious reason is that accountants and works managers may belong to professional institutions which establish minimum levels of competence in their respective jobs and which, in doing so, set standards for common core activities. Although the influence which professional bodies extend over their members differs in degree, they nevertheless provide an outline of the scope of the activities and the standards to which these activities should be executed.

Unlike some managerial jobs, which have to be carried out in every business, the job of management development evolved principally in the larger companies and so not all companies employ someone in this capacity. When they do, what they expect of them varies enormously. The management developer might, for example, be expected to give advice on a range of different topics or perhaps recommend external development resources. Alternatively he could well be expected to provide a practical service himself. He might fill the role of administrator or be an educator. He might be an experienced industrial manager or have no practical managerial experience whatsoever. He might have a doctoral degree or be without the most elementary qualification.

The need for the function of management development has always been linked with 'change', or more particularly, the pace of change. There is a vague acceptance that in times of rapid change, neither the change itself, nor the impact of the change on the management job, can be left to chance. Somehow it has to be controlled. The range of activities covered by the job in any given organization tends to have been determined by a random fusion of the personalities of those present at the time, the availability of a schema, and the needs of the parent organization. Not surprisingly therefore management development has become a highly personalized activity.

Another factor which has played a significant part in the evolution of management development is that the first generation of practitioners in the USA and the UK tended to be either managers, who for one reason or another had been attracted to the job, or academics. The academics – who were usually American psychologists or sociologists – were prompted by the nature of their professions to publish the successful aspects of their work. Despite the fact that the views they expressed were often generalizations made from circumscribed events, their views were nevertheless widely accepted by management developers having a more practical origin, and whose principal needs were firstly for a theory of management, and secondly for development material of any kind.

The realization that the published theories and training materials were not necessarily always relevant to all conditions was yet to come. Much more subtly, the need to understand the essential difference of repeating the content of a developmental programme as distinct from the process was rarely understood. What is more, the depth of experience required to deal effectively with the infinite variety of content (what is said and designed to be met) was almost universally lacking. Finally the vital importance of the context in which content emerges was rarely, if ever, considered. Yet another shortcoming in past management development practices is now apparent as it becomes clear that the cherished beliefs held about the nature of management work owe more to an unquestioned academic mythology than to practical observation. In short, the application of skills developed by a person working in one set of circumstances were not easily transferred to another person working in quite different circumstances. The extraordinary thing is that we should ever have thought that they could be.

Despite the varied origins of management development, there has evolved over the years, through the publication of experience, seminars, movement of personnel between companies and so on, a measure of common ground. The foundation of this common ground has been the notion that managerial performance must somehow be measured against some standard reference. Individual companies have differed widely as to how this should be achieved and there has consequently been much discussed and written on such matters as the relative effectiveness of performance appraisal *vis-à-vis* personality assessment, how potential is recognized, and potential for 'what'.

Notwithstanding the fact that there has yet to be any conclusion to these discussions, other elements of the management developer's job have produced commonly accepted criteria. Firstly, there has been general acknowledgement that management development makes sense only when undertaken in the context of a company's strategic business plans. Secondly, that concern for management falls within the wider ambit of manpower planning, which considers both the acquisition and disposition of all the human resources required by the business plans. Thirdly, that management development needs to have an objective theory which brings its many activities into a coherent focus. The history of these theories indicate a trend from relative simplicity to relative complexity.

More oblique frames of reference which have superimposed themselves on the above theories have been supplied by business strategies such as the 'marketing concept', an ideal somewhat trivialized by its rallying cry of 'The right product in the right place at the right time at the right price'. This in turn has been superseded by the competition concept which adds to the previous market orientation the total activities of competing products and businesses in our markets. In addition to the impact made by these concepts, which affect the boundary between the firm and its environment, there has been the rethinking of roles made necessary by the changes in our social climate.

It is by the establishment of management development as a legitimate business activity, rather than as an educational luxury, which is how some would see it, that its adherents hope to secure the adoption of practices which many would regard as critical to Britain's industrial and commercial future.

THE NATURE OF MANAGEMENT DEVELOPMENT

The many different functions carried out within organizations can be classified in terms of their position on a theoretical scale which would have core activities at one extreme and peripheral activities at the other. Core activities can be defined as those which would always be considered if organizational changes were being contemplated. Peripheral activities, on the other hand, would rarely, if ever, be considered in similar circumstances. The scale can be seen to measure the relative importance attributed to the functions. On such a scale, management development has usually been located at the peripheral end; it is regarded as dispensable in hard times. One clear reason for this evaluation is the essentially long-term nature of the activity; it cannot be seen to produce immediate benefits. Due to the short-term 'fire-fighting' nature of middle management responsibilities it is often difficult for the management developer to exert sufficient influence to persuade middle managers to raise their sights occasionally.

Long-term development projects are also susceptible to changes in personnel who occupy significant managerial positions. Consequently even though a group of managers are convinced of the necessity to develop themselves and their staff, and development programmes are designed and implemented, new senior managers may well bring with them different attitudes and priorities as a result of which projects already embarked on are cancelled. Thoughtfully prepared and often costly plans may well seem incomprehensible and irrelevant to newly appointed senior managers preoccupied by the need to demonstrate their competence quickly. When this happens credibility, not only of any kind of developmental venture but also of management itself, is often put to the test.

Other problems arise due to the fact that management development is an educational activity in a non-educational environment. Even educational institutions specifically designed to promote learning have their problems. Education in an industrial environment not sympathetic to the need to learn, even on occasions openly antagonistic towards it, is infinitely more difficult.

Add to this the fact that management development practitioners never have the authority to compel other managers to attend their programmes (supposing this was even desirable), then the task of sustaining management development programmes can become, at times, truly formidable.

Despite these limitations, or more probably because of them, both teaching and learning techniques in industry are frequently more adventurous and efficient than they are in the traditional learning institutions. Management developers have frequently grasped the whole educational apparatus in short order. Unhindered by stereotyped thinking, and faced with the necessity of making learning both stimulating and relevant, the management developer is becoming increasingly regarded as the truly avant-garde educator.

MANAGEMENT TASKS

Managers and organizations

Firstly, there is a need to understand how the tasks carried out by managers develop within a particular organization. It is still unusual for today's managers to have entered industry or commerce as trainee managers. The more usual path is for managers to have entered an organization to carry out some function such as selling, manufacturing, designing, accounting and so on. It is because some are thought to perform relatively better than others that they are given added responsibility. In other words the usual introduction to management is via promotion through a function. Initially therefore promotion frequently means more responsibility in the function in which the person was originally employed. There comes a stage however when promotion brings with it a quite different set of responsibilities which can be grouped under the heading of administration. Administrative tasks relate to organizational structures, systems, procedures and the management of people. The newly promoted manager now finds himself confronted by the need to carry out tasks for which he has had little or no preparation.

Consequently the situation, frequently found in industrial organizations in the UK, is one in which the typical manager finds himself with two broad groups of responsibilities; one for which he has had long preparation and a record of successful application and a second for which he is unprepared and for which he may ultimately be found to be unsuited. A recent survey of some one hundred managers showed that while every one of them had received formal training for their functional responsibilities only one had received formal training in administration. Significantly this training had been received at a time when the manager had been a serving officer in the armed forces. It is also true that there is little evidence of informal training for administrative responsibilities, a condition which perhaps reflects the degree of importance attached to this category of activities. The other aspect of administration, the management of people, has a chequered history in the United Kingdom. Although contentious it is probably true to say that this form of training has leaned too heavily on psychological concepts which managers were taught and then expected to implement unaided. Since the application of the concepts to widely differing conditions was and still is the crux, it is not at all surprising that the tangible returns from the investment in time and money in such training have been insignificant. The corollary of this is that the developmental needs of managers lie more in the area of application than in the learning of concepts. Busy executives seem to find practical techniques more helpful though perhaps less interesting, than philosophical discussions. If the technique actually works, and if the manager is sufficiently interested, then he may want to understand the underlying theory, but what he really *needs* in the first place is practical help. The subdivisions of the management job are shown in Figure 15.1.

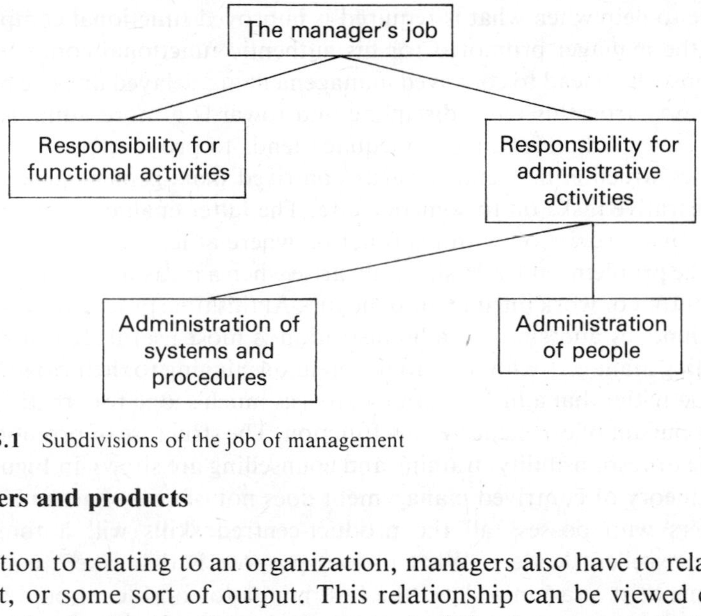

Figure 15.1 Subdivisions of the job of management

Managers and products

In addition to relating to an organization, managers also have to relate to a product, or some sort of output. This relationship can be viewed on two different levels. Firstly, there is the output of the department, that is, the functional output at a specific level in the organization hierarchy. Experience indicates that a manager who lacks the skills necessary to deal with the output of his department is in a far less favourable position to manage effectively than one who has these skills. This seems to be true regardless of other favourable attributes the manager may have. An important reason for this seems to be that natural authority plus the ability to motivate and relate to others flow simply and unaffectedly from a manager's product-centred skills. Managers who lack these skills must somehow contrive their authority and their ability to relate and motivate others from whatever sources seem expedient. Contrived authority, for example, can be achieved by using formal power, withholding information, or manipulating the fear of being overlooked for promotion, having a poor assessment, missing a salary increase, and so on. It is perhaps necessary at this point to explain that in the present context 'contrive' is intended to mean 'devise or plan' and not to infer deviousness or intrigue.

The implications arising from the integration of Figure 15.1 and the concept of contrived management are profound for the management developer at least. It would seem that, other things being equal, initial promotion within a function produces few problems for the person whose upgrading results from genuine functional excellence. However for the 'high-flyer' moving quickly through the management grades, and who is consequently denied the time necessary to develop functional excellence, the problems of authority, communication and the motivation of subordinates are very real. Courses on leadership and communication and motivation theory do little to help when what is required is improved functional competence.

For the manager promoted for his authentic functional competence the problems which lead to contrived management are delayed until he begins to move away from his basic discipline and towards a more administration-centred role. Administrative inadequacy tends to provoke personal coping strategies which either tend towards contrived management or offloading administrative tasks on to someone else. The latter enables the manager to prolong his association with his function where at least he feels safe. Here again the problems of leadership only arise when a measure of incompetence in the output of work intrudes into the job. At this time practical assistance in the techniques and skills of administration is most useful. It is also worth reminding managers who seem to be intent on clinging to their original functional activities that administration offers as much scope for creativity, flair and the pursuit of excellence as any function. The structure of promotion and the type of responsibility, training and counselling are shown in Figure 15.2.

The theory of contrived management does not of course assume that the managers who possess all the product-centred skills will automatically become excellent leaders. What it does propose is that where managerial problems exist at a junior level the first points to consider should be those concerned with product knowledge. Where doubt exists about a manager's competence in the field of departmental output, this is a good place to start development activity. In those situations where the skills related to departmental output are well developed, but where the manager has problems, then attention can be switched to other skill areas such as social skills. The theory would also suggest that where managerial problems exist at a more senior level, and functional competence is recognized, then the first step should be to analyse the manager's competence with his new administrative and business responsibilities. If shortcomings are detected here then, once again, this is a good place to start.

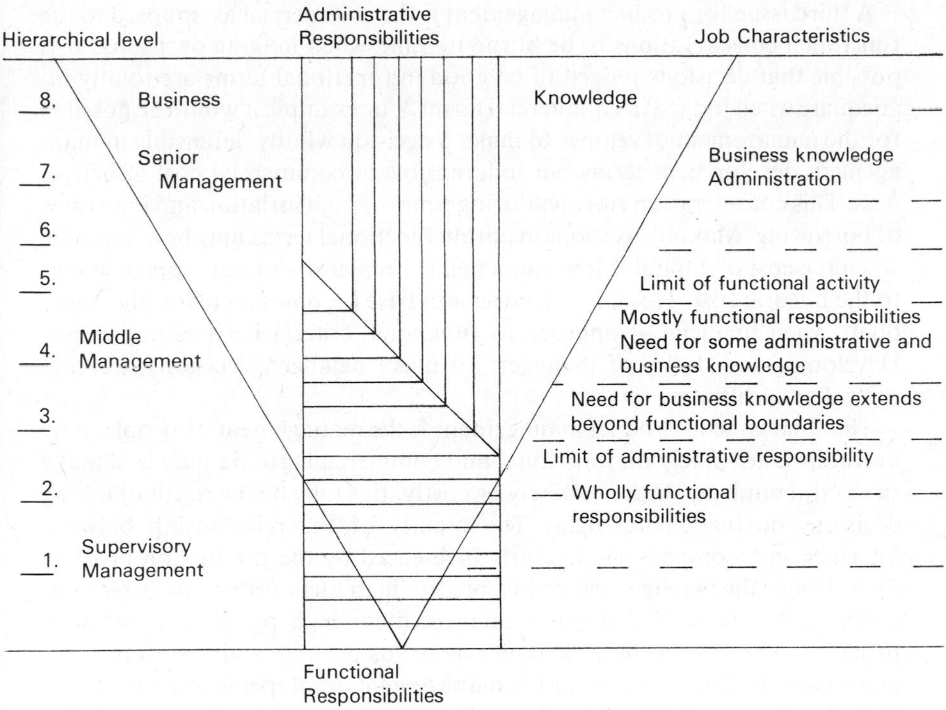

Figure 15.2 Schematic diagram of managerial responsibilities

This structure of thinking about training and counselling indicates that sound functional training is vital at the early stages of a career. It also shows that it is not until the manager has made some progress that the need for business knowledge extends beyond the bounds of functional responsibility. There is also quite clearly a stage at which functional excellence is superceded by the need to demonstrate excellence in administration and a wider business knowledge. Failure to do so may lead to the coping strategies outlined earlier.

A second level at which managers relate to the product is that of the final productive output of the organization: for example, machine tools, food products, designs, news, advertising materials, crude oil and so on. In some cases there will be a close association between departmental and organizational output while in others there will be none. The importance of the nature of this relationship cannot be overestimated because it will significantly influence the extent to which the manager identifies with his company, his industry or his profession. For example, consider the significance of this relationship for the production manager of an organization manufacturing a specialized product made by no other company in the country, and in comparison, for the manager of computer operations in a large multinational company.

A third issue for product management is the commercial as opposed to the functional considerations to be borne in mind when making decisions. It is possible that decisions judged to be good in functional terms are totally inadequate when judged in commercial terms. For example it would be possible for the management developer to make a decision wholly defensible in management development terms but indefensible in commercial cost-effectiveness. This consideration emerges during times of high inflation and high rates of borrowing. Making decisions in purely functional terms may be acceptable when the cost of capital is low and when the replacement cost approximates to the historic cost. However this decision base becomes increasingly inadequate when financial as opposed to functional criteria become important. Developing the ability of managers to make balanced decisions becomes critical at such times.

The final issue in product management is the management of people. Any decisions taken solely on functional and commercial criteria may well make successful implementation unlikely or costly, this may be the result of taking decisions on inadequate data. The quality of the relationship between manager and worker is significantly influenced by the production process. For instance the management of low profit–high turnover products requires a different approach from the management of high profit–low turnover products. The first of these examples demands positive and therefore autocratic control. The problem for the management developer is often to ensure that in such cases the manager differentiates between those decisions affecting products and those which concern people. In the second example immediate control is less important and the relationship between manager and worker more relaxed. It is in this kind of process, typified by high costs and high technology, that many of the worker participation experiments have succeeded.

Another significant factor determined by the product is that the association between an operator and the materials he uses are much affected by the time span of the association and the extent to which the operator applies skills to the process. Quite clearly the management of workers applying skills

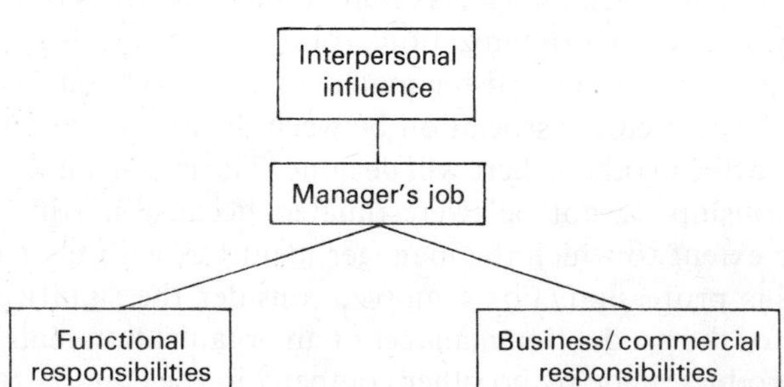

Figure 15.3 Skill areas which should be identified by the management developer

over long periods to the same product is essentially different to the management of workers who have an association with a product which lasts only a few seconds and upon which they exert little influence.

Most problems arising from the management of people who are not only not motivated by their tasks but positively alienated from them, develop from the management of people employed on repetitious short cycle time tasks which, apart from being monotonous, are also susceptible to a wide variety of factors which interrupt the rhythm of work.

The nature of the connection between manager and product raises important issues for the management developer wishing to develop management skills. The areas in which he must identify skills will be associated with functional excellence, commercial ability and interpersonal influence. These skill areas are shown in Figure 15.3.

MANAGEMENT SKILLS

Despite the fact that management skills are frequently referred to in the field of management development, the fact remains that employing the word 'skill' in this context is no more than ambiguous conversational usage. What is usually meant by skill in these circumstances is really knowledge of tasks. A working definition of 'skill' is essential if skills are to be developed and it is this working definition which forms the first of the three elements in this group of concerns which shape the nature of the management developer's skills. At its most basic level a working definition of skill explains the process by which a manager relates to the tasks he performs. A number of specific factors seem to be involved. Firstly there is the cognitive and affective capacity – knowing and feeling, of what it is, and how it feels – to be able to consistently carry out an intention. Associated with this is the knowledge of the plans, rules, procedures, processes, algorithms – call them what you will – which actualize the inner knowing and feeling.

Mental models

The first of the two factors outlined above are often referred to as models. Man is assumed to build an internal representation or model of reality as he presently knows it. The model can usefully be thought of as existing in three separate stages although in reality the three combine into one consolidated blend. The states in which the model can exist are determined by the source and characteristics of the incoming data. The nearest to reality is the enactive model which deals with data which originate from within the person and which therefore deal with bodily states and feelings.

The second state of the model is shaped by inner representations of our experience of external reality and owes as much to the nature of the mind and the structure of the senses as it does to the external phenomenon revealed by the sensory experience. The models established from sensory experience are often referred to as 'iconic' in deference to the dominance of the visual sense. However, sensory models are also built on the auditory sense; they are supported by our olfactory and tactile senses as well, the importance of which are easily underrated.

The third state, furthest removed from direct experience, is made up of models built on the abstract linguistic and numerical symbols of external reality. Paradoxically the further a model is removed from reality the easier it is to communicate its nature to another person. This is due to the fact that we communicate in the same abstract terms as those which constitute the symbolic model. Iconic models on the other hand have to be converted into symbolic form as a prerequisite to communication, a difficult task. However, the task is made easier by expressing the content of the iconic model in terms of diagrams or shapes or by the use of analogues. This technique seems to simplify the communication process because it allows the symbols to be shaped by the ideas as an alternative to the difficulty of fitting the ideas into predetermined symbolic forms. Enactive models, being constructed as they are from reality itself, seem to defy communication. All the models are a notion of 'how things are' or 'how things feel' and can only be developed from personal experience. One cannot develop a model of how it is and how it feels to ride a horse until one has had direct experience of doing it. But having a notion in the form of a model is of little value unless there is some mechanism via which the notion can be employed or operationalized.

Operating programmes

From a practical point of view it is extremely useful to think of a model and the operating mechanism as being distinct entities. The distinction arises from the view that while the model is an internal representation of external reality, the operating programme is the process by which the logic embodied in the model is organized into skilled performance via the sequencing and timing of routinized behaviours. From a knowledge of the consequences of actions taken in the world we build models out of our constructions of the reality of what it is, and how it feels, to carry out these actions. The model therefore faithfully reflects our sensory experience and is essentially part of the process which converts inputs into outputs. The operating programme on the other hand is a plan, or a process, or an algorithm, or a set of rules, or whatever which is abstracted and detached from its parent model.

Because the model is shaped by sensory experience it can never extend beyond experience itself. The detached operating programme however is free from this constraint. By reflecting backwards on actions already taken and forwards in imagination on how events might have turned if the actions taken had been different, the learner is able to invent a 'better' way of acting in the future. When a suitable opportunity arises the learner can act, in what to him is a novel way, and which has been developed from reflections on the consequence of past actions and on the imagined likely outcomes of alternative acts. When the modified actions have been taken, sensory experience will update the model, and may even carry the model ahead of the anticipated outcomes. Model and operating programmes can then be seen to progress towards skilled performance by 'leap-frogging' or moving out of phase with each other. This process continues until the imagination can no longer produce consequences in any way superior to those already achieved in reality and which are now included in the model. Additionally the inner model of external reality will have been developed to the point at which sensory experience can no longer provide data which are capable of improving it. At the point at which the learner stops learning, because he believes he has learned, the model and programme are as near one another as his level of motivation causes him to believe is necessary.

Another important aspect of skilled intellectual performance is the process by which the skilled performer builds his model of reality. Events in the world are not passively received but actively sought, selected or distorted by being differentially emphasized, heightened, excluded or suppressed. It follows that every individual can be viewed as a product of the ways in which he has personally construed reality in terms of his unique purposes and intentions. Personal construct theory would propose that man continually constructs and reconstructs meaning in a manner he finds personally valuable in terms of his purposes. The great benefit to the management developer of this particular psychological theory is its attendant technique of Repertory Grid (Fransella and Bannister, 1977). This technique allows him to elicit from his client managers the way in which their individual constructs are mapped on to specific events. From this information a whole series of developmental activities can be applied (Thomas *et al.*, 1978).

A final practical issue left for the management developer to consider is the equally important enactive model which has resulted from the input of information from within the person. The development of an inner model of external reality cannot in fact be separated from the contiguous development of a model of the internal condition. Perception is as much conditioned by the sensory experience provided by an inner source as it is from an external one. It follows that gaining an insight into the inner thoughts and feeling of the managers with whom he is working is vital information for the management developer.

The heuristic integrant

Two further elements of skill remain; while it is convenient to think of them as separate strands they nevertheless combine to form a single thread. The

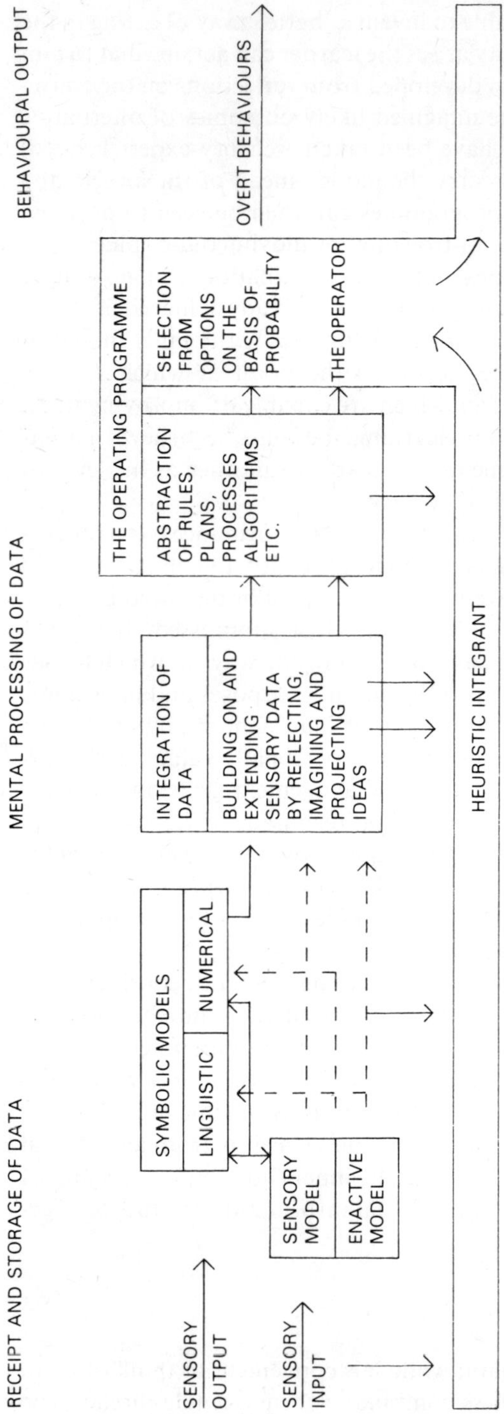

Skill acquisition is achieved via a number of different routes at each stage in the system.
For example:

Importation	Mental through-put	Output
Listening	Thinking	Speaking
Looking	Feeling	Acting
(Reading)	Choosing	(Writing)

Figure 15.4 Diagram of functions in the mental model

first of the strands is the heuristic integrant, a term which describes the process by which current performance is always being improved. The pace of improvement slows down considerably after the point at which the learner considers himself to be performing adequately. However, actual improved performance, or the evolution of greater flexibility, derived from either starting a task from different points or by following different routes from a single point, continues for a long time.

The proposal has been made that it is useful to acknowledge a qualitative difference between the model, that is awareness based on sensory experience, and the operating programme, that is awareness based on thinking which has extended beyond sensory experience. It will also be argued later that an additional and quite separate model originates from the imaginative faculty and which is a projection of 'What it will be like when I am skilled'.

The heuristic integrant uses all available sources, sensory experience,

Notes to Figure 15.4

(1) Sensory data can be converted into linguistic and/or numerical form.

(2) Some sensory inputs which directly enter into the symbolic model, e.g. reading, are a form of vicarious experience and therefore qualitatively different to direct experience.

(3) The enactive model is directly related to both the sensory and symbolic model, i.e. inputs to either are linked to contiguous enactive inputs.

(4) The content of the model held in symbolic form can be translated into iconic form at the integration stage. Words and concepts also help to shape the sensory experience they name and so make some of our experience possible.

(5) Interaction between sensory and symbolic models facilitates the development of a key aspect of skill, namely the extension of either linguistic or unverbalized discriminations, together with their appropriate responses, to the level demanded by skilled performance. An example is provided by the woodcarver. An unskilled person might look at an object and say, 'the object is made of wood', thereby discriminating between that object and others of a similar form made from other materials. A more knowledgeable person might further discriminate by adding that the object was made from a hardwood and so discriminate between the object and similar ones made from softwood. The level of discrimination could be further refined by noting that the object was made of mahogany and not any other hardwood. Further refinement still could identify the object as being made of Sapele mahogany and not, say, Honduras mahogany: each of these discriminations being made possible by interaction between the iconic and linguistic models. An even more refined level of discrimination, arrived at by sight and touch, could lead the skilled wood carver to identify the extent to which the Sapele mahogany had been dried by seasoning: discrimination between many possible levels of dryness at a completely sensory and unverbalized level of analysis. Significantly, this sensory discrimination could provoke the woodcarver to say to himself, 'This grain will be tricky', and so link together two vital aspects of modelling, firstly the role of words in shaping sensory experience and secondly the role of words in shaping actions abstracted from purpose.

(6) The heuristic integrant is active across the whole range of the system integrating data from the importation, mental process and behavioural output stages.

(7) The operator selects from possible options on the basis of the probability of likely outcomes assessed in terms of all the data gathered by the heuristic integrant. The role of the operator is explained in part by Kelly's theory of personal constructs. Constructs are not descriptive of meanings or personality but explain the reference axis or the dimension of appraisal via which reality, in the form of the model, is known. Importantly, constructs also describe the action pathways along which the person is free to travel. Thus we can act on the world only in those terms in which we know it. The heuristic integrant and the operator are thus mutually interdependent.

personal and supplementary feedback, thinking and anticipation to promote learning.

The operator

The second strand is what I have termed 'the operator'. The operating programme is a serial process in which the completion, or frustration, of one activity triggers off the next. The mechanism which determines the order and timing of each separate act, and which is influenced by purpose, is descriptive of the operator. Some evidence now exists to show how the operator works.

The work of McKnight (1977), which is based on Repertory Grid technique, is particularly helpful. After eliciting a number of constructs from a range of elements McKnight proceeds to show how purpose serves to arrange the relative 'weighting' of each construct in such a way that it is possible, from an analysis of the weightings, to predict the likely actions of the person when the purpose is known. If we consider how values, meanings and the constructions we place on things are mapped on to events in the world, it is clear that their relative importance, as determined by our changing intentions, will vary and so enable us to respond in many different ways on the basis of a limited range of values, meanings and constructs. It also explains why one person will respond in different ways to the same event in different circumstances and why a number of people respond differently to the same event in any given circumstance.

Subroutines

The final element of skilled performance is the common base of routine behaviours upon which all operating programmes draw. It is likely that these subroutines form a hierarchy in a learning organism. At the apex of the hierarchy of subroutines will be operating programmes now relegated to subroutine status, while at the base will be relegated behaviour long reduced to automatic actions, the outcome of skills learned in a previous less mature state. The test of whether an action is under the direct control of an operating programme or subroutine depends on the answer to the question, 'Is there a conscious value judgment associated with the act?' If there is, the act is a consequence of an operating programme, while if the act is a mechanistic respondent behaviour it will be associated with a subroutine.

The executive programme

The mechanism which selects the most appropriate skill in any given situation would be called the executive programme if the computer analogy is maintained. In its turn the executive programme would also be the overt actualization of a superordinate executive model. Skill would then appear to be organized in three fundamental levels; executive, operational and routine. Experience with the model however would seem to indicate that the divisions between these levels are sometimes blurred.

Operating skills and subroutines do not necessarily exist on discrete levels; it seems to be possible that at the boundary between conscious and unconscious behaviour an individual manager may have developed some actions to the point where they have been related to routinized behaviour while actions of a similar status are still consciously executed. The executive programme seems to operate at the task level in the work situations and at the level of the game in leisure pursuits. For example, although the number of tasks which make up a job vary widely, the term skill is normally employed at the task level.

A task which forms part of many managerial jobs is problem-solving. Accordingly the task of problem solving would have an executive programme having the responsibility for ordering the sequence and timing of a range of operating programmes. In addition to the conscious application of its own set of abstracted rules the operating programme also has access to a bank of subroutines. It follows that at any one time the manager exercising his problem-solving skill could be employing a mixture of both consciously and unconsciously applied behaviours. For example when presenting a problem to a group in such a way as to promote their individual problem-solving behaviours the manager could, while carefully and consciously choosing his words, control his eye contact and facial expressions by the automatic and unconscious employment of subroutines.

Similarly for the golfer the executive programme would operate at the level of the game. Individual skills controlled by operating programmes would be called up at the discretion of the executive programme within the constraints imposed by the rules of the game. Putting would constitute a skill and so be under the specific control of its own operating programme. When called into action the golfer exercising his putting skill could, while consciously applying a rule abstracted from his mental model – say assessing the lie of the green – be at the same time unconsciously controlling both his stance and the way of holding the club through the use of the relevant subroutines.

The definition of skill, from the above description of skill in use, would need to take a form such as 'the optimum application of both conscious and unconscious behaviours to the solution of a problem'.

The concept of a hierarchy permeates the whole structure of thought about skilled behaviour. Subroutines at the base of the pyramid seem to form their own hierarchy. Individual skills cluster into associations, with some skills subsumed under other skills. The many hierarchies of skill combine to form an important part of the structure of total awareness which determines the individual person's concept of self. It is important that the management developer appreciates that all models and programmes are not only finite but often extremely limited. The elaboration of existing models and programmes is therefore a key feature of individual learning.

ACQUISITION OF SKILL

Learning and training

In addition to a model of skill the management developer must have a model of skill acquisition. The model of skill acquisition should consider skill acquisition not only from the teacher's point of view but also, and probably more importantly, how skill acquisition appears from the learner's point of view.

The first consideration for the management developer is 'What needs to be learned?' Traditionally this question has been answered by two statements. The first would be derived from an analysis of any shortcomings in the way in which managers are carrying out current tasks. The second would be established from a consideration of how future managerial tasks might differ from current tasks after reviewing possible changes in the organization's direction envisaged in the organization's strategic plans.

However, developing managerial skills, as opposed to developing the ability to carry out individual tasks, changes the focus of the analysis. In task analysis the unit of analysis is one task. In skills analysis the unit of analysis is one skill which may be included within the boundaries of many tasks. In task analysis the focus is on the whole task and therefore attracts the risk of confusing the rules from a number of different skills, all of which have *natural boundaries*, in contrast to tasks which have *artificially imposed boundaries*. In skills analysis, the focus is on the development of an inner model and on the evolution of the operating programmes and subroutines. Focus on skill means a quite different focus of what has to be learned, and on the essential differences of learning from experience or learning by being taught by a skilled performer.

There are important differences between learning by being taught and learning from one's own experience. Essentially the process of learning from experience begins with the learner's first attempts to carry out an intention and from which the person develops an inchoate model which accurately reflects the experience gained from the first attempt. From this model, rules can be abstracted which form a springboard for the imagination which is free to range ahead of experience. From the balance of probabilities of the likely outcomes of alternative actions, modified rules can be formed and applied as circumstances allow. The sensory experience from the application of the modified rules updates the inner model, and so the cycle continues. Briefly experiential learning proceeds from action to modelling, and from modelling to rule abstractions, and then on to a modified action (Kolb and Fry).

In contrast to this sequence, the process of learning by being taught begins when rules abstracted from the model of a skilled performer are learned by the novice. The meanings of the words used to describe the rules, and the meanings of the concepts encapsulated in the rules must be exchanged by teacher and learner so that, even though agreement and equal comprehension is not reached regarding the meaning which should be attached, the base from which a common understanding can develop is laid. The rules (or more commonly a subset of rules) are then applied to the task by the learner. From this experience the learner forms an inchoate model which faithfully mirrors current performance. In its simplest form the situation may be represented as shown in Figure 15.5. As this learning cycle continues the state of the learner's model develops and finally stabilizes at the point where the rules abstracted from the learner's model approximate to the rules provided by the teacher during the first stage of the learning process. At this last stage, the teacher and learner will truly share the meanings to be attached to experience and the learner will fully understand all the implications contained in the teacher's supplementary feedback. At this point also the stress and instability which always accompanies the learning process in adults, and which arises

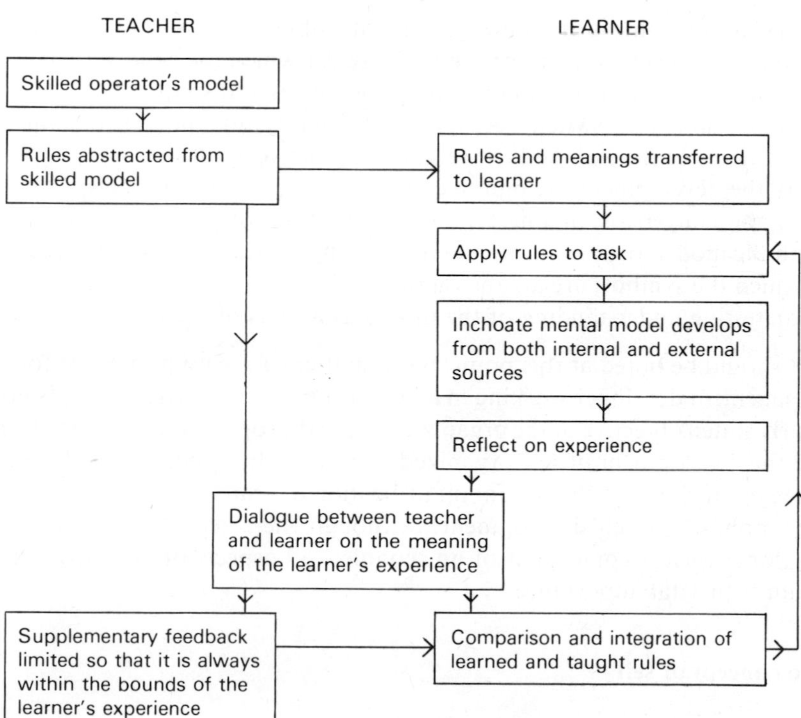

Figure 15.5 The process of learning from a skilled performer

from the need to move away from the certainties of what we know to the uncertainties of what we do not know, finally ceases and is replaced by the mental tranquillity, and oneness of operator and task which is the hallmark of skilled performance.

Whether the learning of skills is achieved from experiential learning, or by being taught, a skill-centred working model of learning should include three important themes. Firstly there is what has to be learned, expressed in both 'rules' and 'modelling' terms. Secondly it must embody a view as to how and when the learning takes place, both for fitting new learning into an existing framework of skills and also for modifying the framework itself. Thirdly it should recognize the similarities and the differences in the learning styles and strategies of individual learners.

Learning and skill

A working definition of skill enhances the possibility of developing a learning model because it provides an insight into the means by which the essential aspects of skill may be individually encouraged. Some of the important components of skill may be listed as:

(1) The attachment of meanings to events, objects, situations, etc. that are relevant to the achievement of the purpose for which the skill is used;
(2) the learning of rules, procedures, processes and so on;
(3) the ability to switch between, and fluently manipulate, the various components of the skill and the relationship between them;
(4) the development of cognitive and affective maps or models;
(5) the conversion of one type of model to another, e.g. converting a symbolic model to an iconic model by creating mental images of the realities of which the symbols are an abstraction; and
(6) testing understanding of the model as well as of the rules.

It should be noted at this point that a matter of great importance for the management developer working in an environment in which learning is not a clearly stated objective of the organization are the topics of 'learning to learn' and the development of self-organized learning. This is because each contributes significantly to the maximum utilization of scarce resources by placing the emphasis on self-development. Although the role of the management developer then becomes that of an 'enabler' all aspects of skill acquisition retain their vital importance.

The concept of self

The concept of self (Maslow, 1968) has at least one important link with skill which is useful to the management developer. The concepts of skill can be seen to stand at the apex of a hierarchy of everything of which the self is aware. Included in this hierarchy are the many aspects of skilled performance. Among other things our self-concept seems to play an important role when we are deciding what we may tackle successfully and what is realistically beyond our capacities. New skills as yet unacquired but, in the view of our self-concept, attainable, become the subject of wishful images which provide a self-prescribed standard as a target for our aspirations.

When we attempt to develop new skills the updated sensory model is contrasted with the ideal model of the wishful image which reflects the level of aspiration provided by the self-imposed view of one's personal efficacy. The acquisition of skill seems, in part, to be a matter of increasing the correspondence between the two models. This view of skill acquisition is close to the view of self-efficacy provided by Bandura (1977) and has connections with concept of scripts developed by Berne in transactional analysis theory. It is also clearly related to Maslow's growth motivation.

This particular facet of skilled performance is of particular interest to the management developer because it impinges on two factors, both of which are crucial to judgments commonly made regarding a manager's future. These are the judgments made about potential, which should hinge on the manager's capacities to develop skills and on judgments having to do with a manager's level of aspiration. Linking the acquisition of skills with the potential for future development, as evinced by the manager's capacities, together with the level of aspiration, as established by the counselling which should accompany performance appraisal, provides a broad unifying structure upon which development can be based (Figure 15.6).

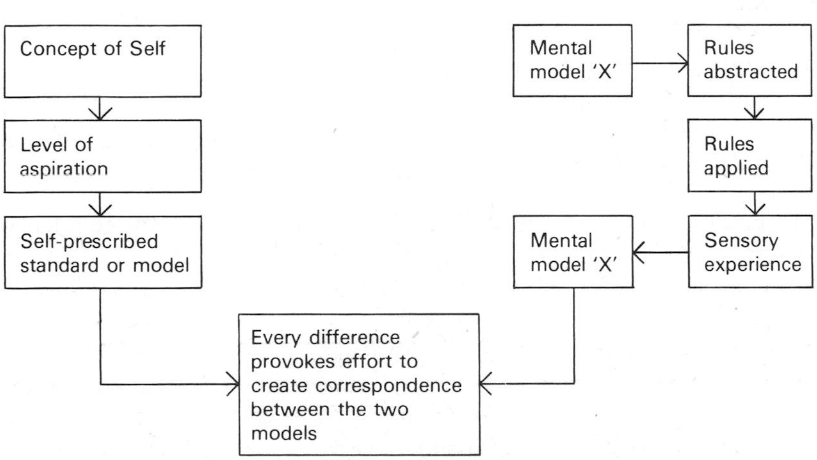

Figure 15.6 Development is based on linking skills and aspirations

MANAGEMENT TRAINING

Although the application of the theory of skilled performance outlined above is fundamentally the same for all topics it may change substantially in emphasis from case to case. In some topics for example the emphasis will be on acquisition routes; listening, feeling and speaking, and the development of the iconic model. While the other acquisition routes and models will certainly be in use, their role will be a relatively lesser one. In other topic areas, accountancy for example, the initial emphasis will be on reading, thinking, choosing and writing. The model to be developed initially will be the symbolic, in both of its forms – numerical and linguistic. The emphasis will change later as forging links between the symbolic and iconic models becomes the central issue.

It will be useful, at this point, to take accountancy training for non-accountants, as the topic around which to describe a typical application of a programme design, centred on skill acquisition rather than on the acquisition of knowledge. Knowledge acquisition involves rule learning only. A programme centred on tasks, on the other hand, will involve learning a range of skills. One of the attractions of skill acquisition immediately becomes apparent. It is a more meaningful *unit* than either knowledge or task acquisition because the domain of the topic is a natural one and not one imposed by a task boundary which is a function of organization nor does it exclude the important aspect of model building from sensory experience. It may be noted here that one of the many major problems yet to be tackled in the use of skill-centred programmes is the lack of a taxonomy of skills for common tasks. However, important as this deficiency undoubtedly is, it does not prevent the management developer from concentrating on the acquisition of skills which have possible applications to many tasks. Such is the case provided by accountancy for non-accounting managers.

Meaning derived from personal experience

The initial problem to be dealt with when developing experienced managers in contrast to educating undergraduates taking business degrees is that what has to be learned must be fitted into the existing knowledge structure. Each individual manager's experience is both unique and private to him. As sensory experience accumulates it becomes the subject of 'self talk' as parts of it are converted into symbolic form. The words used in self talk may be self-generated or may be words in common usage to which the manager imparts his own meaning. Learning from experience inevitably results in the manager building symbolic models in which the meanings attached to events, objects, situations or people is likely to be both personal and capricious. Should anyone doubt this and need to be convinced, simply ask a group of experienced managers to write down their definitions of a number of terms in common use. It is important that the management developer is conscious of the many mental adjustments which experienced managers have to make when first exposed to formal learning.

Rules and meaning transferred to the learner

The first problem faced by the management developer is where to begin. Formal tests or informal discussions can quickly identify the extent of current understanding and so indicate a useful level at which to start the development process. Given the time, it is always better to go back to the very beginning and start by sharing meanings about basic words. Meaning exists at many different levels and so initial discussions must be limited to 'first-order' meanings. For example, first-order meanings for some phrases would be:

Direct cost. A cost conveniently associated with a product, cost centre, project, etc.
Prime cost. The sum of all direct costs. The basic unit of cost.
Indirect costs. Costs not conveniently associated with a product, cost centre or project, etc.
Factory overhead. The sum of all factory indirect costs.
Total factory cost. The sum of prime costs and factory overheads.

These definitions are limited and over simplified. However they do serve as a focus of discussion and provide the base on which second-order meanings can be built. Second-order meanings can be generated by answers to questions such as:

Why are some costs conveniently associated with products while others are not?
What criterion is used to determine where the split occurs?
Why do managers need to be clear about these definitions?
What use can be made of the information?

Other words and their first-order meanings can now be added:

Fixed costs. Costs which are fixed in total over a given time period or production run. Costs not affected by changes in the level of activity.
Variable costs. Costs which vary in total as the level of activity varies but which are fixed per unit.

The management developer should treat these definitions as the focus for discussion, which when understood lead into the expansion afforded by second-order meanings. These may be elicited by asking:

How do fixed costs affect unit cost as the production volume varies?
How do variable costs affect unit cost as the production volume varies?

Once again the answers to these questions should not be regarded as right or wrong but treated as vehicles carrying meanings which are far more important than the words themselves. When the meanings of words are clear it is time to introduce basic concepts into the programme. The concepts should be limited to those which can be fully explained by the words covered by the previous work. Typical concepts to introduce at this stage would be:

Full costing or full absorption costing. Defines products cost as both direct and indirect costs. Because indirect costs are not conveniently associated with products they must be allocated to products on some useful basis. Allocations are always estimates.

Marginal or direct costing. This method of costing clearly defines product cost as direct cost only; that is, it is limited to those costs which are conveniently associated with the product. Indirect costs are not charged to the product. It is the amount, at any given volume of output, by which aggregate costs are charged if the volume of output is increased or decreased by one unit. This definition clarifies the link between direct and variable costs.

Contribution. The excess of selling price over variable cost. The excess is the contribution made by sales revenue towards fixed costs and profit. Fixed costs, that is costs not affected by changes in production volume, are also usually indirect costs, that is costs not conveniently associated with a product. However some fixed costs have a direct and, for that reason, a variable element.

Full understanding of these terms reinforces the fluent use of the meanings attached to words. The learners should be encouraged to explain these concepts by diagrams and interlinking shapes.

Development of rules and the operating programme

Subsequent to the attachment of meanings to words which are appropriate to the purpose in hand, and the development of understanding of related concepts, comes the application of rules to a novel situation. This follows from Figure 15.6 which indicates the sequence of skill acquisition by a person being taught. This stage is not possible until a limited understanding of the meanings of words and concepts has been established. The learner at this time needs constant reminders and props which support him during the difficult period, when, for the first time, he attempts to apply his learning to a situation.

The management developer must invent problems which can be solved by current knowledge. Calculating the cost of a product in both marginal and full costing terms would be appropriate at this stage. Each problem should be designed to demonstrate some point. After the completion of the problem there should be a period of reflections on 'What have I learned so far?' Each succeeding case must be more difficult than the last and build on the lessons learned. A formal session each morning which reviews not only 'what I learned yesterday', but also, 'the issues I had difficulty with yesterday' reinforces yesterday's learning, highlights misconceptions and errors, and keep the instructor aware of real progress. During these periods of reflection the learners should be encouraged to express themselves through diagrams and shapes as well as words.

With growing first hand experience the group can be invited to invent their own rules, procedures, algorithms, plans or whatever, which reflect the growth of their own inchoate sensory models.

The development of the mental models

The principal concern for the management developer at this stage is the direction of the managers undergoing the skill acquisition process, towards the conscious exploration of the relationships which are beginning to develop between their sensory and enactive models and the symbolic data they are using. For example managers can be asked to draw the relationships which they see existing between direct, indirect, fixed and variable costs. The resulting shapes are frequently extremely revealing. Levels of both comprehension and misunderstanding can be clearly seen. Verbal descriptions are much easier to 'fudge' than shapes. The process can be seen as:

(1) clarifying meanings of words;
(2) clarifying meanings of concepts;
(3) abstracting rules;
(4) applying rules to problems;
(5) drawing diagrams of perceived relationships;
(6) discussing diagrams with skilled performers;
(7) removing misunderstandings and misconceptions;
(8) revealing negative feelings associated with specific words or shapes;
(9) removing learning blocks; and
(10) revising rules (inventing new rules).

These ten stages guide the learner through the four phases of:

(1) abstraction of rules;
(2) experimental application of rules;
(3) sensory enactive experience; and
(4) reflection.

At the level of skill acquisition learning is dominated by the need to build inner models of external reality and to abstract rules from the sensory experience. The rules, at first tentatively provisional, are progressively modified and elaborated until a stabilized point is reached at which they can be confidently 'firmed up'. These rules which may take the variety of forms already mentioned, i.e. rules, plans, processes, algorithms and so on, now become the operating guide lines of the manager. Their meaning is validated by the close ties which exist between the operating programme and the enactive, sensory and symbolic models of which they are an expression. Further experience will result in the fine tuning of both models and programmes as the manager follows the path towards continuous authentication of his knowledge of the world. At the same time many of the actions consciously applied during the early stages of learning will subside into routine behaviours.

There is no limit to the extent to which the model building and rule abstraction process can be taken. From the earlier learning regarding the meaning of basic words such as direct and variable cost and the introduction of basic concepts, the manager's model and rules of accountancy can be extended to cover more advanced concepts. Examples of these would be: draw a diagram which indicates the situation called overtrading; abstract rules from the diagram which would prevent this situation from developing; or, given a substantial discrepancy between planned and actual sales mix, design a figure which demonstrates the effect this variance could have on working capital, cash flow, finished goods, stock, warehousing, factory scheduling, operating profit, etc. The only limitations are the needs of the managers and the inventiveness of the management developer.

CONCLUSION

The skeletal propositions made in the introduction to this chapter now have some covering. This fact should permit the reader to attach greater meaning to the first page than he did originally. The ambiguous use of the word 'skill' conceals a wealth of potential growth in the work of the management development practitioner. Hidden beneath this simple word is a new world of meaning which can greatly enhance the insight the management developer has both for the work in which he is involved and for the skills he needs to develop in order to work effectively when developing his colleagues. The word 'skill' has different connotations for the academic researcher and the practical management developer. The academic strives for the integrity of concepts. The management developer on the other hand seeks organizational utility. In a world dominated by short-term thinking he is never free to pursue exclusively long-term improvements. He must be seen to achieve, not in his own terms, but in the terms of the organization in which he works. Paradoxically, while he attempts to convince others of the need to divert some scarce resources from short-term to long-term goals, he often feels a resentment toward the short-term intrusion which this activity introduces into his own long-term world.

The emergence of the management developer has been described as a response to a challenge to industrial efficiency brought about by the accelerating pace of change. Over the last decade or so the management developer has moved from an almost total reliance on others towards a state of self-reliance. However, he still has a very long way to travel on the road from his original embryo state to mature professionalism. It has been argued that some of his difficulties at least arise because he is an educationalist with long-term aims in a goal-orientated environment in which education is only a means to an end. In a highly complex job he needs some kind of structure to assist him in the task of distinguishing the wood from the trees. The basic structure proposed includes models of management. Many are needed to reveal the many dimensions of the management job. Additionally he must have a model of skill – a natural and ubiquitous unit of behaviour. Both this model and his model of skill acquisition, or learning, must be compatible with each other and with his models of management. Armed with this structure he can state his case with greater confidence.

The model of skill used in this paper proposes a fundamental division between knowledge gained from sensory experience and states of knowledge reached after this basic material has been subjected to the many varieties of thought process. In support of this proposition the view has been expressed that man's knowledge of the world cannot extend beyond his experience. Thoughts which mull over past events and project into the possible outcomes of alternative acts in the future, while constituting a valid source of subsequent behaviour, are viewed as qualitatively different to previous experience. This distinction forms the base on which the concepts of mental model and operating programme are built.

The operating programme is projected as the actualizing mechanism which integrates all sources of knowledge and continuously abstracts rules which guide all forms of purposive behaviour. The inner models of external reality are limited by sensory experience and provide the essential logic encapsulated by the operating programmes. The heuristic integrant describes the never-ending, ubiquitous process which constantly sifts through all experience and all thought processes for cues which indicate a need to update either models or their actualizing programmes. This process is seen to be inextricably linked to the mechanism which ultimately makes a selection from the available options and which uses purpose as the key criterion. This second process was labelled 'the operator'. Ultimately skill was viewed as functioning on three distinct levels. The executive level selected the skill most appropriate to the situation from the total repertoire of skills; once selected the skill in current use was supervised by an operating programme which actualized the essential logic provided by experience. The operating level was seen to work at the conscious level. Behaviours reduced by long use to unconscious acts were proposed to be working at the routine level.

Skill acquisition had a variety of possible routes, all of which were part of a cyclical process. Experiential learning moves from model building to rule abstraction while learning by being taught moves in the reverse direction, from rule appreciation to model building. The model of skill acquisition elevates the conceptual framework within which a management developer works above that provided by task or knowledge centred programmes. It is perhaps analogous to the relationship which existed between the Model T Ford and horse transport. It is hoped that skill acquisition will develop in the near future at the same pace as the early automobile.

Acknowledgement

I would like to thank Philip Moorhouse and Laurie Thomas for the many hours of stimulating conversation concerning the nature of skill which they have both provided.

References and further reading

Bandura, A. (1977). Self-efficacy: Towards a unifying theory of behavioural change. *Psychol. Rev.*, **84**, 191

Fitts, P. M. and Posner, M. I. (1967). Human Performance. (Belmont: Brookes–Cole)

Fransella, F. and Bannister, D. (1977). *A Manual of Repertory Grid Technique.* (New York: Academic Press)

Gagné, R. M. (1971). *The Conditions of Learning.* (New York: Holt, Rinehart & Winston)

Harri-Augstein, S., Thomas, L. and Chell, N. (1978). *Learning to Learn – Conversational uses of Grids and 'Structures of Meaning' in Developing Man-management Skills.* (Brunel University, London: Centre for the Study of Human Learning)

Kolb, D.A. and Fry, R. *Towards an Applied Theory of Experiential Learning.* (Cambridge, Mass.: MIT)

Maslow, A. H. (1968). *Towards a Psychology of Being.* (New York: Van Nostrand)

McKnight, C. (1977). Repertory Grids, Values and the Prediction of Behaviour. Presented at the *Construct Theory and Repertory Grid Workshop, Occupational Psychology Section of the British Psychological Society*, September, 1977, Brunel University, London

Miller, D. A. (ed.) (1973). *Communication, Language and Meaning.* (New York: Harper Colophon Books)

Prince, G. M. (1976). *Mindspring.* (Chemtech)

Robb, M. D. (1972). *The Dynamics of Motor Skill Acquisition.* (New York: Prentice Hall)

Thomas, L. and Harri-Augstein, S. (1978). *The Self Organised Learner.* (Brunel University, London: Centre for the Study of Human Learning)

Watts, A. W. (1978). The Way of Zen. (Harmondsworth: Pelican)

Welford, A. T. (1976). *Skilled Performance; Perceptual and Motor Skills.* (Glenview: Scott, Foresman)

16
Final Discussion

W. T. SINGLETON

ORGANIZATIONS

In the first chapter, *Systems Theory and Skill Theory*, the importance of the system environment and the interactions between system levels was emphasized. It seems clear from the preceding chapters that the management system conforms to these general principles. There are obviously differences between the one manager on a farm which has a total of four or five workers, and a manager within a National Health Service employing a million people; but size is only one of many factors.

Every organization attempts to generate a consistent culture or climate or style. This is achieved by selection and training of entrants, by rewards for conformist behaviour and by sanctions on non-conformist behaviour. This climate seems to be very similar in the public services – armed forces, universities, health and social services, local and national government and international organizations – but different on the farm and in manufacturing industry. This is not because the cost discipline is different. This seems to apply with consistent force in all organizations; all find that demands and ostensible requirements exceed available resources and so one primary task of management is economy and careful allocation of resources.

The manager is always accountable, usually within the organization, for the resources for which he is responsible. He is always required, as McGinnis puts it, to give an account of his stewardship. This raises the criterion problem. It is at its most obscure in the social services and in international organizations. Cumella points out that Social Service managers have no readily definable objectives or criteria of success. Castle mentions the difficulties of accountability in international activity where objectives are very generally phrased and where they apply only to groups or teams, the individual can never be blamed. However, even in organizations with products which can be counted or weighed success is not straighforwardly assessable because of what Moorhouse calls the unknown states of nature; it is never obvious how great was the management achievement in a given production because the obstacles which had to be overcome are not readily comprehended. The same applies to the farm where the vagaries of weather are such that sometimes a poor or good performance is genuinely bad or good luck respectively rather than a reflection of level of competence. The McGinnis approach is to insist that objectives must be agreed in the interests of the individual as well as of efficiency; Cumella, accepting that there are no measurable objectives and no criteria, proposes that the careful construction of a role is the alternative. Hedge and Pendleton make a similar point in suggesting that the planner no longer pursues an ideal state as an objective but rather he attempts to understand and facilitate the process of change. The accountability issue is further confounded by the increased emphasis on the achievement of consensus within the organization. This is emphasized most strongly by Richardson for the Health Service on the grounds of the close interdependence of different services for patients; in the Civil Service, McGinnis prefers to emphasize participation but not necessarily consensus so that responsibility is not confused.

It is interesting to note that Castle is able to suggest that social and cultural differences between nationals of different countries can easily be exaggerated but nevertheless there can be influences on management style in attitudes to authority and responsibility, property, work, women and government, and in traditions to do with education, intellectual activity and justice. Wilson and Randell point out that in an effective organization, care is taken to check that the organizational requirements from an individual match reasonably with his aspirations.

The objectives of an organization, like those of an individual, are continuously adjusted by a kind of general audit of resources and constraints in relation to objectives; a constraint may be negative in the sense of a resource inadequacy but it may also be positive, e.g. internal attitudes or external market forces. Nevertheless there is an underlying constancy which is partly to do with the human needs the organization was set up to meet and is partly also to do with style, values and ways of doing things; e.g. a university short of funds may decide to market expertise but it would never attempt to market icecream, while a manufacturing organization might sell technology but it would not attempt to market psychotherapy. Cumella points out that the evidence that an organization is not effective is usually clearer than the evidence that it is effective. Randell suggests that explanations of effectiveness can be at the economic, the social or even the religious level. Singleton proposes that the indicator of progress of a university organization is the sum of the progress of the members of that organization. Plumb considers that the farmer determines his objectives in a hybrid trade-off between profit and quality of life: the permanent constraints on his activities are land, labour and capital; the dynamic constraint is the weather. Moorhouse describes the objective of a manufacturing unit as the requirement to make enough at the right cost: the constraints are finance, efficiency and legislation. The town planner is unusual in having no control of or responsibility for finance but he has exceptionally definitive legal constraints and constraints from public opinion, both directly and through the elected representatives. A hospital has an unusual constraint in that it never ceases to function, which causes serious maintenance problems and accentuates costs. In hospitals, universities and social service departments the impossibility of specifying detailed objectives causes serious difficulties in setting criteria for allocating resources; the solution in each case is to go on doing what was done before with minor adjustments in the face of internal forces (usually ambitious individuals) and external forces from changes in societal economic or social beliefs and attitudes. In the armed forces, the Civil Service, and international organizations the determination of objectives is left to the politicians who, in turn, respond to societal forces.

In speed of change, manufacturing organizations are probably the most flexible although as Wilson points out the individuals who are agents of change are undertaking considerable risks in terms of their own careers. Plumb rightly emphasizes that the oldest occupation – farming – has in the UK an admirable record of change in absorbing new technology particularly over the past thirty years.

As befits the youngest occupation, marketing seems to take the most trouble to clarify ends and means. Burnett identifies the essence of marketing as the matching of controllable resources to uncontrollable forces in the environment. The controllable activities are market research, forecasting, planning of products, distribution, sales and promotion. The objective can be market penetration, product development, market development or diversification, or any mix of these. He quotes the Boston Grid which assumes that the degree of success of an organization and its likely future can be described in essentials by two parameters: market share and market growth. In large organizations profit-making can be assigned as an objective and an indicator to geographic units but marketing usually remains a central function. Accountability can determine the structure of the organization; in particular a matrix structure can be used to encompass usually two but sometimes more than two kinds of accountability. Burnett relates the stages of growth of an organization to its basic culture: organizations usually begin in a 'power' mode with one or more entrepreneurs firmly holding the functional control centrally; as the organization grows it moves into a 'task' culture with separately definable functions as complementary parts of the whole, and finally it may move into a 'role' culture where tasks are too diffuse to be kept separate and many individuals are interchangeable. The role culture is comfortable and will function well enough if the environment is stable; there is a premium on reliability and little incentive for innovation.

MANAGEMENT

There seem to be at least three separable levels of management function. In a large organization these will be different people but in a small organization two or three levels may be within the activities of one individual; e.g. on the farm there is often only one manager but he may rely on an outside organization, such as the National Farmers Union, to do some of the long term thinking, policy making and negotiation with government for him. These are the functions of *upper management*, while *middle management* is concerned with reconciling long term objectives and short term demands and *lower management* is a mixture of thinking and doing, often involving coping with emergencies. Captain Page is able to describe the qualities needed at these three levels with unusual clarity partly because the Navy has entry only at the bottom of the management ladder and partly because the relatively unambiguous concept of rank provides benchmarks for the different levels. Managers in the lower levels up to Commander are, to use his graphic phrase, 'tough, arrogant and ambitious'. Middle managers, Commanders and Captains, achieve success by intellect, restraint, foresight and stamina. The upper managers, Admirals, are farseeing, politically sensitive, calculating, resistant to stress and highly tolerant of uncertainty.

This last seems to be a key characteristic of the top manager; it is his responsibility to cope with massive swings in the environmental forces – changes in government, in relations between nations, in societal norms, in economic activity and so on – and yet he is the guardian of what Singleton calls 'the spirit of the enterprise' which has taken a long time to build up and which must not be dissipated. His job is to cope with the environment in its widest sense but he must also keep in contact with internal constraints and changes; this is more of a pleasure because it is more familiar and more predictable. Hence the Admiral likes to visit a ship, the Vice Chancellor enjoys a dialogue with some students and the Chairman or Managing Director still needs to visit the geographical units and even chats with the lads on the shopfloor. However, these pleasures must be rationed because as Captain Page points out there is always a danger of weakening the authority of middle and lower management by short-circuiting communications. The chain of command may appear tiresome to those at the extremes but it is essential to those in between. He lists the sources of uncertainty as future resources, changing technology and changing objectives. In *The Social Services*, Cumella points out that there is uncertainty about the total role which emerges as unclear relationships with other services such as health, the police and other branches of local government. Looking at the negative aspects of management Wilson describes the characteristics as overtight control, low creativity, under-utilization of resources, slow decision-making, low risk-taking, poor productivity and poor management development.

Burnett suggests that, in industrial organizations, the optimal kind of top management changes as the organization and its environment change; the key variable is the switch from a supply dominated market to a demand dominated market. In the early years when supply is the key requirement the top manager is likely to be an engineer – a maker of things; but he gradually gives way to the financier – the maker of money. At about this point, supply overtakes demand, and thus the top manager needs to be a salesman; eventually he gives way to the marketeer. The marketeer becomes dominant not only because the demand is dominant but also because with accelerating technical change, products and businesses have a shorter life cycle.

Upper management copes with external uncertainty more readily perhaps because there is less internal uncertainty, they can identify with the organization, they are senior enough for authority to be undisputed, and they are insulated from internal emergencies. The stress on the middle manager comes from internal insecurity, from the backstop role of having to pick up serious emergencies or issues which lower management cannot cope with and from the role ambiguity of being halfway between the policy issues of upper management and the resource issues of lower management. Castle lists the tasks as directing work, ensuring compliance with directives, helping to determine policy, representing and negotiating. Cumella considers that middle managers, heads of operational units, have a key role because their policy directives from above and their measures of success from below are so indefinite. Hedge and Pendleton enumerate their functions as: being responsible for decisions, setting goals, devising strategies and deploying resources. Chell considers that middle managers are fire-fighters but Richardson sees this emergency-coping role as the essential and desirable characteristic of the lower manager. Page and Richardson are suspicious of the orthodoxy that managers should avoid emergencies by anticipation; this is not possible in a turbulent environment. Resources are not available to be deployed to cover everything that might happen. Crises are bound to occur and the manager grows in stature by coping with them. To do this he needs authority and Chell distinguishes derived authority from contrived authority.

Authority can be derived from obvious functional competence and this is one reason why lower managers find it difficult to reduce their activities in the function from which they were promoted. On the other hand promotion quickly leads to responsibility for functions in which the individual does not have extensive personal experience and he must then start to rely on contrived authority from the structure of the organization. The 'high-flier' meets this issue more quickly than do others. In *Management of Military Organization*, Page points out that authority is diminished and other organizational issues are confused by the practice of 'role splitting' or 'personal assistantships' or 'one over one' management. This is meant to give the junior of the two more exposure and experience but it usually leads to more problems than it solves.

In the Civil Service and in other large organizations some distinction is made between policy, administration and management. Although these overlap, their separate existence does throw some light on general management tasks. McGinnis quotes the aphorism that management is action through people and administration is action through paper. Richardson suggests that administration is about the present and managing is about the future. Singleton implies that in universities, administration is what non-academic managers do. Another way of illustrating the distinction is by the analogy of players in orchestras and players in games. The administrator plays in an orchestra: there is a conductor and someone else wrote the score but there remains considerable creativity in the musicians' interpretation of the music. In the Civil Service, the composer is the policy-maker and the politician is the conductor; they are both open to much more criticism as individuals than is the musician/administrator. Managers are, by contrast, games players: they score goals and their team wins or loses matches, and there are corresponding rewards and sanctions. The general implication is that administration works through comprehensive independent guidebooks and managers write their own guidebooks. Still, as McGinnis points out, guidebooks tell you what to look for rather than what to see. Clarifying what to see is the task of the leader.

LEADERSHIP

Leadership is much more than crisis management although it is often in crises that the leader first demonstrates his potential. Leadership is required to set the objectives and the style of any organization at any level. The leader formulates and articulates ways of doing things and why they need to be done. The style of the organization is the internal manifestation of leadership, while the external manifestation is in the ambassadorial role. Burnett suggests in Chapter 12 that for industrial organizations the operational leadership and the organizational style are functions of the phase of business development. Similarly Chell points out that the low profit/high turnover business requires a different style from the high profit/low turnover business – the former is usually autocratic, whereas the latter can be more democratic. Most of the advanced worker participation schemes have been in high cost high technology industries. By contrast Castle sees the leader of an international organization as a person who imposes his own personality both internally and externally. Page puts leadership behaviour as the key factor in the process which relates the individual to the organization. Functional leadership involves the dynamic balancing of task requirements, individual needs and team maintenance needs but this is different from personal leadership which involves fast intuitive decisions, risk taking, coolness under stress and general mastery of the situation. He is properly concerned that the armed forces in peacetime may lose the art of developing personal leaders and may come to rely too much on safe, mediocre system-users.

The ambassadorial role is mentioned in one form or another in almost every chapter. It can be described as leadership or merely as one facet of management at all levels. It involves representation outside the group and communication between levels. The competent manager must be able to communicate the views of those he represents upwards in the hierarchy of the organization, either to gain resources or to get routines changed, and correspondingly as a link in the chain of command he must also be able to communicate downwards to those he leads. This communication across a boundary is often his most difficult task and to do it successfully he must generate both above him and below him a belief in his honesty and integrity as well as his competence. Success is dependent on style, on how it is done rather than what is done: it is an affective as well as a rational process.

MANAGERS

It is easier to describe abilities, attributes and qualities rather than skills: as McGinnis puts it 'qualities you have; skills you exercise'. Plumb lists the abilities as technical, man-management, communication and information processing: the manifestations of skill are in innovation, timeliness and good husbandry. Singleton mentions the rational processing of information and setting of goals with precise timing and phasing in implementation. Richardson identifies the abilities to communicate and motivate, while Cumella proposes: judgement of people – in particular prediction of their behaviour on inadequate evidence – the ability to deal with an individual as an individual and not as one of a category of individuals the complementary ability to perceive a set of individuals as a whole to judge to delegate to be aware of subordinates' successes. Hedge and Pendleton enumerate planning, representation and work control: planning involves political sensitivity, monitoring, organizing and determining strategy; representation involves communication upwards and downwards; and work control involves monitoring in terms of standards of quality and speed.

The Civil Service requires trained, accountable and participative individuals who are capable of defining tasks, marshalling resources, measuring achievement and rendering an account of activities, either their own or those of others. The qualities sought by formal selection are literacy, numeracy, intelligence and personality. McGinnis describes the basic skills as awareness including sensitivity, flexibility but maintenance of direction, and getting and deploying information. Castle mentions intellect, diplomacy and administration with skills in language, communication, social interaction and bureaucracy manipulation: the qualities needed are integrity, conviction, courage, drive, imagination and technical grasp. Wilson again mentions timing of activities, either as a catalyst or a participant, a high tolerance of uncertainty together with an inner self-confidence, diagnostic and design skills and the ability to detect nonsenses in goals, structures, roles and methods. Singleton lists an enduring technical expertise, conceptualizing ability and the ability to detect significant cues in real situations which are full of irrelevancy.

MANAGEMENT SKILLS

The above attempts to describe the attributes of a manager are informative, particularly in view of the underlying consistency across very different occupations but they tell us little about how the manager does his job and how he can learn to do it better.

One universal function is that managers make decisions and moreover these choices invariably have to be made on incomplete data. The available evidence has to be supplemented by less definitive information from the real situation, by the conglomerate of earlier experience and by personal inclination. To do this last effectively Plumb points out that the manager must understand himself and his preferences. Plumb and Chell mention that information comes from integrated sensory experience: it is not always merely metaphorical to say that the choice smells right. The limitations of data and data manipulations are graphically expressed by Moorhouse who notes that keeping the score is quite different from playing the game. Managers are rarely worried by inadequate knowledge; as Randell points out, this will be readily admitted but, by contrast, no manager will admit to lacking skill. The obvious necessity for making decisions and the difficulties of how to make them may obscure the more subtle skill of when to make them – that is, the ability to create or identify significant choice points. Hedge and Pendleton talk about navigating through a terrain of conflicting pressures, picking approaches and endpoints, while Moorhouse describes the same process as finding an optimal path through a decision tree and, at a more practical level, as reducing an objective to a daily requirement. Cues as to when a control action is needed may come either from the data or from the real situation. Moorhouse mentions that a manager receiving evidence puts it into three categories: fits expectations therefore needs no action; is so remote from expectation that it is probably in error and therefore must be checked; and between these two extremes, indication that action may be needed. For cues from the real situation, Singleton suggests that the ability to detect an important signal in a welter of noise is a key feature of skill in specific situations. Superficially different, but in fact closely related, is the ability to detect the essential form of the issue and to identify it as within a category for which there is an adaptive reaction if not a solution.

So far, in identifying relevant data, in combining information from the real situation with abstract numerical information and in identifying triggers for action along a conceptual path towards his objective, the manager is behaving just like any other process controller such as a pilot. The action phase is quite different; the manager cannot press buttons and operate controls so that mechanisms carry out his orders precisely. He has to operate through other people. People are not as obedient as hardware mechanisms so the manager's position is in many respects more complicated. He has to take account of what his subordinates can do and will do (this latter is the social skill area). On the other hand these other people have some grasp of what he wants to do and they will filter instructions accordingly; when he makes a mistake they might remedy it or at least ask him to check again. His communication can be much more sloppy than with hardware because they have their own concepts of what is needed. One facet of the manager's skill is to decide how and what to communicate in order to get the most effective action; the optimal mix of means and ends in his instructions is a manifestation of his skill.

This applies at all levels of management; as in other skills, the differences between levels are more obvious on the perceptual side. The lower manager is dealing mainly with the real situation and with all the short-term perturbations which crop up as input, processing or output problems; these can be to do with materials, energy, information or people. The middle manager is operating on a longer time scale and so he relies more on abstract data and less on the real information which arrives in real time. Thus he needs more extensive experience to draw on which can help to integrate those hybrid sources of information. He is less subject to the stress of emergencies but he has his own stress source in the conflicts between long term and short term demands. Short term demands scarcely reach the senior manager at all; he is essentially dealing with the long term and, correspondingly, his data are mostly abstract. His stress source is uncertainty because he must operate in relation to an environment over which he has little or no control and which, in present day society, is liable to extreme turbulence.

All levels of managers have in common the basic organizational problems of matching demands to resources, of making decisions on incomplete evidence, of identifying appropriate paths and tasks in decision networks and of taking action through other people. They all seem to be capable of arriving at the key decisions intuitively and to check them later by logic and the deployment of evidence; this is a function of the inherent uncertainty and it does suggest that the basic mode of operation in skill terms is by the enactive or body-image extension process. This is less obvious for more senior managers but it still forms the basis of functioning. Moving up the management hierarchy, the more there are indications of pictorial modelling and finally symbolic modelling as in graphs and balance sheets. Correspondingly the higher the level the less the detail the bigger the total picture and the longer the time scale under consideration. Finally the higher up the hierarchy he is, the more the manager has a choice in the use of his own time and resources, and so, if he is to be effective, the more he must know himself.

MANAGEMENT DEVELOPMENT

The practical purpose of the study of management skills is to improve managers. The formal processes for doing this are selection, appraisal, training and development. As Chell points out, to do these things systematically, we need a model of skill acquisition as well as a model of skill.

Randell and Chell agree that in principle one can either start with conceptual development and use the concepts to improve practice, or one can start by improving practice and consolidate this by developing supportive concepts. Neither way is easy as a complete process; as Randell points out knowledge can sometimes be acquired by insight but skilled performance can be improved only by laborious procedures demanding considerable and continuing effort. Thus the primary requirement is that a manager must be convinced that he needs to improve and must want to improve. The consensus seems to be that at present, management training and development is weakest in the practical and experiential aspects. The Management Schools provide adequate expertise in techniques which support managers but not so much in management as such. Chell suggests that we need improved methods to facilitate the move from practice through models to rules. This he calls the experiential approach as opposed to the reverse which is the traditional teaching approach. Skill concepts are useful aids to generalizing because skill boundaries are more natural than task boundaries which are necessarily specific and artificial: the study of skills is the exploration of processes by which managers relate to tasks. As Chell put it, the oneness of the operator and the task is the mark of skill.

The central issue is the improvement of communication. This follows from skill theory in that management skills are fundamentally enactive and these cannot be communicated abstractly. They can only be demonstrated. An organization is, by definition, a collective enterprise and the overall performance is a function of individual skills and communication between individuals. Communication facilitates and is facilitated by the coherent pursuit of the objectives which give meaning to the enterprise.

There are also some implications for job and task design for managers. The art is to design different jobs (laterally and longitudinally in terms of the management hierarchy) where the roles overlap in a manner such that intercommunication is both facilitated and minimized.

Notwithstanding these generalizations it is important also to note that almost all the authors mentioned that there are extensive individual differences.

CONCEPTS OF SKILL

The academic purpose of study of management skills is to improve the theory of skill. The method followed in this book, like that in the other books in this series, has been to start with the general (systems theory) and move to the particular (skill theory) and also to start with particular management occupations and look for common features which will generalize back into skill theory.

The simplest kind of skill is expressed in a movement controlled in the context of a purpose. This seems to be done by creating an internal record of what is intended before the action takes place, followed by continuous feedback of data about what actually happens as it happens, and after it has happened, this feedback is compared with and assimilated into the record so that the record remains, modified in terms of degree of success and available for a better attempt next time. This is how skill is acquired. This continuously developing record is called a schema.

More complex series and sets of movements develop under the control of increasingly complex schema until the standard human range of enactive or body-image skills is available. These skills are universal but they are also private; there is no symbolism and so there can be no communication other than primitive gesticulation and simulation of activity. They are 'inside-looking-out' but they can be extended from the inside outwards by using mechanisms and people as extensions of the body image most readily at the output level. At an early age the human infant, aided by the dominance of the visual system, finds it possible to shift to 'outside-looking-in' schema where he himself is seen as no longer necessarily at the centre of events but as part of a total scheme. The individual now has pictorial images which are more general and more flexible and has an improved communication facility through the drawing of pictures which can have shared meaning with other individuals. These pictorial models follow the same principles as enactive schema: they grow and develop; they are continuously modified in the light of new data but these data need no longer involve active participation; the individual can now be a spectator; but still his learning is mostly dependent upon action which is personal manipulation of the picture. With increasing experience these pictures can become more symbolic; they can become icons – three dimensional portraits which need only contain the necessary facets for that individual – until finally they become abstract as in languages.

Thus, there is a hierarchy of skill foundations in body-image, pictorial and symbolic schema or enactive, iconic and abstract schema – these are just two different sets of bench markers for the same series. They do not indicate a simple hierarchy of skills because schema can be hybrid. There can be an enactive base with iconic and abstract overtones as in management skills. For skills of this type discussion and learning are particularly difficult because the basis is inexpressible except by the action of the skilled individual. Hence the importance of action as the basis of management development. The manager operates by manipulating the real situation and he can do this most readily by using an enactive schema which directly accepts data from what is happening in practice as a result of his actions but he must have symbolic additions because he can use abstract data particularly to facilitate thinking beyond the immediate situation.

This description has avoided the question of where the purposes come from and how they are represented. One can envisage that the structure of the schema might contain the short term purpose, and higher level records – pictures and symbols – might represent the endpoint, but there remains the puzzle of how and why particular endpoints are regarded as desirable. This is at least partially a social phenomenon and will be taken up in the next book.

CONCLUSION

In the first volume it was concluded that man is conceptually a model builder and categorizer and operationally a mapmaker and navigator. In the second volume it was concluded that aspirations are a key feature of skills because they set the boundaries. The individual reacts not just to the external world but also his personal internal world which he must therefore understand and appreciate if he is to be effective. The skilled practitioner preserves a nice balance of attention to the external world and attention to himself and his personal reactions.

In the study of managers these concepts remain fitting. Not surprisingly there is a new emphasis on communication between people and it becomes clear that an unavoidable impediment to this is the foundation of management in body-image schema – in the personal reaction to the consequences of action. Individual differences are thus re-emphasized; sensitivity to them is crucial in all organizations which are dependent on the complementary collective efforts of individuals.

Partly because of the difficulties of communicating and understanding what a manager does and how he does it the skill appraisal method in this book has been to rely entirely on practitioners describing what they have found by discussion with other practitioners and what they personally have experienced.

Author Index

Bold numerals refer to names cited in reference lists at chapter ends

---

Subject Index